India in the World Order
Searching for Major-Power Status

Two highly regarded scholars come together to examine India's relationship with the world's major powers and its own search for a significant role in the international system. Central to the argument is India's belief that the acquisition of an independent nuclear capability is the key to obtaining such status. The book details the major constraints at the international, domestic and perceptual levels that India has faced in this endeavor. It concludes, through a detailed comparison of India's power capabilities, that India is indeed a rising power, but that significant systemic and domestic changes will be necessary before it can achieve its goal. *India in the World Order* examines the prospects and implications of India's integration into the major-power system in the twenty-first century. Given recent developments, the book is extremely timely. Its incisive analysis will be illuminating for students, policymakers, and for anyone wishing to understand the region in greater depth.

Baldev Raj Nayar is Emeritus Professor of Political Science at McGill University in Montreal. He is the author of over a dozen scholarly books dealing with international relations, political economy, comparative politics and South Asia.

T.V. Paul is Professor of Political Science at McGill University. His publications include *International Order and the Future of World Politics* (with John A. Hall, 1999), and *The Absolute Weapon Revisited: Nuclear Arms and the Emerging International Order* (1998).

Contemporary South Asia 9

Contemporary South Asia has been established to publish books on the politics, society and culture of South Asia since 1947. In accessible and compehensive studies, authors who are already engaged in researching specific aspects of South Asian society explore a wide variety of broad-ranging and topical themes. The series will be of interest to anyone who is concerned with the study of South Asia and with the legacy of its colonial past.

India in the World Order
Searching for Major-Power Status

Baldev Raj Nayar
McGill University

T.V. Paul
McGill University

PUBLISHED BY THE PRESS SYNDICATE OF THE UNIVERSITY OF CAMBRIDGE
The Pitt Building, Trumpington Street, Cambridge, United Kingdom

CAMBRIDGE UNIVERSITY PRESS
The Edinburgh Building, Cambridge CB2 2RU, UK
40 West 20th Street, New York, NY 10011–4211, USA
477 Williamstown Road, Port Melbourne, VIC 3207, Australia
Ruiz de Alarcón 13, 28014 Madrid, Spain
Dock House, The Waterfront, Cape Town 8001, South Africa

http://www.cambridge.org

First published 2003

Printed in China by Everbest Printing Co.

Typeface Plantin (Adobe) 10/12 pt.   *System* QuarkXPress®   [MAPG]

A catalogue record for this book is available from the British Library

National Library of Australia Cataloguing in Publication data
Nayar, Baldev Raj.
India in the world order: searching for major power status.
Bibliography.
Includes index.
ISBN 0 521 82125 8
ISBN 0 521 52875 5 (pbk.)
1. India – Foreign relations – 1984–. 2. India – Defenses.
I. Paul, T. V. II. Title. (Series: Contemporary South Asia
(Cambridge, England); no. 9).
327.54

ISBN 0 521 82125 8 hardback
ISBN 0 521 52875 5 paperback

Contents

Acknowledgements

In researching and writing this book, we have received immense help from several individuals and institutions in different countries. Thanks to their assistance and cooperation, our field-research trips to Beijing, Berlin, London, Moscow, Paris, Tokyo and Washington, DC, proved to be highly fruitful. In these capitals, we met with officials and scholars who shared their views with us on India and its relations with their countries. We conducted three trips to India, in 1998, 2000 and 2001, and several Indian scholars and serving and retired officials lent their time to meet and share their expertise with us during one-on-one interviews, seminars and round-tables.

We thank Stephen P. Cohen and Dinshaw Mistry for organizing a special workshop for us at the Brookings Institution, Washington, DC, in December 1999, and also Ambassador Teresita Schaffer at the Center for International and Strategic Studies, Washington, DC, and David Welch at the University of Toronto for conducting work-in-progress seminars. Our trip to China in the summer of 2000 was made possible through the help of Venu Rajamony, a dynamic Indian diplomat, who along with his gracious wife, Saroj, provided us great hospitality. Yang Wenjing and Hu Shisheng acted as our interpreters and hosts during our visit, which was sponsored by the Chinese Institute of Contemporary International Relations (CICIR). In the summer of 2000, T.V. Paul conducted field trips to Bangalore, Hyderabad and Thiruvananthapuram – India's information-technology centers – and gained first-hand ideas on how India is changing in this area. For their help in arranging the meetings, he especially thanks Colonel M. Vijayakumar, Director, Software Technology Parks of India (STPI), Hyderabad; Dr. S. Rajagopal, of the National Institute for Advanced Studies (NIAS), Bangalore; Ammu Joseph and Sheeba Thayil in Bangalore; T.V. Varkey in Kottayam; T.V. Mathew in Muvattupuzha; and Johny Lukose in Thiruvananthapuram. We also thank Itty Abraham, Kanti Bajpai, Michel Fortmann, T.J.S. George, Tetsuya Kataoka, Pierre Martin, Amitabh Mattoo, James Putzel, Robin Ramcharan, Julian

Schofield, P.O. Varghese and K. Vijayakrishnan, who were most forthcoming in helping us with our research.

During December 2001, T.V. Paul conducted an extensive field-
research trip to several Indian cities. The following institutions and indi-
viduals deserve special mention: P.R. Chari at the Institute of Peace and
Conflict Studies; Charan D. Wadhva and Nimmi Kurian at the Centre
for Policy Research; V.R. Raghavan at the Delhi Policy Group; Manoj
Joshi and Sidharth Varadarajan at the *Times of India*; Chinmaya
Gharekan at the United Services Institution (all the aforementioned in
New Delhi); Shrikant Paranjpe at the Department of Defence and
Strategic Studies, University of Pune; Gopal G. Malavya and Lawrence
Prabhakar at the University of Madras; G. Gopakumar at the
Department of Political Science, University of Kerala,
Thiruvananthapuram; Raju Thadikkaran at the Mahatma Gandhi
University, Kottayam; P.T. Thomas and R. Gopalakrisnanan at
Samskrithi, Cochin; Rajesh Kharat at the Department of Civics and
Politics, University of Mumbai; Purushottam Bhattacharya at Jadavpur
University, Kolkotta; and Satish Sahney at the Nehru Center in
Mumbai.

We benefited greatly from four panels on India that we organized at
the American Political Science Association meeting (Atlanta, August
1999), the International Studies Association meeting (Los Angeles,
March 2000, and New Orleans, 2002), and the South Asia Conference
at the University of Wisconsin – Madison (October 2000). We thank the
panelists and discussants at these meetings, especially Stephen P.
Cohen, Harold Gould, Ashok Kapur, Raju G.C. Thomas, Tim Hoyt,
James Wirtz, Douglas Lemke and Edward Kolodziej. Graduate students
who provided research assistance include: Cori Sommerfeldt, Marc
Lanteigne, Bill Hogg, Mathew Moss, Pushkar, Maren Zerriffi and
Shantarene Shungur. Mrinalini Menon deserves special praise for her
dedicated work in formatting and typing several changes in the manu-
script. Financial support was made available by generous grants from
the Social Sciences and Humanities Research Council of Canada
(SSHRC), the University of Montreal–McGill Research Group in
International Security (REGIS), and the Fonds pour la formation de
Chercheurs (FCAR). Cambridge University Press editors Marigold
Acland, Paul Watt and David Barrett provided excellent support.

Last but not least, we owe immense gratitude to our families for bearing our absences during field-research trips and providing moral support throughout the undertaking. T.V. Paul thanks Rachel, Kavya and
Leah, while Baldev Nayar thanks Nancy, Sheila and Tom, Kamala and
Jaswinder, and Sunita and Steve.

1 Introduction: India and Its Search for a Major-Power Role

This book investigates the dynamics of the interaction between the world's major-power system and India's attempt to enter it, and the prospects of India's integration into that system as well as its implications for world politics. Although having long been an issue of some importance in the postwar international system, India's search for a major-power role has gained special significance in the light of its nuclear tests in 1998. In this work, we attempt to answer the following three principal questions: What are the sources of the conflict between the world's major-power system and India over India's attempt to enter that system, and what is the extent to which there is convergence and divergence among the existing major powers over that question? What factors are responsible for the largely muted, moderate and stretched-out – rather than activist, confrontational and precipitous – nature of India's aspiration to a major-power role? And what are the prospects for India's peaceful entry into the major-power system in the twenty-first century?

In answering these questions, we provide a largely international-system-level analysis, although domestic and individual-level factors are given their due importance as well. First, the central argument is that India's foreign-policy behavior has been driven by the desire to achieve major-power status, and that the sources of the conflict between India and the major-power system have been fundamentally systemic, given on the one hand India's extant status as a rising power, its potential capabilities, and therefore its perceived "status inconsistency", and on the other the adverse impact that India's entry would have on the power positions of the present major powers and their allies, both regionally and globally. The convergence and divergence among the existing major powers over the question of a new entrant is likely to depend on the degree of polarization and the type of alliance patterns in the international system, and the manner in which their interests are affected by the acceptance of that entrant into their ranks.

Second, India's moderate posture, at least until recently, in relation both to role assertion and, correspondingly, to the building up of its

1

capabilities has been a function of: internally, its sociopolitical heterogeneity, and uneven and limited economic development, and the related constraints on developing and consolidating a national identity
appropriate for a major power; and externally, the policy of "regional
containment" pursued by one or more major powers in relation to
India. We use the term *regional containment* to denote a set of constraining policies pursued by the major powers, especially the United States
and China, such as alignment with and arms supplies to India's smaller
regional adversary, Pakistan, which have helped to balance and neutralize the Indian power position within South Asia. It also includes continued economic and technological sanctions, and the creation and
maintenance of international regimes meant to arrest India's development of military capabilities, especially in the nuclear and missile technology areas, precisely the capabilities that are necessary (but not
sufficient) for obtaining major-power status. Containment in this case is
not the system-wide hard containment characteristic of the intense mil-
itary-political-technological denial and nuclear deterrence associated
with the Western/US policy toward the Eastern bloc during the Cold
War era.

In other words, regional containment is limited containment with a
small c, while global containment is containment with a capital C. Some
policies that the US had adopted to contain Russian and Chinese power
in Asia also limited the expansion of India's power capabilities and influence regionally and internationally. This result could be characterized as
"indirect regional containment." A good example of this is the US support to Pakistan in its intense struggle to expel Soviet forces from
Afghanistan in the 1980s. The US aim here was largely to bleed the
Soviet Union but, when the former sought Pakistan's help, it meant the
rearming of Pakistan, whose main rivalry was with India and not with
the Soviets.

Regional containment in India's case is a limited strategy, as the powers imposing it have simultaneously pursued engagement and economic support in nonsecurity areas to the regional state that is targeted by
such a policy. Regional containment may be specific to military capabilities, unlike the hard containment of the communist bloc during the
Cold War, which involved all key aspects of interstate interactions and
was system-wide.

Theoretical underpinnings

India's nuclear tests in May 1998 had their immediate origins in its
longstanding concerns over national security in relation to China and
Pakistan and their military alliance relationship. However, a key under-

lying reason for the acquisition of nuclear capabilities that often goes understated is the enduring and deep-rooted aspiration of India for the role of a major power, and the related belief that the possession of an independent nuclear capability is an essential prerequisite for achieving that status. These two elements, national security and national role, however, are not necessarily unrelated, for major powers often see their national security tied to the acquisition and maintenance of capabilities that would enable them to protect their national autonomy and role. This autonomy is especially crucial in the military realm, as major powers by definition are those states that are least vulnerable to direct military coercion or attacks, and are most capable of deterring any potential attacks and of defending their security from other major and minor powers. India's search for a major-power role has a long history over the period since independence, and has manifested itself intermittently in various forms. We argue that it is the long-term aspiration for a major-power role that explains the thrust for self-reliance in economic and defense planning pursued by successive Indian governments since 1947, even when some of the policies were not bringing the desired results immediately. Economic, security and political autonomy have been interlinked as goals in the policies pursued by the Indian elite of all political persuasions, whether they clearly articulated this linkage or not.

What are the bases for India's aspiration, if not outright claim, to major-power status? The answer would seem to lie in certain national attributes, of which the elite seems cognizant. Chief among these are: India's existing geopolitical status (subcontinental size and large population); hegemonic presence in the Indo-centric South Asia region; the perception of India's potential economic and military power; and a long and sustained nationalist struggle, which fostered the thrust for foreign-policy autonomy and the tenacity to achieve it. There is also a sense among the Indian elite and informed public that India, as one of the world's largest and most enduring civilizational entities, ought to have a leadership role in the international arena. Although India's contemporaneous material capabilities in some areas may be relatively weak vis-à-vis present-day major powers, there is additionally the belief that it is a matter of time before this situation changes and that, in the interim, nonmaterial attributes could compensate for material weaknesses. However, just as there is a tenacious drive apparent on the part of India to acquire a major-power role, there is an even more powerful resistance to it on the part of the existing major powers, principally the US and, in recent years, China, even though such resistance has been masked in the language of world order and normative concerns. This resistance is explainable in the light of the fact that the international system is largely managed by a loose oligarchy based on differentiation in power.

A sharp hierarchical distinction in this system can be, and is, drawn between *great powers* (subjects, or *system-determining* states) and *minor powers* (objects, or *system ineffectuals*).[1] We use the terms *great powers* and *major powers* interchangeably, although we are sensitive to the different dimensions of power that make a state a leading actor in today's international order as compared to the nineteenth or early twentieth century international order dominated by European powers. Similarly, we also use the terms *world order* and *international order* interchangeably, although we are aware of the distinction made by scholars between the two concepts.[2]

To attenuate the sharpness of the distinction between major powers and minor powers, one can posit an in-between category of *independent centers of power* (or *system-influencing states*) in respect of states that do not have the leverage to influence the course of the international system as a whole, but which possess enough capabilities to have a considerable degree of foreign-policy autonomy and the capacity to resist the application of unwelcome decisions, especially in the realm of security, in their own regions. While great-power states have system-wide or global influence, mostly based on global power-projection capabilities, independent centers of power are often dominant or pre-eminent in a certain region. They may also be referred to, in Martin Wight's terms, as *great regional powers*, or as *middle powers* in view of their status as lying in between major and minor powers.[3]

In an anarchical international system, struggles for power occur, sometimes intensely, other times in more muted fashion or less visibly, especially among states that wield the highest levels of capability.[4] Typically, established major powers resist the emergence of a new major power, for to accommodate others in a similar role is to diminish one's own power, and to that extent lose some control over one's own national security and welfare, unless the rising state bestows a substantial addition to the capabilities of some major power in the international system. Rather, the tendency among established powers is to extend their own

[1] Jack Levy, *War in the Great Power System 1495–1975* (Lexington: The University Press of Kentucky, 1983), 16–17; Robert Keohane, "Lilliputians' Dilemmas: Small States in International Politics." *International Organization*, 23 (Spring 1969), 291–310.

[2] See, for instance, Hedley Bull, *The Anarchical Society* (New York: Columbia University Press, 1977), 8–20.

[3] Martin Wight, *Power Politics*, edited by Hedley Bull and Carsten Holbraad (Leicester, UK: Leicester University Press, 1978), chs 1–5.

[4] John Herz, "Idealist Internationalism and the Security Dilemma," *World Politics*, 2 (January 1950), 157–80; Robert Jervis, "Co-operation under the Security Dilemma," *World Politics*, 30 (January 1978), 167–214.

power as far as possible, to exercise dominion over others, and to reduce middle powers to the status of objects. In the contemporary era, since the possession of nuclear weapons and their delivery systems is a defining characteristic of major powers, such powers tend to seek to deny or deprive middle powers of such instruments, often under the garb of concern for world order and international stability. On the other hand, for those middle powers that have the potential to become major powers, entrance into the exclusive club of subjects is also a compelling goal. Status inconsistency (that is, the discrepancy between increasing status aspiration and ascribed status) puts pressure on rising states to work toward the alteration of the system, sometimes intensely, while at other times less so.

However, the aim of entering the major-power system is not simply for reasons of status or prestige, but rather for national survival and welfare, for middle powers are constantly confronted with the prospect of domination by the major powers. Aspiring middle powers are also cognizant of the fact that power (military capabilities) and plenty (economic capabilities) often go hand in hand. Some military powers may bandwagon for a period of time, long or short, with a major power that is most significant for their security and welfare, because their extant capabilities may be weak, even as their role aspirations remain dominant in the perceptions of the elite and sections of the public. However, the contrary impulses of major powers and rising middle powers often set them on a collision course, and the story of the graduation of a middle power to the status of major power has usually, at least in the past, been written in blood and fire even as it has been accompanied by much demonizing of the rising power. The resolution of this conflict between the major-power system and the challengers to that system as it exists thus represents a significant problem for study in international relations.

A typology developed by George Liska is useful here. Although the precise terms are not his, Liska holds that great powers typically choose from among three policies to follow toward a middle power that is pre-eminent in a region: *containment, satellization* and *accommodation*.[5] In regard to the first of this policy trilogy, he states:

Great powers can treat and have reason to treat individual middle powers as regional rivals, and be led to help still lesser states to contain them under the pretense of restraining, unilaterally or co-operatively, all Third World conflict.

[5] George Liska, "The Third World: Regional Systems and Global Order," in Robert E. Osgood *et al.* (eds), *Retreat from Empire* (Baltimore, MD: The Johns Hopkins University Press, 1973), 326.

In contrast to containment, the policy of accommodation leads to the devolution of regional responsibility to "apparently constructively disposed middle powers." Finally, a great power may adopt the policy of satellization, under which it endeavors to subordinate the foreign policy of the middle power to its own by way of acquiring an interventionist capability, such as aid or trade dependence, in the internal and external affairs of the target country. None of these policies is exclusive of the others, and a great power may use elements from each, at varying levels in different cases, depending on the state in question.

A middle power, faced with the strategies of containment and satellization on the part of the great power, may decide that the pursuit of an independent foreign policy is too costly and it may choose to bandwagon or accept the position as a foreign-policy satellite of the great power. Or it may simply accept the great power's leadership role with the expectation that it would receive economic and security side-payments; that is, market access and security protection. On the other hand, if it chooses to persist with a foreign policy of independence, the middle power may adopt a short-term policy of alliance, to the extent that the power configuration in the international system allows it, in order to cope with the pressures of containment and satellization. If the possibilities of alliance are not open, however, there may be no alternative but to become satellized. Even if the possibility of an alliance is available, some middle powers may still want to pursue a longer-term policy of building economic and military capabilities for the purpose of assuring foreign-policy autonomy under possible adverse circumstances in the future. For historical reasons, some middle powers may focus more on economic than on military capabilities. In such cases, the role of security provider could be delegated to the great power or to a collective alliance, as there may be immense payoffs in terms of free-riding. The security-protection role could also bring market access, as the protecting power may delegate some of the economic activities to the protected power. Thus, elites with clever strategies, as in the case of Japan and Korea vis-à-vis the US, may well use security cooperation as a great opportunity for economic advancement and endeavor to build their military capabilities as well. But even in these cases, middle powers may still be sensitive to questions concerning their power position in the international system and endeavor to build their military capabilities incrementally.

At base, the conflict between major powers and rising middle powers is part of the larger problem of power transition in the international sys-

---

⁶ A.F.K. Organski and Jacek Kugler, *The War Ledger* (Chicago: University of Chicago Press, 1980).

tem, but one which in the postwar period has acquired an aberrant aspect. Historically, in the 500-year-old modern international system, great-power status was often obtained through war.[6] Many historians of international diplomacy view the rise and fall of great powers as the major characteristic of international politics since the dawn of the modern state system in the seventeenth century.[7] In this phenomenon relating to the fate of great powers, war was the key system-changing mechanism because rising powers believed that they could obtain their goals without incurring too heavy a cost to themselves. However, the advent of nuclear weapons has transformed the nature of state behavior among the major powers, for the escalation of conflict to nuclear war would mean the destruction of the belligerent states; in effect, nuclear weapons have probably made war unthinkable and obsolete among the major powers.[8]

At the same time, even as nuclear weapons have provided security to their possessors, the nuclear powers have attempted to deny the possession of such weapons to new states through the creation and fostering of a nuclear nonproliferation regime. The aim here has been to bar new nuclear weapons states (NWSs) from emerging in order to preserve indefinitely the power position of the existing nuclear powers in the international system. Many small states accepted this regime, as it offered them certain benefits, most notably closer relations with the US, and support for civilian nuclear-energy programs. Some middle powers, such as Canada and Australia, have also become promoters of the regime for reasons of self-interest, as their security is provided by the US, or they genuinely want to prevent other states, especially their neighbors, from acquiring nuclear weapons.[9]

However, in their endeavor to construct and perpetuate an unequal nonproliferation regime, the major powers have encountered the most stubborn and sustained opposition from India. The consistency and persistence of this opposition marks India, in its own perception as well as in that of others, as distinctive among all the non-major powers. The impulse for this opposition springs largely from power considerations; that is, the underlying fear of the Indian elites that the strengthening of the regime would permanently bar India's entry into the major-power

[7] Paul Kennedy, *The Rise and Fall of Great Powers* (New York: Random House, 1987).

[8] John Lewis Gaddis, *The Long Peace: Inquiries into the History of the Cold War* (New York: Oxford University Press, 1987); Robert Jervis, *The Meaning of the Nuclear Revolution* (Ithaca, NY: Cornell University Press, 1989). See also John Mueller, *Retreat From Doomsday: The Obsolescence of a Major War* (New York: Basic Books, 1989).

[9] See T.V. Paul, *Power versus Prudence: Why Nations Forgo Nuclear Weapons* (Montreal: McGill–Queen's University Press, 2000).

league. The use of normative language by the Indian elite, such as sovereign equality or nondiscrimination, can be viewed as simply the nonviolent means that a rising power resorts to when it views the international regime as being constructed precisely to arrest its growth. An interesting contrast with India's behavior is the virtual acceptance of the nonproliferation regime by many smaller developing states as well as middle-ranking allies of the US, who see no chance of their obtaining a major-power role in the international system. The opposition by India to the regime culminated in the nuclear tests of 1998. In the aftermath of the tests, the Big Five of the UN Security Council, and their associates in G-8, NATO and EU, attempted, although not for too long, to prevent India from deploying its nuclear and missile capability, or from achieving a major-power role, through such means as economic sanctions and political condemnation. Within two years of the tests, however, New Delhi seemed to have weathered the sanctions, especially in the economic realm, and was engaged in strategic dialogue with all major powers; but its desire to obtain major-power status remains to be fulfilled.

The historical record shows that the present saga of conflict between a rising middle power attempting to assert a major-power role and the status quo states trying to constrain that effort is nothing new. What is new, however, is that the possession of nuclear weapons by India and by the five declared NWSs has altered the range of actions that either side can undertake in the pursuit of its goals. In the past, coordinated condemnation and coercive economic sanctions were preliminary to gunboat diplomacy and war against a challenger to the international order. Today, partially due to the potential for incalculable destruction and partially because of the "nuclear taboo," neither side is willing to engage in violent action that may escalate into nuclear conflict.[10] Could it be that the application of economic sanctions and diplomatic pressures has in the contemporary era become the moral equivalent of war, while the capacity of the targeted state to survive and overcome the economic sanctions and diplomatic pressures is the modern-day test for graduation to the rank of major power? The empirical answer to this question has yet to emerge.

As Kal Holsti argues, one of the main weaknesses of the present international order is the absence of a peaceful mechanism for rising powers to gain acceptance in the international hierarchy.[11] Moreover, the status quo is often viewed as legitimate and, accordingly, there is a built-in bias

---

[10] T.V. Paul, "Nuclear Taboo and War Initiation in Regional Conflicts," *Journal of Conflict Resolution*, 39 (December 1995), 696–717.

[11] Kalevi J. Holsti, *Peace and War: Armed Conflict and International Order* (Cambridge: Cambridge University Press, 1991), 339.

against an aspiring power. Established powers legitimize their position over time, and they resent the rise of new powers unless the latter augment their own power position in the international system. Thus, the pertinent question that arises is how India may be deterred from entering the major-power system, or how it may be integrated into that system with the fewest possible negative consequences for world peace and stability. The current great powers may find it hard to keep India, which holds one-sixth of humanity, from playing a major role in international politics when the clamor for democratic global governance is likely to increase in the twenty-first century. Moreover, with the pace at which the Indian economy has been growing since 1991 – an annual average of 5 to 7 per cent – India is poised, barring any economic meltdown, to become the third-largest world economic power behind the US and China by the end of the second decade of the twenty-first century. The Indian claim for major-power status is based on the realization among its elites that no other state in the developing world holds such actual and potential power capabilities. Demographic, military and economic changes will also result in the relative decline of the present-day major powers. Further, if New Delhi makes little headway in gaining a major-power role, the status inconsistency between role ambition and ascribed status is likely to widen as India makes stronger strides in nuclear and space technologies as well as economic development, in part provoked by the very sanctions imposed against it.

India: A status-inconsistent nation?

India is a rising power by several indicators of capability, although this power is yet to be fully realized or recognized by key actors in the international system. These indicators include the world's second-largest population, the fourth-largest army, the fourth-largest economy in 2000 (in terms of purchasing power parity (PPP)), the eighth-largest industrial economy, the world's largest pool of scientists and engineers after the US, and a middle class double the size of that of Japan and growing. In the past, these raw indicators have been extremely critical in deciding the rank of states. Since the economic reforms began in 1991, the Indian economy has grown at an annual average of 5 to 7 per cent, placing India among the world's better-performing economies in terms of GDP growth rate.[12] This growth was reflected in India replacing Germany in 2000 to become the fourth-largest economy in PPP terms. This change placed the Indian economy behind only the US, China and

---

[12] World Bank, *India: Sustaining Rapid Economic Growth* (Washington, DC: 1997), xiii.

Japan, but ahead of Germany, Russia (formally the Russian Federation), UK and France.[13] These achievements have been noted by many leading Western scholars who see India as a rising power. For instance, Henry Kissinger predicts that in the twenty-first century the international system will be dominated by six major powers: the US, Europe, China, Japan, Russia and probably India. Similarly, Samuel Huntington foresees that during the coming decades, "India could move into rapid economic development and emerge as a major contender for influence in world affairs."[14] Norwegian scholar Johan Galtung even predicts that India and the European Union are on their way to superpower status.[15]

Although an independent actor for over five decades and a vibrant democracy in comparison with almost all developing countries, India has been less integrated into the world order than one would expect for a country of vast size, long history, and actual and potential economic capabilities. Despite substantial achievements, a discrepancy exists in India's accomplishments and aspirations, on the one hand, and its ascribed status on the other. Differently put, India remains less integrated in the international order than most other major actors of similar power capabilities at comparable stages of their development. The major powers of the international system, especially the US, have been somewhat instrumental in the isolation of India, although India's own polices and strategic choices, especially in the economic arena, have been part of the reason for its lack of integration as well.

India exhibits some characteristics of a status-inconsistent nation. Its leaders often speak of the second-class treatment it receives in comparison with China, especially from the US and its allies.[16] Its achievements and its ascribed status in the international system increasingly do not match. Although India has not yet mounted any violent challenge to the order, it has had serious disagreements with several international-order

---

[13] World Bank, *The World Development Report, 2000/2001* (Washington, DC: 2001), 274–5.

[14] Henry Kissinger, *Diplomacy* (New York: Simon & Schuster, 1994), 23–4; Samuel P. Huntington, *The Clash of Civilizations and the Remaking of World Order* (New York: Simon & Schuster, 1996), 121. Huntington classifies India as a core state in the emerging international order of eight core civilizations. *ibid.*, ch. 9.

[15] Johan Galtung, "On the Way to Superpower Status: India and the EC Compared," *Futures*, 24 (November 1992), 917–29.

[16] As one report put it, "there is a lingering resentment that the United States treats India as if it were not important, and a very strong sense that India has at least as much claim as China to the status of great power." Flora Lewis, "The World-Class Muddle in Seattle was a Failure of Politics," http://www.IHT.com, December 10, 1999.

norms promoted by the status quo powers. India's challenge has been confined primarily to diplomatic means, and is reflected most prominently in the acquisition of nuclear and missile capabilities in violation of the nonproliferation regime, and in its voting behavior in international institutions. Being a democracy and a nuclear weapons power, India is highly unlikely to resort to war as a mechanism to challenge the status quo in the near or medium terms. However, New Delhi has pursued nonviolent and diplomatic means to oppose some elements of the international order designed to keep its power status confined to the lower ranks. These include the persistent and vocal opposition to the nuclear nonproliferation and missile-control regimes, the articulation of norms that enhance international equity, fairness and justice, and the promotion of a new international economic order and sovereign equality of states.[17] Despite its vociferous championing of global norms of justice, India often finds itself isolated by the major-power system, especially on core issues that affect its security and economic prosperity.

India's isolation or limited integration is vivid in several important areas. Three such areas are: international institutions and regimes; technology, especially the nuclear and space fields; and the world economy.

United Nations and other international institutions

India is the world's second-most populous country and it is fast headed to become number one in population by the second decade of the twenty-first century. It is home to about one-sixth of the world's population. Yet it has only limited say in the way international governance is conducted. Although India is an active member of many global institutions, such as the World Trade Organization, the World Bank and the International Monetary Fund, and it has been occasionally successful in influencing the decisions of these bodies, in general it does not, like most developing countries, get much hearing in them.

India is also the world's largest democracy, patterned after the British parliamentary system of government. The people of India hold many fundamental freedoms that citizens of Western democracies enjoy. It has generally been a supporter of many important norms of international relations, especially those relating to sovereignty and the peaceful settlement of disputes. From its very inception, India has been a major contributor to UN peacekeeping operations. Since the end of the Cold War in 1991, India has emerged as one of the most active troop contributors

---

[17] On this, see Baldev Raj Nayar, "India as a Limited Challenger," in T.V. Paul and John A. Hall (eds), *International Order and the Future of World Politics* (Cambridge: Cambridge University Press, 1999), ch. 11.

for such peacekeeping. In 1998, it became the largest troop contributor, while in 1996 and 1999 it was the second-largest contributor.[18] India is also a major recipient of refugees from other states, as it has a fairly liberal refugee policy, but it has not been a producer of refugees itself, an incredible achievement for a state that holds over 1 billion people of immense diversity. The political turmoils within India have also produced few internal refugees.

During much of the Cold War era, India was a forceful leader of the developing states and represented their views through the Group of 77 and the nonaligned movement. In that role, India mobilized the developing world and provided a certain amount of bargaining power to the lower-ranking members of the international system. It was a key player in the New International Economic Order (NIEO) negotiations held under the auspices of the United Nations Conference on Trade and Development (UNCTAD) in the 1970s.[19] India still retains a key role in some of the international institutions, especially those relating to international trade, and a limited but significant role in lending institutions like the World Bank and IMF. For instance, at the December 1999 WTO ministerial meeting in Seattle and the November 2001 meeting in Doha, India led the developing nations and made a significant impact in preventing the developed countries from forcing their agenda on the conference, especially concerning issues relating to labor, environment, and market access for agricultural products.[20] The Group of 15 (G-15) developing countries that took a leading role in the conference was India's main source of bargaining power. India has also been a member of the G-20 forum, comprising finance ministers from key developed and developing countries, to deal with global financial issues and to prevent crises similar to the 1997 East Asian crisis. Yet there has been great reluctance to include India as a permanent member of the UN Security Council. The Western countries, as well as those developing countries that want Japan and Germany to be included, have opposed India's permanent membership.[21]

---

[18] http://www.globalpolicy.org/security/peacekpg/data/pk001-1.htm.

[19] Marc Williams, *Third World Co-operation: The Group of 77 in UNCTAD* (London: Pinter, 1991), 97–8.

[20] Lewis, "The World-Class Muddle in Seattle"; Chidanand Rajghatta, "Maran Holds Sway: India Sits Pretty at WTO," http://www.Indian-express.com, December 2, 1999; "Input from India Critical: WTO Chief," http://www.hinduonnet.com, January 12, 2000; Paul Blustein, "142 Nations Reach Pact on Trade Negotiations," http://www.washingtonpost.com, November 15, 2001.

[21] This has been slowly changing. By early 2000, four permanent members – US, UK, France and Russia – had supported India's candidature to a greater or lesser degree, at least theoretically, while one, China, stood aloof from the issue. This verbal support is yet to materialize in concrete action, however.

The limited nature of India's inclusion in global governance has been largely because of power politics. While the US and its Western allies strongly push, in the aftermath of their triumph in the Cold War, the liberal agenda of democratizing countries internally, they have been the most emphatic opponents of democratizing global institutions. In this respect, they act mostly as realists, who do not share many of the Wilsonian idealist principles of international governance. In many respects, they are against translating internationally the democratic values they hold dear in their domestic societies. Many Western liberals also support the hierarchical nature of international institutional governance. To them, the dominance by Western liberal states is essential to carrying out the liberal agenda; that is, democratization, free trade, and the maintenance and preservation of the liberal pacific union.[22] US realist scholars have long argued that the demands for change in international institutions and regimes are driven by power considerations of the developing countries – that is, to improve their structural position in the international system – and that therefore they are not in the interest of the developed countries.[23]

Technological arena

The second area where India's isolation is clear is in the technological arena, especially nuclear and space-related technologies. This isolation was institutionalized when the Nuclear Nonproliferation Treaty (NPT) was concluded in 1968, much against the opposition of India. The treaty legitimized the nuclear weapons of the five permanent members of the UN Security Council, who had acquired nuclear weapons by 1967, while it forbade all other countries from becoming NWSs. Article 9 of the NPT defined a nuclear weapons state as one which had "manufactured and exploded a nuclear weapon or other nuclear explosive device prior to 1 January 1967."[24] Among the countries that were affected most by this treaty was India, because it had no major-power allies to provide a security umbrella, even as it had an enduring conflict with China, a declared NWS, whose capability was legitimized by the NPT. India's plea for a comprehensive disarmament treaty encompassing all states, or the provision of guaranteed security assurances to non-nuclear states,

---

[22] On this theme, see Michael W. Doyle, "A Liberal View: Preserving and Expanding the Liberal Pacific Union," in Paul and Hall (eds), *International Order*, 19–40.

[23] Stephen D. Krasner, *Structural Conflict: The Third World against Global Liberalism* (Berkeley: University of California Press, 1985).

[24] For the text of the treaty, see William Epstein, *The Last Chance: Nuclear Proliferation and Arms Control* (New York: The Free Press, 1976), 316–21.

was rejected by the NWSs. Instead, they insisted that India not develop nuclear weapons and remain an underdog in the international nuclear order.

The Indian leaders viewed the NPT as a highly discriminatory instrument and unanimously opposed India's accession to it. All political parties in India were intensely hostile to the treaty, and a national consensus emerged against signing it. This Indian defiance resulted in the imposition of sanctions and restrictions on technology transfer by supplier countries. While many erstwhile opponents of the treaty, including Brazil, Argentina and South Africa, joined it in the 1990s, India has been persistent in its opposition to it, despite being the target of severe sanctions and denial of technology and materials. This opposition is primarily driven by systemic reasons. No other country views itself as a rising power more than India does in the contemporary international system, and no other country perceives that it has the most to lose by acceding to a discriminatory treaty which will keep it down as a permanent underdog nation. These perceptions were again evident in the negotiations for the Comprehensive Test Ban Treaty (CTBT) in 1996, when India was alone in opposing it, mainly because the treaty made it obligatory for all forty-four states with a nuclear power reactor, including India, to ratify it as a condition for its coming into force. The Indians were clearly worried that adhering to the treaty would foreclose their nuclear-testing option, while it would allow the P-5 states (the five permanent members of the UN Security Council) to conduct laboratory-type or subcritical-level tests.[25]

The technological isolation of India began most clearly in the wake of its 1974 nuclear test. In fact, most of the stringent instruments of the nonproliferation regime commenced with the Indian test. In 1977, the Carter administration elevated nuclear nonproliferation to the "centerpiece of his foreign policy and singled out South Asia as a particularly important target," and by the 1990s the US policy in South Asia was largely focused on the issue of nuclear proliferation.[26] The London Suppliers Club guidelines, the *Nuclear Non-Proliferation Act*, the missile-control regime – all these were heavily aimed at retarding the Indian

---

[25] On the Indian objections to the treaty, see Arundhati Ghose, "Negotiating the CTBT: India's Security Concerns and Nuclear Disarmament," *Journal of International Affairs*, 51 (Summer 1997), 247–8. See also T.T. Poulose, *The CTBT and the Rise of Nuclear Nationalism in India* (New Delhi: Lancer's Books, 1996).

[26] Stephen Philip Cohen, "The United States, India and Pakistan: Retrospect and Prospect," in Selig S. Harrison, Paul H. Kriesberg and Dennis Kux (eds), *India and Pakistan: The First Fifty Years* (Washington, DC: Woodrow Wilson Center Press, 1999), 198.

nuclear and missile programs.[27] The nuclear powers and their allies made every effort to isolate India and deny it the technology necessary for both military and civilian programs in the nuclear and space fields. This isolation was strengthened temporarily in 1998 following the Pokhran tests, when the US and its Western allies imposed economic sanctions on India.

India has also been under sanctions, especially by the Western countries, in the area of space and missile technology. India's space program, although largely intended for civilian purposes, came under sanctions because of the possible military applications of space technology, especially in the area of missile development. The embargoes that have been largely associated with the Missile Technology Control Regime (MTCR) have helped to increase the cost of and, more importantly, to delay India's space program, but none has been able to halt the program.[28] In fact, by 2001 India had put in place some key satellite programs and launch vehicles under the Polar Satellite Launch Vehicle (PSLV) and Geostationary Satellite Launch Vehicle (GSLV) series. It has become a key space power with the ability to launch and deploy satellites in different geosynchronous orbits. In recent years, India has emerged as one of the few nations with high-resolution, remote-sensing satellite technology. Indian scientists have also set their eyes on the moon, as part of their next round of space programs.

Thus, despite the technological and economic sanctions, India has built up a substantial nuclear and space capability, which is the most successful in the developing world but still not on par with that of the five major powers. Its behavior thus far has not been as irresponsible as nonproliferation analysts often portray. India has not supplied nuclear materials to any potential nuclear states, nor has it engaged in selective proliferation, as most of the current nuclear weapons powers have done. This restraint has not earned India any kudos, however. Part of this anomaly is that India has rarely used its technology as a lever to gain access to the MTCR, nor have the Western countries shown a willingness to accept a new space power into their ranks by inviting India, which possesses the fifth-largest space program in the world.

---

[27] Virginia I. Foran, "Indo-US Relations after the 1998 Tests: Sanctions versus Incentives," in Gary K. Bertsch, Seema Gahlaut and Anupam Srivastava (eds), *Engaging India: US Strategic Relations with the World's Largest Democracy* (New York: Routledge, 1999), 40–76.

[28] Dinshaw Mistry, "India's Emerging Space Program," *Pacific Affairs*, 71 (Summer 1998), 151–74.

Economic sphere

The third area where India's isolation is most evident is the economic realm. Unlike the previous two areas, where isolation was imposed by outside powers, economic isolation has largely been self-imposed. Until 1991, the Indian economy was on a low-growth trajectory and was one of the most insulated in the world.[29] India's share of less than 1 per cent of total global trade and relatively low levels of foreign direct investment are good indicators of its lack of integration with the world economy. For more than four decades, India's technology and products remained inferior to international standards. However, the economic isolation grew out of the desire of the political elite for autonomy or less dependence on outside powers.[30] The reasons for an autarkic economic policy are often portrayed as internal, while the underlying systemic causes of such a policy tend to be ignored. A state may pursue economic autarky partly because of its desire to become a major power, since the ability to withstand economic pressures from abroad is a crucial precondition for obtaining a leadership role in the international system. This strategic consideration was the key to the mercantilist and neomercantilist philosophies of the principal European powers, as well as Japan, in the past. However, in recent years this strategy seems to have become outmoded, as economic autarky does not guarantee the economic and technological wherewithal necessary to keep a power equal to or ahead of its competitors and peer states. In fact, a great power can decline precipitously as its autarkic economic policies make it economically noncompetitive, as happened in the case of the Soviet Union in the early 1990s.

The liberalization of the Indian economy that began in 1991 has somewhat changed its situation of relative economic isolation. Although the immediate catalyst for the reform was the balance-of-payments crisis in 1991, another consideration, although often not stated, may have been strategic; that is, the fear that India was falling behind China.[31]

---

[29] During the period from 1950 to 1990, India's average annual GDP growth rate was 3.71 per cent, which in per capita terms amounted to only 1.5 per cent overall, given the high level of population growth. Meghnad Desai, "Capitalism, Socialism, and the Indian Economy," in Kalyan Banerji and Tarjani Vakil (eds), *India: Joining the World Economy* (New Delhi: Tata McGraw–Hill, 1995), 191.

[30] For evidence on this point, see Baldev Raj Nayar, *Globalization and Nationalism: The Changing Balance in India's Economic Policy, 1950–2000* (New Delhi: Sage, 2001), ch. 2.

[31] On this, see Jalal Alamgir, "India's Trade and Investment Policy: The Influence of Strategic Rivalry with China," *Issues and Studies*, 35 (May–June 1999), 105–33.

Since 1991, India's integration into the world order is more evident in the economic domain than in the institutional or technological areas. This disparity is largely because economic integration required only unilateral reforms, whereas in the other two areas integration depends to a great extent on the policies of other key states. The results of liberalization have been fairly positive as major improvements have occurred in the country's foreign-exchange reserves, foreign direct investment, and equity markets. The Asian financial crisis during 1997–98 affected India in a limited way only, as did the Western economic sanctions imposed following the 1998 nuclear tests. During the 1990s, India's GDP grew at an average rate of almost 6 per cent, a substantial if not too high a rate, only to slow down to 4 per cent in 2000–01, despite the global recession and the technology stock meltdown in the US.

The historical dimension: The past as prologue

The status inconsistency between role aspiration and actual role that is evident in India's case at present is, however, characteristic of the entire period since independence, although the precise extent to which it is manifest may vary. Two distinct phases can be demarcated in the interaction between India's search for a major-power role and the major-power system. One phase extends from independence in 1947 to the early 1960s, when there was a stark divergence between ambition and material capabilities. The lack of material capabilities fundamentally resulted from the heritage of some two centuries of British colonialism, which left the country economically underdeveloped and dependent, overwhelmingly rural (85 per cent), food-scarce and famine-prone, and illiterate (87 per cent). What is astonishing is that, despite the handicap of the lack of material capabilities, the Indian elites attempted to play a leadership role on the basis of *soft power,* defined in terms of diplomacy and ideological appeal, rather than *hard power,* defined in terms of economic and military capabilities.[32] This pattern of behavior constitutes an important intellectual puzzle, and leads to such questions as: What factors made India assert a leadership role through the nonaligned movement while lacking in economic and military capabilities? Can personality, cultural/civilizational and historical-experience variables provide a convincing explanation for the ambition in the absence of corresponding capabilities? It would seem that India's behavior pattern was a function of the leadership's perception of the country's potential as a future major power, the anticolonial nationalist ethos of the leadership,

---

[32] Joseph Nye, *Bound to Lead: The Changing Nature of American Power* (New York: Basic Books, 1990), 191.

and the Gandhian value system – all these prevented India from either joining any military bloc or remaining passive on critical global issues. At the core of it, though, lay the systemic roots of a large, emerging state attempting to carve out a leadership role in the international system through normative means, as its elites seemed keenly aware that material capabilities were in short supply for the time being, but that they would improve with the passage of time. The civilizational factor also served as a powerful basis for a claim to a leadership role. But a frontal assault on the systemic power structure was evidently impractical and imprudent, whereas a low-risk normative assault offered the possibility of achieving gradual change.

However, the pursuit of an activist role by India was perceived by the US as serving to circumscribe its influence in the developing world, and it provoked Washington to undertake a policy of regional containment aimed against India, in order to squash its putative leadership role, through building up Pakistan militarily and siding with it in the South Asian regional conflict. Washington was, no doubt, also greatly motivated by the Cold War conflict with Moscow and wanted to use Pakistan as a base to conduct espionage in regard to Soviet nuclear activities, and to develop Pakistan as a frontline state against feared Soviet expansion into South-West Asia. America's regional containment of India was only partial, as the US simultaneously attempted to engage India, albeit in a limited fashion. Because of its larger bipolar rivalry, the US provided substantial economic aid to India to prevent it from a fuller alignment with the Soviet Union, especially during the late 1950s and early 1960s. However, the US military build-up of Pakistan led India to focus more directly on questions of national security. India's activist global posture was thus patently premature and unrealistic, in that India revealed its hand of ambition for a major-power role before having acquired the necessary capabilities for that role.[33] It is noteworthy, nonetheless, that partly in reaction to US actions and partly in response to its own inner impulses, India launched on a policy of counterbalancing regional containment through cultivating friendships with China and, subsequently, the Soviet Union on the political and diplomatic, but not military, plane, as well as on a long-term plan of building an industrial-scientific base for the acquisition of economic-military capabilities. These actions and reactions increased the role of superpowers in the affairs of South Asia, and the larger systemic rivalry was also played out in the region.

[33] Ashok Kapur, "Indian Strategy: The Dilemmas About Enmities, the Nature of Power and the Pattern of Relations," in Yogendra K. Malik and Ashok Kapur (eds), *India: Fifty Years of Democracy and Development* (New Delhi: APH Publishing Corp., 1999), 341–72.

In the first phase, then, the challenges for India were, internally, to build up economic and military capabilities and, externally, to cope with the policies of regional containment and satellization. This phase ended with the India–China War of 1962, which showed up the basic unrealism of a policy based on soft power and forced India to come to terms with the proposition that the pursuit of a major-power role in the absence of hard power, or military capabilities, was a chimera. The transformation of India from a Gandhian-idealist posture to a realpolitik state was thus forced on it by systemic and subsystemic forces; that is, the failure in war with China and the intense balance-of-power politics pursued by regional adversaries with the aid of extraregional major powers.

The second phase, which starts with 1962 and lasts until 1998, represents a long period during which India attempted to adapt to the requirements of a power-driven international system. Domestically, this phase represents continuity with the earlier one in terms of building economic and military capabilities. In the course of building such capabilities, however, India had to overcome a concatenation of challenges pertaining to economic crises, political turmoil, military conflict and several insurgencies. Externally, too, the phase represents continuity, in that India had to cope with the challenge of regional containment, now directed by both the US and China, whether independently or collaboratively, but it also had to avoid being handcuffed by the imposition of international normative regimes, aimed precisely at thwarting the rise of middle powers to the status of major powers. The second phase marks a long period of transition, which culminated in India's defiance of the major-power system through its nuclear tests.

This second phase is most interesting as a transitional period. It evidences a race between two powerful impulses. On the one hand, India was engaged in a tenacious, though slow-paced and protracted, drive to build its economic and military capabilities and to retain its nuclear option unless the major powers would agree to a time-bound program for the universal elimination of nuclear weapons. On the other hand, the existing major powers hastened precisely to foreclose India's nuclear option, by rapidly pushing through the installation of an international regime organized around the permanent extension of the NPT and the finalization of the CTBT, while retaining their own nuclear monopoly and refusing to commit themselves to the elimination of nuclear weapons. Additionally, the major powers applied both de jure and de facto sanctions against India on the transfer of dual-use technology in the nuclear, missile and electronic areas.

Notwithstanding the phase culminating in India's nuclear tests, what is noteworthy is the fact that India's drive to resist the imposition of unequal nuclear regimes and to build its capabilities, even though not yet concluded, was stretched out over a very long period and was marked by ambiguity, moderation and restraint; it was largely reactive and basically lacking in direct confrontation with the major-power system. India's behavior did not evidence an emphatic assertion of power or an open confrontation with the major-power system, as had been seen in the case of China in the 1960s. The important intellectual puzzle that arises is as to why a middle power eager to enter the major-power system remained restrained and reactive. What were the factors responsible for this particular pattern of state behavior? First and foremost, it would seem that the constraints derived from the lack of economic and military capabilities adequate for a major-power role, especially in respect of nuclear and missile capabilities. This raises the further question as to why the build-up of capabilities was tepid in the first place. It would seem that the answer to that question lies in: internally, India's sociopolitical heterogeneity and the related constraints on developing a national identity appropriate for a major-power role; and externally, the policy of regional containment pursued by one or more major powers, through both counterbalancing alliances and the construction of new international regimes aimed to prevent new nuclear or space powers from arising in the system.

The future

The nuclear tests in May 1998 inaugurated a third phase in which India removed the earlier ambiguity characterizing the two dimensions of its search for a major-power role and its possession of nuclear weapons capabilities. One significant question here relates to the reactions of the major-power system, both collectively and severally by its constituents, and the measures undertaken to counter the challenge along both dimensions.

A final set of questions pertains to the existing opportunities and constraints in the interaction between the major-power system and India that are likely to promote or thwart change in the present structure of the major-power system, or to enhance or dissipate India's ambition to become a major power. Are the major powers prepared to incorporate or integrate independent-minded new members into the major-power system beyond symbolically accommodating only their subordinate allies? Correspondingly, can India be truly said to have the capabilities for a major-power role? Is it a complete power or only an incomplete power? What, indeed, is the appropriate measure of capabilities: aggregate power, or per capita indices? How does the India of today compare in capabilities with China at the time of its incorporation into the major-power system in 1972? Is the disparity in capabilities between the US and other members of the major-power system (China, Russia, UK and France) smaller or larger than the disparity between India and one or more of the other members? If integration is barred, what other policies are open to the existing major powers for adoption in relation to India? Isolation? Marginalization? Benign neglect? What are the prospects for success of such policies?

Methodology

By the very nature of the subject matter pertaining to the struggle for the acquisition of a major-power role in the contemporary period, the approach has to be that of an inductive single-case study, for there are not very many new viable claimants, especially from the developing world, for the role. Indeed, India is perhaps sui generis today in this regard, and it may well be a case of Indian exceptionalism. Ian Lustick outlines how, since the end of the nineteenth century, there have been no additions to the club of great powers, because of the capacity of the "existing great powers to interrupt the dynamic interaction of war and state building that had helped bring them into existence as such and [relatedly] to the new, dense, and increasingly constraining network of anti-belligerency norms in the international arena."[34] Remarkably, however, by way of exception to the general rule on barriers to entry, he notes that "China, India, and Brazil are examples of very large countries that may now, or soon, be legitimately considered 'great powers'." Since China is already recognized as a major power, while Brazil has chosen to remain in the orbit of the US rather than assert itself to be an independent center of power, only India can be genuinely regarded as pursuing the search with some degree of determination and is therefore deserving of study by its very exceptionalism in the contemporary era. This does not mean that in the future other middle powers will not arise with major-power ambitions. Japan and Germany (perhaps under the EU umbrella) are two potential candidates which are at present, however, constrained by a host of historical factors in asserting their position.

Importantly, there are comparative elements to the study as well. We look at the five current major powers – US, Russia, UK, France and China – and examine when and how they acquired major-power status. In addition, the power capabilities of key regional states – India's current reference group – are assessed.

[34] Ian S. Lustick, "The Absence of Middle Eastern Great Powers: Political 'Backwardness' in Historical Perspective," *International Organisation*, 51 (Autumn 1997), 653–83.

The series of questions that the interaction between India and the major-power system raises, not only in respect of the immediate present, but also in regard to the more recent postwar period, requires a scholarly analysis that is both diachronic and synchronic. For the diachronic part, reliance is based on secondary works and the memoirs of decision-makers, while the synchronic focus on developments in the third period is based on, apart from reports in the media, discussions with policy-makers and analysts in the capitals and intellectual centers of the major powers. Of course, the combination of synchronic and diachronic dimensions, of thematic analysis and historical narrative, and of the intellectual products of two authors, makes occasional repetition in the text unavoidable.

Our work is very much influenced by classical realist ideas, especially those relating to the international system and balance of power, although we are not dogmatic about the claims of one international-relations paradigm or another. Classical realism, it seems to us, provides the best framework for explaining the rise and fall of major powers. We have also been influenced by power-transition theories, especially those that deal with the economic and military causes and consequences of the rise and fall of major powers. Although we agree with neorealists on the role of nuclear weapons and polarity, we diverge from them in that we believe that, while system structure is important, state actions and strategies are influential as well.[35] The grand strategies of rising powers and established powers may, in part, determine what sort of system develops in the international arena. Structure, generated by power distributions, is very important, but outcomes are partially determined by the strategic choices of individual states as they intervene between systemic forces and international order. Further, the classical realist notion of *prudence* has great relevance in the age of nuclear and other weapons with immense destructive power. Within a realist framework, we pay special attention to systemic forces.

Our systemic focus is posited on the belief that the security behavior of a state is largely determined by its position in the international system, and that this position is affected by the interactions between it and other major powers, as well as those among the major powers themselves. This belief is consistent with the three characteristics of a systemic approach identified by Robert Jervis. They are: first, outcomes may not be due to the attributes of actors; second, as units are interconnected, changes in some parts of the system can produce changes in others; and, third, relations between two actors are conditioned, in part,

---

[35] For the neorealist position on system and structure, see Kenneth Waltz, *Theory of International Politics* (New York: Random House, 1979).

by the relations between each of them and other actors in the international system.[36] However, the behavior of key actors – that is, major powers – produces the maximum effect in its implications for smaller powers. States placed differently in the international system may have different security concerns, even though security and prosperity are primary motives of all states. Thus, major powers tend to have global interests, while the security concerns and interests of most middle powers and small powers are concentrated in a given region. An aspiring major power also perceives its security as being tied to the larger balance-of-power processes occurring in the international system, involving other established powers, even when it is focusing largely on its immediate neighborhood. Therefore, as an aspiring major power, India's state behavior can best be understood by using a framework with a largely systemic focus.

Significance

This study has major significance for scholarship on international relations and foreign-policy-making. The public and scholarly interest on India is likely to increase as India attempts to advance its economic and military power, especially nuclear and missile capabilities, and as the established powers attempt to constrain or utilize Indian capabilities before the middle of the twenty-first century. Demographic and economic changes will automatically thrust India into becoming one of the largest world actors, and yet not fully accredited in a leadership role in the international system. How a democratic India can be peacefully integrated will be crucial for international order and peace in the next century. The Indian case will, in fact, be a test case for peaceful systemic change as well as whether international governance can at best be partially democratized.

Most importantly, the peaceful integration of India into the major-power system would remove a likely source of potential conflict in the international system – that associated with power transitions. The rise and fall of major powers, or power transition, forms an important subject in political realism and diplomatic history, while peaceful change is crucial for a liberal global order, especially with respect to international governance. The generic problem of power transitions arises from the

---

[36] See Robert Jervis, "Systems Theories and Diplomatic History," in Paul Gordon Lauren (ed.), *Diplomacy: New Approaches in History, Theory, and Policy* (New York: Free Press, 1979), 212–44; and Robert Jervis, *System Effects: Complexity in Political and Social Life* (Princeton, NJ: Princeton University Press, 1997).

fact that the modern international system has been characterized by the rise and decline of major powers. History tells us that political units that amass superior material capabilities – military, economic and technological – attempt to refashion their environment according to their interests and ideals. In this process, the international system often generates intense conflict, especially between rising and established powers. In the past such conflicts had led to world wars, resulting in power transitions. Wars occurred because the challenging nations were dissatisfied with their status, while the system leaders were reluctant to make changes in their privileged positions until they were forced to do so.[37] Rising powers that challenged the established powers were often not sufficiently integrated into the norms of the international order upheld by the status quo powers. The lack of integration of rising powers into the international system has adverse consequences for international order, as it can generate pressures within the rising state to alter the status quo, sometimes through violent and at other times through nonviolent means.

The lack of integration can also be reflected in the status inconsistency of rising powers. Status-inconsistency theorists have argued that the international system generates stratification similar to that in domestic societies where interactions between top-dog and underdog actors lead to conflict. Galtung, who pioneered the argument, contends that "aggression is most likely to arise in social positions in rank-disequilibrium. In a system of individuals it may take the form of crime, in a system of groups the form of revolutions, and in a system of nations

---

[37] A variety of historical-structural theories exist on the subject, and they all point to the violent nature of power transitions. Dominant under this category are Gilpin's hegemonic stability, Organski's power transition, and Modelski's long-cycle theories. See Robert Gilpin, *War and Change in World Politics* (Cambridge: Cambridge University Press, 1981), 10–11; A.F.K. Organski and Jacek Kugler, *The War Ledger* (Chicago: University of Chicago Press, 1980), 20–3; and George Modelski, "The Long Cycle of Global Politics and the Nation State," *Comparative Studies in Society and History*, 20 (April 1978), 214–35. Diplomatic historian Paul Kennedy underlines war and imperial overstretch as the principal mechanisms through which the rise and fall of major powers occur. See his *The Rise and Fall of Great Powers: Economic Change and Military Conflict from 1500 to 2000* (New York: Random House, 1987). On the basis of historical evidence, critics point out that not all power transitions have led to wars. For one such critic, only power transitions associated with high levels of dissatisfaction on the part of the challenger have generated wars. John A. Vasquez, "When are Power Transitions Dangerous? An Appraisal and Reformulation of Power Transition Theory," in Jacek Kugler and Douglas Lemke (eds), *Parity and War* (Ann Arbor: University of Michigan Press, 1996), 35–56.

the form of war."[38] Thus, the discrepancy between a nation's achievements and its ascribed status at the international level can be a cause for conflict.[39] The generation of status inconsistency tends to be slow but, when it occurs, lateral pressure may result; that is, the country may become more assertive, aggressive and revisionist vis-à-vis its neighbors and other significant powers. Ultranationalist groups may gain control of the society, and they may undermine the democratic fabric of the rising power. Thus, systemic pressures can have tremendous internal consequences for a rising power. In this century, such internal transformations have occurred in Japan and Germany, largely as a result of status inconsistency generated by external systemic pressures.

Although some status inconsistencies have led to wars in the past, violence need not be the only mechanism through which a status-inconsistent nation challenges the international order. In India's case, nonviolent challenge is the most likely route, given the nation's history and general ethos. A nonintegrated rising power may challenge the status quo through a variety of means, such as pursuing assertive and belligerent policies, building up arms, and breaking or not observing norms created by the status quo powers or even engaging in limited wars.[40] In the nuclear age, nuclear-armed rising states are unlikely to resort to a frontal assault similar to the way Germany and Japan did in the 1930s, but a general dissatisfaction may be expressed through other mechanisms and policies that are inimical to the interests of established powers. Such policies could include the extension of economic and political support for revolutionary regimes, and the supply of weapons to states or groups that oppose the status quo powers. Opposition could also be mounted through violation of, or nonadherence to, treaties created by the top-dog countries to arrest the growth of rising powers from enhancing their power capabilities. The fundamental challenge for any international order is to attain change without actual war or a major systemic conflict similar to the Cold War. In this respect, the reconciliation of status and achievements as well as the integration of rising powers by the top-dog nations matter most for a peaceful international order. This book has thus relevance to several aspects of international order, most

---

[38] Johan Galtung, "A Structural Theory of Aggression," *Journal of Peace Research*, 1 (1964), 98–9.

[39] Michael D. Wallace, *War and Rank among Nations* (Lexington, KY: Lexington Books, 1973), 18, 72; Manus I. Midlarsky, *On War: Political Violence in the International System* (New York: The Free Press, 1975), 94, 110, 141.

[40] For an interesting discussion of China in this context, see Thomas J. Christensen, "Posing Problems without Catching Up: China's Rise and Challenges for U.S. Security Policy," *International Security*, 25 (Spring 2001), 5–40.

prominently theories of power transitions, balance of power, containment, deterrence and nuclear weapons.

The scheme of the book

In the next chapter, we look at what constitutes major-power status in the modern world, especially the military, economic and perceptual dimensions of that status. We explore the issue of both the hard-power and soft-power resources and the favorable systemic conditions required for acquiring and maintaining major-power status. The power positions of the five current major-power actors are examined briefly. In addition, the chapter also makes a brief comparison of India with other regional powers in its reference group – Brazil, Indonesia, Nigeria and Pakistan – in order to see the validity of India's claim to major-power status. Chapter 3 explores the constraints and opportunities, international and domestic, that India faces in entering the major-power league.

Chapters 4, 5 and 6 deal with the ups and downs in India's efforts to acquire a leadership role since independence in 1947. The period 1947 to 1962 is marked by the quest for a major-power-equivalent role without hard-power resources. Was the high level of resort to international norms an effort by India to use soft power to acquire a leadership role? Did the defeat in the India–China War of 1962 abruptly change this strategy? In the period subsequent to that war, India's efforts at adjustment represented a long march to building capabilities or hard-power resources amid severe challenges. Although these efforts took place in the context of conflict with regional rivals Pakistan and China, the underlying desire to be taken seriously by the major powers is evident. The end of the Cold War saw India come under severe pressures to nullify its nuclear option. These pressures proved counterproductive, with India reacting with the most assertive action to date in search of major-power status through its nuclear tests.

The concluding chapter discusses the implications of the Indian case for international-relations theory and foreign-policy-making, in India and in the other major powers in the world system. The chapter argues that the peaceful integration of India into the major-power system may be vital for the attainment of peace, stability and prosperity as well as democratic international governance in the twenty-first century

2 Major-Power Status in the Modern World: India in Comparative Perspective

A longstanding foreign-policy goal of India's elites has been to achieve major-power status for their country in the international system. Despite variations in the intensity of this ambition, in the application of the means to achieve it, and in the willingness to take hardline positions, this thread has been common in the policies of Prime Minister Jawaharlal Nehru and his successors, especially Indira Gandhi and Atal Bihari Vajpayee. Although Nehru often spoke against great-power politics, underneath his idealism lay a submerged realism about the potential of India to become a major power in the international system. Such a desire was evident in his pursuit of nonalignment, in his autarkic economic-development strategy, which placed heavy emphasis on the public sector and heavy industry, and in the prominence he gave to science and technology. The building up of the nuclear and space programs by Nehru and his successors has also been driven largely by the desire to become a major power.

Among India's political parties, the Bharatiya Janata Party (BJP) has been the most outspoken articulator of the goal of having India achieve a major-power position. Unlike the Congress leaders, the BJP top brass has not been ideologically constrained in proclaiming major-power status as an explicit part of its core policy objectives. One of the key reasons for the nuclear tests in 1998 by the BJP-led government was to achieve the party's longstanding objective of major-power status for India. From the point of view of the BJP, all major powers in the international system are currently nuclear weapons powers and it was imperative for India to declare its nuclear capability in order to assert its major-power position.[1] Despite this desire, India's power position at the

---

[1] Indian strategic analysts have noted the connection between nuclear weapons possession and major-power status. See Raj Chengappa, *Weapons of Peace: The Secret Story of India's Quest to be a Nuclear Power* (New Delhi: Harper Collins, 2000), 130; and K. Subrahmanyam, "India and the Changes in the International Security Environment," in *India's Foreign Policy: Agenda for the 21st Century*, vol. I (New Delhi: Foreign Policy Institute and Konark, 1997), 71.

beginning of the twenty-first century remains somewhat ambiguous and unfulfilled. Although Western scholars have noted the increasing economic and military capabilities of India, most still see it only as a "potential power," or a "power in the making," rather than an actual major power. A major study of great powers in 1999 suggests that although India, with the world's second-largest population and nuclear capabilities, could be considered as the eighth great power (following Germany and Japan), its power still remains potential because the radius of its influence is confined largely to South Asia. Further, its trading capacity is low. But the author concedes that if India can achieve a sustained economic growth rate of 10 per cent and if it succeeds in the area of national integration and unity, "then it could be a great power in the twenty-first century."[2] In many senses, India is still viewed neither as having attained the wherewithal of a major power, nor as being ready to make the effort and sacrifice necessary to make the country a major power. Some Indian analysts, on the other hand, assert that India will be a major power in the twenty-first century.[3]

In this chapter, we explore the claim of India for major-power status and compare that claim with the five established major powers as well as key regional powers among whose ranks India is often placed. In order to make this comparison, we first assess the elements that constitute major-power status in the modern international system. These elements are in flux as we begin the twenty-first century and, therefore, the changing nature of the power resources required for the acquisition and sustenance of major-power status needs to be assessed. This assessment is followed by a discussion of the power capabilities of the present-day major powers – US, Russia, France, UK and China – and the two leading economic powers, Japan and Germany. The chapter looks at India's present and potential power resources in comparison with these leading states. Comparisons are also made with a few of India's reference group of middle powers – Brazil, Indonesia, Iran, Nigeria and Pakistan – countries that have been accorded somewhat similar status in the international system as regional powers. This comparison should enable us to see whether India's power capabilities and potential capabilities would elevate its status from a regional power to a major power in the twenty-first century.

---

[2] Robert A. Pastor, "The Great Powers in the Twentieth Century," in Robert A. Pastor (ed.), *A Century's Journey: How the Great Powers Shape the World* (New York: Basic Books, 1999), 25.

[3] See Bhabani Sen Gupta, "India: The Next Great Power," in *India's Foreign Policy*, 129.

Major-power status: The power ingredients

Since the sixteenth century, the European-led international system has witnessed the rise and fall of major powers. This process occurred largely through major wars that engulfed several countries in many theaters of the globe. The winners with the necessary military and economic attributes were accorded major-power status in the postwar settlements, while the vanquished in most instances lost such status altogether. In the modern international system, the following states were accorded major-power status at some point or another: Spain, Portugal, Sweden, the Netherlands, Austria–Hungary, Germany, Japan, France, England, Russia, the United States and China. Of these, Spain, Portugal and the Netherlands had lost such status by the eighteenth century following their defeat in wars or loss of colonial empires, and shrinkage of their territories in Europe. Austria–Hungary also did not retain the position after its defeat in World War I. The conclusion of World War II resulted in the removal of major-power status from Germany and Japan and the awarding of that status to China. The five permanent members of the UN Security Council were the winners of World War II and the major-power status of these states since 1945 has remained unaltered. No new additions have been made to this group of nations and no state has exited formally from it, although the power capabilities of Russia have considerably weakened since the early 1990s, while those of the UK and France have stagnated since the 1960s. Until now, the international system has devised no peaceful mechanism for the orderly entry of a new major power or for the peaceful exit of a declining power. A disjunction thus exists between the historic record and reality in the contemporary international system. One thing is clear: in the long run, the relative power positions of states do change, and it is imperative for a peaceful international order that new powers be accorded their legitimate position in the international system.

At this point, it is important to know what power ingredients are necessary for acquiring and maintaining major-power status. Some definitions of *major power* are useful here. Most conventional definitions emphasize military power as the key ingredient of major-power status. This is because, historically, economic power followed military power, or the latter was essential to acquire the former. More importantly, actors with the most physical power to hurt, deprive, deny, or provide military security to others could wield dominant status. Weaker actors often succumbed to the wishes of the militarily strong major powers. As we will see subsequently, this overemphasis on military power to determine major-power status is now waning, as there is recognition among national leaders and analysts alike that superior economic and technological capabilities are essential for gaining and maintaining a leadership position in the international system. Yet military power still remains the final arbiter of international politics and the background condition for a leadership role, although major powers have been reluctant to exercise it vis-à-vis one another overtly, largely due to the nuclear revolution. In fact, there has perhaps been a waning of major wars in the international system.[4]

Following the traditional parameters of power, Jack Levy provides a succinct discussion of major-power status. He defines a *great power* as a state "that plays a major role in international politics with respect to security-related issues. The Great Powers can be differentiated from other states by their military power, their interests, their behavior in general and interactions with other Powers, other Powers' perception of them, and some formal criteria."[5] Superior military power is measured in terms of the military capability vis-à-vis other states that allows a great power to project power globally, be invulnerable to military attacks by non-great powers, conduct offensive and defensive operations beyond its region, come to the support of its allies, and wage aggressive wars. Great powers hold global or continental interests and their security goals go beyond territorial defense, and include the maintenance of balance of power and order in the international system. Great powers defend their interests aggressively with the aid of a wide range of instruments, including frequent use or threat of use of force, continuous diplomatic interactions with other powers, and formation of alliances and counteralliances. Further, great powers are differentiated through perceptions that others hold of them and perceptions they hold of themselves with respect to their status.[6] As Levy puts it: "Equal perception and treatment of one another are among the most important criteria of Great Power rank, for perceptions determine behavior." Finally, for Levy, great-power status is formally accorded by international treaties or conferences, along with privileges such as veto power and permanent membership in key decision-making organs of international organizations.[7]

The ingredients of major-power status that Levy identifies are crucial, and were the most critical in determining such status in the period up to the end of World War II. During the Cold War era, these elements

---

[4] On this, see Raimo Varnynen (ed.), *The Waning of Major Wars* (forthcoming).

[5] Jack Levy, *War in the Modern Great Power System, 1495–1975* (Lexington: The University Press of Kentucky, 1983), 16.

[6] For Keohane, a great power is a "state whose leaders consider that it can alone exercise a large, perhaps decisive impact on the international system." Robert O. Keohane, "Lilliputians' Dilemmas: Small States in International Politics," *International Organization*, 23 (Spring 1969), 291–310.

[7] Levy, *War*, 17–18.

held sway in determining major-power rank as well, but in a limited way. Strictly speaking, only two superpowers, the US and the USSR, could be considered as major powers during the Cold War period, as their behavior and power position typified the classical characteristics of major-power status. The other three – UK, France and China – were second-tier major powers; that is, states holding some or several parameters of power capabilities, but without the global reach of the superpowers. Since the 1970s, but most prominently with the end of the Cold War in the 1990s, new conceptions of major-power status have emerged that take into account the changing nature of power in the international system. Samuel Kim presents one such definition of great-power status. To him, a great power is:

a state that easily ranks among the top five in the primary global structures – economic, military, knowledge, and normative – and that enjoys relatively low sensitivity, vulnerability, and security interdependence because of massive resource and skill differentials and relative economic self-sufficiency. A great power is a strong state with the ability to mobilize the country's human and material resources in the service of its worldview and policy objectives.

There is also a "behavioral requirement of great power status: a great power is and becomes what a great power does."[8]

The structural power approach provides another framework for determining a state's power position in the international system. As Susan Strange characterizes it, structural power consists of four elements. A state commands structural power if it: possesses the capacity to threaten, defend, deny or increase the security of other states from violence; controls the system of goods and services; determines the structure of finance; and exerts the highest influence over the acquisition and dissemination of knowledge.[9] A major power that wields structural power ought to have the military and economic capabilities to "choose and shape the structures of global security and political economy within which other states have to operate."[10]

The power-transition school provides a simple but nuanced definition of power, and the relative positions of states can be assessed using its

---

[8] Samuel S. Kim, "China as a Great Power," *Current History*, 96 (September 1997), 246.

[9] Susan Strange, "The Persistent Myth of Lost Hegemony," *International Organization*, 41 (Autumn 1987), 565.

[10] T.V. Paul, "Power, Influence and Nuclear Weapons: A Reassessment," in T.V. Paul, Richard Harknett and James Wirtz (eds), *The Absolute Weapon Revisited: Nuclear Arms and the Emerging International Order* (Ann Arbor: University of Michigan Press, 1998), 21.

approach. It defines power as "the ability to impose on or persuade an opponent to comply with demands." Such power for a state derives from a combination of three elements:

the number of people who can work and fight, their economic productivity, and the effectiveness of the political system in extracting and pooling individual contributions to advance national goals. How much "power" these capabilities endow a state with generates the ability to project influence beyond its borders.[11]

Based on the preceding discussion, we select ten key elements as essential for a new power to claim major-power status in the new millennium. These form the ingredients of a comprehensive national power capability that are sought by major powers, or that those who already possess them eagerly attempt to maintain. Four of these – military, economic, technological/knowledge and demographic – are hard-power resources, while the other six – norms, leadership role in international institutions, culture, state capacity, strategy/diplomacy and national leadership – are soft-power resources. Nye, who coined the terms *hard power* and *soft power*, defines soft-power resources as less coercive in nature and as derived from cooptive power, which is the "ability of a nation to structure a situation so that other nations develop preferences or define their interests in ways consistent with one's own nation. This type of power tends to arise from such resources as cultural and ideological attraction as well as the rules and institutions of international regimes."[12] Soft-power resources, by their very intangible nature, are difficult to measure. Each of these elements may affect or influence the others, and one may be a prerequisite for gaining the others. Yet sometimes a country may be economically powerful but militarily weak, or vice versa. Often, great economic strength is a prerequisite for building a strong military and sustaining it. But if a major power overspends its wealth on the military and overextends itself too quickly, it could decline after a period of time. This outcome occurs because the state is likely to fail in wealth creation and technological innovation, which are essential to sustain its relative power position.[13] Soft-power resources such as state capacity, strategic/diplomatic strength and quality of national leadership are extremely important in converting a state's latent capabilities into actualized power. A current major power failing in all these dimen-

[11] Ronald L. Tammen *et al.*, *Power Transitions: Strategies for the 21st Century* (New York: Chatham House, 2000), 8–9.
[12] Joseph S. Nye, *Bound to Lead: The Changing Nature of American Power* (New York: Basic Books, 1990), 191.
[13] Paul Kennedy, *The Rise and Fall of the Great Powers* (New York: Random House, 1987), xvi.

sions can lose its effective power over time, even though it may retain the juridical status as a veto-holding member of the UN Security Council. Geography or strategic location is another factor, but its significance is weaker than often claimed, partly because a rich and powerful country by its very strength makes its geographic location strategically important for others in the international system. Moreover, aircraft carriers, long-range missiles and aircraft, and overseas bases have made geography less of a factor in determining a state's power position. With the arrival of the information age, especially the Internet, the ethnic diasporas that sometimes augment the power of their mother countries, and the increasing militarization of space, geographic distances have shrunk to some extent.[14] However, favorable geographic conditions help to provide effective defenses against external aggression and can thus increase national power. Further, the geostrategic location of a state may attract the attention of other major powers for economic or balance-of-power reasons.

A criticism may be raised in lumping the different power resources together, since various international-relations paradigms emphasize the differential value of these resources. Our position is that power capabilities are not static and that, during different eras, different elements gain prominence. However, we hold that hard-power resources are still the most significant power elements in world politics, as soft-power resources tend to grow along with them. Even among the hard-power resources, two resources stand out for major-power status: military and economic capabilities. Further, almost all militarily and economically superior states use soft-power resources to further their global influence and legitimize their position. In the twenty-first century, relations with neighbors and other major powers may be heavily influenced by economic and other soft-power resources, even though military power is likely to remain in the background as a key factor in determining a country's structural position in the international system. Despite the overwhelming importance of military power, if a major power ignores its economy, it is bound to fail in the long run, as wealth and military strength go hand in hand.

There may be variations in the extent to which a state holds each of the ten power resources at a given point in time. It should be noted that such variations, indeed, exist in the power positions of the present-day major powers. For example, we can note the differences in the power positions of the US versus all the others; Russia versus UK, France and China; and China versus the rest. The US is the only superpower commanding a strong capability in all of the ten areas of power identified

---

[14] We owe this point to Itty Abraham, pers. comm., October 2000.

here, and can therefore be referred to as a "complete power." In this respect, the remaining four are second-tier major powers possessing a majority of the crucial power resources, albeit at relatively lower levels.

One important caveat can be made at this point. Even if a state ranks high in the ten indicators of power, it may still not obtain major-power status, given that the status has to be accorded to it by the other major powers through formal recognition of it by treating it as a major power and by giving it membership in key international decision-making groups and organizations. Major-power status has been a systemic position, a recognition often accorded at the settlement that follows a major war. In the past, a candidate major power had to make great human and material sacrifices in order to obtain this status. It also had to decide whether the costs and benefits of such an endeavor were worth it, and it had to pursue its objectives relentlessly and actively. Further, favorable systemic conditions had to arise for a power to receive recognition from other states. In the nuclear age, the international system has yet to find a viable alternative to war in order for a rising power to achieve major-power status. In some sense, alternative mechanisms for the rise and fall of major powers are yet to be evolved and, unless found, their absence could become a major source of conflict in the twenty-first century.

How do the major powers measure up?

The present-day international system is dominated by five powers – US, Russia, UK, France and China – and the two economic giants, Germany and Japan. The first five are recognized as major powers as a result of their victory in World War II, and the according of this status came in San Francisco in 1945. They hold different power attributes, but they have one thing in common: in relative terms, their power attributes are still largely unmatched by almost all other states in the international system. However, the United States is the only truly global hegemonic power; the others are second-tier major powers.

Of the present-day major powers, the US holds the supreme position, due largely to the fact that it wields all the ten power ingredients strongly. To paraphrase Keohane, it is a "system-determining"[15] actor with tremendous global reach. The rise of the US as a world power occurred in the twentieth century due largely to its victory in two wars, World War I and World War II. Yet it was a power reluctant to enter the global arena

---

[15] Keohane, "Lilliputians' Dilemmas," 295.

until the middle of World War II, largely due to domestic constraints.[16] Following the Japanese attack on Pearl Harbor in 1941, the US began to actively defend its allies and wage war against the Fascist Axis. After the war, the US emerged as one of the two superpowers, but economically far more powerful than the Soviet Union. The US helped to create the postwar international order largely through a network of military alliances and economic institutions that bestowed it primacy and a hegemonic leadership role.

The power of the US results from both hard-power and soft-power resources. Militarily, the US was the first to develop nuclear weapons and build a strong triad of intercontinental ballistic missiles (ICBMs), long-range aircraft and submarines. Through a network of alliances and overseas bases, it has managed to acquire the ability to rapidly reach any corner of the world, and to engage in simultaneous offensive and defensive military operations globally. It has also been a victor in almost all wars that it has fought in the twentieth century (except in Vietnam and to a certain extent Korea), and this gives it the aura of indomitable power in its own and others' perceptions. In the 1990s, the US increased its offensive capability immensely. During the 1991 Persian Gulf War and the 2001 Afghan War, there were hardly any US casualties from enemy action; the few that occurred were mainly due to friendly fire or accidents.

In economic power, the relative position of the US has declined over time, but in absolute terms it remains the world's largest market, the biggest source of investment, and leader of the global financial system. Demographic factors also favor the US. Its population of 270 million (in 2000) is ideal for a major power. Its ability to attract talented immigrants from all over the world to fill jobs in its corporations, universities and research institutions, to innovate products and to draw in huge amounts of foreign investment, allow it to maintain a high standard of living. Its economic power is also a function of the superior position that the US dollar enjoys as the lead currency in the global financial system. Despite problems of racial discrimination, especially toward African-Americans, the American dream has been an unusually powerful magnet for people of all nationalities to come to its shores. Among immigrant countries, the US has been the most successful in sharing its

[16] Fareed Zakaria, *From Wealth to Power: The Unusual Origins of America's World Role* (Princeton, NJ: Princeton University Press, 1998). On the rise of the US, see also Geoffrey Perret, *A Country Made by War: From the Revolution to Vietnam: The Story of America's Rise to Power* (New York: Random House, 1989); and Foster Rhea Dulles, *America's Rise to World Power 1898–1954* (New York: Harper & Row, 1955).

wealth with people of all colors and creeds. The US power position is also a function of its commanding lead over soft-power resources, especially in terms of knowledge, culture, ideas and diplomacy. The last-mentioned resource has been crucial in its dominant position in international institutions, such as the UN, WTO, World Bank and IMF, and military alliances, especially NATO.

In sum, the US has been more or less a "complete power" and commands all the elements of structural power as articulated by Strange. It is likely to remain so in the foreseeable future, although long-term relative decline is possible. For the US, the favorable factors are all present at the beginning of the twenty-first century. In fact, the end of the Cold War, which occurred mostly on its terms, strengthened the US position in the global system. The US is also helped by its indomitable lead in information technology and the revolution in military affairs (RMA). It is likely to maintain its military edge in the foreseeable future, with its emphasis on missile defense and space-based military systems. The expansion of US military power to outer space, where it enjoys a dominant position, would help prolong its capabilities well into the next century. Substate actors, such as terrorists, may still mount limited asymmetrical challenges to the US, but they are unlikely to weaken its power position.

The key challenger to the US, Russia, presents a different picture. The erstwhile superpower's power position declined substantially following the collapse of the Soviet Union and the dismantlement of the Warsaw Pact in 1991. This decline is visible in all the ten power resources identified previously. Russia's military, economic and demographic capabilities have shrunk considerably. However, Russia is still treated as a major power, as it retains the military capacity to deny security to others, if it chooses to do so. Most importantly, it is the only power that can still decimate the entire United States through a nuclear attack. Although its conventional military capability has declined, it still holds assets to cause insecurity to the neighboring regional states as well as the European countries.

During the Cold War, Russia enjoyed most of the elements of global power. Militarily, it was somewhat on par with the US during the 1970s and 1980s, with the triad of nuclear and conventional forces stationed in Eastern Europe. Its conventional capability was very high, and it was a producer and exporter of large numbers of new military systems on a global scale. Although inferior to the US navy, the Soviet navy could still sail in most of the world's oceans. Economically, the Soviet Union was weaker compared to the Western states, but held enough strength to assist many developing countries in Asia, Africa and Latin America, and to control economically and politically the vast areas of Eastern Europe through the Comintern and the Warsaw Pact alliance system. In terms of soft power, the ideology of communism provided the Soviet Union with powerful influence over allies, and leftist parties around the world spread its message. Russian literature and culture also had a powerful influence worldwide.

With the dismantlement of the Soviet Union in 1991, Russia's super-power position has withered away. Since then, Russia's economy has shrunk, its population has been declining rapidly, and its territorial depth has been reduced considerably. However, in its long history Russia has declined several times, only to recover later. Although some argue that this time Russia will remain in the backwaters,[17] it is not totally inconceivable that Russia may bounce back economically, militarily and politically if proper reforms take place.

The second-tier major powers – UK, France and China – offer different pictures. The rise of the United Kingdom as a global power occurred due to favorable geography, early military and technological innovations, and astute diplomacy, which included playing the role of a balancer in the balance-of-power politics of Europe.[18] In its heyday, the British Empire controlled a quarter of the world's living space and population, and dominated the sea-lanes throughout the globe. Two devastating wars – World War I and World War II – caused the decline of Britain, while the decolonization process – which began with India's independence from it in 1947 – divested the British Empire of its "hegemonic power" status.[19] Yet Britain retained many assets of a major power, in both hard-power and soft-power resources. Its military remains one of the most dynamic and innovative – in weapons, tactics and global reach. This was proven in the 1981 Falklands War, in which the British navy 14,000 kilometers away from its home territory defeated an enemy. Although the British economy has had its ups and downs,

[17] See Jack Snyder, "Russia: Responses to Relative Decline," in T.V. Paul and John A. Hall (eds), *International Order and the Future of World Politics* (Cambridge: Cambridge University Press, 1999), 147; and Jeffrey Taylor, "Russia is Finished," *Atlantic Monthly*, 287 (May 2001), 52.

[18] On the rise of British power, see John Bowle, *The Imperial Achievement: The Rise and Transformation of the British Empire* (London: Secker & Warburg, 1974); M.L. Dockrill and Brian McKercher (eds), *Diplomacy and World Power: Studies in British Foreign Policy, 1890–1950* (Cambridge: Cambridge University Press, 1996); and Walter Besant, *The Rise of the Empire* (London: Horace Marshall & Son, 1897).

[19] On the British decline, see Keith Robbins, *The Eclipse of a Great Power, Modern Britain* 1870–1992 (New York: Addison–Wesley, 1994); and Lawrence James, *The Rise and Fall of the British Empire* (New York: St. Martin's Press, 1994).

it regained momentum in the 1990s, partly due to the policies initiated by Margaret Thatcher and sustained by her successors. A close alliance relationship with the US gives Britain tangible benefits in both military and economic terms, while its veto-holding membership in the UN Security Council, its culture and its language endow it with worldwide appeal.

Thus, in the soft-power resources area, Britain continues to excel, although at a diminished level. To its good fortune, the US became an English-speaking country and its language became the lingua franca for multiethnic societies and regions such as Europe, Middle East, South Asia and East Asia. And now English has also become the lead Internet language. The British position in the Commonwealth provides it with some influence, but no longer greatly significant. In the 1990s, Britain increased its role in the EU, partially with the hope that it would regain its influence through involvement in an integrated Europe. As the twenty-first century advances, the relative position of Britain in hard-power resources is bound to decline as its birthrate falls, and other world economies, including that of India, acquire increasing strength, placing the UK in a lower relative power position. This decline would mean that the UK would ingratiate itself more with the US and, to some extent, the EU as vehicles for retaining its power status.

In ways similar to the UK, France enjoys several hard-power and soft-power resources. The rise of France in Europe was helped by both military and technological factors.[20] Although weakened considerably by World War II and the loss of its colonies in the 1950s and 1960s, France has managed to maintain a strong army, navy and air force, and a limited nuclear deterrent, or the *force de frappe*. France is also a major producer and exporter of arms to the world market. France's soft-power resources are still salient, although much of the global position of the French language has been eroded, due largely to the increasing use of English. French culture, cuisine and fashion have an international appeal, despite the fact that the appeal is confined to certain strata of the global rich. France has increasingly realized that its power cannot be retained single-handedly, and it has strengthened its position through the EU and the articulation of a cooperative multipolar world, where it

---

[20] On the rise, decline and limited resurgence of France, see Stanley Hoffmann, "France: Two Obsessions for One Century," in Pastor, *A Century's Journey*, 63–89; Philip Gordon, *A Certain Idea of France* (Princeton, NJ: Princeton University Press, 1993); Edward Kolodziej, *French International Policy under De Gaulle and Pompidou* (Ithaca, NY: Cornell University Press, 1974); and William I. Hitchcock, *France Restored: Cold War Diplomacy and the Quest for Leadership in Europe, 1944–1954* (Chapel Hill: University of North Carolina Press, 1998).

has increasingly viewed India as a partner. Through its affiliation with francophone Africa, it retains some amount of influence in the affairs of the African continent.

Among the P-5 members, China is the newest addition to the major-power ranks, although some Western analysts view it as a rising power which has yet to obtain the hard-power or soft-power resources needed to claim full major-power status.[21] When China acquired its permanent membership of the UN Security Council in 1945, it did not possess many of the ingredients necessary for it to become a major power. It was a fortunate confluence of factors – its membership in the victorious alliance and strong US support – that helped it to attain that position. Up until the early 1980s, China and India had several similarities, especially in economic terms. For instance, their per capita incomes had been somewhat similar for well over three decades. But since then the rapid growth of the Chinese economy has enabled China to double its capabilities vis-à-vis India.

China's acceptance as a major power occurred largely after the 1950s, when it managed to avert defeat in the war against the US in Korea. China's role in Vietnam and its support for armed struggles worldwide, and as a supplier of military and economic aid to such movements, had also strengthened its position. The 1964 nuclear test allowed China to enter the nuclear club well before the 1968 Nuclear Nonproliferation Treaty closed the club to new entrants. The most significant change in Chinese global-power position occurred following the US striking an alliance with it in the 1970s against the Soviet Union. In 1972 the US under the Nixon administration restored diplomatic relations with China, and soon China was accepted as a real P-5 member in the UN Security Council. The acceptance of Beijing by the US, through giving it a key role in the global balance-of-power game, and the opening of the US market to Chinese goods, enabled China to improve both its military and its economic power in the international arena.[22] Moreover, the economic investments by Chinese expatriates or by neighboring countries with large Chinese populations also helped the growth of the Chinese economy.

In terms of hard-power resources, China has the world's largest standing army (although much of its weaponry may be obsolete), a

---

[21] Gerald Segal, "Does China Matter?" *Foreign Affairs*, 78 (September–October 1999), 24–36.

[22] On China's ascendance, see Thomas W. Robinson and David Shambaugh (eds), *Chinese Foreign Policy: Theory and Practice* (Oxford: Clarendon Press, 1994); and Lowell Dittmer and Samuel S. Kim (eds), *China's Quest for National Identity* (Ithaca, NY: Cornell University Press, 1993).

limited nuclear deterrent, and the world's fastest-growing economy.[23] China's economic growth rate of 8 to 12 per cent provides it with the most robust opportunities to emerge as a superpower in the twenty-first century. Estimates in 2000 placed the Chinese economy as number two in the world, ahead of that of Japan. China's GNP is estimated at $4.112 trillion[24] compared to Japan's $3.042 trillion in PPP terms.[25] Some have argued that the rise of China may constitute the most important trend in twenty-first century international politics,[26] and if not managed properly it could become a major source of rivalry and conflict in the international system.

The two economic powers, Japan and Germany, are also viewed as potential major powers, as they can obtain the necessary military capability in a short period of time. But at the moment they remain only economic powers, because their military capacity is constrained by various internal and external factors. The rise and decline of Japan as a major power has been one of the most violent stories of the first half of the twentieth century. Japan's rise to major-power status occurred due to conscious grand strategies adopted by its elite, especially during and after the Meiji Restoration. Japan's defeat of Russia, a reigning European major power, during the 1904–05 Russo-Japanese War, and its important role as an ally of the UK up until the end of World War I, also helped it in its attainment of major-power status.[27] Following its defeat in World War II, Japan adopted a trading-state strategy, giving primacy to economics over unilateral military build-up.[28] It accepted a constitutional ban on building up armed forces for offensive operations in return for the US security umbrella.

---

[23] In recent years, China has embarked on the modernization and expansion of its nuclear capabilities. See David E. Sanger and Erik Eckholm, "Will Beijing's Nuclear Arsenal Stay Small or Will it Mushroom?" http://www.nytimes.com, March 15, 1999.

[24] Throughout the book, figures are in US dollars unless otherwise stated.

[25] *World Development Report 2000–2001*, cited in http://www.hinduonnet.com, September 12, 2000.

[26] See Nicholas D. Kristof, "The Rise of China," *Foreign Affairs*, 72 (December 1993), 59–74.

[27] See Meirion and Susie Harries, *Soldiers of the Sun: The Rise and Fall of the Imperial Japanese Army* (New York: Random House, 1991); and David H. James, *The Rise and Fall of the Japanese Empire* (London: George Allen and Unwin, 1951).

[28] See Kenneth B. Pyle, *The Japanese Question: Power and Purpose in a New Era* (Washington, DC: The AEI Press, 1992); and Richard J. Samuels, *Rich Nation, Strong Army: National Security and the Technological Transformation of Japan* (Ithaca, NY: Cornell University Press, 1994).

Japan typifies some of the pitfalls of the rise of a new major power in the international system, and holds, to some extent, a lesson for rising powers such as India. Its rise was opposed by established powers that saw in Japan's efforts a major challenge to their supremacy and material wealth. Japan then initiated a bloody war, which ended with its total defeat in history's first and only atomic attacks. Defeat was followed by the occupation of the country by the US and the transformation of Japan into a liberal democracy. The Japanese case is also important for illustrating the mistakes that status quo powers need to avoid vis-à-vis rising powers. These powers failed to adopt proper deterrence and reassurance policies prior to the war, while Japan was asked to forgo all its territorial conquests in Asia in return for no war and a reduced status in the international order.[29] Following the war, Japan adopted an economics-first strategy, which was crystallized in the Yoshida Doctrine.

At the beginning of the twenty-first century, Japan remains a partial power. Its economy has weakened, although it retained the number-two position after the US until 2000. Although well-trained and committed, the Japanese workforce is shrinking and its productivity is declining. If Japan does not allow mass immigration, its population is poised to decline from "126 million today to 100 million in 2050 and 67 million in 2100." For one writer, "Japan steadily lost its capacity for what the economist, Joseph Schumpeter called 'creative destruction'."[30] In the security area, Japan's reliance on the US has shown no signs of decrease, although some modifications have been made to the capabilities and operations of the Self-Defense Forces. Part of Japan's difficulty in becoming a normal power is due to its inability to come to terms with its past, especially with respect to properly apologizing to and compensating its Asian neighbors that bore the brunt of Japanese aggression.

In similar ways to Japan, Germany also typifies the dangers of a rising power attempting to hasten its passage to major-power status and to take on other established powers all at the same time. The rise and decline of Germany as a major power has been written in two bloody wars in the twentieth century, which redrew the map of Europe as well as the contours of world politics. Germany became powerful following its unification in 1870. Subsequent industrialization helped to increase German power rapidly, culminating in a strong military position in the early 1900s. In order to quicken its rise, Germany devised strategies

---

[29] T.V. Paul, *Asymmetric Conflicts: War Initiation by Weaker Powers* (Cambridge: Cambridge University Press, 1984), ch. 4.
[30] Nicholas D. Kristof, "For Japan, Signs of Diminished Influence in Next Century," http://www.IHT.com, August 2, 1999, 1–6. See also Michael J. Green, "The Forgotten Player," *National Interest*, 60 (Summer 2000), 47–9.

based on the Schlieffen Plan and the blitzkrieg during the world wars, but each time ended up fighting on two fronts simultaneously, thereby weakening its military position.[31]

After its defeat in World War II, Germany adopted a trading strategy and a political strategy based on the economic and political integration of Europe. The NATO alliance, although chiefly meant to contain the Soviet bloc, also ensured that Germany would not become a major power again through a unilateral military build-up.[32] In return for nuclear protection by the US, and in order to present a low-profile and nonthreatening military posture, Germany foreswore nuclear weapons.[33] With the end of the Cold War, Germany improved its position as the peaceful reunification of East and West Germany consolidated the state. Despite the reunification, Germany is still a contained power, both internally and externally, and it is unlikely to rearm and become a traditional major power in the foreseeable future. Germany, however, has been championing the creation of a European Union more like a federal United States, with the hope that, being the leading power in the EU, it will have a major influence in global affairs.

India in comparison with the major powers

Compared to the present-day major powers (US, Russia, China, UK and France) and major economic powers (Germany and Japan), India's capabilities present a mixed picture with respect to the four hard-power resources discussed previously. Among all the regional powers, however, India holds the highest promise and potential in acquiring and exerting power from the three sources in the medium and long terms. According to one analysis, should India, "with a population of 1 billion, increase its per capita productivity and then efficiently extract resources from its population, it would be on a trajectory to eventually challenge international leadership in the latter half of the 21st century."[34] The comparison with respect to soft-power resources is more difficult to make. However, India's advantages in these areas are many and they are discussed later.

---

[31] On Germany's rise and decline, and resurgence as an economic power, see Joseph Joffe, "Germany: The Continuities from Frederick the Great to the Federal Republic," in Pastor (ed.), *A Century's Journey*, 91–138.

[32] See David Calleo, *The German Problem Reconsidered: Germany and the World Order, 1870 to the Present* (Cambridge: Cambridge University Press, 1978), 2.

[33] See T.V. Paul, *Power versus Prudence: Why Nations Forgo Nuclear Weapons* (Montreal: McGill–Queen's University Press, 2000), ch. 3.

[34] Tammen *et al.*, *Power Transitions*, 20.

Table 1 *Relative demographic, economic and military positions of major and selected regional powers, 1999–2000*

Country	Population (millions)	Surface area (,000 sq. km)	GNP ($ bn)	GNP at PPP ($ bn)	Per capita ($)	Per capita at PPP ($)	Ave. annual economic growth % (1998–99)	Military expenditures ($ bn)	Armed forces (active)
USA	273	9,364	8,351.0	8,350.1	30,600	30,600	4.1	275.5	1,365,000
Russia	147	17,075	332.5	928.8	2,270	6,339	1.3	56.0	1,004,000
UK	59	245	1,338.1	1,234.4	22,640	20,883	1.7	36.9	212,450
France	59	552	1,427.2	1,293.8	23,480	21,897	2.4	37.1	294,430
China	1,250	9,597	980.2	4,112.2	780	3,291	7.2	39.5	2,470,000
Japan	127	378	4,078.9	3,042.9	32,230	24,041	1.0	40.8	236,700
Germany	82	357	2,079.2	1,837.8	25,350	22,404	1.2	31.1	321,000
India	**998**	**3,288**	**442.2**	**2,144.1**	**450**	**2,149**	**6.9**	**14.2**	**1,303,000**
Brazil	168	8,547	742.8	1,061.7	4,420	6,317	-2.0	16.0	287,000
Indonesia	207	1,905	119.5	505.0	580	2,439	1.9	1.5	297,000
Iran	63	1,633	110.5	325.2	1,760	5,163	2.1	5.7	513,600
Pakistan	135	796	64.0	236.8	470	1,757	3.6	3.5	612,000
Nigeria	124	924	37.9	92.2	310	744	3.0	2.2	76,500
Egypt	62	1,001	87.5	206.2	1,400	3,303	5.7	3.0	448,500

Source: Compiled from the World Bank, *Entering the 21st Century: World Development Report 2000/2001* (Washington, DC: The World Bank, 2001); and the International Institute for Strategic Studies, *The Military Balance 2000–2001* (London: IISS, 2001).

In the military realm, India's conventional capabilities may not equal those of any of the present five major powers. However, India can certainly boast of the third-largest armed forces after China and the US and, in aggregate numerical measures, its forces may surpass those of France, UK, Japan and Germany. On the other hand, India's long-range deployment capabilities beyond the region are limited relative to the five major powers. The rapid-deployment capabilities of India are sufficient to deal with minor powers in the Indian Ocean region, but beyond that the capability dims in comparison with the major powers. Active defenses on two fronts – one with a smaller yet determined adversary, Pakistan, and the other with a major power, China – weakens Indian power-projection capabilities beyond the region. In addition, in qualitative measures of military capability, India is still a regional power, as it is heavily dependent on external suppliers for major weapons systems such as fighter aircraft and advanced munitions. India's biggest weakness here lies in the areas of both naval and long-range air-power capabilities, as well as ICBMs, the areas precisely where India is likely to improve its position in the twenty-first century. The military expenditure of India in US-dollar terms is the lowest of all the major powers, as well as that of Germany and Japan. This, however, hides the purchasing power parity (PPP) factor and the cost of each serviceman, given that salaries and expenditures on India's servicemen are perhaps the lowest compared to the aforementioned set of countries.

With respect to economic position, in 2000 India became the fourth-largest economy in the world in PPP terms. India's GNP of $2.14 trillion in PPP terms is larger than that of Russia, UK, France and Germany. Its GNP in PPP terms is approximately 25 per cent that of the US, and 52 per cent that of China. In the long run, India may even excel all major powers except the US and China, as Japan is now on a slow growth trajectory. In PPP terms, India's economy is more than twice that of Russia, a powerful indicator of the extent of Russia's economic decline. The countries that are ahead of India are the US, China and Japan. But in actual dollar terms, the GNP is only $442 billion, which is relatively smaller than that of all the major powers except Russia.

In PPP terms, at $2,149 India's per capita income is the lowest in the reference group of major powers. In dollar terms, the per capita income of $450 is the lowest in the entire reference group. Nearly 30 per cent of Indians (more than 300 million) live below the poverty line. The Indian middle class of some 300 million by itself has a much higher per capita income, but that does not modify the aggregate capability of the nation. India's economic position is relatively weak, and it is the Achilles heel of India in achieving major-power status. In terms of economic competitiveness, in 2000 India ranked forty-ninth, a small improvement from 1999 when its rank stood at fifty-second.[35] The weakness in this regard is critical because other elements of power, such as military capability and the productivity of the population, tend to increase largely along with economic advance.

Demography is both an asset and a curse for India. As the world's second-most populous country, India compares only with China. The Indian states of Uttar Pradesh (176 million), Bihar (104 million), Maharashtra (94 million), Madhya Pradesh (83 million), West Bengal (80 million), Andhra Pradesh (77 million), and Tamil Nadu (63 million) individually hold more population than the UK (59 million) and France (59 million). Uttar Pradesh's population is larger than that of Russia (147 million), and more than double that of Germany (82 million). The approximate size of the Indian middle class – 300 million – is larger than the population of all the major powers except China, although in terms of purchasing power this middle class is much weaker than its counterparts in all the major powers, except perhaps Russia. India also contains one of the largest pools of skilled workers, especially in the information-technology area, which can be a major asset, both economically and politically. The productivity of the Indian workforce, however, is much lower than in almost all the states in the comparison group.

Demography is the bane of most of the present-day major powers, except the US and China. Falling birthrates and aging populations in Russia, UK, France, Germany and Japan mean smaller numbers of workers unless these countries allow a large influx of immigrants and innovate in such a way that their technologies and factories do not require great human resources in order to function. Although numbers alone are not a great predictor of the military strength of a nation, in order for a major power to keep its position it needs an optimum number of men and women to run its factories and service its industry and, more importantly, its armed forces. A caveat is in order, however. A largely unskilled and illiterate populace is not a boon but a bane for a country's power capability, as typified by India's present-day condition.[36]

India's closest competitor, China, presents an interesting comparative picture. In aggregate terms, China is larger in every indicator presented here. China's population is nearly 250 million more than India's, and its

---

[35] World Economic Forum, *Global Competitiveness Report* (Geneva: The World Economic Forum, September 2000).

[36] India's low rank of 115 in the human development index in 2001 (an improvement from the 128th rank in 2000) tells this story most vividly. "India Moves up in UNDP's Human Development Index," http://www.timesofindia.com, July 10, 2001.

GNP (in both dollar and PPP terms) is nearly double, as are the armed forces and military expenditures. However, the differential in per capita income in PPP terms is only one-third more for China. China's advantages lie in other indicators not presented here. In foreign trade, foreign-currency reserves, foreign direct investment (FDI), economic productivity, and human resource development index (such as poverty level, literacy and health), China has made much more progress than India. This is partly due to the fact that China initiated economic reforms over a decade before India, and the Chinese communist regime had paid more attention to human development than had successive Indian governments. For instance, in 1998 China received $43.75 billion in FDI (India, $2.63 billion), and $42.67 billion in net private capital flows (India, $6.15 billion), while its merchandise exports were worth $183.81 billion (India, $33.63 billion).

Some other economic indicators are also relevant here. In 1998, 70 out of 1000 Chinese had telephones (India, 22), 272 owned TV sets (India, 69), and 8.9 owned personal computers (India, 2.7). In 1997, on a per capita basis, the Chinese consumed 714 kilowatt-hours of electric power to the Indians' 363 kilowatt-hours. In 1999, China's stock markets had a capitalization of $330 billion to India's $184 billion. In 1999, China held $157.73 billion in foreign-exchange reserves, to India's $32.67 billion. In human development, the differences are even more glaring, except in higher education: public expenditure on health as a percentage of GDP (1990–1998: China 2.0; India 0.6); access to improved water source (1990–1996: China 90 per cent of population; India 81 per cent); percentage of population with access to sanitation (1990–1996: China 21; India: 16); infant mortality rate per 1,000 live births (1998: China 31; India 70); public expenditure on education as a percentage of GNP (1997: China 2.3; India 3.2); population below poverty line (China 6 per cent in 1996; India 35 per cent in 1994); adult illiteracy rate as a percentage of population (1998: China, males 9, females 25; India, males 33, females 57); and life expectancy at birth (1998: China, males 68, females 72; India, males 62, females 64).[37]

India in comparison with other regional powers

India's power capabilities, except in respect of per capita income, are appreciably higher than those of the other regional powers (Brazil,

---

[37] These statistics are from World Bank, *World Development Report 2000–2001* (Washington, DC: 2001).

Indonesia, Iran, Pakistan, Nigeria and Egypt).[38] In geographical size, the only relevant state for comparison is Brazil, which covers 2.6 times India's area. Yet Brazil's population of 168 million is less than the population of India's largest state, Uttar Pradesh (176 million in 2001). The Indian middle class of 300 million is larger than the entire population of any of the other regional powers. The largest among the other regional states in population is Indonesia, with 207 million people. However, this population is divided along ethnic, linguistic and religious lines, competing for power and economic benefits. Worse than India's situation, Indonesia is plagued by separatist movements, especially in Irian Jaya, Aceh, Riau and Ambon. Indonesia is also troubled by the weakness of its political institutions, which hampers its coping with its internal ethnic diversity. Indonesia had considerable economic successes during the 1980s, but fell into the Asian financial crisis of the 1990s and has not recovered from it. Indonesia's key role in ASEAN provides it with some institutional power in the region, but it has also limited Indonesia's military development, for any dramatic upsurge in spending or military posture would upset its neighbors.

Pakistan's population of 135 million is only one-seventh of India's (smaller than Uttar Pradesh's population of 176 million), a fact often ignored by many analysts and journalists who bracket these two states in the same category. In physical terms, Pakistan is only one-quarter of India's size, while Pakistan's total GNP is nearly one-seventh of India's. Only in the area of per capita income (not adjusted in PPP terms) does Pakistan appear better ($470 compared to India's $450), although this is likely to change in India's favor in a few years, given the present differential growth rates of the two countries. Pakistan has attempted to balance India through the acquisition of sophisticated weaponry, including nuclear arms, and aggressive low-intensity warfare, especially waged through Kashmiri insurgent groups and Afghan Mujahids. Further, Pakistan has formed a de facto alliance with China and, in the past, off and on with the US to counterbalance India.

None of the regional powers in the group presented here hold aggregate raw military capabilities comparable to India's. In terms of the total number of armed forces, India holds third position among all the states, way ahead of all the regional powers. In terms of military expenditures, India ranks highest among all the regional powers except Brazil. The lower labor costs in India, however, mask India's real military spending.

---

[38] For a comparative assessment of the positions of India, Indonesia, Pakistan and Brazil, among other regional states, see Robert Chase, Emily Hill, and Paul Kennedy (eds), *The Pivotal States: A New Framework for U.S. Policy in the Developing World* (New York: W.W. Norton, 1999).

In regard to GNP in dollar terms, India has the largest economy among all the regional powers listed here, except that of Brazil, while in PPP terms India's GNP is double that of Brazil. In per capita income in dollar terms, almost all the regional powers except Nigeria rank higher than India. If India continues its current rate of economic growth for over a decade or so, per capita income will improve substantially, although several other regional states will still be ahead of India for years to come.

India's prospects

The discussion so far indicates that India is a rising power in terms of hard-power resources, and is the leading candidate among the regional powers to obtain a major-power position as the twenty-first century advances, although its present power position is relatively weak compared to the existing major powers. Moreover, it still has not asserted its position unequivocally as a global power. However, India is changing rapidly and is strengthening its position in almost all indicators of power capability identified previously. The level of improvement varies from one area to another.

India's claim for second-tier major-power status would be based on its relative position in the four elements of hard-power resources and perhaps in all of the six soft-power resources discussed here. It is probably the only Asian power that can effectively balance China in the future, as Japan, the other power in the region, is constrained by several factors in its ability to militarily assert itself. Moreover, as Stephen Cohen points out, "unlike the people of other middle powers such as Indonesia, Brazil, and Nigeria, Indians believe that their country has both a destiny and an obligation to play a large role on the international stage. India, and China, after all, are the world's only major states that embody grand civilizations."[39] In fact, India's claim to major-power status is very much rooted in the fact that the country is one of the "world's oldest and largest civilizations," as well as in the self-image that "India is entitled to recognition as a leading global power and a regional sphere of influence centered in, but not necessarily restricted to, South Asia and the western Indian Ocean and its island states."[40]

An important study on power transitions concludes:

Largely overlooked by Western strategists, India has the key components for

---

[39] Stephen P. Cohen, "India Rising," *Wilson Quarterly*, 24 (Summer 2000), 46.
[40] Selig S. Harrison and Geoffrey Kemp (eds), *India and America after the Cold War* (Washington, DC: Carnegie Endowment for International Peace, 1993), 20.

rapid power growth: a large population coupled with the dynamics of an emerging free marketplace. India can ride the rapid phase of the endogenous growth trajectory if it broadens its economic base, curbs population growth, successfully manages the rural-urban migration, and increases governmental political capacity. A formidable list of challenges, but similar in many ways to those faced by the United States in the late 1800s and by China today.

It adds:

If India meets these challenges, its power potential is enormous, competing with that of China and the United States. It is not mere speculation to project India and China as superpowers in the mid to late part of this century.[41]

Huntington also states that Asian economic growth in the coming decades could be led by China and India, and that the latter "could move into rapid economic development and emerge as a major contender for influence in world affairs."[42]

Hard-power resources

Military power: With respect to military power, India's ability to provide or deny security in the South Asia region has always been high. With the nuclear capability and the acquisition of long-range delivery systems, this domain of power capability has increased and will increase further, albeit incrementally, over the years. Over time, this capability will likely cover the Middle East, Central Asia, East Asia and Australasia. On the conventional front, the acquisition of a blue-water navy may be essential to increase power-projection capabilities beyond the Indian Ocean region. As long as oil remains a key strategic material coveted by all states, especially by the industrialized states, the Persian Gulf and the Indian Ocean region will remain important geopolitically. India's adjacent strategic location thus offers a certain level of advantage in military terms if it succeeds in developing a substantial naval presence in the region.

India's military power-projection capabilities are poised to improve if New Delhi's ambitious missile acquisition plans fructify. India already possesses the 1,500-kilometer Agni I missile, which was tested in February 1994. The Agni II and Agni III missiles will increase India's military reach to the Far East, Middle East and Central Asia, as well as

---

[41] Tammen *et al.*, *Power Transitions*, 180.
[42] Samuel P. Huntington, *The Clash of Civilizations and the Remaking of the World Order* (New York: Simon & Schuster, 1996), 121.

Australasia. The Agni II mobile intermediate-range ballistic missile (IRBM), with a range of 2,000 kilometers, was tested twice (in May 1999 and January 2001) and is expected to be inducted into the Indian arsenal in 2002. Another version of Agni II, with a range of 3,500 kilometers, will allow India to target deep into Chinese territory. Extended to its maximum range at 2,200 to 2,400 kilometers, Agni II can deliver nuclear warheads to Chinese cities like Xi'an, Chengdu, Chongqing, Guiyang and Nanning, and possibly Hong Kong if deployed from extreme north-eastern India. In 2001, India still lacked the ability to hit Beijing or Shanghai, and therefore its deterrent posture vis-à-vis China was not fully credible. In order to obtain this capability, India may have to wait until the 5,000-kilometer-range Surya is tested and deployed.[43]

India's BJP-led government has embarked upon air-based and sea-based delivery systems for the nuclear deterrent since it returned to power in 1999, and India's missile capabilities are poised to improve in the near future. According to reports in May 2000, India is planning to acquire ICBM capability by extending the Agni II to a 5,000-kilometer-range missile (renamed Surya I) in 2002 and 12,000-kilometer-range missile (Surya II) in 2003, the range of which will be eventually extended to 20,000 kilometers.[44] The nuclear capability has improved India's deterrent power vis-à-vis other major powers, but nuclear weapons are not tantamount to more usable conventional power-projection capabilities. A blue-water navy with several aircraft carriers and nuclear-powered submarines would dramatically increase India's power-projection capabilities from the Indian Ocean to the Pacific and beyond. This, however, would require a substantial increase in defense expenditures, a feasibility if India's economy strengthens appreciably.[45] However, the navy should have adequate defensive systems, as it could become a target of missiles being acquired by many of the regional powers.

The BJP-led government seems to be keen to modernize the Indian armed forces. The 28 per cent hike in defense spending in the 2000–01 budget, the purchase of new frigates, submarines and a Russian aircraft carrier, as well as the updating and purchase of Mirage 2000 aircraft and Su-30 strike aircraft, and acquisition of T-90 tanks, all show that defense modernization is under way.[46] In June 2001, it was reported by

---

[43] Amitabh Mattoo, "Strategic Significance of the Agni-II Test is Stressed," *India Abroad* (April 23, 1999), 2.

[44] "India Set to Test Launch ICBM, Says Report," http://www.timesofindia.com, May 5, 2001.

[45] Varun Sahni, "India as a Global Power: Capacity, Opportunity and Strategy," in *India's Foreign Policy*, 25.

[46] Timothy D. Hoyt, "Indian Military Modernization, 1990–2000," unpublished paper, Georgetown University (July 2000).

the US journal *Defense News* that India would spend $95 billion during the next fifteen years to buy new weapons, while retaining its defense spending at $15 billion per year.

The most important weapons systems will be bought from or coproduced with Russia, which already supplies nearly 70 per cent of India's military hardware imports. The Indian air force is getting the biggest share of the spending, $30 billion, followed by the army, $25 billion, and the navy, $20 billion. These figures suggest that India is slowly expanding its focus beyond its land borders in South Asia. India plans to upgrade its existing MiG aircraft, induct the retrofitted aircraft carrier *Admiral Gorshkov* in 2005, and acquire another aircraft carrier and Krivak-class frigates from Russia.[47] In June 2001, India and Russia signed several deals for weapons systems, including the licensed production of 140 fifth-generation Su-30MKI jets in India. This is in addition to the fifty fourth-generation Su-30 India has already purchased from Russia, some of which will be upgraded to Su-30MKI.[48] India is also likely to buy Russian S-300 air-defense systems to cover the entire country. The commissioning of three Russian-built Krivak II-class stealth frigates will strengthen Indian naval capability, especially vis-à-vis Pakistan. Radar-evading stealth ships are now being built in India as well.[49] The India–Russia cooperation in military systems received a further boost in June 2001 when India tested a jointly developed supersonic cruise missile, PJ-10, with a range of 500 kilometers. In 2001, the two countries were planning to market this missile.[50]

The nuclear capability, although it may not immediately add to power and influence, can help to get the attention of the other major powers. As Bracken argues: "Atomic bombs on missiles get the West's attention. If the country is big and powerful, it earns Western engagement."[51] However, India has to be careful here not to engage in overblown rhetoric, confrontational military postures and rapid build-up, especially of long-range missiles, which can result in adversarial responses from the major powers. Further, Pakistan's acquisition of nuclear capability somewhat nullified India's advantages, as it does serve, under certain

---

[47] Chidanand Rajghatta, "India to Spend $95 bn on Arms over the Next 15 years," http://www.timesofindia.com, June 13, 2001.

[48] Rajat Pandit, "India, Russia Agree on Joint Defense Production," http://www.timesofindia.com, June 4, 2001.

[49] "3 New Frigates to Strengthen Indian Navy," http://www.timesofindia.com, June 1, 2001.

[50] Vladimir Radyuhin, "India, Russia to Market Missile," http://www.hinduonnet.com, June 15, 2001.

[51] Paul Bracken, *Fire in the East: The Rise of Asian Military Power and the Second Nuclear Age* (New York: Harper Collins, 1999), xii.

circumstances, as a "great equalizer" for the weaker party between two otherwise unequal powers. Despite these constraints, the nuclear capability has increased India's political and diplomatic bargaining position with the other major powers, as evident in the strategic dialogues that New Delhi has been engaged in with all of them. Major powers tend to respect the power capabilities of eligible states, especially if they see the potential of the rising power in augmenting their own strategic position, globally and regionally.

Economic power: India will become a leading economy by the middle of the twenty-first century, if the growth rate continues at the present level. This outcome is possible because at a growth rate of 6 to 7 per cent per annum the GNP will double every ten years or so. Although economic disruptions may occur due to business cycles and domestic political crises, an average growth of this level is possible, as the post-1991 experience shows. A quadrupling of the economy in the space of thirty to forty years could dramatically alter India's power position in this area, especially given the prospect that many developed countries are unlikely to grow at that rate. As discussed before, economic power is the area where India's power potential remains high. With an annual economic growth rate of 6 to 7 per cent the Indian economy can become number three in the next decade. India's share of world trade and global product total remains low, but this situation may also change. Moreover, once the Indian economy doubles its size, the percentage of the population living below the poverty line, which in 2001 was around 26 per cent, could decrease to 15 per cent within a decade, while there would be improvements in education, health and social-service sectors. These achievements are possible only if the Indian government actively pursues a strategy of high economic growth and human development. Further, they also presume that the world economy will not enter into prolonged periods of recession.

One positive dimension of the Indian economic reforms has been the fairly reasonable consensus over the reform process among the various political parties in India, barring the extreme left and the extreme right, who are in a minority. The BJP, after advocating *swadeshi* (economic self-reliance), has largely embraced the economic-reform agenda of the Congress Party and other previous coalition governments and carried it further. However, despite the formal homage to the vaunted consensus on reform, the severe partisanship in India's political process has blocked rapid progress on this front. As a consequence, the second stage of reforms remains yet to be actively pursued.

Technology: Technology is linked to both economic and military power. India has made major strides in some areas of technology, while in others it still lags behind. Although India boasts the world's third-largest pool of scientists and has developed impressive indigenous technological capabilities, its record of applying those capabilities to solving the country's problems has been less than impressive. It pays enormous attention to high-end technology, such as space and nuclear capability, while it neglects low-end technology for higher quality of life. For instance, newer technology for infrastructure facilities is relatively absent in India and, as a result, India's roads and other infrastructure facilities remain primitive not only by world standards, but by the standards of many developing states. However, the high-end technologies are critical for its aspirations for major-power status.

In the space and nuclear technology areas, for example, India has been making major strides. In fact, it is emerging as the fifth or sixth of the leading space powers in the world. Its space program has succeeded in placing different types of satellites in space, and in developing and deploying different types of launch vehicles. With the Polar Satellite Launch Vehicle (PSLV) launch, India has been able to place heavier remote-sensing satellites at higher altitudes. In May 1999, India launched the PSLV-C2 space vehicle, which successfully placed a Korean satellite and a German satellite, along with an Indian satellite, in polar sun-synchronous orbits. This was the second operational flight of the five or so planned flights under the PSLV program.[52] In October 2001, India successfully launched PSLV-D3, which placed three satellites into orbit. One of these satellites is reported to be for intelligence data gathering.[53] Prior to PSLV, the satellite launch capability was limited to light payloads and low-earth orbits (altitudes of 300–450 kilometers), which was not sufficient for major military or commercial applications.[54] On April 18, 2001, India used the Geostationary Satellite Launch Vehicle (GSLV) to place a 1.53-tonne communications satellite in orbit at 36,000 kilometers in space, although its functioning has not been up to the expected level. With this launch, India joined an exclusive club of space powers – US, Russia, China and the European consortium – that have successfully launched satellites into this orbit with their own launch vehicles. As a result, the Indian space agency, ISRO, hopes to gain a bigger share of the $10 billion global communications

[52] http://www.hinduonnet.com, May 27, 1999.
[53] http://www.hinduonnet.com, October 23, 2001;
     http://www.timesofindia.com, October 23, 2001.
[54] Dinshaw Mistry, "India's Emerging Space Program," *Pacific Affairs,* 71 (Summer 1998), 151.

business.[55] Although ISRO has begun to earn foreign exchange by providing low-earth satellite facilities to mobile-telephone companies, by leasing out transponders to Intelsat and by furnishing remote-sensing data, the amount is still limited.[56] Indian scientists claim that India has the ability to send an unmanned polar orbiter to the moon with the "capability to fly around the moon for about five years, conducting experiments and transmitting images back to earth," and they plan to launch a lunar expedition in the future.[57] However, compared to the space agencies of the major powers, the Indian space agency's record in terms of average annual launches has been poor, while in terms of generation of technology India lags behind the other major space powers by ten to twenty years.

India is likely to progress as a key space-faring nation in the years to come. Although an increasing number of countries are likely to launch space programs, only Israel and Brazil are likely to follow India's evolutionary route to advanced satellite-launch capability.[58] Even in these cases, financial considerations may well keep them from progressing much further than their present light-payloads launch capability. The challenge for India is, however, in placing heavier communications satellites into orbit on a sustained basis. India's emerging space capabilities will likely give it a key role in the future international system, especially if space becomes militarized and there is competition among the major powers for space-based military capabilities. The US plans for missile defenses include the militarization of space. India is among a handful of countries with the wherewithal to achieve space capabilities necessary for building its own defense systems in case of such an eventuality. Speculatively, one can posit that, just as naval power determined great-power status during the past five centuries, outer space may emerge as the next frontier of major-power competition, and that the control over this sphere may determine the relative position of a state. India is well-poised to obtain a leading position in outer space, both in military and civilian terms, a possibility that is missing for almost all other regional powers.

Among the new technologies, knowledge-related technology is where India's major hope for future success lies, and information technology

[55] Raj Chengappa, "India is Now a Space Power," http://www.india-today.com, April 28, 2001.
[56] http://www.india-today.com, April 28, 2001.
[57] Srinivas Laxman, "India can Aim for the Moon Now," http://www.timesofindia.com, May 8, 2001.
[58] Mistry, "India's Emerging Space Program," 174.

(info-tech, or IT) is India's greatest asset in the knowledge sphere.[59] In fact, by 2000 India had emerged as a leading player in the global IT arena and it is likely to improve its position in the coming years. According to some estimates, by 2008 India's IT industry is likely to earn $87 billion in revenues, which would form 7.5 per cent of India's GDP, even as the domestic market for software and services would be around $18 billion. IT services (especially in banking, manufacturing, retail distribution and health care), software products, IT-enabled services (in customer interaction, financial processing, accounting and data-management services) and e-business are the areas that are likely to bring the most revenues. If actual achievement matches the estimates, it will represent an exponential growth for the Indian IT industry from the level of $4 billion in 1998. The compounded annual growth rate during the period from 1995 to 2000 was 56.5 per cent for software-industry revenues and 62.3 per cent for software exports, while the domestic market grew by 46.8 per cent. The compounded annual growth rate for the entire IT industry in India was over 42 per cent during the five-year period.[60] In 2000–01, despite the global economic slowdown, Indian software exports grew by 55 per cent in dollar terms. Total software exports were estimated at $6.2 billion, while the software and service industry produced an annual revenue of $8.26 billion. India exported software to 102 countries, and one out of every four global multinational corporations outsourced their critical software requirements from India.[61] India has thus emerged as one of the most favored investment destinations for multinational corporations for the outsourcing of their software requirements. India's competitive advantage over other countries such as China, Ireland, Israel and the Philippines lies in a high-quality workforce and superior offerings, cost-benefit edge, a decade-long experience in the area, widespread fluency in English, and supportive government policy.[62]

The information age has provided India a major opportunity to leapfrog technologically and economically in a short period of time. Scholars and businessmen, including leaders of the IT industry, who were interviewed in Bangalore, Hyderabad and Thiruvananthapuram,

[59] On the policies that led to India's achievements in software industry, see Richard Heeks, *India's Software Industry: State Policy, Liberalisation, and Industrial Development* (New Delhi: Sage Publications, 1996).

[60] For the preceding data and analysis, see, "NASSCOM–McKinsey Study: Strategizing for the boom," http://www.voicendata.com/feb00/boom.html, March 4, 2001.

[61] http://www.nasscom.org/articles/sw_export_growth.asp.

[62] NASSCOM, "MNCs Growing, Growing, Grown!" http://www.nasscom.org/articles/mnc.asp.

argued that info-tech might allow India to bypass the industrial revolution and yet emerge as a powerful global economic force. India is in the throes of the first stage of a revolution, for which it possesses several advantages over other potential competitors. IT does not require large amounts of capital and physical infrastructure, it does not create huge environmental problems, it is human-resource oriented and, moreover, it can improve India's international image. India has already achieved a high international profile in this area. Others argue that the IT revolution has allowed Indian companies to integrate with the world's leading companies of all kinds, as a back-end and front-end supplier of software, software services and IT-enabled services. It has also generated competition among the states within India. As one Indian industrialist put it, the IT revolution has brought "suddenly a quantum jump in the socioeconomic status of thousands of Indians and their families from all sections of the society. Whether they are city-born or village-born they ought to be professional in order to survive in this industry."[63]

Info-tech has great potential for expansion and, thereby, for advancing India's economic development at a faster pace. In 2000, some 2.8 million people were working in IT[64] and the potential exists for multiplying this number five to six times over the next decade. However, India needs to leverage its power and influence through IT, which could be a major source of hard and soft power. A country can project power through institutions, ideas and culture, as well as through information technology. Other areas of science and technology will also improve as a spillover from the successes in IT. Moreover, IT-based industries result in increased revenues for the localities they are situated in and, thereby, help the economic development of those areas, especially in the service sector. The head of Motorola's Hyderabad operations suggests that each IT job brings in four or five non-IT jobs. There has been no backlash against IT, as it is proving to be a great equalizer in society and it helps to bridge some social sectors.[65]

Demographics: India's relative position in population will change dramatically because of the projected decline of population in most of the industrialized countries. These countries will increasingly need Indian immigrants with higher technical education. As a result, emigrants from India will likely hold considerable money power and per-

---

[63] Interview with K. Balaji, Hyderabad, June 23, 2001.
[64] "Indian IT Sector Growing at Breakneck Speed,"
   http://www.hinduonnet.com, March 22, 2001.
[65] Interview with Sandhya V. Kode, Hyderabad, June 23, 2001.

haps political influence in key countries such as the US, a trend that has become manifest since the second half of the 1990s. These immigrants have begun to assert themselves politically in the US even as they have engaged in linking with Indian industries back home, especially in the information-technology area. Domestically, as the size of the Indian middle class increases, the economic power of India will also improve. However, nearly 30 per cent of India's population live below the poverty line and are mostly illiterate, thereby pulling down India's relative power position in the short and medium terms.

The demographic situation in India has begun to improve. According to census data, the Indian population stood at 1.03 billion in 2001. The most notable feature of the census data was the decline in the annual rate of population growth between 1991 and 2001 to 1.95 per cent; indeed, between 1997 and 1999 the growth rate was 1.6 per cent. There was also a decline in the total number of illiterates, while the gap between male and female literacy rates narrowed.[66] Indian official data also paint a rosy picture on poverty reduction. On the basis of survey data, the Indian Planning Commission in February 2001 claimed that the percentage of people living below the poverty line fell to 26.1 per cent of the population in 1999–2000, from 36 per cent in 1992–93.[67] In the information age, demography may become an asset for India, because countries without an adequate demographic base may not be able to accomplish much in the software industry area, since the raw material for info-tech industries is a literate, productive, technically trained workforce that can innovate at a rapid pace and readapt to changing circumstances.

Soft-power resources

In terms of soft-power indicators, India's position is significantly high in some areas while it has considerable potential in others. Soft-power resources are increasingly important, as they complement hard-power resources. They also provide a less costly means for exercising and preserving a state's power externally, as the use of military power has become increasingly difficult in an increasingly interdependent and globalized international system.

[66] C. Rammanohar Reddy, "India's Population," http://www.hinduonnet.com, March 31, 2001.
[67] "Only 26% Indians are Poor: Claims Plan Panel," http://www.timesofindia.com, February 23, 2001.

Normative: Norms offer legitimacy to the power position of a major power, and they have been used, often selectively, by countries such as the US to legitimize their international status. India's normative influence has been reasonably high in the developing world. India has been a consistent voice on behalf of the underprivileged for global equality and a new international economic order. This stance has been manifest in India's positions at world trade talks and in UN forums. However, its normative influence has witnessed ups and downs, especially during the 1960s, when India adopted a more inward-looking, regionally oriented foreign policy after its defeat by China. India's normative strength needs further augmentation in order for it to claim a global leadership role. What India can offer as new in a normative sense is an aspect that is likely to reverberate among power centers of the world. India's track record as a democracy for more than five decades, and its positions on global equity and further democratization of international governance, may provide some normative power in the years to come. However, some of these normative positions may clash with the interests of the powerful actors, especially the US. Some positions – for example, global nuclear disarmament – may also undermine India's own power, although they provide a good foil for India to pursue its nuclear weapons program. India may have to rely on diplomacy and a clear articulation of its goals in order to advance its position further in this area. It needs the support of like-minded states, which is possible only if it can offer something in return. However, without hard-power resources, the articulation of norms becomes a hollow exercise, as powerful actors tend to ignore options that are not congruent with their interests.

Institutional: India has been working toward achieving permanent membership for itself in the UN Security Council. India's role in other forums, such as the international financial institutions and international economic regimes, is limited but not inconsequential. India exercises institutional power intermittently through its leadership in G-77, G-20 and the nonaligned group. India's contributions to UN peacekeeping operations also provide it with some institutional influence. The acquisition of permanent membership in the Security Council will dramatically improve the Indian power position in this respect. India's future institutional power will depend on how much support it can amass among like-minded developing states, some of whom also covet the same UN Security Council seat that India is seeking. But, going by any possible benchmarks for membership, India's claim for a UN seat is the strongest of them all, and the denial of that claim is likely to generate intense status discrepancy and nationalism within India, especially if any other developing country is inducted instead of India. Institutions have emerged as a source of power for the major powers. Established powers often use institutions to legitimize their position. Rising powers such as China have also been increasingly using institutions in order to further their power ambitions. To achieve greater institutional power, India would need a permanent seat in the UN Security Council and membership in other key global decision-making forums.

Cultural: India's influence in terms of cuisine, art, music, film and dance is likely to expand with the increasing globalization in the cultural sphere. India has yet to make wider use of its cultural accomplishments globally; increasing involvement in the international entertainment and culture industry by Indian artists is likely to give India more prominence than it enjoys today. In fact, in the area of culture India offers one of the more dynamic alternatives to the Western cultural ethos, a point recognized by French government officials who were interviewed in Paris. The increasing globalization of media, especially television and the Internet, provide India a great opportunity to disseminate its culture across the world. The increasing presentation of Indian culture, especially movies, on Asian television networks, such as Hong Kong-based Star TV, show that the trend has already begun, even if it is at a modest level for the moment. These networks seem to have realized that in order to attract millions among audiences in India and other parts of Asia, they have to include Indian cultural programs, a trend that is strongly evident to travelers to Asia in recent years.[68] In fact, the Indian film industry has emerged as the second-most important globally after Hollywood. Millions of viewers of all ethnic origins in Asia, the Middle East, Africa and Europe watch Bollywood movies, and listen to Hindi songs. Although, in sheer numbers, India produces the largest number of films – over 800 a year – it collectively earned only $300 million in 2001, compared to $10 billion by the Hollywood film industry. However, "with improving production values, advertising and distribution, it may not be long before Bollywood hits the billion-dollar mark."[69] In order to make the Indian cultural presence felt internationally, Indian corporations and other agencies need to push their products

---

[68] Some analysts believe that India's cultural influence, especially among ethnic Indians, is higher worldwide than Chinese cultural influence. Segal, "Does China Matter?" 34.

[69] Chidanand Rajghatta, "Bollywood is India's Instrument of State Policy," http://www.timesofindia.com, January 12, 2002.

more vigorously, while synthesizing ideas and assets from other cultures into them.[70] They also need to gain access to the main global media outlets, such as cable TV and telecommunication networks.

In the sphere of literature, India has major achievements to its credit. Many key contemporary writers of English literature are Indian or of Indian origin, and their themes relate to India or Indians living abroad. The list is not exhaustive, but some of the prominent names include Mulk Raj Anand, R.K. Narayan, Anita Desai, Arundhati Roy, Salman Rushdie, Vikram Seth, Abraham Verghese and Jhumpa Lahiri. These prominent Indian or India-inspired authors have made a powerful impact in the field of English literature during the past three decades. The command over the English language provides India and Indians a unique avenue to exert influence in this sphere, an avenue missing in the case of China, Japan or even Germany.

In fashion, India-inspired designs have been increasingly popular in the West, although most designers in this field originate from the UK or the US. Mass marketing of such designs may take a while, but it is not an impossible prospect.[71]

State capacity: Although scholars differ on what constitutes state capacity, it is often measured in terms of the ability of a state to extract and use resources from the population, and to have effective and legitimate control over the population.[72] Effective state capacity is essential for generating loyalty and discipline among the workforce and the armed forces, as well as for engendering a national ethos necessary for obtaining greatness in the international arena. This is an area in which India ranks rather low, partly because of the inability of the Indian state to develop adequate strength.[73] India is often called a *soft state*, a state that fails to enforce enacted policies, for the state authorities are often "reluctant to place obligations on people. This reluctance, which often derives from the economic, social and political structure" of the country, "is then excused and, indeed, idealized. ... The abstention from compulsion has thus been permitted to masquerade as part of the mod-

---

[70] M.D. Nalapat, "Culture on Diplomacy: India Inc. Needs US-Style Chutzpah," http://www.timesofindia.com, March 19, 2001.

[71] "Indian Style, Western Cut," http://www.timesofindia.com, July 23, 2000.

[72] See Kal Holsti, *The State, War and the State of War* (Cambridge: Cambridge University Press, 1996), 99–106; and John A. Hall and G. John Ikenberry, *The State* (Minneapolis: University of Minnesota Press, 1989), 97.

[73] Some scholars even argue that India has been in a perennial crisis of governability. See Atul Kohli, *Democracy and Discontent: India's Growing Crisis of Governability* (New York: Cambridge University Press, 1991).

ernization ideals."[74] The soft state in India is a serious handicap in building and mobilizing hard-power resources, and to a large extent explains Indian diffidence in asserting power in the international arena.

Strategy and diplomacy: Strategy and diplomacy are areas where India's soft-power potential lies but has not been fully utilized by India's governing elite. A crucial concept here is that of *grand strategy*, which refers to the collection of military, economic and political means and ends with which a state attempts to achieve security. Under this concept, the political leadership assesses all the resources at the disposal of a state and arrays them effectively to achieve security, prosperity and power in both war and peace.[75] The grand strategy of a state must identify likely threats to national security, and it must devise political, economic, military and other remedies to confront those threats. And it must look beyond war, as war is only a means to an end, the end being peace, prosperity and status. For an aspiring major power, an effective and appropriate grand strategy is essential to take the state to its desired objective. Grand strategy, in contemporary times, must focus not only on military security, but also on economic security; it should attempt to increase the wealth of the country, as economic capability is equally important in gaining and retaining a state's power position in the international system. A grand strategy is often an intervening variable in translating a state's power capabilities into actual power and influence in the international system.

The earlier strategy of nonalignment followed by Nehru and his successors helped India in a limited fashion to establish a role in global institutions and to bargain on issues between the North and the South. However, without hard-power resources and under the weight of Cold War competition, this strategy exposed India's vulnerabilities. The anti-hegemonic theme was good in terms of creating periodic Third World solidarity, but it alienated the US and other Western countries, who attempted to contain and balance India by propping up a weaker Pakistan. With the end of the Cold War, Indian strategy changed to some extent as India began to give up some of its Cold War-era global objectives and to think more in terms of its national interests by engaging

---

[74] Gunnar Myrdal, *Asian Drama: An Inquiry into the Poverty of Nations*, vol. I (New York: Pantheon, 1968), 66–7.

[75] Barry R. Posen, *The Sources of Military Doctrine: France, Britain, and Germany between the World Wars* (Ithaca, NY: Cornell University Press, 1984), 25. Another broader definition of grand strategy is by Thomas Christensen, which we discuss in Chapter 4.

with the US, especially under the BJP-led government. The government's partial endorsement of the US national missile-defense plan in 2001 was significant, since most of the US allies and others have opposed it.

National leadership: Effective national leadership is another soft-power resource that is critical to translate other power resources, both hard and soft, into international influence. Historically, great leaders have sometimes compensated with their leadership skills for deficiencies in hard-power resources. Effective leaders serve several functions for an aspiring major power. Leaders shape a country's intentions and strategies and they affect the behavior of other states toward their state. Leaders are also very important in helping to shape the domestic and international politics of a state when conditions are fluid internally and externally.[76] Over the years, India's international influence rose and then waned and waxed with the kind of leadership it possessed. India's international influence in the 1950s was largely due to the commanding leadership of Jawaharlal Nehru. Strong leaders like Indira Gandhi did exert some influence overseas, but often the Indian political elite, especially in coalition governments, has been excessively focused on domestic politics. Indian political leaders have to develop better ideas and strategies and take an active role in global affairs if they wish to gain major-power status for their country.

Despite its limitations, India's strategic position had improved appreciably by 2000. Many reasons are ascribed for this change. Most of all, the US has increasingly perceived India's potential in balancing China. "Economic liberalization, growth, changes in strategic environment, nuclear tests, measured response to Pakistani provocations" – all these have earned India the status of a "mature regional power." But, as Ayoob adds, this has been achieved without much forethought or strategic preplanning.[77] The strategic dialogue with the US and other major powers has also helped India in clarifying its objectives, but sustaining the dialogue would require concrete policy postures and accomplishments. The change in the international environment after the terrorist attacks on the US on September 11, 2001, has opened up new oppor-

---

[76] Daniel L. Byman and Kenneth M. Pollack, "Let us Now Praise Great Men: Bringing the Statesman Back in," *International Security*, 25 (Spring 2001), 107–46.

[77] Mohammed Ayoob, "India and the Major Powers," http://www.hinduonnet.com, May 30, 2000, 1–4. For an earlier assessment of the absence of strategic thinking in India, see George K. Tanham, *Indian Strategic Thought: An Interpretative Essay* (Santa Monica, CA: Rand Corporation, 1992).

tunities and constraints for India; over the long term, it may work in India's favor, as the war against terrorism could help reduce the threats that India faces, and it may also bring the US and India closer.

Classical realists pay enormous attention to diplomacy as an instrument in augmenting and shaping national power. For instance, Morgenthau defines diplomacy as the "art of bringing the different elements of national power to bear with maximum effect to further the national interest." As a rising power, India should find Morgenthau's nine essential rules of diplomacy most relevant.[78] India has an impressive diplomatic corps that played a major role in international forums in the 1950s and 1960s, and still plays a key role in global negotiations. However, due to larger geopolitical factors and domestic constraints, this resource has not been effectively utilized. Further, Indian diplomacy has yet to attune itself to realpolitik or balance-of-power thinking that is necessary for an aspiring major power, for some of the residual Gandhian and Nehruvian ideas persist in the diplomatic language and behavior of the country.

Conclusions

This chapter has identified several parameters of power, both hard and soft, that are necessary for a major-power state to achieve and maintain its power position in the international system. It has discussed the power positions of the five major powers. A comparison has been made between India and these powers, as well as between India and a select group of regional powers. In the comparison with the present-day major powers, India offers a mixed picture. In some measures of power, its position is appreciably high and is likely to increase with the passage of time, while in others it remains low or skewed. Among the regional and middle-power states, none is comparable to India in almost all the indicators of power. The discrepancy between India and the other regional powers is likely to widen in the twenty-first century, favoring India's emergence as a major power with both hard-power and soft-power resources akin to that of the present second-tier major powers.

The Indian elites have long perceived India's potential for a major role. This perception has been manifest in the sustained policies of nation-building pursued by Nehru and his successors. Often, they pursued their goal of a major-power role through resorting to soft-power resources and through appealing to norms, even as they fostered the building up of technological and military capabilities. Yet India faces

---

[78] Hans J. Morgenthau, *Politics among Nations*, 4th edn. (New York: Alfred A. Knopf, 1967), 542–8.

formidable challenges and constraints in gaining a leadership role comparable in significance to the five leading actors of the international system. The next chapter elaborates on these challenges and constraints and their historical roots.

3   The Constraints on India: International and Domestic

The rise of a new state to the status of a major power has invariably been turbulent. In fact, almost all of the present-day major powers have achieved their status through victory in war with other major powers. Major-power status is often accorded to the leading members of a winning coalition in a postwar settlement. All the current major powers, or the five permanent members of the UN Security Council (the P-5), were in such a coalition at the end of World War II. Although China was not a leading member in this coalition, it was part of the war against the Axis powers and was accorded the status due to US insistence. The major-power system has, however, been frozen since 1945, and with no third world war in sight it may remain so in the foreseeable future. As discussed in the previous chapter, India, with its subcontinental size, large population, economic and military strength, leadership role among the developing countries, and diplomatic activism at the UN and other international forums, is indeed the strongest contender for future major-power status among all the potential candidates from the developing world. In the developed world, Germany and Japan remain strong contenders, but several structural, normative and institutional factors act as constraints on their projecting or actively asserting their position in the short and medium terms.

In this chapter, we explore the broader reasons – international and domestic – for the restrained and diffident manner in which India has asserted its position, and the reluctance of the major powers to accord India a leadership role. At the international level, we look specifically at three aspects: systemic factors, subsystemic (regional) factors, and the international image of India. At the domestic level, we focus, among other things, on economic and cultural constraints that have hampered India from developing the national identity required for a major power. The chapter concludes by arguing that, among all these factors, the systemic constraints are the most crucial, since an eligible state's position in the international system and its relationship with the existing leading actors are most pivotal in its securing a leadership role. However, factors at other levels, especially domestic, can act in tandem with systemic-level variables in constraining a country such as India from obtaining major-power status.

International-level explanations

Systemic constraints: Major powers and their balancing acts

A systemic-level explanation would hold that postwar international orders are created by the winners of major wars, and that whichever nations gain leadership roles is determined at the settlements after the wars by the winning major powers. The current international order is largely the creation of the victors of World War II. India missed the boat in 1945 because, when the new international order was created, it was still a British colony; and since then it has been struggling as a late arrival in the international system. Although India was the "Jewel in the Crown" of the British Empire and was about to gain independence, the British did not make much of an effort to give India a leading role in the UN system by awarding it a permanent membership of the Security Council. This neglect occurred despite the fact that tens of thousands of Indian soldiers died for the British Empire, fighting in many theaters of the world. Toward the end of World War II, the size of the Indian army stood at 2.5 million troops along with 8,300 Indian and 34,500 British officers. This was history's largest volunteer army to that time. It played a significant role in South-East Asia (especially Burma and Malaya), North Africa, East Africa, Italy, Greece, Syria and Iraq. The Indian army's casualties were 24,338 dead, 64,000 wounded, 12,000 missing and 80,000 taken prisoner.[1] India's participation in World War I was equally significant. Over 1.3 million Indians served in the army during the war (877,068 as combatants and 563,369 as non-combatants). The Indian army participated in overseas theaters such as France, Belgium, Gallipoli, Salonika, Palestine, Egypt, Mesopotamia, Aden, Somaliland, Cameroon, East Africa, Persia, Kurdistan and the Gulf of Oman. In fact, the Indian army constituted the largest contingent from any British colony.[2]

---

[1] *The Oxford Companion to the Second World War* (Oxford: Oxford University Press, 1995), 564.

[2] Over 53,486 Indians died in the war, while 64,350 were wounded and 3,762 were missing in action. See S.D. Pradhan, "Indian Army and the First World War," and Krishan G. Saini, "The Economic Aspects of India's Participation," in DeWitt C. Ellinwood and S.D. Pradhan (eds), *India and World War I* (New Delhi: Manohar, 1978), 55, 143–5.

Unlike China, which was recognized as a major power due to the intervention of the US, India had no active sponsor at the San Francisco conference in 1945 that created the UN and its key organs. The US was not an enthusiastic supporter of Indian independence, largely because it did not want to upset relations with its chief wartime ally, Britain. This lack of enthusiasm was also caused by the antiwar position of the Indian National Congress. The Congress leadership declined to suspend its independence struggle during the war, even though it was totally opposed to the fascist alliance. The 1942 decision by the Congress leaders, it has been argued, to go to

prison rather than actively support the war effort [causing a shift in the Roosevelt administration's support for Indian independence]. Roosevelt ceased pressuring the British to grant independence, a choice that disillusioned many Indian nationalists – and one that prefigured later disappointments when Washington was forced to choose between other allies and a nonaligned India.[3]

Thus, from a systemic point of view, the policies of the US were the most critical in determining India's position in the international order that emerged during the Cold War era.

During the first two decades of the Cold War era, India attempted fairly successfully to carve out a leadership position through, first, the Afro-Asian and, later, the nonaligned movements. This position helped India to obtain a reasonably strong role in the UN system, especially in relation to the UN efforts at decolonization. During the 1970s, India acted as a spokesman for the developing countries, in venues such as the United Nations Conference on Trade and Development (UNCTAD), on the creation of a new international economic order. However, the nonaligned movement never reached the cohesion of a power bloc, nor was it effective in fundamentally transforming global governance at the UN. India's activism in the nonaligned group, however, led to opposition to it by the US and lack of support from other Western powers. India's defeat in the 1962 war with China weakened New Delhi's position among nonaligned states as well. Meanwhile, the Soviet Union was initially not favorably disposed toward India, but Indo-Soviet relations changed in the mid-1950s and solidified prior to India's 1971 war with

[3] Stephen Philip Cohen, "The United States, India and Pakistan: Retrospect and Prospect," in Selig S. Harrison, Paul H. Kriesberg and Dennis Kux (eds), *India and Pakistan: The First Fifty Years* (Washington, DC: Woodrow Wilson Center Press, 1999), 190. See also Harold A. Gould, "U.S.–Indian Relations: The Early Phase," in Harold A. Gould and Sumit Ganguly (eds), *The Hope and Reality: U.S.–India Relations from Roosevelt to Reagan* (Boulder, CO: Westview Press, 1992), 17–42.

Pakistan.[4] The Soviet support for India helped to increase Western suspicion and hostility toward India.

In sum, from a systemic point of view, India's unwillingness to play the global balance-of-power game and its apparent lack of relevance in the Cold War rivalry (unlike China after 1972) resulted in less prominence for India in the international power system. Indian leaders, especially Nehru, often rejected balance of power as an appropriate strategy to achieve peace.[5] Even when India played a balance-of-power game (most significantly in 1971), it was not as part of the ideological struggle between the superpowers, but with the purpose of establishing India's regional preponderance in South Asia, then challenged by a triangular alliance of the US, China and Pakistan.

The US, especially during the early years of the Eisenhower administration, adopted a hostile attitude toward India and aligned itself with Pakistan. This alliance continued during much of the Cold War era, sometimes more closely than at other times. Despite the fact that India was a democracy and was more than three and a half times larger (until 1971) than Pakistan, Washington treated India and Pakistan on par as regional powers, while tilting toward Pakistan on many crucial issues, adversely affecting India's security and prosperity. India's unwillingness to join hands with the West in its struggle against communism, along with Pakistan's eagerness to be part of the Western alliance, was the underlying reason for this policy. The supply of sophisticated arms to Pakistan that began in the mid-1950s was the most direct and continuous manifestation of the anti-India policy, which forced India to acquire expensive weapons systems from other producers. Although Washington may have been primarily motivated by the desire to strengthen Pakistan as part of its containment policy toward the Soviet Union, as well as gaining bases in that country, an important motive appeared to be to keep India regionally contained as well.[6] Many US analysts do not accept this view. To historian McMahon:

the rationale for the U.S. arms deal with Pakistan was framed especially by America's perceived military and political vulnerabilities in the Middle East and

---

[4] For the Soviet position on India up to 1970, see Bhabani Sen Gupta, *The Fulcrum of Asia: Relations among China, India, Pakistan and the USSR* (New York: Pegasus, 1970), 65–91.

[5] Nehru's nonalignment policy and his opposition to balance-of-power strategies are discussed in the next chapter.

[6] For this position, see Baldev Raj Nayar, *Superpower Dominance and Military Aid: A Study of Military Aid to Pakistan* (New Delhi: Manohar, 1991).

the possibility of acquiring at a later date base sites in Pakistan; those concerns had little or nothing to do with India.[7]

However, McMahon's in-depth study cites several primary documents that reveal the extent of anti-India sentiments held by a wide range of US decision-makers, especially Secretary of State John Foster Dulles and Vice-President Richard Nixon, and how these decision-makers simultaneously viewed the aid to Pakistan as a way to teach Nehru, the champion of nonalignment, a lesson in order to make sure that more developing countries did not follow the Indian lead. Further, the type and quantities of weapons transferred to Pakistan had little relevance to deterring the Soviet Union. Part of the difficulty in this debate is the tendency of analysts to use the term *containment* largely the way it is used in explaining Western policies toward the Soviet Union and its allies. The other possible use of limited *regional containment* is often ignored in these analyses.

Washington's position on aid to Pakistan was supported by other Western major powers, especially Britain, even when the Western nations contributed economically to India's development, out of fear that India's economic collapse would result in the further spread of communism in the developing world. Over time, the working of the balance-of-power process is evident specifically in relation to India. In the 1971 Bangladesh War, the US tilt toward Pakistan became even more overt as the realpolitik-oriented Nixon administration actively pursued a pro-Pakistani policy, while employing coercive diplomacy to pressure India not to attack West Pakistan.[8] The most significant element of this policy was the dispatch of the US Seventh Fleet, led by the USS Enterprise, to the Bay of Bengal in an apparent effort to coerce India. Although India declared a cease-fire two days after the fleet entered the bay, its decision actually may have had little to do with the dispatch of the fleet. However, the episode left a deep scar on the US–India relationship and the attitudes of the Indians toward the US.[9]

In its active military hostility with Pakistan and China, India had only the Soviet Union to rely upon, which weakened its nonaligned credentials

---

[7] Robert J. McMahon, *Cold War on the Periphery: The United States, India and Pakistan* (New York: Columbia University Press, 1994), 177.

[8] For the Nixon–Kissinger coercive diplomacy toward India, see William Burr (ed.), *The Kissinger Transcripts* (New York: The New Press, 1998), 46–57.

[9] For the events leading to this episode and an evaluation, see David K. Hall, "The Laotian War of 1962 and the Indo-Pakistani War of 1971," in Barry M. Blechman and Stephen S. Kaplan (eds), *Force without War* (Washington, DC: The Brookings Institution, 1978), 135–221.

even further. The position of all the major powers, except the Soviet Union after 1971, was thus antithetical to India gaining a leadership role during the Cold War period. Soviet support alone was not sufficient to impart a leadership position for India, given that any effort by Moscow to elevate India's status would have resulted in Western opposition. Western powers often perceived India as pro-Soviet and were critical of its nonaligned position in many areas of international relations. The US–India relations are especially significant here. It is a puzzle as to why the US and India, the world's two largest democracies, could not get along and why they regarded themselves as inimical to each other's regional and global strategic interests.

Explaining the US–India estrangement: In a major comprehensive work on India–US relations, based on previously classified documents and on interviews, US diplomat-historian Dennis Kux provides a straightforward historical account of the mutual estrangement between the democratic superpower and the world's largest democracy. Kux contends, however:

India and the United States were not at odds because, as some assert, there was too little dialogue, or a lack of mutual understanding, or were serious misperceptions, or because Indians and Americans have trouble getting along with each other. On the contrary, I believe that Washington and New Delhi fell out because they disagreed on national security issues of fundamental importance to each.[10]

What Kux does not explain or explore is what lay behind their disagreement on "national security issues of fundamental importance," which has been sustained over half a century. The argument here is that they disagreed because they occupied different structural positions in the international system and the global power hierarchy, and acted accordingly to promote their interests within those parameters of power.

There is an inherent dynamic of conflict between major powers and independent-minded middle powers that are ambitious and unwilling to accept the dominance of the former. Major powers are driven to resist the emergence of new such powers, since the accommodation of others to a similar role reduces their own power and, thus, control over their own national security and welfare. Quite the contrary, existing major

---

[10] Dennis Kux, *India and the United States: Estranged Democracies, 1941–1991* (Washington, DC: National Defense University Press, 1992), xii–xiii.

powers endeavor to extend their power as far as possible, to bring others under their domination through spheres of influence, and to reduce middle powers to the status of *objects*. On the other hand, for middle powers the goal of entering the exclusive club of *subjects*, or major powers, is also a compelling one, provided they have the potential for it. That goal is compelling, not for reasons of prestige as is often presumed, but for purposes of national survival and welfare, since middle powers constantly face the prospect of domination by the major powers. In order therefore to avoid domination by the major powers, middle powers seek to add to their capabilities. However, the very addition of such material capabilities, undertaken for the purpose of national security, serves to elevate their status. The thrust for *role elevation* to major-power status is thus an almost ineluctable consequence of the structural position of eligible middle powers in the international system. The contrary impulses of existing major powers and eligible middle powers – to exercise dominion over others for the former, to avoid domination for the latter – often set them on a collision course. Consequently, the graduation of an eligible middle power to the status of major power has in the past been invariably accompanied by violence. However, rivalry and competition among the existing major powers may at times facilitate the emergence of some middle powers as subjects.

   In Chapter I, we called attention to the typology that the international-relations theorist George Liska has presented about the policies that major powers typically choose in their posture toward middle powers. Chief among them is containment, while the other two are satellization and accommodation. Often, the underlying purpose of a major power in the containment of a middle power under the garb of controlling conflict in the developing world is to reduce its international influence as a claimant to a subject role, to subordinate its foreign policy to that of the major power, to raise the costs for it of seeking foreign-policy autonomy and, crucially, to prevent its rise to the status of a major power. The principal instrument in the regional containment of a middle power is the shaping of a balance of power in the region that favors the major power. This is accomplished through a policy of alliances, tacit or explicit, or both. Containment is not necessarily the only policy that a major power may pursue toward a middle power. It may be supplemented by satellization through the generation of dependencies in the middle power; the key instruments for this purpose are economic aid and military alliances. Finally, there is the policy of accommodation; under it, major powers "proceed either unilaterally or jointly progressively to devolve regional responsibilities to apparently constructively disposed middle powers." However, a critical consideration for major powers in adopting this policy is whether the middle power is "loyalist" or "rebellious."[11]

Major powers need not be rigid in the application of these policies, for that is a matter of some delicacy or flexibility in practice. For example, the containment of a middle power may be modified by the need to be contingently supportive of its target in the cause of the containment of another power that is perceived to be a greater threat. Or regional containment may be limited to a particular region and to specific issue-areas, and need not be of the dimensions of a system-wide military-political-technology denial that characterized Western policy toward the Eastern bloc during the Cold War era. Regional containment may also be supplemented with economic aid and be narrowly focused on technology or military capability. There can also be variations in the intensity with which such policies are applied to specific regional powers. It should be understood that to analyze these policies in respect of a major power in its relations with a middle power is not to assign motives, but only to draw out the policy consequences of specific location in a structurally differentiated international system.

The US military aid to Pakistan starting in 1954 has to be seen in the light of this policy typology; it was a necessary US riposte to contain India's assertiveness in playing a global role, which was taken to impinge on US interests. Most US scholarship has focused on the containment of the Soviet Union as the cause for US military aid to Pakistan. Sufficient and compelling evidence has been provided elsewhere in favor of the proposition, theoretically consistent with Liska's typology, that India itself was the target of US regional containment, albeit in terms of military balancing and technology denial as opposed to economic denial.[12] Although earlier such a proposition has met with criticism at the hands of US scholars, it is noteworthy that, with the passage of time, at the end of the twentieth century one of the US's foremost political scientists, Samuel P. Huntington, stated in a matter-of-fact manner:

In terms of power, the United States and the secondary regional powers have common interests in limiting the dominance of the major states in their regions. ... The United States ... has worked with Pakistan to balance India in South

[11] George Liska, "The Third World: Regional Systems and Global Order," in Robert E. Osgood *et al.*, *Retreat From Empire* (Baltimore, MD: Johns Hopkins University Press, 1973), 326.

[12] See Baldev Raj Nayar, "A World Role: The Dialectics of Purpose and Power," in John W. Mellor (ed.), *A Rising Middle Power* (Boulder, CO: Westview Press, 1979), 117–46; and Nayar, *Superpower Dominance and Military Aid*.

Asia. In all these cases, cooperation serves mutual interests in *containing* the influence of the major regional power.[13]

Others have concurred with this view, although less emphatically. For instance, according to Selig Harrison, the mindset of the US decision-makers in the 1950s was that India was an economic "basket case" and yet it was taking "independent positions," and it therefore "needed to be put in place." The US, he believes, has been reluctant to see the rise of any other independent power centers, not just India. However, he acknowledges that Nixon and Dulles did hold notions of containing India.[14] Another American scholar, who has seriously studied US–India relations, Harold Gould, argues that John Foster Dulles was instrumental in the strident opposition by the US to India's nonaligned position. In his view, the method that Dulles adopted:

was to try to diplomatically isolate India to cut it off as much as possible from Western sympathy and support in the context of the United Nations and other international bodies and at the same time to inhibit its capacity to be of any strategic value to the Communist bloc. The last effort took the form of recruiting Pakistan into the *cordon sanitaire* that Dulles was determined to erect around the perimeters of Soviet and Chinese Communist power.[15]

As US–India relations began to improve in 2001, US officials started to publicly state views that agree with this position. For instance, in July 2001, Deputy Secretary of State Richard Armitage remarked that the US has "never had a balanced policy in South Asia," and that the US–Pakistani relationship was "relatively false ... based against someone else – *in the first instance India* and their relationship with the Soviet Union and later against the Soviet occupation of Afghanistan."[16] This is in line with a much earlier declaration by the then US Ambassador to India, Robert Goheen, who stated in 1977:

The events of the last decade have brought it about that whether you look at it in geographical terms, in military terms or in economic terms, India and Pakistan really aren't competitors any more. India is clear and away the preeminent nation in the subcontinent, *so that game we played for many years of trying*

---

[13] Samuel P. Huntington, "The Lonely Superpower," *Foreign Affairs*, 78 (March–April 1999), 35–49; emphasis added.
[14] Interview with Selig Harrison, Washington, DC, December 16, 1999.
[15] Gould, "U.S.–India-Relations," 35.
[16] S. Rajagopal, "India and Pak Not on Par: US," http://www.hindustantimes.com, July 5, 2001; emphasis added.

to balance one off against the other – that's a dead game. And that was a terrific cause of friction between India and ourselves.[17]

Unfortunately for India, however, such retrospective reassessments did not put an end to the policy of regional containment.

The US–Pakistan military alliance that was initiated in 1954 was of momentous importance to the international politics of South Asia and to India's power position in the region. The military aid to Pakistan made that country technologically superior to India in military equipment. That aid also set in motion a process of reorientation of India's foreign policy in the direction of cultivating the Soviet Union, though initially only diplomatically rather than militarily, to counterbalance the alliance. Notwithstanding India's declarations to the contrary, nonalignment had, in effect, become modified, demonstrating in the process that balancing is an inescapable process among states, even when they may profess antagonism to it. As friendship reactively developed between India and the Soviet Union, the US responded by providing extensive economic aid to India to counter Soviet influence; the economic aid thus partly compensated India for the US military aid to Pakistan.

Even though the US may have been eager for the alliance, Pakistan had ardently courted the US for it. The weaker party in the asymmetric India–Pakistan dyad borrowed capabilities to balance off the larger power's superior position in the region, using the Cold War rivalry as a timely opportunity. Why Pakistan should have been so ardent on balancing with external support has been a function of the region's geopolitical structure, history and culture. Since Pakistan has been the fulcrum for the intervention of external powers in the affairs of the subcontinent, its role needs to be examined in some detail, a task we undertake in a subsequent section of this chapter.

Once formed, the alliance between the US and Pakistan saw some ups and downs. As Pakistan drew closer to China after the India–China War of 1962, the US began to have misgivings about the alliance. In the India–Pakistan War of 1965, the US took a neutral position between the two belligerent states and let the Soviet Union handle the aftermath of the war by getting them together at Tashkent. However, with Richard Nixon in the White House in 1969, the alliance saw a revival and Washington used the good offices of Pakistan to open relations with China. In the India–Pakistan War of 1971, a de facto triple alliance between the US, China and Pakistan became evident. During the second half of the 1970s, there was another cooling off in the relations

---

[17] William Borders, "Mr. Goheen in Delhi: On Both Sides, New Ideas," *New York Times,* October 2, 1977; emphasis added.

between the US and Pakistan – indeed, considerable tension – as a result of the Pakistani drive for nuclear weapons and the military coup d'état under General Zia ul-Haq. Soon, however, the military alliance was revived once again, with Pakistan assuming the role of a frontline state in the US effort to oust the Soviets from Afghanistan after their intervention in 1979. Not only did the US once again provide massive military aid to Pakistan and rearm it with technologically superior weaponry, but it also now adopted a permissive approach to Pakistan's development of nuclear weapons. Only with the collapse of the Soviet Union did the US begin to distance itself from Pakistan.

The military alliance with Pakistan was not the only instrument in the regional containment of India by the US. From the early 1970s, the US emerged as the most outspoken opponent of India's acquisition of nuclear and space capabilities. The Nuclear Nonproliferation Treaty (NPT) was the most important manifestation of this opposition. Missile control was another; it was added in 1987 through the establishment of the Missile Technology Control Regime (MTCR), which sought to restrict transfer of space and missile technology from industrial countries to developing states, including India. The US opposition to India's acquisition of nuclear and space capabilities also derived from systemic factors. In fact, there is somewhat of a consensus among analysts that the single most important issue that prevented an India–US rapprochement, even in the post-Cold War era, was the nuclear one, signifying the pivotal role that security calculations play in major-power behavior, especially in US foreign policy. The nuclear issue generated negative perceptions among US decision-makers vis-à-vis India, which became well-entrenched as the years passed by. The US assumed that India was a "revisionist state destined to be at odds with the United States, a status quo global power," that "India is obstinate about the Nuclear Nonproliferation Treaty," that it was "vulnerable to technology-denying efforts, and that it can be equated with its neighbor, Pakistan." These perceptions led to policies which were viewed by the Indian elites as antithetical to their interests. For instance, "the American tendency to equate India and Pakistan, especially pronounced in the past, artificially reduces Indian security concerns, making any wider strategic calculations by India appear unreasonable."[18]

From the US perspective, India posed the most significant challenge to a near-universal regime through its advanced nuclear capabilities in the developing world, and by its powerful normative arguments against

[18] See Deepa Ollapally and Raja Ramanna, "U.S.–India Tension: Misperceptions on Nuclear Proliferation," *Foreign Affairs,* 74 (January–February 1995), 13–18.

the regime, which struck at the heart of the unequal world order that the US has championed. The US position on the regime gradually received support from almost all the nuclear holdouts, barring India. Sections of the US elite viewed nuclear proliferation as dangerous to global security, and they simply could not understand or appreciate Indian security concerns. To them, India was a proliferator, and an obstruction to the regime, period. By their treatment of India, they also wanted to make an example out of New Delhi for other nuclear "wannabes." By isolating India, they aimed to have other eligible states, such as Brazil and Argentina, curb their nuclear ambitions.

Nonproliferation analysts rarely explore the key underlying reasons for India's acquisition of nuclear and space capabilities, nor do they broach the question of the impact of such capabilities on power distribution in the international system. This stance has resulted in supply-side approaches and short-term policy pronouncements which do not take into account the roots of the nuclear issue. Over the years, the US and other nuclear powers have come to the conclusion that the spread of nuclear weapons to smaller states would undermine their structural dominance, as nuclear weapons, under certain conditions, would serve as a "great equalizer," for nuclear weapons would limit the ability of conventionally superior powers from intervening in the affairs of the regional powers.[19] One of the key attributes of a major power is its ability to punish a weaker actor militarily without receiving punishment in kind in return. Nuclear possession by a weaker actor can put significant constraints on the major power's ability to intervene and punish. It can also reduce the power of nuclear umbrellas, since threatened regional states may opt for independent capabilities in order to offset a local rival's nuclear capabilities.

The NPT was a powerful institutional and normative arrangement that the nuclear-armed powers and their associates initiated in order to stem the tide of proliferation. By creating two classes of states with two types of responsibilities and by selecting the cut-off date of January 1967, the treaty purported to stop any new nuclear power from emerging legally. By its very structural position, India became the most outspoken opponent of it, as the treaty did nothing to allay India's security concerns vis-à-vis China and, later on, Pakistan. Further, by subscribing to this treaty, India would have perpetually forfeited its claim to major-power status, which to the Indian elites was something unacceptable. Once acceded to, it would have become extremely difficult to exit from the treaty, as North Korea found out in the early 1990s, even

[19] Robert W. Chandler, *The New Face of War* (McLean, VA: Amcoda Press, 1998), 13, 228.

though legally under the terms of the treaty a signatory could withdraw after giving three months notice in the event of a supreme national-security threat. The Indian opposition to the NPT regime has always been couched in terms of normative goals, such as its failure to promote sovereign equality, equity between "haves" and "have-nots," and global disarmament. However, the fundamental, though unstated, reason has been structural, which the Indians allude to but rarely make explicit. India has viewed the continued possession of nuclear weapons by the P-5 as legitimizing their major-power status while keeping India as a lower-ranking power perpetually.[20] India's advocacy of moral norms, such as sovereign equality, came from a state that has viewed itself as thoroughly disadvantaged under the present dispensation. Its conflict with the major powers on the nuclear issue has been a structural conflict par excellence.

An astute and long-term analyst of India–US relations, Selig Harrison, captures the essence of this structural conflict: "The conflict between India and the United States over the NPT not only reflects disagreement on nuclear matters, as such, but also underlines what may prove to be incompatible views concerning the nature of the global power structure ..." The US wants to restrict the ownership of nuclear weapons to a small group of states for power reasons, but:

it is India's goal to escape from second class status in world affairs and receive recognition commensurate with its position as one of the world's oldest and largest civilizations, constituting nearly one fifth of the human race. Since nuclear weapons still constitute the principal coin of power, this quest for equitable status has prompted India to perfect its ability to assemble and deliver nuclear weapons, unless and until the existing nuclear weapon states make credible progress toward a nuclear free world.

Harrison adds:

Many Indians have what might be called a "post-dated self-image." They are confident that India is on the way to great power status and want others to treat them as if they had, in fact, already arrived. By the same token, to many Americans, India's ambitions are pretentious nonsense, given its widespread poverty, and New Delhi should be prepared to deal with the United States on the basis of the actual power relationship now existing between the two countries.[21]

[20] Jaswant Singh, "Against Nuclear Apartheid," *Foreign Affairs*, 77 (September–October 1998), 41–52.
[21] Selig S. Harrison, "A Nuclear Bargain with India," paper presented at the conference "India at the Crossroads," Southern Methodist University, Dallas, Texas, March 27, 1998, 6–8.

In the post-Cold War period, Indian concerns with respect to nuclear weapons increased. The 1991 Gulf War, the 1995 NPT extension in perpetuity and the 1996 CTBT negotiations all magnified India's structural difficulties in the international arena. An advocate of the Indian deterrent and a former Indian army chief, General K. Sundarji, stated that India needed nuclear weapons "to dissuade big powers from lightly pursuing policies of compellence vis-à-vis India. The Gulf War emphasized once again that nuclear weapons are the ultimate coin of power. In the final analysis, they could go in because the United States had nuclear weapons and Iraq didn't."[22]

However, despite its vehement opposition to the nonproliferation regime, India failed to assert its role as a nuclear weapons state (NWS) for well over three decades, for a variety of domestic, international and idiosyncratic reasons. Still, it continued to maintain nuclear ambiguity. India's vacillation in declaring itself as an NWS or in building up a credible nuclear deterrent until May 1998 allowed the major powers and their allies to treat India, along with a number of other states, as a threshold state and thus a candidate for sanctions by the supplier countries. As a result of its ambiguity and vacillation, India not only lost a chance to develop a credible nuclear deterrent but it also heavily undercut its civilian nuclear-energy program. In contrast, China has succeeded in gaining access to both civilian and military nuclear technology.[23] The NWSs and their associates hoped that India would fold up its nuclear weapons program under continued external pressure.

India's systemic aspirations were thus hampered by the fact that, as a nuclear weapons power, it was a latecomer. It was not an NWS by 1968 when the NPT was finalized. By the time India detonated a nuclear device in 1974, it was too late to receive recognition, since the NPT had proclaimed that only those states that had tested a nuclear device by 1967 were to be accepted as NWSs. The norm of nonproliferation had taken strong roots globally by then, and by 1998 it was even stronger. The 1974 test was a pivotal event, as it galvanized the US and its allies to tighten the screws on nonproliferation. Much of the US legislation on the subject came into being after the 1974 Indian test.

Besides the element of India's own major-power aspirations in building nuclear capabilities, its nuclear behavior is not explainable without reference to Chinese security policies vis-à-vis India, and the larger bal-

---

[22] Cited in Selig S. Harrison and Geoffrey Kemp, *India and America after the Cold War* (Washington, DC: Carnegie Endowment for International Peace, 1993), 21.

[23] C. Raja Mohan, "India and the Sino-US Nuclear Deal," *Hindu*, August 21, 1997, 1.

ance-of-power relationship that developed between China and Pakistan as well as between China and the US. Among the nuclear powers, China merits particular mention here, as India's relationship with Beijing was significant in a whole gamut of external constraints that faced India in its bid for achieving a leadership role.

China: China is the second key major power that constrains the extension of India's power in South Asia and beyond. Except for a brief period in the 1950s, Chinese policy toward India has been predominantly one of containment, although since the late 1980s the policy has become a mixture of containment and engagement. When he died in 1964, Prime Minister Nehru left behind for India a deeply troubled relationship with China. Prior to independence, Nehru had a utopian belief in the common destiny of Asia, especially in respect of China and India as the carriers of Asia's two great civilizations. He even envisioned a political federation between the two countries. After independence, rather than assuming a natural rivalry between the two largest states of Asia, he pursued an active policy of befriending China, marked by a considerable degree of naïve sentimentalism.[24] More damaging was his neglect of the defense of the borders with China and the failure to extend the administrative jurisdiction of the state to the territories that India formally regarded as its own. When Nehru finally awakened to the Chinese occupation of vast areas of India's territory, albeit regions disputed by China, it was too late.

In 1962, as India sought to strengthen its new de facto borders and to counter what it regarded as creeping expansion into India's territory, China resorted to a massive punitive strike that left India reeling. The resultant military defeat for India was shattering in its consequences. First, it was a major personal and political blow to Nehru, from which he never recovered; he died within less than two years of the violent conflict.

Second, its most fundamental impact was to tear India away from the unrealism partially characteristic of Nehru's foreign policy; the unrealism had already been to some extent eroded as a result of US military aid to Pakistan, but the war with China was a most searing and

---

[24] Nehru and his defense minister, V.K. Krishna Menon, held naïve expectations regarding China. See Michael Brecher, *India and World Politics: Krishna Menon's View of the World* (New York: Praeger, 1968). Nehru believed that "by allowing Indian control up to the McMahon Line without any protest for so many years, the Chinese acknowledged *de facto* acceptance of this boundary." M.J. Akbar, *Nehru: The Making of India* (London: Penguin Books, 1988), 542.

transforming experience with long-term significance. More immediately, the military defeat undercut the basis of Nehru's foreign policy, which had underlined the virtues of peaceful coexistence and nonalignment. After the earlier lofty disdain for the emphasis on the military instrument in the West, it was deeply humiliating for India, as well as Nehru personally, to be put in a position to ask for protection and military aid from the US and its allies. It was humiliating for the Indian elites to tolerate a high degree of US intrusiveness in Indian decision-making for defense, with the US ambassador allowed to act as if he were an imperial proconsul.

Third, the military defeat drove India into a dependency on the Soviet Union for arms. Fourth, it deflated the image of India in the developing and nonaligned world, which now saw it as dependent on the superpowers despite its pronouncements to the contrary. The consequent diminished role of India on the international scene was especially galling when juxtaposed against its earlier activism. Fifth, India's doubling of its defense expenditures in response to the conflict resulted in serious destabilizing consequences for the economy and, therefore, for the polity, at least in the short term. Sixth, the conflict laid the basis for future cooperation and collusion (which would unfold over the subsequent decades) between India's two adversaries, China and Pakistan, to the serious detriment of India's security interests. It offered China the opportunity to follow the example first set by the US to contain India regionally through the instrumentality of Pakistan.

Since 1963, China has actively sided with Pakistan in the latter's conflict with India. It even gave hints of opening up a second front against India during Pakistan's wars with India in 1965 and 1971, although it failed to follow through on its threats. In June 1963, Premier Zhou Enlai had openly declared that China would defend Pakistan throughout the world. A month later, Foreign Minister Zulfikar Ali Bhutto echoed Zhou's statement before the Pakistan National Assembly by announcing that any attack on Pakistan by India "would no longer confine the stakes to the independence and territorial independence of Pakistan," but would also involve "the security and territorial integrity of the largest state in Asia."[25] Chinese collusion with Pakistan, as well as its limits, became manifest in the India–Pakistan War of 1965. As the tides of the war began to turn against Pakistan, China made limited moves on its border with India.[26] In 1971, China was once again supportive of

---

[25] See *Dawn* (Karachi), June 18, 1963; Zulfikar Ali Bhutto, *Foreign Policy of Pakistan* (Karachi: Pakistan Institute of International Affairs, 1964), 75; and T.V. Paul, *Asymmetric Conflicts: War Initiation by Weaker Powers* (Cambridge: Cambridge University Press, 1994), 118.

Pakistan during the Bangladesh War. Pakistani Foreign Minister Zulfikar Ali Bhutto publicly stated that China would intervene on Pakistan's side in the event of an Indian attack. During the war, however, China confined its backing to material and political support. Toward the end, Beijing threatened a crisis in Sikkim on the China–India border, but this was only after a cease-fire had been announced between India and Pakistan.[27]

The most significant containing behavior on the part of China vis-à-vis India has been in the form of supply of nuclear and missile technology, components and materials to Pakistan. The China–Pakistan nuclear and missile supply relationship has persisted for well over two decades, even after China had signed on to the NPT and had agreed to observe the missile-control regime. According to Robert Ross, China continues its support for Pakistan by supplying nuclear and missile technology, because:

China views a credible Pakistani deterrent as the most effective way to guarantee the security of its sole ally in Southern Asia against Indian power. ... In this respect, China's relationship with Pakistan is similar to America's relationship with Israel.[28]

The China–Pakistan nuclear cooperation began in the 1970s during the tenure of Zulfikar Ali Bhutto as prime minister of Pakistan. This cooperation reached its peak in the 1980s and early 1990s, when Beijing assisted Pakistan in building its nuclear capabilities. The precise nature of the Sino-Pakistani nuclear cooperation is not fully known, but US intelligence sources have long contended that the Pakistani nuclear-bomb project would not have come into being without the active support of China. This support included: a secret blueprint for a nuclear bomb in the early 1980s; highly enriched uranium; tritium; scientific advisers; and key components for a nuclear-weapons production complex. As a report in the *New York Times* presented it:

Beginning 1990, Pakistan is believed to have built between 7 and 12 nuclear warheads – based on Chinese designs, assisted by Chinese scientists and

[26] Yacov Vertzberger, *The Enduring Entente: Sino-Pakistani Relations 1960–1980* (New York: Praeger, 1983), 37.

[27] See Richard Sisson and Leo E. Rose, *War and Secession: Pakistan, India and the Creation of Bangladesh* (Berkeley: University of California Press, 1990), 252–3.

[28] Robert S. Ross, "Engagement in U.S. China Policy," in Alastair Iain Johnston and Robert S. Ross (eds), *Engaging China: The Management of an Emerging Power* (London and New York: Routledge, 1999), 193.

Chinese technology. That technology included Chinese magnets for producing weapons grade enriched uranium, a furnace for shaping the uranium into a nuclear bomb core, and high-tech diagnostic equipment for nuclear weapons tests.[29]

According to a *Time* magazine report in 1997, the CIA had discovered that China had helped Pakistan to set up a factory to manufacture M-11 surface-to-surface missiles near Rawalpindi, in addition to supplying thirty ready-to-launch M-11s that were stored at the Sargodha air base near Lahore. These missiles, each with a warhead of 500 kilograms and a range of 300 kilometers, would be ideal for Pakistan's nuclear weapons and could be targeted on Indian cities close to the Pakistani border.[30] Even after Pakistan's nuclear tests in 1998, China is reported to have continued its assistance to Pakistan by helping to establish the 50-megawatt Khushab reactor, which will produce weapons-grade plutonium, "although such a help is in direct violation of article III of the NPT."[31] The Sino-Pakistani collaboration was evident in a high-level Pakistani delegation visiting China immediately after the Indian tests in May 1998, with the aim of gaining nuclear guarantees and politico-military backing. Although the precise nature of the proffered Chinese support is not clear, it is believed that China was not opposed to Pakistan conducting nuclear tests in response to those of India. However, no open security guarantees were apparently forthcoming from Beijing. Pakistan then conducted its own nuclear tests, claiming that it needed an autonomous atomic capability to deter India.

Indian analysts believe that China has been pursuing a strategy of simultaneous containment of and engagement with India. Indian strategic analyst K. Subrahmanyam has argued that the Chinese threat to India is indirect:

If China can transfer nuclear and missile technologies to Pakistan and thereby countervail India, there is no need for China to pose a threat to India. China can continue to be friendly with India but at the same time lock India in a nuclear standoff with Pakistan. It can also treat both Pakistan and India in the same category as regional powers, not in the same class as China, which is a global player.[32]

[29] Tim Weiner, "U.S. and China Helped Pakistan Build the Bomb," *New York Times,* June 1, 1998, A6.
[30] Douglas Waller, "The Secret Missile Deal," *Time,* 149 (26), June 30, 1997.
[31] K. Subrahmanyam, "Eight Months after the Nuclear Tests," paper presented at McGill University, February 16, 1999.
[32] K. Subrahmanyam, "Understanding China: Sun Tzu and Shakti," *Times of India,* 5 June 1998, 7.

Senior Indian diplomats in Beijing concur with this view. For one Indian official, China has been trying and will try to "keep India in a box" until there is a settlement of the India–Pakistan conflict; the Chinese have learned lessons from the US with respect to Pakistan and have "strong compulsions" to place India and Pakistan together; and they were eager to play the balancer's role even after Sino-Indian relations began to improve in 1988.[33]

There seems to be some truth in the contentions of the Indian analysts. The Chinese containment strategy involves a de facto alliance with Pakistan and gradual military build-up in the Indian Ocean/Bay of Bengal region through establishing military bases in places such as Myanmar.[34] The Chinese policy of containing India through the military build-up of its neighbors has been noted by Western analysts as well. Quoting Chinese sources, Iain Johnston has argued that the dominant Chinese motivation in arming Pakistan has been to "help divert Indian military resources away from China."[35] The engagement policy has involved reduction of tensions in the border region, a series of high-profile visits between China and India, and periodic proclamations in official and unofficial statements about the traditional friendship between the two countries. Since 1988, joint working groups have been negotiating confidence-building measures and ways to promote mutual cooperation. Although the engagement policy received a severe setback with the Indian nuclear tests in 1998, it was resumed two years later.

Regional (subsystemic) constraints: Pakistan's balancing acts

The enduring and protracted conflict between India and Pakistan has considerably undermined India's strategic significance because, in the perceptions of the West and the developing nations, India's asymmetric conflict with a smaller neighbor made Pakistan into an equal of India. Islamabad's success in bringing in extraregional powers to its support, and its capacity to create crises and wars, while keeping the Kashmir conflict boiling through its active support of the Kashmiri liberation movements, has in some respects weakened India's power position in the global system. Pakistan's ability to attract the support of external

---

[33] Interviews, Beijing, June 13, 2000.

[34] Ashok Kapur, "China and Proliferation: Implications for India," *China Report*, 34 (3–4), 1998, 401–17. See also Nimmi Kurian, *Emerging China and India's Policy Options* (New Delhi: Lancer Publishers, 2001).

[35] Alastair Iain Johnston, "International Structures and Chinese Foreign Policy," in Samuel S. Kim (ed.), *China and the World: Chinese Foreign Policy Faces the New Millennium* (Boulder, CO: Westview Press, 1998), 63.

powers and to be an activist challenger to India, despite its smaller size, has largely been a function of the region's geopolitical structure in which both Pakistan and India are located, and also of Pakistan's own grand strategy, which has roots in its particular social and ideological ethos.

Whether called the Indian subcontinent or South Asia, the region constitutes a geopolitical fortress, bounded in the north by the mountain ranges of the Himalayas and in the south by the Indian Ocean. Apart from its geopolitical unity, the subcontinent also constitutes in some measure a single civilizational complex which has endured over some three millennia. However, for much of its history the subcontinent has not been united under a single comprehensive political system. It was only with the British conquest that a single political system was imposed that was coextensive with the geopolitical unity of the subcontinent. In their concern for India's security, the British evolved a strategic design which provided a double line of defense, one internal and the other external. The design's central element was the policy of "reverse slopes," under which other powers such as China and Russia were to have no presence on the Indian side of the Himalayan ranges; that aim was accomplished through the effective subordinating by Britain of the Himalayan states. Additionally, the British established an iron fence of buffer states (such as Tibet, Afghanistan or Iran), located on the reverse slopes of the Himalayan ranges, so that no major power would have direct control of the territory around India, even on the other side of the Himalayas. The end of British colonial rule in 1947, however, resulted in the collapse of the single central political authority through the partition of the subcontinent into the two large states of India and Pakistan. Moreover, the partition laid the basis for the reversal of the reverse slopes design; it established an institutionalized basis for the external intervention by outside powers, with Pakistan, as a possible base for such intervention, representing a serious vulnerability for India.

Despite partition, and the resultant loss of huge territory in its western and eastern parts, India emerged as the pre-eminent power in the subcontinent. Indeed, the region is singularly Indo-centric, not only because India lies geographically at the center of the region flanked by the other states, which physically do not touch each other, but also because, with some three-quarters of the population and territory of the region, it is no exaggeration to say that in a geopolitical sense India is South Asia. As a consequence of its position, India's conception of its security has been a *geopolitical and regional* one, rather than simply a national one. For, given its position, the threat to India's security is likely to come, in the first instance, from the relatively weaker states in the region rather than from outside powers. A serious threat to India arises if its neighbors within the subcontinent are weak and unstable, thus inviting outside intervention inside the South Asian geopolitical fortress, or if they become willing proxies for outside powers. As the US strategic analyst Wayne Wilcox once pointed out, India "fears the disintegration of Pakistan, which might involve foreign powers in the resulting 'vacuum' and would open the subcontinent's flanks to external powers, possibly involving India in a conflict for which it has neither the capacity nor the vital interests to fight." It was understandable for him, therefore, that "India must count upon Pakistan's being relatively able to manage its own territories," though not so strong as to challenge India itself. At the same time, India being the pre-eminent power in South Asia, it was not surprising that it "sees its security as a function of South Asian regional security and regional security requires Indian leadership and strength."[36] India thus views its preponderance as a source of stability as opposed to instability and war. This Indian view has a strong pedigree in international-relations theory. One school, opposed to balance-of-power theory, argues that peace is maintained only when satisfied status quo states are militarily preponderant, whereas war is more likely when dissatisfied challengers approximate their capabilities with the dominant power.[37] As a status quo power, India holds the view that smaller powers have nothing to fear as long as they do not challenge India's dominant status on the subcontinent.

India's security and defense measures in relation to its neighbors therefore have been primarily accommodative and defensive, and at times reactively adversarial. This pattern of behavior on the part of India may also be the consequence of the dominant component of the region's civilization in the form of Hinduism, as well as of the nature of India's democratic political system, which encourages accommodation – primarily internally and, as an extension of internal policy, also externally – but it is in some measure built into the larger geopolitical structure of the region. At the same time, given its conception of regional security, India has, in a local version of the Monroe Doctrine, been strongly opposed to intervention by outside powers in the affairs of the region except in support of its own position. This stance has often led to criticism by the smaller states in the region, who from time to time have

---

[36] Wayne A. Wilcox, "India and Pakistan," in Steven L. Spiegel and Kenneth N. Waltz (eds), *Conflict in World Politics* (Cambridge, MA: Winthrop Publishers, 1971), 240–60.

[37] See A.F.K. Organski, *World Politics*, 2nd edn. (New York: Alfred A. Knopf, 1968), 364, 366; Inis Claude, *Power and International Relations* (New York: Random House, 1964), 56; and Erich Weede, "Overwhelming Preponderance as a Pacifying Condition among Contiguous Asian Dyads, 1950–69," *Journal of Conflict Resolution*, 20 (September 1976), 395–411.

accused India of "heavy handedness" and "hegemony" in its relations with the neighbors. However, among the smaller states, only Pakistan has been somewhat successful in constraining Indian power, since India rarely achieved overwhelming preponderance in relation to it. Where India has had overwhelming preponderance, the consequence has been some form of hegemony.

India's existential pre-eminent position in the subcontinent, however, evokes in the smaller states within the region the specter of Indian domination, and therefore a strategy for weakening and countering India comes naturally to them, and in particular to the most capable state, Pakistan. Again, as Wilcox had underlined, "the strategic paradox in South Asia is that all Pakistani strategies in the end are based upon a diminution of Indian unity, will, or relative power," and that "Pakistani leaders see their national security as a function inversely proportional to India's strength."[38] Toward this end, Pakistan has pursued a strictly *national and counter-regional* strategy, seeking to neutralize India through counterbalancing it by inviting foreign intervention in the affairs of the subcontinent. A key element in this strategy of Pakistan's has been from the very beginning the attaining of *parity* with India, whether on its own or through the intervention of external powers. The founder of Pakistan had himself given expression to the logic of parity, and he did so even before the founding of the state; on May 21, 1947, M.A. Jinnah told a Reuters correspondent:

A weak Pakistan and a strong Hindustan will be a temptation for the strong Hindustan to try to dictate. I have always said Pakistan must be a viable Pakistan and sufficiently strong as a balance *vis a vis* Hindustan. I am, therefore, deadly against the partition of Bengal and Punjab and we shall fight every inch against it.[39]

It was in line with this aim to "balance" India that Jinnah was totally against a "moth-eaten" Pakistan – that is, one without the entire Punjab and the entire Bengal and Assam – and, if he could not get the entire Bengal, he was even ready for an independent one, as it would cut down India's power. Equally, for the same reason, Jinnah sought to prevent the princely states from joining India, encouraging them instead either to accede to Pakistan or to assert their own independence, with the intent to keep the rest of the subcontinent Balkanized. The "parity principle" is thus rooted in the strategic thinking of Pakistan's founder prior to partition. Subsequently, after partition, the aim of parity became immedi-

---

[38] Wilcox, "India and Pakistan," 240–60.
[39] Cited in A.G. Noorani, "The Sub-Continent: Some Pakistani Perspectives," *Economic and Political Weekly,* September 11, 1976, 1500–4.

ately manifest in territorial terms in respect of the princely states of Kashmir and Hyderabad, where Pakistan attempted to achieve balance with India through the conquest of the former and support for the independence of the latter. The pursuit of parity did not end with Jinnah, but became a cornerstone of Pakistan's strategic posture; as G.W. Choudhury, who served as a minister in Pakistan's federal cabinet from 1969 to 1971, put it, "one of the basic objectives of Pakistani foreign policy has always been to attain parity with India in politics and diplomacy if not in military might."[40]

If parity is the end, then "pursuing an active alliance policy invoking external balancers to keep India from asserting its paramountcy," as Wilcox phrased it,[41] has been one of the principal means. Foiled in the attempt to keep India territorially Balkanized or to fully acquire Kashmir, Pakistan sought to obtain superior weaponry as a means to parity through military alliance with the US; the alliance became the "long nourished American equalizer."[42] The origins of Pakistan's alliance policy can also be traced to Jinnah. Unlike Nehru, who set his face against alignment, Jinnah took the position that "we shall certainly establish friendship and alliances, which will be for the benefit of all those who may enter into such an alliance."[43] Since then, any strengthening of India has been viscerally an anathema to Pakistan, since it forecloses the possibility of parity. Accordingly, Pakistan has taken upon itself the task of opposing the rise of India as a major power. Even the secession of Bangladesh did not lessen Pakistan's ardor for parity. Witness the statement by Lieutenant General A.I. Akram of Pakistan in the mid-1980s as an indication of Pakistan's determination to resist India's possible emergence as a major power:

Pakistan thus became an obstacle in India's march to greatness. If Pakistan would not accept India as a great power, the rest of the world was not likely to do so either. Pakistan had to be removed from the path of the Indian march to glory, but Pakistan had no intention of being so removed. This led the two countries on a collision course, and they collided again and again.

They are still on the same collision course, in spite of the reduction in size of Pakistan, which is partly compensated for by the internal weakening and disruption within India and the rise of divisive elements in that country. This state

---

[40] G.W. Choudhury, *India, Pakistan, Bangladesh, and the Major Powers: Politics of a Divided Subcontinent* (New York: The Free Press, 1975), 13.

[41] Wilcox, "India and Pakistan," 257–8.

[42] Pervaiz Iqbal Cheema, "American Policy in South Asia: Interests and Objectives," in Stephen Philip Cohen (ed.), *The Security of South Asia: American and Asian Perspectives* (Urbana: University of Illinois Press, 1987), 123.

[43] Noorani, "The Sub-Continent," 1500.

of affairs is likely to continue so long as India retains its designs of hegemony over South Asia, preeminence in Asia, and a great power role in the world.[44]

The hope and aim of weakening India emerges repeatedly in Pakistani expression. The key underlying objective seems to be the territorial reorganization of the subcontinent, and it appears that parity in power is only a way-station to that objective. One leader who served in the last cabinet of East Pakistan states:

And for the rest of the subcontinent, also, a confederation with West Bengal and Assam on one side and South India on the other, flanked by North India, as an independent state, with Sikhstan in East Punjab and Hariyana would also help restore those values, bringing lasting peace instead of bloodshed in the region. *One day again the whole subcontinent will come under Muslim rule, including Kashmir.*[45]

This assessment was similar to the advice that Zulfikar Ali Bhutto was given, as war approached in 1971, in a top-secret message by one of his confidantes in the president's office on the assumption that Bhutto would soon be installed as prime minister:

once the back of Indian forces is broken in the East, Pakistan should occupy the whole of Eastern India and make it a permanent part of East Pakistan. ... This will also provide a physical link with China. Kashmir should be taken at any price, even the Sikh Punjab and turned into Khalistan.[46]

The perception that India is an unnatural state in view of its large size compared to the other states of the region, and that it should therefore be reduced in size, is widely and deeply held among the Pakistani elites. A Pakistani expert in geopolitics, who has lectured at the country's strategic think-tanks, expresses the sentiment more forcefully:

But who will balance India – expansionist, hegemonic, nuclear Akhund Bharat? As undivided and one, expansionist, nuclear and hegemonic, it is a total menace to Afro-Asian and world peace. Cut to size, it falls in line with the subcon-

---

[44] Lt. General A.I. Akram, "Security and Stability in South Asia," in Cohen (ed.), *The Security of South Asia*, 163–80.

[45] Akhtaruddin Ahmad, *Nationalism or Islam: Indo-Pakistan Episode* (New Delhi: D.K. Agencies, 1982), 320; emphasis added.

[46] Stanley Wolpert, *Zulfi Bhutto of Pakistan: His Life and Times* (New York: Oxford University Press, 1993), 162.

tinental pattern of small and medium, non-nuclear states. The world may realize the blessings of the *Balkanization* of Bharat one day.[47]

With such perceptions, Pakistan understandably refused to follow India's regional strategy, which would have certified Indian pre-eminence in the region. Instead, Pakistan adopted an ambitious and activist "stalling diplomacy" in collaboration with outside powers in order to deny India regional leadership and to weaken it, hoping for India's eventual political decay under the pressure. To quote Wilcox again:

If Pakistan can stall, its diplomats can hope that internal strains within India will progressively weaken the central government and finally lead to a fragmentation that will make it possible for a united Pakistan to seize its opportunities.

But Pakistan has engaged in more than "a stalling diplomacy." It has adopted extraordinarily ambitious goals in relation to India in terms of parity and destabilization, and it has demonstrated readiness to use violence to achieve its ends. Fear of the larger state has not been its only motivation; far from it, high ambition has been a principal characteristic of its strategic posture toward India. As Wilcox, who as an analyst was friendly to Pakistan, acknowledged:

Most India–Pakistan interstate conflict since 1947 has been generated by Pakistan. The weak party in this situation is also the revisionist power, and at times it has pursued what Boulding could characterize as "rational aggression," "the deliberate, planned conflict or game of ruin" against India, in the calculated hope of relative benefit.[48]

Another US foreign-policy analyst would seem to agree:

The most striking feature of Pakistan's foreign policy was its extremely ambitious goals. Here were two unorganized and impoverished pieces of territory, as yet a nation in name only, seeking to gain security through strength rather than accommodation and to wrest a sizable area away from a neighbour four times as large.[49]

In brief, it is obvious that there is a fundamental asymmetry in the

---

[47] Ikram Azam, *Pakistan's Geopolitical and Strategic Compulsions* (Lahore: Progressive Publishers, 1980), 141; emphasis added.

[48] Wilcox, "India and Pakistan," 257–8.

[49] William J. Barnds, *India, Pakistan and the Great Powers* (New York: Praeger, 1972), 71.

strategic outlooks of the two major states of South Asia; for Pakistan a weak or, better still, a fragmented India is an aim, a hope and an opportunity, whereas for India a weak Pakistan is a threat and an occasion for concern and forbearance. Indeed, the circumstance of Pakistan being weak or weakened can be used by it and its friends as an effective bargaining chip against India. While the other smaller powers in the subcontinent adopt a stronger or milder version of the national and counter-regional strategic design in order to counterbalance India, they do so at the political level and are reluctant to see India destabilized, perceiving in such an eventuality a threat to their own well-being. On the other hand, Pakistan has pursued the strategic design with extraordinary tenacity, ingenuity and stamina, even at severe costs to itself; Pakistan's international behavior demonstrates remarkable persistence with the design, despite the vast changes over its history as a state. In this sense, Pakistan is a profoundly revisionist or dissatisfied state in contrast to India, which is a status quo or satisfied power except at the global level, and that too in a moderate manner. As Wilcox expressed it, "Pakistan continues to be the state with the greatest interest in the destruction of the status quo, no matter who is its guarantor."[50]

Consistent with its strategic perceptions vis-à-vis India, Pakistan's grand strategy, as it has been manifest in its state behavior over the course of the half-century and more since its creation, has focused on three areas: seizing the initiative in generating violent conflict with India; mobilizing external resources for such conflict through alliances with one or more of the major powers in order to overcome its relative weakness in respect of India; and fostering destabilization of India through covert support to subversive and secessionist groups within that country.

In regard to the element of exercising initiative in war-making, Pakistan launched the first violent conflict with India hardly three months after its creation in 1947 through supporting a tribal invasion of Kashmir and then directly participating in the consequent war with India. In the international negotiations at the UN over the war, Pakistan was able to get the support of the UK and the US; even though India retained nearly two-thirds of the state, the issue was not conclusively settled and remained a long-term cause for repeated future conflicts. About two decades later, Pakistan started armed skirmishes in the Rann of Kutch in order to test India's will and preparedness, and then inducted a massive force of commandos into Kashmir with the purpose of detaching that state from India; in the process, it precipitated the India–Pakistan War of 1965, the result of which was largely a military

---

[50] Wilcox, "India and Pakistan," 259.

stalemate. Again, half a dozen years later, Pakistan sent 10 million refugees fleeing into India through its genocidal military operations against the autonomy movement in its eastern wing. As its military position became unviable in the face of the rising guerilla forces fighting for the independence of Bangladesh, Pakistan attacked air bases in northern India in a desperate move to extract itself from its hopeless situation. The consequence of that attack was the India–Pakistan War of 1971, which resulted in the emergence of an independent Bangladesh out of Pakistan's eastern wing.

However, the three wars between the two states did not result in shifting the power asymmetry decisively in India's favor. Although the 1971 war was more conclusive than the previous two – since it brought about the dismemberment of Pakistan even as India held 92,000 prisoners of war and over 13,000 square kilometers of Pakistani territory – India could not translate its victory into a favorable settlement. The Simla Agreement of 1972 did not make for any dramatic change in Pakistan's attitude or strategic posture toward India. In fact, the war and the Simla Agreement resulted in reinforcing the militaristic aspect of the Pakistani polity and the power of the Punjabi aristocratic elite within Pakistani society. Moreover, Pakistan was no longer constrained by its eastern wing, which had lain separated from it by over 1,600 kilometers of Indian territory. Indeed, as Pakistan felt emboldened by the large-scale military aid from the US and by its acquisition of nuclear capabilities during the 1980s, it launched a low-intensity conflict against India in 1989 through brazenly aiding the insurgency in Kashmir in an effort to bleed India white. In 1999, the conflict escalated into a limited war with the invasion of armed forces from Pakistan in the Kargil sector of Kashmir. Even though India was able to force a Pakistani withdrawal, with the diplomatic support of the US, the denouement of this war led straight to a military coup d'état in Pakistan.

The reason that Pakistan has been able to take the initiative in violent conflict with India, despite its much smaller size (it is only less than one-quarter the size of the latter), is that it still constitutes a substantial middle-sized state. If it were located in the Middle East, it would be the largest state in population, and in territory (except Saudi Arabia), in that region, including such states as Iran, Iraq, Syria and Egypt. Besides this, Pakistan has possessed several assets in its struggle against India. Two such assets have been Pakistan's decisive ability to attract external support, and the determination of its landed gentry and army – both dominated by the Punjabis – who view conflict with India as the very raison d'être of their power. Moreover, the Pakistani army has always held a sense of superiority, which was especially strong during the 1960s, when its top brass believed that one Pakistani soldier was equal to five Indian soldiers.[51] Pakistan has also counted on external allies coming to its rescue, on the terrain favoring its guerilla operations in Kashmir, on its strategy of limited aims at any one given time preventing India from escalating conflict to full-scale war, and on obtaining a favorable political settlement through inflicting severe pain on India.[52] In addition, Pakistan has relied on the ideological elan of its single-religion polity defeating an ideologically less cohesive India, given the latter's abundant religious and ethnic diversity.

In the second area of alliance-making to balance India, Pakistan initially relied on the UK, with which for many years the Muslim League had had a tacit alliance against India's Congress Party. Soon after its creation, Pakistan also began to court countries in the Middle East for allies in an effort to construct an Islamic bloc to be headed by Pakistan in order to counter India. Largely disappointed in this endeavor, it turned to the US and formed an alliance with it in 1954, which brought massive amounts of military aid for the re-equipment and modernization of its armed forces. Pakistan received modern jet fighters that could outfly any Indian aircraft and Patton tanks that could outgun any Indian armor. Pakistan became "America's most allied ally," joining the Baghdad Pact, CENTO and SEATO. After the India–China War of 1962, there began Pakistan's de facto alliance with China, which has continued into the twenty-first century. This alliance provided Pakistan military aid by way not only of conventional weaponry, but also of nuclear and missile capabilities. Moreover, the alliance gave Pakistan diplomatic leverage against India through China exerting pressure on India in bilateral relations and in international organizations. In addition, from the 1960s, Pakistan became more active in the Islamic bloc and has been able to mobilize political support against India on issues of concern to it.

The third area of Pakistani effort, directed at the destabilization of India, is a more recent development that can be traced to the early 1980s. In part, it reflects the skills and resources garnered by Pakistan from the support that the CIA provided for the activities of the Afghan guerillas against the Soviet forces in Afghanistan, with the Pakistani army's Inter Services Intelligence (ISI) – Pakistan's equivalent of the CIA – serving as the conduit for such support. Pakistan aided the separatist movement among the Sikhs in the Indian Punjab for an independent Khalistan. The ISI has been fairly active in penetrating India,

---

[51] Stephen Philip Cohen, "Arms and Politics in Bangladesh, India and Pakistan," *Special Studies*, 49 (New York: Council on International Studies, State University of New York at Buffalo, 1973), 26.
[52] For these Pakistani calculations, see Paul, *Asymmetric Conflicts*, ch. 6.

occasionally engaging in terrorism, airplane hijacking, distribution of counterfeit currency notes, and other destabilizing acts. The ISI has been able to establish a network of operations through the Pakistani diplomatic missions in Nepal and Bangladesh. This strategy has been fairly successful, as the Indian state is slow to react and its borders are porous. Further, since 1989, the insurgency in Kashmir has intensified, making it possible for increased Pakistani involvement.[53] India's dissuasion strategy is not very effective, as "India's punitive power is not seen as credible or backed by requisite political will."[54] More than this is the apparent difficulty in combating asymmetrical challenges posed by subnational groups with guerilla and terrorist strategies. Since the 1980s, Pakistan's acquisition of nuclear weapons has also constrained India's retaliatory options. An emboldened Pakistan believes that, through nuclear weapons and the ability of subnational groups to penetrate India, it has acquired a major bargaining strength vis-à-vis India, and that it can force India to concede Kashmir if it insists on the territorial dispute as the central issue in any peace negotiations. This brinkmanship-style bargaining position of Pakistan was evident in the failed Agra summit negotiations between the two states in July 2001.

The enduring conflict with Pakistan has had, no doubt, an adverse impact on India's power position, regionally and globally. Cohen has argued that two generations of US policy-makers came to see South Asia as a region beset by "war and intractable conflict" and "[f]or long periods South Asia simply vanished from America's strategic map, and apathy, rather than engagement, was the norm." He adds: "Without either a threat to the region by an outsider or a threat to regional stability brought about by an Indo-Pakistani war, Washington tended to regard South Asia as a strategic side show."[55]

Perceptual-level factors: The world image of India

The systemic and subsystemic factors are only part of the international-level constraints. A perceptual/ideational-level explanation would hold that India has been a victim of pervasive cultural biases and racism prevalent in the global system. India's inability to obtain a leadership

---

[53] On this, see Reeta Chowdhari Tremblay, "Kashmir: The Valley's Political Dynamics," *Contemporary South Asia*, 4 (1, 1995), 79–101; Raju G.C. Thomas (ed.), *Perspectives on Kashmir: The Roots of Conflict in South Asia* (Boulder, CO: Westview Press, 1992); and Sumit Ganguly, *The Crisis in Kashmir* (Washington, DC: Woodrow Wilson Center Press, 1997).

[54] Brahma Chellaney, "Too Hard for a Soft State," http://www.hindustantimes.com, May 2, 2001.

[55] Cohen, "The United States, India and Pakistan," 193–5.

position would thus be regarded as the result of the widely held stereo-typical and negative images of India, especially in the West.[56]

The international system until 1945 was a European-dominated sys-tem. Many elements of this system continued beyond 1945, as the dom-inance of the Europeans, especially the Anglo-Saxons, persists even beyond the end of the twentieth century. Asia, in particular, was domi-nated by European colonial powers whose "political domination brought in its train a doctrine of racialism and a feeling of European sol-idarity as against the Asians."[57] To some, the Europeans, especially the English and the French, and later the US, created and perpetuated *ori-entalism* in literature, the arts, the social sciences and many other walks of life, often belittling the contributions of non-Europeans to human progress. Edward Said defines orientalism as "a system of knowledge about the Orient, an accepted grid for filtering through the Orient into Western consciousness." Orientalism has allowed European culture to be perceived as dominant. It perpetuates the idea that European identi-ty is "a superior one in comparison with all the non-European peoples and cultures." Said argues that the relationship between the Occident and Orient is a relationship of "power, of domination, of varying degrees of complex hegemony." Further, "Orientalism depends for its strategy on this flexible positional superiority, which puts the Westerner in a whole series of possible relationships with the Orient without ever los-ing the relative upper hand." Said views "Orientalism as a dynamic exchange between individual authors and the larger political concerns shaped by the three great empires – British, French, US – in whose intellectual and imaginative territory the writing was produced."[58] India, in particular, has been a target of orientalist attitudes because of British rule of the country and the attendant dominant-subordinate relation-ship spanning more than 200 years. Said's citation from John Stuart Mill, who worked at the India Office for several years, is poignant. In his *On Liberty and Representational Government*, Mill warns that his views could not be applied to India because the Indians were "civilizationally, if not racially, inferior."[59] The US elite also shared this mindset. For instance, Theodore Roosevelt believed that the British rule in India had been one of the "mighty feats of civilization, one of the mighty feats to

---

[56] On this, see Ronald Inden, *Imagining India* (Cambridge, MA: Blackwell, 1992).

[57] K.M. Panikkar, *Asia and Western Dominance: A Survey of the Vasco da Gama Epoch of Asian History, 1498-1945*, abridged and revised edn. (London: George Allen & Unwin, 1959), 14. The original version of this book was pub lished in 1953.

[58] Edward W. Said, *Orientalism* (New York: Vintage Books, 1979), 5–15.

[59] Said, *Orientalism*, 14.

the credit of the white race during the past four centuries" of "expansion and dominance."[60]

It appears that the modern international system has actively discouraged non-Western countries from gaining leadership roles. The lack of membership of the Ottoman Empire in any of the councils of Europe in the nineteenth century, although it controlled one-quarter of Europe,[61] is an example. It took the defeat of Russia in the Russo-Japanese War of 1904–05 for European countries to show Japan any respect. Even then, it was the context of Japan's importance in the 1910s in balancing Russia and in the Anglo-Japanese alliance that gave Japan the major-power status.[62] Similarly, the Korean War was probably an important turning point for China to receive some semblance of recognition. India and Indians have generally been berated in the international arena due to the persistence of orientalist cultural stereotypes generated during the British colonial era. Postwar writings, including those by Indian expatriates such as V.S. Naipaul and Nirad Chaudhuri, have often helped to generate negative images of India.[63] The discourse on postcolonial development also marginalized large areas of the developing world such as India as "backward, deficient, inadequate, behind"; it equated "development" with "adulthood" and "underdevelopment" with "infancy and immaturity."[64]

Although since the 1970s systematic racism in the US toward Indian expatriates has declined considerably, US policy-makers, who are largely drawn from the white upper strata of society, in general seem to hold stereotypical views on India and Indians, drawn heavily from British discourses, à la the Kipling legacy. The portrayal of India by US academic textbooks, media and academic writings has been consistently negative and stereotypical: "The Asia Society, in a review of 300 school text books in use in 1974–75, found that the presentation of India was the most negative of all Asian countries."[65] Again: "According to a State

---

[60] Howard K. Beale, *Theodore Roosevelt and the Rise of America to World Power* (Baltimore, MD: The Johns Hopkins University Press, 1956), 164.

[61] Samuel P. Huntington, *The Clash of Civilizations and the Remaking of World Order* (New York: Simon & Schuster, 1996), 52.

[62] Panikkar, *Asia and Western Dominance*, 292.

[63] See V.S. Naipaul, *India: A Wounded Civilization* (New York: Vintage Books, 1976); and Nirad C. Chaudhuri, *The Autobiography of an Unknown Indian* (London: Macmillan, 1951).

[64] Akhil Gupta, *Postcolonial Developments: Agriculture in the Making of Modern India* (Durham, NC: Duke University Press, 1998), 11.

[65] *Asia and American Textbooks* (New York: Asia Society, 1976), cited in Arthur G. Rubinoff, "Congressional Attitudes toward India," in Gould and Ganguly (eds), *The Hope and Reality*, 156.

Department analysis, American attitudes concerning India focus on disease, death and illiteracy more than for any other country."[66] Studies on US images of India suggest that both informed and uninformed people have held consistently negative images about India. During the first decade of Indian independence (1947–1956), the images were largely negative, partly due to the geographical, cultural and political remoteness of India. A work on US perceptions of India notes:

American and Indian civilizations appeared to Americans as opposite extremes of one spectrum of values by which they judged themselves and others. America was the "richest country in the world," and India the "poorest." (The rich and the poor always find communication difficult, except in the mechanical process of giving and receiving.) America was preoccupied with material "abundance," and India specialized in spiritual quests and offered religious panaceas for its "starving" people. ... India was another world, incredible, fabulous, and the concerns of its people escaped the understanding or even the imagination of Americans.[67]

Another influential comparative study of US images of India and China observes that the differences in US perceptions are:

rooted partly in the effect of relative cultural values, the Chinese being long seen ... as "closer" – pragmatic, down-to-earth, hardheaded – and the Indians, or more particularly, the Hindus, as much more exotic, much more violently different, as indeed Hindu culture is from Anglo-Protestant and most other forms of Western culture.[68]

There was a period of US elite interest in India from the late 1950s to the early 1960s, when many liberals, who were impressed by India's commitment to democracy and were driven by humanitarian and strategic concerns, supported the US providing substantial aid to India. The apex of this period was during President Kennedy's term in office. However, US foreign-policy-makers soon changed their view of India, which resulted in the resurfacing of negative images, this time more for security and strategic reasons.[69] US relations with China and Pakistan

---

[66] *United States–Indian Educational and Cultural Relations* (Washington, DC: Department of State, Bureau of Educational and Cultural Affairs, 1982), cited in *ibid.*, 156.

[67] Charles H. Heimsath, "American Images of India as Factors in U.S. Foreign Policy Making," in Michael L. Krenn (ed.), *Race and U.S. Foreign Policy during the Cold War* (New York: Garland Publishing, 1998), 101.

[68] Harold R. Isaacs, *Images of Asia: American Views of China and India* (New York: Harper Torchbooks, 1972), xxvi.

[69] For the changing attitudes, see *ibid.*, 271–89.

and India's friendship with the USSR, the 1971 Bangladesh War, India's nuclear testing in 1974 – all contributed to hostile perceptions and images of India. Academic interest in India also waned over time, partly due to the restrictions imposed by the Indian government on US scholars.

In recent years, the negative images of India have been reflected most prominently in the nuclear nonproliferation discourse and policies. An MIT anthropologist, Hugh Gusterson, characterizes the nuclear nonproliferation discourse in the West as "orientalist," especially vis-à-vis India. India has been portrayed as part of the "other" who cannot be trusted with nuclear weapons. Gusterson sees the legitimization of this discourse occurring with the establishment of the NPT regime in 1970: "Thus in Western discourse nuclear weapons are represented so that 'theirs' are a problem whereas 'ours' are not." To him:

the dominant discourse that stabilizes this system of nuclear apartheid in Western ideology is a specialized variant within a broader system of colonial and postcolonial discourse that takes as its essentialist premise a profound Otherness separating Third World from Western countries.

It is the binary opposition that produces the Orient as a mirror image of the West.[70] The Indians also seem to agree with Gusterson. A former Indian military chief, General Krishnaswami Sundarji, who also pioneered several concepts of Indian nuclear strategy in the 1980s, put it bluntly at a US arms-control conference in 1993: "The trouble with you Americans is you think that just because I have a brown face I should not have nuclear weapons."[71]

Despite the economic successes of the 1.7-million-strong Indian expatriate community in the US, which forms the single wealthiest ethnic group in the country in terms of per family income, there has been no powerful constituency for instilling a positive image of India, similar to the Jewish community with respect to Israel, up until the late 1990s. As India has been open to international media reporting, the West most often saw the bleak side of India, thus giving it a low image and perceptual value in international public opinion. Western media consistently reported negatively on India, helping to create a basket-case image of the country in the world's perception. The continuous negative coverage of India by the Western media has helped to embed India's

---

[70] Hugh Gusterson, "Nuclear Weapons and the Other in the Western Imagination," *Cultural Anthropology*, 14 (1999), 114.
[71] Cited in Chandler, *The New Face of War*, 26. See also Jaswant Singh, "Against Nuclear Apartheid," *Foreign Affairs*, 77 (September–October 1998), 41–52.

"civilizational exceptionalism" in the Western mindset. India has thus become a foil for the Western media and intelligentsia to demonstrate the West's cultural superiority.

The constraints on India's power position at the international level only tell part of the story, however. In order to develop a more comprehensive understanding of the issue, a discussion of these constraints needs to be supplemented by an analysis of the domestic-level constraints, as factors at these two levels often work in tandem and reinforce each other.

Domestic-level constraints

Economic and social weaknesses

Domestic-level explanations for India's difficulties in obtaining a major-power role focus on India's economic weakness, its problems of national integration, its sheer size and diversity, its cultural constraints, and its inability to develop a grand strategy appropriate for a state seeking a major-power role. In other words, these unit-level factors are regarded as having thus far constrained India from making a powerful thrust internationally for a leadership role.[72] India's failure to achieve international recognition has thus been attributed to the socioeconomic policies pursued by the Indian state for well over four decades. According to a leading US scholar of South Asia, "India is not recognized as an equal by the great powers" because:

post-independence economic development policies have not succeeded in turning India into an economically powerful country and have failed to improve the lives of its people in a manner that the industrialized and post-industrial societies of the world would recognize as sufficient, though the general well-being of some segments of the poor has increased somewhat over the years.[73]

Although, since independence in 1947, India has made considerable progress, it lags behind in removing its social and economic maladies, such as mass poverty, malnutrition, child labor, regional and gender-based inequalities, and rural–urban disparities. Although the population below the poverty level is claimed to have come down to 26 per cent in 1999–2000, this still makes for a staggering 260 million extremely poor

---

[72] See, for instance, Sandy Gordon, *India's Rise to Power* (New York: St. Martin's Press, 1995), chs 1–5.
[73] Paul R. Brass, "India: Democratic Progress and Problems," in Harrison, Kriesberg and Kux (eds), *India and Pakistan*, 40.

people.[74] A country with such high levels of social and economic deprivation, the argument goes, is unlikely to gain much international respect, let alone major-power status.

The economic policies that independent India adopted were greatly driven by a desire to make the country self-reliant and strong industrially and militarily, yet these policies failed to produce sufficient results. The Indian elites believed that the best way to achieve national power and welfare was through autarkic economic policies. Given their experience with colonialism, they assumed that close economic relations with the West would lead to poverty and loss of independence. They adopted, therefore, an inward-oriented strategy of economic self-reliance through import-substitution and building heavy industries, a policy which had some resemblance to the Soviet economic model. This led to the elites paying less attention to international economic forces and trade with other countries.

Export-led growth was not on India's national agenda for a long time. A trading-state strategy was not adopted, as the large internal market consumed most of the products made in India. Indian political leaders and economic planners were driven by the notion of "export pessimism," even when countries in East and South-East Asia were changing during the 1960s and 1970s to an export-led growth strategy. As a consequence, India's share of global trade declined over time and remained abysmally below 1 per cent of the total global trade volume, even when international trade was expanding rapidly. In 2000–01, India's exports were $43 billion, which is less than 0.7 per cent of world exports. Even if India succeeds in raising them to the projected $75 billion export level by 2004, they would still remain below 1 per cent of global exports at that time.[75]

Foreign direct investment (FDI) is another area where India's position has remained weak as compared to China's. Even after several years of economic reforms, FDI peaked at $3.6 billion in 1997–98, only to decline subsequently. FDI has been a major source of China's wealth and power, as the US companies investing heavily in China have been the source of pressure on US politicians to engage China. A survey by a key global consultancy firm in December 2000 found that the government bureaucracy acted as a major deterrent against FDI in India.[76] FDI is hampered by the higher transaction costs in India, compared to countries like China:

[74] "Only 26% Indians are Poor, Claims Plan Panel,"
http://www.timesofindia.com, February 22, 2001.
[75] "From Short-termism to Strategy," http://www.hinduonnet.com, April 2, 2001.
[76] *India Abroad,* December 1, 2000, 19.

Anyone doing business in India runs up against what might be called institutionalized friction. Whenever he ventures beyond an environment under his own control to one controlled by others, he needs to watch out. This happens every time he petitions a bureaucrat, signs a contract, goes to court or even turns a light switch.[77]

Although India's policies of industrial self-reliance helped to economically strengthen it in an incremental fashion, they did not go far enough for the country to attain a major economic role in the global arena. The Nehruvian strategy of planned economic development was heavily dependent on state enterprises, many of which over the years ran on losses and had to be massively subsidized by the state. Initially, agriculture was neglected, which caused severe food shortages until the Green Revolution in the late 1960s eradicated the problem to a great extent. Other deficiencies in economic policy included unrealistic estimates of fiscal revenue, lip-service to employment generation, lack of attention to primary and secondary education, and inadequate facilities for training skilled workers:

A disproportionate share of resources was devoted to higher education, and no dedicated effort was made toward attaining universal primary schooling. The legacy of these deficiencies is that India's labor force at the end of the century has noticeably low levels of literacy and skills compared to workers in East Asia, Southeast Asia, and much of Latin America, although its cadres of engineers and technicians are the largest in the developing world.[78]

India's economic growth has also been hampered by poor tax revenues. The narrow taxation base and the weaknesses in collecting even the direct taxes resulted in a very low GDP/direct-tax ratio and thereby low revenue from this key source. Millions of Indians, especially wealthy farmers, do not pay any income tax at all.[79] Moreover, governments at the center, state and local levels accumulated large fiscal deficits in order to provide subsidies on the supply of water, power, food, fertilizers and fuel, often to farmers who could afford to pay. The electricity sector is especially notorious for unjustifiable subsidies and mismanagement. Power outages are so common that even metropolitan cities go without electricity for hours or days, affecting industrial production and quality

---

[77] "A Survey of India's Economy," *Economist*, June 2, 2001, 9.

[78] John Adams, "India: Much Achieved, Much to Achieve," in Harrison, Kriesberg and Kux (eds), *India and Pakistan*, 69.

[79] I.G. Patel, *Economic Reform and Global Change* (New Delhi: Macmillan, 1998), 9; Prem Shankar Jha, *India: A Political Economy of Stagnation* (Bombay: Oxford University Press, 1980).

of life. The problem is caused by the way state electricity boards (SEBs) buy and generate electricity and distribute it to a variety of consumers, especially farmers, at low prices, and the widespread theft as well as losses in transmission, which are estimated at 30 to 40 per cent of the total electricity generated.[80]

Studies show that corruption remains a major problem for India. According to a report by the watchdog group Transparency International, in 2000, India ranked twenty-first from the bottom in a list of ninety countries for the level of corruption. Another study by an Asian consultancy service in 2001 rated India as the third-most corrupt state among a group of twelve Asian countries, preceded only by Vietnam and Indonesia.[81] Official corruption is rampant in every walk of life. Citizens and business establishments often have to pay bribes for getting any small official clearance or utility connection. Although corruption is a universal phenomenon, its impact is felt more widely in the daily lives of the people in India.

A large population can, of course, have long-term benefits for a major power, but in India's case this is one key resource that has been under-utilized by successive Indian governments. Moreover, despite India being self-sufficient in food, several Indian states, especially in the north, have general undernourishment levels worse than sub-Saharan Africa.[82] In March 2001, India's population crossed 1.027 billion mark. The literacy rate stood at 65.38 per cent (75.85 per cent for males and 54.16 per cent for females). Although this rate marks an improvement, one-quarter of the male and half of the female population still remain illiterate after fifty years of independence. Women's education and health are areas where progress has been slow. Child labor is rampant in India and compulsory education has been absent from government policy. An influential study by Myron Weiner argues that India's economic constraints are not the main cause of the lack of attention to compulsory primary education, but rather "the belief systems of the state bureaucracy" – shared widely by "educators, social activists, trade unionists, academic researchers, and more broadly, by members of the Indian middle class" – that "excessive and inappropriate education for the poor would disrupt existing social arrangements." There is a widespread belief that education of the poor would lead to increased unemployment

[80] "Red Tape and Blue Sparks," in "A Survey of India's Economy," *Economist*, June 2, 2001, 10.
[81] "Nigeria Most Corrupt Country," http://www.hindustantimes.com, September 18, 2000; "India No. 3 in Corruption," http://www.hindustantimes.com, March 20, 2001.
[82] Amartya Sen, *Development as Freedom* (New York: Anchor Books, 2000), 102–3.

and that the "lower classes should work with their hands rather than with their heads ..." Thus, despite the rhetoric:

India's policymakers have not regarded mass education as essential to India's modernization. They have instead put resources into elite government schools, state-aided private schools, and higher education in an effort to create an educated class that is equal to educated classes in the West and that is capable of creating and managing a modern enclave economy.[83]

Comparative studies of selected East Asian countries and India suggest that human development is one of the areas where India lags behind these countries tremendously. The East Asian countries, such as Korea, Taiwan and Singapore, succeeded in economic development, partly due to the importance they gave to education at the primary and secondary levels as well as technical education. In India's case, primary education remained a low priority of the state. A high proportion of Indian students drops out of schools before completing fourth grade. Further, the proportion of students in technical and vocational-training programs in India has been significantly low compared to East Asian countries and, as a result, a large section of the workforce does not possess basic education or the technical skills required for building industrial competitiveness.[84]

India's economic weaknesses are very much apparent in the development of the country's infrastructure. These weaknesses are especially noticeable in roads, power-distribution grids, ports and telecommunications, although the last of these has shown some improvement in recent years. India is self-sufficient in food but, due to lack of adequate storage and distribution facilities, nearly 250 million to 300 million people remain undernourished. Despite achieving food self-sufficiency, "no industry is being as thoroughly hobbled by government intervention as agriculture. That is the biggest reason for the persistence of poverty." As a special report in the *Economist* points out:

India does much to discourage the efficient storage, distribution and processing of food. Its aversion to market has left a lot of people hungry. ... Shortcomings in infrastructure hit agriculture harder than any other industry. Farm produce lacks an adequate chain of refrigerated warehouses and transporters, and deteriorates on long and bumpy rides from farm to consumer. About 20 percent of

---

[83] Myron Weiner, *The Child and the State in India* (Princeton, NJ: Princeton University Press, 1991), 5.

[84] Pradeep Agarwal *et al.*, *Policy Regimes and Industrial Competitiveness: A Comparative Study of East Asia and India* (Houndmills, UK: Macmillan, 2000), 272.

total agricultural output, and 40 percent of fruits and vegetables, is lost along the way.[85]

The agriculture sector is even hampered by land reforms in several north Indian states, such as Uttar Pradesh and Bihar. The earlier land reforms had helped the Green Revolution of the 1970s, "but it is now thwarting consolidation of land holdings that have become too fragmented." And mechanization in agriculture is difficult: "That is one of the main reasons why India's rice and wheat yields are just a third of international levels."[86]

Governmental services at all levels in India remain below acceptable levels. At the local level, India's much-touted *panchayats* (village councils) and municipalities have not worked well. Their performance in the areas of jurisprudence, local infrastructure and sanitation has been extremely poor. A traveler to India instantly notices the filth that accumulates in India's main cities and towns, and the absence of proper public sanitation and sewerage systems. The inefficiency of local administrators is so apparent that even India's financial capital, Bombay (or Mumbai), has an extremely primitive system of garbage collection and disposal. Narrow and poorly maintained roads choke traffic in Indian cities and towns, while the leaded gasoline used in outmoded cars and trucks makes for enormous amounts of polluting substances in the atmosphere, making breathing tough in most Indian cities. A large segment of the urban population lives in slums, making Indian cities teem with people competing for limited public utilities and resources.

Thus, India's domestic-level constraints, it can be argued, have kept the country away from obtaining a leadership position in the international arena.

Cultural constraints

Along with economic weaknesses, cultural constraints, to some, have also been holding India back from realizing its potential as a major power. These cultural factors have inhibited India from developing a national identity appropriate for a major-power actor on the world stage. Socially, the unique caste system has kept a large majority of Indians economically and socially deprived. The system also perpetuates

[85] "A Survey of India's Economy," 14.
[86] *ibid.*, 16.

inequalities in land distribution and high levels of illiteracy, with low political participation among the lower-ranking castes.[87] In recent years, the lower castes have started gaining political power in some of the north Indian states, especially Uttar Pradesh and Bihar, but the Indian political elite is still heavily drawn from the upper castes. Moreover, caste-based and religion-based conflicts are present in most parts of the country.

Rosen has argued that caste divisions have also had a debilitating effect on India's military power, as this dominant aspect of the Indian social structure affected the Indian army during both the pre- and post-independence eras.[88] However, Rosen's thesis suffers from several drawbacks. First, Rosen ignores the fact that the Indian army, albeit under British leadership, played a pivotal role in both world wars. In World War II, it stopped the Japanese army's march toward South Asia and defeated that army in South-East Asia, before any other power did so.[89] Second, the Indian army is still the most disciplined and most unified segment of Indian society. India's failures in conflicts with China and in Sri Lanka are poor examples for proving that social stratification was the cause of these debacles. In the first case, it was the surprise attack by China, combined with poor strategy, tactics, equipment, leadership and training of soldiers, that caused the Indian rout. In the second case, the fight was with a well-entrenched guerilla force. In fact, few modern armies, including those of the US, Russia and Israel, have succeeded in defeating well-organized guerilla forces. Third, Rosen ignores the successes of the Indian army, especially in 1971. India's victory in Kargil in 1999 could be added to this list. The bottom line is that, although culture and caste-based social stratification constrain India's military preparedness, they are not key determinants in the military's performance. Rather, it is the lack of resources and sustained attention of the political and bureaucratic elites that have constrained the army for a long period of time. Since the BJP-led government began to focus on military modernization, and the economic liberalization brought in larger resources, Indian military strength and offensive power have been improving, although incrementally, making it virtually impossible for an outside power to conquer India, a rare achievement for a country that has been an easy target of external aggression over the millennia.

To some, the predominant Hindu cultural values also inhibit India's

---

[87] For a good set of analyses of the caste system, see Dipankar Gupta (ed.), *Social Stratification* (Delhi: Oxford University Press, 1991).

[88] Stephen P. Rosen, *Societies and Military Power: India and its Armies* (Ithaca, NY: Cornell University Press, 1996).

[89] Jaswant Singh, *Defending India* (New York: St. Martin's Press, 1999), 19–20.

emergence as a major power. An analysis by Tanham about the absence of strategic thinking in India contends:

To Indians, life is much more complex and less optimistic than in prevailing Western thought. They accept logic as one influence on life, but only one. Other influences include emotion, tradition, intuition, and fate. Accordingly, life is unknowable, but man must strive to follow his dharma. Fate is something to be dealt with, but also to be accepted.

He adds:

The Indian view may be seen as a realistic and pragmatic approach to life, but it also can lead to a passive, almost fatalistic, acceptance of life. Many argue, however, that dharma requires that an individual strive to fulfil his moral obligations. Although most Indians deny that they are fatalists, the acceptance of life as it comes carries considerable weight among believers.[90]

From the perspective of Tanham's analysis, then, the general cultural ethos, with a certain passiveness in life as a dominant characteristic, has become embedded in the state as the political and bureaucratic elites of India have imbibed its values in their outlook.

Although there is some merit in Tanham's contention, he ignores the fact that Indian leaders, despite their lack of concrete strategic theorizing, have held certain precepts, one of them being independent development, and another the consistent search for major-power status even in the face of severe constraints. Further, their immediate strategic concerns have been regional, and one could argue that India, like any other emerging power, has been going through a period of internal and regional focus. The US also had a very narrow strategic view up until the early twentieth century, when only the two world wars shattered its isolationist policy and brought it out as a key international player.

For some scholars, the Gandhian legacy also made India weak at the international level because the international system is very much dominated by military power and power politics. India gained independence largely through the Gandhian nonviolent strategy, and has been tremendously influenced and constrained by this historical political culture. Thus the lack of a forceful pursuit of major-power status can be attributed to the legacy of nonviolent struggle against imperialism and its extension of power politics. A country with nonviolent values has little chance to enter the major-power system, which is based on power

---

[90] George K. Tanham, *Indian Strategic Thought: An Interpretative Essay* (Santa Monica, CA: Rand Corporation, 1992), 17.

politics, even though there is much merit to the nonviolent strategy that it had adopted to gain independence from the colonial power. The Gandhian legacy has created a certain Indian exceptionalism compared to the large states of the international system, especially China. According to Indian strategic analyst K. Subrahmanyam, Gandhi and Nehru broke with the Kautilyan realpolitik tradition in Indian history, while China has been continuously following the realist tradition set by Sun Tsu. Some Indian leaders, especially Indira Gandhi, occasionally resorted to Kautilyan statecraft, but the foreign-policy establishment has been heavily influenced by the normative ideals advocated by Gandhi and Nehru, which often questioned power politics in international relations.[91] India thus became an aberration of sorts, a state with immense potential power capability, but one that chose not to realize that power for ideological reasons. As one Indian analyst puts it:

India's bark – which has traditionally taken the form of high-pitched moralizing – has always been worse than its bite. This moralizing helps to sustain illusions of national grandeur among the country's self-serving elites. Even as it seeks a permanent UN Security Council seat, India presents itself as unwilling to suffer pain to achieve national goals, or to inflict it on those that flagrantly undermine its security.

He adds: "India needs to remember that a major power is one that can withstand and inflict pain."[92] For well over half a century, India remained the world's biggest "underachiever."[93] The Indians wanted power and status but they were unable to comprehend fully the requirements of the game of power politics, or they were pretending to transcend it, often falling victim to the games of other key actors in the international system. Decision-makers in Islamabad, Beijing, Washington and Moscow often compelled them to make choices based on power politics, as such actors never accepted the Indian logic of normatively driven international politics. Or they simply viewed Indian claims as "pretentious" and "self-serving."

Thus a proper strategic culture failed to develop in India even after independence. This has historical roots. Jaswant Singh, foreign minister under the BJP-led government, argues that:

[91] Interviews, New Delhi, December 17, 1998. One could argue that Emperor Ashoka, who embraced Buddhism, had already broken with the Kautilyan realpolitik tradition in the third century BC, and that Gandhi was carrying on the Ashokan ideals of nonviolence.

[92] Brahma Chellaney, "After the Test: India's Options," *Survival,* 40 (Winter 1998–99), 94.

[93] "Normalizing India," *Economist,* September 4, 1999, 24.

India's strategic culture got internalized, remained fixated upon curbing within rather than combating the external, and created a yawning chasm of mutual suspicion between the state and the citizen. ... Many influences have contributed to this: an accommodative and forgiving Hindu milieu, successive Jain, Buddhist and later Vaishnav-Bhakti influences resulting in excessive piety and, much later, in the twentieth century – *ahimsa* or non-violence. An unintended consequence of all these influences, spread over many centuries, has been a near total emasculation of the concept of state power, also its proper employment as an instrument of state policy, in service of national interests.[94]

To Singh:

whereas ancient Indian texts on every conceivable subject abound – on art and dance and drama, most abundantly on philosophy – there are none, other than Kautilya, that have detailed the military science of India. There is another factor: of geography, of a sense of territory. Indian nationhood, being largely cultural and civilizational, and Indians being supremely contented with what was theirs feared no loss of it, for it – the civilizational – was as unconquerable as is the spirit. Thus, both were absent: a territorial consciousness, and a strategic sense about the protection of the territory of residence.

Others have contended that there has, indeed, been a realist tradition in India's historical/cultural milieu as embodied in the Indic (Hindu/Buddhist) system on the role of the state, which had a major influence on the historical evolution of security conceptions in Asia.[95]

The absence of a proper grand strategy and, as a result, weaknesses in diplomacy came to intellectual attention in the early 1990s when a study by a Rand Corporation analyst, George Tanham, was published. The report argued that India has a predominantly defensive, ad hoc strategic orientation, focused heavily on the South Asian region, and that India has produced little formal strategic thinking. Although Indians have been seeking global power and influence and are generally dissatisfied with the world not according them influence, they have not articulated their strategic goals clearly and pursued them in a disciplined fashion. They have no overall strategy to deal with even their biggest regional security challenge, Pakistan. Geography, historical experience, culture and belief system, and British rule are discussed in the work as the causes for the absence of strategic thinking. According to the study, geography was the main reason for India's long history of

---

[94] Jaswant Singh, *Defending India* (New York: St. Martin's Press, 1999), 13, 16.
[95] For this, see Muthiah Alagappa, "International Politics in Asia: The Historical Context," in Muthiah Alagappa (ed.), *Asia's Security Practice* (Stanford, CA: Stanford University Press, 1998), 65–111.

nonaggression and nonexpansion outside the subcontinent. However, to Tanham, the most important reason for the absence of strategic think-ing in India is cultural; that is, the "Hindu concepts of time and the mys-tery of life that have contributed to the passive or reactive tendencies in Indian military matters." In modern times, the agricultural basis of Indian culture, the rigid structure of Indian society, and the bureaucra-cy in the form of the Indian administrative services have also con-tributed to this state of affairs.[96]

While there is merit in Tanham's thesis, it is not fully clear whether the absence of strategic thinking in India since independence is largely because of cultural-religious factors. A strong case can be made that the Indian elites that took over power, especially the Congress party lead-ers, loathed power politics and Western realpolitik thinking. Nehru often questioned realpolitik-oriented foreign-policy behavior. Strategic stud-ies and security analyses, which are often associated with realism and the realpolitik tradition, therefore became virtually unfashionable sub-jects to study in the Indian academia for a long period of time. However, if culture and religion are the basis of India's lack of strategic writing, then one can ask: How is it that the Hindu nationalist party, BJP, among all the Indian political parties, has shown the most interest in strategic thinking? One may argue that the Indian state took fifty years or so to come to terms with power politics, and only when a nationalistic politi-cal party gained power did serious strategic thinking become possible. The nation was so focused on internal politics and regional security issues that consistent strategic thinking was missing from the milieu up until the late 1990s, when economic growth and nuclear testing made it possible to think in terms of a global power status a bit more seriously.

Despite Tanham's skepticism, readers of the Indian media and schol-arly writings may have noticed a substantially improved level of strate-gic debate, especially in the post-1998 nuclear era. Indian academic institutions like Jawaharlal Nehru University, and official and semioffi-cial think-tanks such as the Institute for Defense Studies and Analyses and the Centre for Policy Research, do produce fairly good writings on security and strategy. The level of discourse is superior to what one can find in most developing states and, to some extent, in South-East Asia and in East Asian countries such as China and Japan. There is also a vocal group of writers who oppose India adopting power politics, and this brings diversity to the Indian discourse on security, a characteristic that is completely absent in countries such as China. However, most of

[96] Tanham, *Indian Strategic Thought*, 59. Tanham's work generated considerable debate in India; see Kanti P. Bajpai and Amitabh Mattoo (eds), *Securing India: Strategic Thought and Practice* (New Delhi: Manohar Publishers, 1996).

the Indian debate is still conducted through the English newspaper media and the jargon is borrowed from Western discourses, and as a result good books on strategy with long shelf-life are scarce.

Strategic thinking apart, India's difficulties in national integration also had ramifications for its power status globally. Despite major strides in national integration, India is still perceived as a state not sufficiently unified or integrated to form a cohesive and viable political unit, let alone a major power. With its diverse languages, cultures and customs, India has been a divided nation. In the 1950s and 1960s, language-based conflicts were rampant. In the 1980s, violent autonomy struggles occurred in Punjab, Assam and other north-eastern states, and Kashmir. These conflicts have constantly demanded the attention of India's ruling elite, making it impossible for it to make a major thrust at international leadership or to gain respect from other powers. Bradnock avers:

To some observers, India's very diversity severely inhibits the emergence of a coherent national identity. It lacks the rallying cry of fundamentalist religious belief that exists in some Islamic countries. Nor does it have the cultural unity bestowed by a predominant language and universally shared history, as in China. Without such strengths, India, it is argued, with its predominantly Hindu population but with a secular constitution designed to give equal rights to divergent minorities, cannot summon up the nationalist vigor to become a force in the wider world. Rather it will remain locked in introspection, struggling with its own political identity and viability.[97]

However, this view has been contested by others who see Indian democracy, secularism, federalism and language arrangements as sources of strength and unity. The majority Hindu population provides the necessary *staatsvolk*, or a dominant national or ethnic people, for a successful federation and a state with potential power.[98] The Indian language policy of two plus one (English, Hindi and regional language) has been a fairly durable formula for stability.[99] India has come a long way in national integration, compared to many other multinational states in the

---

[97] Robert W. Bradnock, *India's Foreign Policy since 1971* (London: Pinter Publishers, 1990), 12.

[98] For this argument, see Brendan O'Leary, "What Nations can do with Nations: The Iron Law of Nationalism and Federation?" in John A. Hall, T.V. Paul and G. John Ikenberry (eds), *The Nation-State in Question* (forthcoming), ch. 2.

[99] John A. Hall, *International Orders* (Cambridge: Polity, 1996), 129; David Laitin, *Language Repertoires and State Construction in Africa* (Cambridge: Cambridge University Press, 1992), 38.

developing world or even the European Union, an entity somewhat similar in geographical size and diversity.

Some also blame India's cumbersome democratic system for its inability to forge ahead. Despite its merits, Indian democracy tends to support the mediocre. Politicians of all hues have come to rule India, but very few understand or excel in their knowledge about world affairs or economic affairs. Indian politicians, in general, are not driven by a passion to serve their country's interests as a whole. Instead, they tend to take the view that "election to parliament or appointment to the cabinet and the patronage that this brings are victory enough for their state or caste."[100]

Thus cultural explanations focus on India's inherent unit-level constraints for not being able to obtain a major-power role. As we argue below, cultural factors are secondary, although not totally insignificant, in India not realizing its major-power potential.

Conclusions: Major-power status – a systemic condition

Although all the explanations that have been discussed so far have some relevance for understanding India's lack of a major-power role, it is our contention that the most significant factors lie at the systemic level, and are accentuated by subsystemic and domestic-level variables. India's rise and acceptance as a major power have been heavily constrained by two factors: first, the balancing and regional containment of India by the existing major powers, and, second, India's unwillingness to play a key role in the global balance of power, due partly to domestic constraints outlined here, and partly to the weaknesses in its military and economic capabilities.

Although at the beginning of the twenty-first century both these factors are gradually changing, India has been at the "receiving end" of major-power politics and not at the "giving end" as yet. India's independent capabilities (except in the nuclear and missiles areas), although impressive in the regional context, have not been of real consequence to the major-power system, nor are they sufficient for India to mount a challenge to the international order or a forceful claim to major-power status. India's strategic marginality in the systemic conflict during the Cold War era, especially after it adopted a nonaligned posture, and its lack of powerful allies decreased its chances of gaining a key international role. The leadership of nonaligned countries provided limited influence based on soft power, but without adequate hard-power resources this influence was not sustainable. The major powers saw in

---

[100]"Normalizing India," *Economist*, September 4, 1999, 24.

India a limited challenger and a potentially rising power. The major powers, especially the US, viewed India's rise as a leading state negatively and actively discouraged it through political opposition, denial of material and technological assistance, and a sanctions regime that has been in place since the early 1970s. At the regional subsystem level, India's smaller yet determined adversary, Pakistan, has been successful in balancing India through forming alliances with major powers, especially with the US and China. To a large extent, these factors account for India's isolation in the institutional and technological areas as well. However, India's economic isolation has been largely self-inflicted. The adoption of a closed economic model was chiefly in response to the expectation on the part of Indian leaders of adverse systemic influences. They believed that economic autonomy would lead to greater strategic autonomy and an improved power position in the international system, an expectation that, in hindsight, has proven to be wrong.

Arguments that locate India's failure to achieve major-power status at the domestic or cultural level hold some validity. The domestic and ideational-level factors have compounded or magnified the systemic-level constraints. Although economic factors are becoming increasingly important as the world enters the twenty-first century, economic strength alone has not been a guarantor of major-power status. China's economic position when it acquired major-power status in 1945, or when the US accepted it as a major power in 1972, was not all that impressive. Up to the 1970s, with respect to many indicators of economic strength India and China were on par, especially on the basis of per capita income. Russia at the dawn of the twenty-first century is one of the most economically backward major powers. Its superpower position has declined but it is still considered a major power. When the current major powers obtained their position, they had not removed all the problems of economic development; for example, illiteracy and inequality. Further, two of the world's richest countries, Japan and Germany, have not been accorded major-power status. They are major economic powers, but not major military powers. In fact, many of the world's richest nations in terms of per capita income are small states, but their power position is skewed in one direction. Entry of new major powers into the modern international system has been frozen since 1945, partly because no other actor, including India, beyond the five permanent members of the UN Security Council has yet acquired military capabilities that have consequence for the world system. These capabilities include nuclear weapons and missiles that can reach the strategic heartland of all key major powers, and a strong conventional army, navy and air force that can engage in combat beyond the immediate region of the state. Moreover, barring a major realignment of power, the entry of a new power into the major-power system is likely to be difficult, but not implausible.

These arguments are not meant to belittle the role of economics in attaining major-power status. Indeed, economic and military power often go hand in hand. Without economic prowess, no major power can sustain its military power and the capacity to innovate technologically for a long period of time. Similarly, without security generated by self-help or through alliances, no economically strong country can sustain its economic prosperity. The linkage thus goes both ways. In other words, power and plenty go hand in hand.

Perceptual and cultural factors may be relevant in explaining a country's international position, but only up to a point. They may constrain and shape how a nation behaves as well as how others perceive it. But images can undergo dramatic change as the military and economic capacity of the actor improves and the state becomes efficient and innovative. Historically, dominant states viewed challengers as inferior and often branded them as "barbarians," as in the case of the attitude of the Romans toward the smaller challengers, of the Chinese toward the Mongols, and of the Russians and the Americans toward the Japanese in the early part of the twentieth century. However, once the material strength of the challengers improved, their international image and status also improved, as in the case of Japan. There is a strong parallel with the domestic situation in the US, where the Indian expatriate professional community in places like the Silicon Valley came to acquire fairly high social status after it became economically stronger in recent years. Once India's economic and military strength becomes of consequence for other countries, it is bound to receive respect. More importantly, images can change if the hegemonic power comes to the view that it requires the support or sympathy of the rising power as an ally in its struggle against other major powers or rising challengers. The Western media, despite all its professed objectivity, takes its cues from the political and economic elites, and determines "who is with us" and "who is against us," or "who is economically important" or "unimportant to us," in their favorable and unfavorable reporting.

Prior to India's independence, the systemic conflict involving the major powers (UK and US vis-à-vis the fascist alliance) made the Indian independence struggle a nuisance for the Allied powers, despite their public statements in support of national liberation struggles. To the West, the defeat of fascism was more important than the independence of colonies under their control. This factor, and the fact that India was still a colony when the postwar power settlement was made, resulted in India's marginalization in the global institutional hierarchy.

India's power capabilities were limited until the 1970s, and they were of limited consequence to the world order. Since then, India has made efforts to acquire nuclear and missile capabilities, which have been vehemently opposed by the major powers because these are weapons of consequence for the major-power system. During the Cold War period, partly because of the dearth of hard-power resources, India deliberately chose nonalignment, which made it a less prominent participant in the Cold War game. The US became close to Pakistan and helped it in containing India's strategic potential. Although Nehru made some strategically wise policies of exerting soft power, such as diplomatic mediation and active participation in UN peacekeeping operations, these were neither sufficient nor sustained enough to carve a major role for India over a long period of time. The failure in the war with China in 1962 exposed India's lack of hard-power resources. Washington's choice of Pakistan and the continued India–Pakistan conflict over Kashmir partly allowed the US to equate India with its much smaller adversary. India's inward-looking economic policies also made it a less attractive international economic actor. These policies were partly the result of the Indian elites' conception of the best route to attaining self-sufficiency and thereby increasing India's independent role in world politics. In the balance-of-power relationship involving China, the US and Pakistan, India increasingly became pro-Soviet, thereby alienating the West further. The end of the Cold War, a major systemic change, has liberated India from the relationship with the Soviet Union and the socialist mode of development.

By 1991, after winning the Cold War, the US began to focus its attention on other security challenges. To US policy-makers, the spread of weapons of mass destruction became the most prominent threat, and India became a target of opposition despite the increasing economic relations between the two countries. India's strong opposition to the CTBT created a negative impression, but the nuclear tests of 1998 constituted the biggest of all challenges by India. The major powers of the system put enormous pressure on India to abandon its nuclear weapons program but to no avail. The major powers are largely concerned about their monopoly being questioned and are, indeed, uncomfortable about letting a newcomer enter their league. At the beginning of the twenty-first century, India is slowly building up its capabilities in the nuclear and space arenas, and a liberalized economic policy has allowed an average economic growth rate of 5 to 7 per cent throughout much of the 1990s. If the trend continues, India will be a stronger state within a decade or two, but it may still remain somewhat marginalized in the international power hierarchy unless the major powers, especially the US, allow India's entry into their league. From a systemic point of view, India's prospects either way would have considerable ramifications.

The incremental positive changes in India's power position have occurred largely due to systemic factors, including the end of the Cold War and the rise of China as a powerful state in Asia. The US and Indian desire to constrain China has given India a potentially significant role in the emerging strategic picture involving the two countries. These changes have occurred not because of any major changes in cultural or ideational factors within or toward India, but because of the change in systemic/structural conditions, and also in India's economic and military capabilities. Improvements in India's military and economic conditions have resulted in India asserting its foreign-policy goals more effectively, and in other leading powers looking at India as a partner in the particular balance-of-power games that they seek to play in Asia and beyond in the twenty-first century.

In the following three chapters, we examine India's search for a leadership role and the constraints it has experienced, especially the reactions and responses of the major-power system. For purposes of analysis, these chapters are organized along the following periods: 1947 to 1964, 1964 to 1990, and post-1990. This largely historical analysis reveals the constraints at different levels more elaborately, especially at the systemic and regional levels, and also tests some of the arguments presented in this and previous chapters.

4 Nehru's Grand Strategy for a Major-Power Role, 1947–1964

Presiding over modern India's destiny as the country's first prime minister and foreign minister for a long and continuous period of seventeen years, Jawaharlal Nehru played a pivotal role in shaping India's foreign policy, not only for his time but, through his legacy, for the remainder of the twentieth century. Although deeply conscious of India's severe constraints, Nehru was nonetheless convinced that India was destined to be a key player in the international system. Nehru saw his own role as advancing the country along the path of achieving that prospect, through a wide-ranging set of policies. Moreover, he believed that the country's future potential demanded that India play an activist role in international affairs in the here and now in order to secure the interests both of India and of humanity at large. Analysts differ, however, as to whether Nehru was driven in his policy by realism (power politics) or idealism, concepts that he himself explicitly discussed.

One school of thought, most notably represented by the eminent Indian strategic thinker K. Subrahmanyam, holds that Nehru had really been a practitioner of realism and balance-of-power policy.[1] If India under Nehru was, indeed, practicing a balance-of-power policy as between the superpowers, then it follows that Nehru must have considered India to be a major power to assume playing the role of a balancer. Subrahmanyam acknowledged that in the execution of Nehru's policy there may have been errors, but he believed that overall Nehru had acted in accord with the tenets of realism. As against this line of analysis, another school holds that Nehru's policy was one of idealism.[2] That was overwhelmingly the public image of his policy as well. Nehru himself lent credibility to it when he admitted, at the time of the India–China War of 1962, that there was something fundamentally

---

[1] K. Subrahmanyam, "Nehru and the India–China Conflict of 1962," in B.R. Nanda (ed.), *Indian Foreign Policy: The Nehru Years* (New Delhi: Vikas, 1976), 102–30.

[2] See, for example, T.T. Poulose, "Viewpoint: India's Deterrence Doctrine: A Nehruvian Critique," *Nonproliferation Review*, 6 (Fall 1998), 77–84.

wrong with his policy, not just errors in execution, by acknowledging that "we had been living in a world of unreality."[3] That was an admission that he had not paid adequate attention to considerations of power and national security in his foreign policy. If it admittedly flowed out of illusions, his policy could not then be taken to have been based on realism.

One source of difficulty in resolving the contention between the two perspectives is that Nehru was no ordinary statesman; he was first and foremost an intellectual, who often thought aloud and, through a half-century of active involvement in politics, gave expression to his evolving thinking and views in innumerable writings, speeches and statements in multiple settings, and accordingly emphasized different aspects of his actual or projected policy and the rationale for them, depending on the time, occasion and audience. Any effort therefore to reduce the complexity of his thought and policy to make them intelligible in terms of the simple categories of realism and idealism is likely not to do adequate justice to his position. More importantly, Nehru was in office for a long period during the formative stage of India's emergence from colonialism into independence, its consolidation as a new state, and the founding and legitimizing of its institutional structures and policy frameworks in different fields. During his long stewardship, the world underwent many changes, as did his foreign policy. To treat his policy as if it were of a single piece in terms of realism or idealism is to impart it a static quality which is not justified by the facts. It becomes essential, therefore, to differentiate his foreign policy in terms of change over its long course. Here, two periods are differentiated: one from late 1946 to 1954, during which idealism was more prominent, though it did not entirely exclude realism, while the other is from 1954 to 1964, during which, as challenges mounted directly to India's national security, realism became progressively salient.

Even with this differentiated perspective, the focus on foreign policy alone is too limiting to understand Nehru's approach to world affairs, often reduced simply to his nonalignment policy. Nonalignment was only a part of his overall foreign policy, let alone of his national policy. Nehru had a highly integrated view of social affairs, incorporating domestic and international as well as economic and political dimensions. It is a limiting exercise therefore to restrict the analysis of Nehru's vision and endeavor on behalf of India's national interests internationally to merely his policy of nonalignment or even more broadly to his foreign policy. A truer understanding of Nehru's position can be gained

---

[3] Jawaharlal Nehru, *Jawaharlal Nehru's Speeches: Volume V: March 1963–May 1964* (New Delhi: Publications Division, 1968), 198.

by examining what in the international-relations literature is referred to
as *grand strategy*, which has been described as:

the full package of domestic and international policies designed to increase
national power and security. Grand strategy can therefore include policies varying from military expenditures and security alliances, to less frequently discussed policies, such as long-term investment in domestic industrialization and
foreign aid to nations with common security concerns.[4]

This broader perspective of grand strategy avoids the error of treating
foreign policy as if it were an isolated, and even self-contained, enterprise; instead, it forces us to see how the state's chief decision-makers
manage the challenges from the international environment through
policies spanning the polity and economy, not just through foreign policy. In taking this more comprehensive route to gain a better understanding of Nehru's position on India's role in the world, both
contemporaneous and prospective, this chapter is divided into five sections: (1) The political consolidation of a new state; (2) Founding the
foreign policy of independence, 1947–1954; (3) The shift in foreign policy, 1954–1964; (4) The economic strategy for undergirding independence; and (5) Science and technology for strategic autonomy.

The political consolidation of a new state

Foreign policy presupposes a state, but in the case of most developing
countries in the postwar period, an effective state is not a given; it has
often to be created, in the sense of a defined territory and of authoritative political institutions with legitimacy. As a developing country, newly
come to independence, India was no exception. Hardly a year before
India's emergence into independence, as well as a year after it, neither
its territorial extent nor the nature of its political institutions, or for that
matter its very survival, was certain. This dire circumstance was a function both of India's social structure and of the colonial inheritance. At
the same time, the very drive for political consolidation on the part of
the new state had to contend with external powers even as it had implications for foreign policy.

---

[4] Thomas J. Christensen, *Useful Adversaries: Grand Strategy, Domestic
Mobilization, and Sino-American Conflict, 1947–1958* (Princeton, NJ:
Princeton University Press, 1996), 7.

Territorial integration

When India achieved independence from Britain in 1947, it was accompanied by the partition of the country, leading to the formation of Pakistan as a separate state encompassing the Muslim-majority areas in the north-western and eastern parts of the subcontinent. The partition settlement, however, left out of its ambit the 562 princely states scattered across India, which had been under indirect British rule. In consideration of the past loyalty of the princes to the empire, Britain declared that its paramountcy over them would lapse, in effect rendering them sovereign and free to decide their own future. The Indian nationalists regarded this as the parting kick administered to India by the British and as "the greatest disservice the British had done us and the rulers."[5] Disruption, chaos and, indeed, the dissolution of the Indian state right at its birth were writ large in the declaration. As India's chief aide on princely India remarked subsequently, the decision "was fraught with the gravest danger to the integrity of the country. And so the prophets of gloom predicted that the ship of Indian freedom would founder on the rock of the States."[6]

Most of the princely states lay within the political boundaries of India, spread across it in a crazy-quilt fashion. Many of them had aspirations for independence. Soon after the declaration, Travancore, Hyderabad and Bhopal announced their intent to proclaim independence, while the colonial government's own Political Department attempted to create a Third Force consisting of the princely states.[7] Britain itself was implicated in Travancore's push for independence because of its interest in the state's monazite sands for its nuclear program.[8] The developing situation was unacceptable to the nationalist leaders of the Congress Party. There then began in July 1947, under the extraordinary leadership of Sardar Vallabhbhai Patel, the energetic campaign to rapidly bring about the integration of the princely states into India. Largely through persuasion and peaceful negotiations, all but three of the princely states that were relevant to India signed on to the instrument of accession. The campaign was concluded speedily, essentially within three weeks, and earned Sardar Patel the sobriquets of "the Iron Man of India" and "the Bismarck of India." The magnitude of Patel's achievement is conveyed by the important statistic that, while the

---

[5] V.P. Menon, *The Story of the Integration of the Indian States* (New York: Macmillan, 1956), 94.
[6] *ibid.*, 91, 484.
[7] See *ibid.*, 90, 113–14.
[8] A. Martin Wainwright, *The Inheritance of Empire: Britain, India, and the Balance of Power in Asia, 1938–55* (Westport, CT: Praeger, 1994), 99–103.

partition resulted in a loss of an area of 944,595 square kilometers with a population of 81.5 million, the integration of the princely states brought in some 1,295,000 square kilometers with a population of about 90 million.[9]

This achievement, of course, did not earn India any appreciation from Britain, which was angered in particular instances where princes with a long record of loyalty to the empire were pressured to integrate into India; British reactions, in turn, aroused suspicions in India about British intentions. However, unknown to the Indians, the US, too, was miffed at what it saw in the endeavor as an emerging challenge to its new-found domination in Asia; an authoritative but secret document noted in 1950 that:

the vigor and methods which have characterised India's execution of its policy of consolidating the princely states, and its inflexible attitude with regard to Kashmir, may indicate national traits which in time, if not *controlled,* could make India Japan's successor in Asiatic imperialism.

In so characterizing India as a future threat and therefore deserving of regional containment by the US, the statement provided an early omen of the policy course that the US as the global power was contemplating, by immediately adding: "In such a circumstance *a strong Muslim bloc under the leadership of Pakistan, and friendly to the US, might afford a desirable balance of power in South Asia.*"[10]

Notwithstanding the achievement of integration, three princely states proved difficult for India: Junagadh (now part of Gujarat), Jammu and Kashmir, and Hyderabad. As against the British stand, with which the Muslim League agreed, the Congress position was that the disposition of the princely states was for the people, and not the princes, to decide. Despite the diplomatic row that it created between India and Pakistan, the question of the accession of Junagadh was decided by the population revolting to join India and the prince fleeing to Pakistan. In the case of Jammu and Kashmir, the Hindu prince of the largely Muslim state vacillated on which country to join but when, in October 1947, tribesmen and army irregulars from Pakistan almost overran the state in an invasion masterminded by Pakistan, he hurriedly acceded to India. India then ordered its army to intervene to vacate the aggression. With the support of the popular forces in the state, the Indian army recovered

---

[9] Menon, *The Story,* 490.
[10] US Department of State, *Foreign Relations of the United States, 1950: Volume V: The Near East, South Asia, and Africa* (Washington, DC: 1978), 1499; emphasis added. The series is hereafter referred to as *FRUS.*

most of the territory but, before it could finish the job, Nehru's India in a fit of naive idealism went to the UN to complain about Pakistani aggression. It found that the UN was no impartial body, but one caught in geopolitical maneuvering in which the major powers acted with a view to advancing their own interests. Consistent with its past hostility to Indian nationalism, the UK often favored Pakistan and in this policy it was joined by the US. India, however, refused to buckle under the joint UK–US pressure and thwarted, by delay and noncooperation, the imposition of solutions that would put India's territorial integrity at risk.

In the case of Hyderabad, the Muslim prince of an overwhelmingly Hindu state had quixotic visions of independence. In this ambition he was encouraged by Pakistan and by certain British leaders, including Winston Churchill. India exercised extraordinary patience and restraint in negotiations, and made many exceptional concessions. However, believing India "to be very weak and to be incapable of military action now or at any time," the prince and his advisors proved to be obdurate while "the anti-Indian attitude of a section of the British press, and the plea for Hyderabad's independence voiced by some British political leaders, confirmed the Nizam in his uncompromising attitude."[11] Meanwhile, fanatic elements gained control of the administration; they terrorized the population, colluded with Pakistan against India, and adventuristically carried out raids into India and attacked Indian trains passing through the state. Finally, losing patience, India asked its army to march into Hyderabad. With the overwhelming majority of the population hostile to the prince's absolutist regime, his armed forces crumbled quickly, while the Indian army was hailed as liberator.

In the few months before independence, and for several years afterwards, matters relating to territorial integration of the state were clearly at the very heart of domestic and foreign policies. Contrary to popular mythology, Indian actions regarding both Jammu and Kashmir and Hyderabad convincingly demonstrated that India under Nehru, no matter how patient and flexible, would in the ultimate analysis not be deterred from using force where its vital interests were at stake. The vigor with which India's territorial integration was pushed by Nehru and his colleagues was related to their determination to reverse the pattern of India's earlier history, in which external powers set one kingdom against another in order to conquer and control the subcontinent.

Opting for a liberal-democratic federal polity

Even while the leadership was attempting to foil any attempt at the ter-

---

[11] Menon, *The Story*, 348, 369.

ritorial disruption of India through the instrumentality of the princely states, the northern part of the subcontinent sank into a complete breakdown of law and order, indeed anarchy, in the midst of massive rioting, arson and massacres. It is an index of the foresight and dedication of the Indian leadership under Nehru that, despite the daunting multiple crises it faced, it strove to establish the long-term foundations of state power and, toward that end, continued to deliberate on a constitution as the basis of a new institutional framework for the country. By November 1949, India had adopted a constitution that was both daring and complex. At the heart of the constitution was the deep faith of the leadership in the people for their capacity to elect their governors, thus defying the assumptions of democratic theory that a literate and wealthy population was a prerequisite for democracy. The key features of the constitution were the sovereignty of the people, civilian rule through a parliamentary system, a federal structure with considerable autonomy for the states, and rejection of the sectarian or confessional state (a path chosen by Pakistan) in favor of the secular state. The constitution came into effect in 1950, and was soon legitimized through elections in 1951 and further institutionalized under Nehru through the elections of 1957 and 1962. The speed and the dedication with which the leadership evolved a liberal-democratic institutional order and deepened its legitimacy were extraordinary among developing countries.

While the choice of a liberal-democratic order was in accord with the values of the leadership – in turn derived from India's tradition of freedom of the mind, notwithstanding the rigidity of its social system – it also meant that the leadership accepted the implicit consequence in terms of a gradualist approach to social and economic change. Since governance was to be based on the consent of the governed, there could be no revolutionary or blitzkrieg strategy in developing a backward economy or restructuring a traditional society. By the same token, there could be no rapid building up of economic or military capabilities. The Indian leadership thus made an implicit trade-off between democracy and rapid advance in capabilities.

The integrative strategy of ethnic accommodation

Not only did the leadership under Nehru adopt an institutional structure which had as its centerpiece both democracy and the secular state, but it supplemented that choice by an integrative strategy which had as its thrust ethnic accommodation, rather than either assimilation or exclusion. The personal role of Nehru in the development of the strategy can hardly be exaggerated and was, indeed, crucial. However, there are structural aspects of Indian society which were facilitative and supportive of such a policy.

Speculation about India's collapse under the weight of its immense diversity began with its emergence as an independent state. However, the very nature of India's diversity has to a considerable extent mitigated the threat to national unity. For India is not a case of bipolar distribution but, because of its abundant diversity, of multipolar distribution, which tends to largely avoid the problem of domination, actual or perceived, of one group by the other, that is typical of bipolar distribution. Also, multipolar distribution makes achievement of power conditional on bargaining and coalition-building. Moreover, the resultant coalitions are likely to shift and not be permanent; consequently, the issue of domination as between one group and another becomes attenuated. Again, the very multiplicity of diversity makes for the cross-cutting of cleavages, thus diffusing conflicts. In short, India's demonstrated unity is structurally based, though it is not immune to frequent, and at times damaging, jolts.

In the area of foreign policy, the integrative strategy of accommodation reinforces the impact of democracy. For one thing, it also places constraints on any rapid build-up of capabilities and, therefore, on over-ambitious or adventuristic aims in the international system that require the backing of capabilities. For another, it is not difficult for India's elite, already socialized into a strategy of accommodation internally, to extend it externally. Not surprisingly, Nehru's accommodative posture toward Pakistan – which his opponents decried as appeasement – was simply an extension abroad of his internal policy toward the Muslim community among India's many communities.

Overall, it is clear that India's leadership under the stewardship of Nehru displayed political skills of a high order in bringing about the initial political consolidation of the state and laying the foundations of state power. Taken together, its achievements in the realm of territorial integration, instituting a liberal-democratic federal polity and developing the integrative strategy of accommodation, are noteworthy for having been accomplished on short order in the midst of extreme adversity and severe crises. They led to a certain extent to the feeling of Indian exceptionalism among the newly emergent states. In foreign policy, they allowed India to participate in world affairs as a self-confident, politically consolidated state with largely moderate goals. At the same time, the process of territorial integration left behind a trail of suspicion about British, and by extension of Western, intentions in relation to the subcontinent.

Founding the foreign policy of independence, 1947–1954

Nehru came to his office as prime minister and foreign minister in 1947 with a not inconsiderable preparation in political and foreign affairs, having been a long-time leader and molder – second only to Mahatma Gandhi – of one of the most innovative and sustained mass nationalist movements. He had also been the sole spokesman of the nationalist movement to the outside world and the singular formulator of its official positions on world affairs. In the movement's foreign affairs, his usual relationship to Mahatma Gandhi as disciple was reversed; in this sphere, it was he who was the mentor, and Gandhi acknowledged him as such.[12] Nehru was first and foremost an intellectual, and he used his long spells in British colonial jails to reflect deeply on world and Indian history. The results of these reflections were evident in serious books and essays on history and world affairs.

Nehru's foreign policy came to be identified with a single word: non-alignment. However, that term does not do full justice to the entire range and content of his policy, to its intellectual sophistication and to its full implications. Here, in order to understand the content, causes and consequences of Nehru's foreign policy, three aspects of it are examined: the thrust for independence, the penchant for foreign-policy activism, and opposition to power politics.

An independent foreign policy

Although India emerged as an independent state in August 1947, the central thrust and direction of Nehru's foreign policy for India in the specific postwar context had been made demonstrably clear a year earlier, when he became the head of the interim government in early September 1946. Within days of assuming this role, even though still operating under the constraints of colonial rule, he declared the intent of his government to participate in international affairs:

as a free nation with our own policy and not merely as a satellite of another nation. We hope to develop close and direct contacts with other nations and to co-operate with them in the furtherance of world peace and freedom.

More significantly, at that early stage of postwar history, he laid out the basis for what subsequently became the hallmark of independent India's foreign policy by adding:

---

[12] B.R. Nanda, in Surjit Mansingh (ed.), *Nehru's Foreign Policy, Fifty Years On* (New Delhi: Mosaic Books, 1998), 19–24.

We propose, as far as possible, to keep away from the power politics of groups, aligned against one another, which have led in the past to world wars and which may again lead to disasters on an even vaster scale.[13]

This was no one-time declaration for form; Nehru reiterated its central message many times in the subsequent months before independence, both publicly and, more importantly, in internal government documents: India was to stay out of the two power blocs led by the US and the USSR, and it would decide its policy on world issues on the merits of each case.[14] Later, after independence, Nehru's expression of the refusal to join either of the two power blocs became sharper. In this fashion, Nehru endeavored to avoid entangling India in the systemic and structural conflict of the emerging Cold War between the two blocs.

What underlay the refusal to join either power bloc was the fierce determination to be independent and master of one's own foreign policy rather than handing over its management to the superpower leading one bloc or the other. The aim to retain India's foreign-policy autonomy was the most fundamental aspect of Nehru's foreign policy. A subordinate or satellite role was simply unacceptable to him. As he remarked with compelling logic: "What does joining a bloc mean? After all it can only mean one thing: give up your view about a particular question, adopt the other party's view on that question in order to please it and gain its favour."[15] Indeed, so central was the aim of foreign-policy autonomy that Nehru and his colleagues were initially dubious about any formal organizing of even a bloc of nonaligned countries.[16]

Despite the determination to stay out of the two power blocs, Nehru was nonetheless wary about any false notions of a durable equidistance from them; rather, he underlined the importance of national interests as determining the nature of foreign relationships. In a message to the *New Republic* in early 1947, he stated:

We propose to avoid entanglement in any blocs or groups of Powers realizing that only thus can we serve not only [the] cause of India but of world peace. This policy sometimes leads partisans of one group to imagine that we are support-

[13] Jawaharlal Nehru, "Free India's Role in World Affairs," in *Selected Works of Jawaharlal Nehru: Second Series,* vol. I, 404–8. Hereafter, this series is referred to as *SWJN–SS.*

[14] See *SWJN–SS,* vol. I, 492, 539, 573, 576, 580, 594; and *SWJN–SS,* vol. II, 429.

[15] Jawaharlal Nehru, *Independence and After* (New York: John Day Company, 1950), 218.

[16] Sarvepalli Gopal, *Jawaharlal Nehru: A Biography,* 3 vols. (Cambridge, MA: Harvard University Press, 1976), vol. III, 185.

ing the other group. Every nation places its own interests first in developing its foreign policy. Fortunately India's interests coincide with peaceful foreign policy and co-operation with all progressive nations. Inevitably India will be drawn closer to those countries which are friendly and cooperative to her.[17]

Nehru was quite firm on this point. When the US press and other Americans were critical of India's positions at the UN, he pointedly told his aides:

It would have been absurd and impolitic for the Indian delegation to avoid the Soviet bloc for fear of irritating the Americans. A time may come when we may say clearly and definitely to the Americans or others that if their attitude continues to be unfriendly we shall necessarily seek friends elsewhere.[18]

The enormousness of the challenge implicit in India's stance on staying free of entanglements with the two power blocs cannot be exaggerated, for it amounted to throwing down the gauntlet of independence before the two superpowers emergent from World War II. At the time, a defeated Japan and a ruined Europe lay at the feet of the US, while the eastern part of a partitioned Europe was occupied by the Soviet Union. No alternative was seen for states in the immediate postwar period except to join one bloc or the other. For India to have made an open declaration of its intent to maintain its foreign-policy independence was not only innovative but also daring. While India's challenge was addressed to both superpowers, in effect it was meaningful largely in relation to the US. For, having been devastated by World War II and having lost 20 million of its people in the war, the Soviet Union was an insecure and isolated country, contained and confined to its immediate neighborhood by the other superpower. The world immediately after the war was essentially a unipolar system, with the US as the hegemonic power; the bipolar system with two somewhat equally powerful poles was a subsequent, even if not durable, development. It is precisely in this circumstance of the US as the hegemonic power and the assertion by India of foreign-policy independence that were sown the seeds of the largely conflictual relationship between the two states, casting them as adversaries for a long time to come. For a country to have an independent foreign policy – as India had chosen, in what a later foreign minister was to describe as "an act of defiance" and a determined refusal to "bend

[17] *SWJN–SS*, vol. II, 409.
[18] *SWJN–SS*, vol. I, 475.

and crawl"[19] – would, as that policy flowered, be implacably unacceptable to the US with its conception of being the hegemonic power and successor to the British hegemony. In this development, the contemporaneous perception by the US of its existing position and future role was critical.

The emergence of the US as the hegemonic power at the end of World War II, ushering in what many believed to be the American Century or Pax Americana, had generated among most Americans a messianic complex, somewhat similar to that of Pax Romana for the Romans many centuries earlier. Drew Middleton pointed out how after World War II, the US envisioned "an unprecedented expansion of power and influence on a global scale," "one greater in extent than any known to history," and he underlined "the supreme national confidence it promoted in the American people." He continued: "Americans were emboldened to believe that there were no policies they could not implement, no dangers they could not overcome." Not until the military failure in Vietnam did disillusionment occur with such power among "those internationalists who believed in an America destined to dominate Asia and the Pacific."[20]

But until then, the sense of US omnipotence was pervasive in that nation. Dean Rusk gave expression to this feeling of power, saying "when the United States applies pressure on something, anything, it gives."[21] As the hegemonic superpower, the US aimed, then, to extend its influence, power, and domination across the entire globe, restricting the Soviet Union to its own region for a considerable period of time. In this world order, there was no room for other states except as satellites within the US orbit. The thrust for domination in US foreign policy was reinforced and legitimated by a fervent ideology of opposition to communism and totalitarianism.

Against this self-perception of the US, India's pretensions to an independent foreign policy seemed far-fetched and unwarranted, indeed foolhardy, for India was perceived to lack the capabilities commensurate with its claims. By the same token, they stood in contradiction to the requirements of realism in respect of balance between aims and capabilities.

[19] I.K. Gujral, "India's Foreign Policy: Challenges and Perspectives," in Mansingh (ed.), *Nehru's Foreign Policy*, 25–39.

[20] Drew Middleton, *Retreat from Victory: A Critical Appraisal of American Foreign and Military Policy from 1920 to the 1970s* (New York: Hawthorn Books, 1973), 435–46, 213.

[21] Marvin Kalb and Bernard Kalb, *Kissinger* (Boston: Little, Brown & Co., 1974), 65.

Regardless, the determination on India's part at its very birth to pursue an independent foreign policy as the bedrock of its relationship with the world, later to sustain such policy – despite reverses, temporary concessions and vacillations from time to time – during Nehru's seventeen years in office, and further to continue to nurture it subsequently by his successors as a precious legacy, was of momentous significance. It was at core a profoundly revisionist policy. For the endeavor to foster an independent foreign policy was to create implicitly the scope and space for a major-power role, if not now, at least in the future, when capabilities matched the ambition. To proclaim an independent foreign policy was to declare one's capacity, howsoever derived, to stand on one's own, while to join a bloc was to renounce beforehand any future claim to such a role. An independent foreign policy was both a prerequisite to, and a marker of, becoming a major power. Simply put, no independent foreign policy, no major-power role.

Nehru was not unaware of the limitations of India's contemporaneous capabilities, but he believed that to become a satellite or subordinate member of a bloc under a superpower was to forfeit one's independence. To him, an independent foreign policy was at the very heart of national independence; as he proclaimed:

What does independence consist of? It consists fundamentally and basically of foreign relations. That is the test of independence. All else is local autonomy. Once foreign relations go out of your hands into the charge of somebody else, to that extent and in that measure you are not independent.[22]

With the hindsight of history of the last half-century, it is possible to appreciate the intrinsic merit in Nehru's foreign-policy logic. For the assertion of foreign-policy independence is shown to be intimately linked to claims to a major-power role. The last half-century demonstrates that membership in a bloc not only makes for a truncated acquisition of national capabilities (witness Japan and Germany, states which are essentially military protectorates of the US), but also renders difficult any subsequent ambition to break out of the straitjacket of bloc membership, which act is likely to be viewed as rebellious and illegitimate. There consequently has to be a prior and specific assertion to an independent foreign policy to safeguard a possible claim to a major-power role in the future. That, indeed, was the core legacy of Nehru's foreign policy.

---

[22] Gopal, *Nehru*, vol. II, 300; Jawaharlal Nehru, *India's Foreign Policy: Selected Speeches, September 1946–April 1961* (New Delhi: Publications Division, 1961), 240.

Capabilities and culture in the making of foreign policy: If the safeguarding of a future major-power role can be regarded as implicit in the declaration of an independent foreign policy, where did the goal of an independent foreign policy come from? Can it be regarded as having issued, in accord with the position of realism, out of a shrewd assessment of India's capabilities? Some have considered India to have been at independence a successor to considerable capabilities. Bharat Karnad believes that India's founding decision-makers demonstrated an inadequate appreciation at independence of India's inherent strengths and did not evidence a realistic assessment of its capabilities. In his opinion, India did not act in world affairs in accord with its inherited capabilities, which ought to have pointed to a major-power role. Says Karnad:

By the time the Second World War ended, India too had all the characteristics of big power – size, natural resources, a large sterling balance – the debt that the UK had run up during the War – providing hard currency muscle and, above all, military heft. The Indian Army had grown into a force of renown, with Field Marshal Claude Auchinleck acknowledging that without it "the war could not have been won." More impressively, India had developed into "The Western Alliance's Eastern Arsenal" – the source of most of the manpower and of war materiel for the Middle Eastern and South East Asia Commands, and together with its military infrastructure, it had the capacity "to project power" which was exceeded only by the United States, the Soviet Union, Great Britain and, perhaps, Turkey.[23]

This assessment finds an intriguing confirmation in a little-known fact that colonial India's representatives at the British Commonwealth Conference in April 1945 demanded a permanent seat for India on the UN Security Council in recognition of its wartime contribution. Shortly afterwards, Canada, Yugoslavia and Australia raised the issue more openly at the San Francisco conference on the UN charter. The effort proved fruitless, however, apparently because India was not yet independent.[24]

While there may be some merit in Karnad taking an unorthodox position on India as a possible major power, that stance ignores several serious and crippling deficiencies in India's capabilities at the time. First, it fails to take into account the impact of partition on India's strategic situation. The partition set up not only a local rival in Pakistan against

---

[23] Bharat Karnad, "India: Global Leadership and Self-Perception," paper presented at the workshop "India as an Emerging Power," at the United Service Institute of India, New Delhi, January 22, 1999.

[24] M.S. Rajan, *India and International Affairs: A Collection of Essays* (New Delhi: Lancers Books, 1999), 6–7.

India, but also a base for external powers to neutralize India. Indeed, some maintain that the partition of the subcontinent permanently foreclosed the possibility of India emerging as a major power.[25] Second, the unorthodox position on capabilities neglects to appreciate the specific strategic context in which India could make its heavy contribution during World War II. That context was one of India's complete dependence on Great Britain for war strategy and the higher direction of·the war, and on the Royal Navy for its maritime security. Indian officers had not been allowed to advance much beyond the rank of colonel, while India's navy amounted to no more than a glorified fishing fleet. Even after independence, India had to depend on British officers for the higher positions, and at times Britain used the threat of withdrawal of these officers to put diplomatic pressure on India. Third, despite the claims of being the eastern arsenal of the wartime alliance, India was dependent on Great Britain and the US for the supply of heavy and advanced equipment for its army, navy and air force;[26] small arms alone do not a major power make. Behind this dependence lay the fundamental characteristic of the absence of an industrial base in capital goods in India. In truth, India was at independence, in realistic terms, an economic and military appendage of the West.

Basically, India inherited a typical underdeveloped economy, where the per capita income was less than $50 and where agriculture was the main occupation of 70 per cent of the population. The society was in no better shape, with over 80 per cent of the population being rural and illiterate. More distressingly, India was unable to adequately feed its growing population. For more than half a century before independence, India's agriculture had been stagnant. In 1943, several million had died in the terrible famine in Bengal. Indeed, Nehru had to remind his ambassadors not to forget that they were from a poor country.[27] Soon after independence, India was asking the US for the supply of substantial quantities of food and, given India's refusal to align itself with Washington, the conditions under which the US was willing to respond caused considerable resentment in India. Nehru believed one particular bill in the US to be tantamount "practically to converting India into some kind of a semi-colonial country or at least a satellite in the economic sense."[28] In brief, it is hard to see how the contemporaneous

---

[25] Conversation with Professor Stephen P. Cohen, at the APSA annual meetings in Atlanta, Georgia, in September 1999.

[26] Wainwright, in *The Inheritance of Empire,* and on whom Karnad relies to develop his revisionist position, is absolutely clear on this point.

[27] See *SWJN–SS,* vol. I, 575.

[28] Gopal, *Nehru,* vol. II, 137.

economic and military capabilities of the country could be seen as supportive of even the goal of a foreign policy of independence from the two power blocs, let alone that of a big power.

Yet this last assessment cannot be allowed to stand as definitive; Karnad's position is not without some merit. There is first of all the matter of size. With 3.1 million square kilometers, India was the seventh-largest state in the world. Again, after China, India was the second-most populous country in the world; its population was larger than that of the two superpowers combined. More importantly, what matters in international politics is often relative capabilities. When India emerged into independence, China was in turmoil because of the civil war between the Communists and the Nationalists; a defeated Japan was under US military occupation; South America was then, as now, under US hegemony; and much of Asia and Africa was still under colonial rule. It is not surprising that India was therefore seen, even by the US, as "the strongest power in Asia."[29] There was a self-conscious awareness of this aspect even by the Indian leadership; as Nehru told the constituent assembly in March 1948:

I can understand some of the smaller countries of Asia being forced by circumstances to bow down before some of the greater Powers and becoming practically satellites of those Powers, because they cannot help it. ... But I do not think that consideration applies to India.

We are not citizens of a weak or mean country and I think it is foolish for us to get frightened, even from a military point of view, of the greatest of the Powers today.[30]

In this manner, India was different from the other countries that subsequently jumped onto the nonaligned bandwagon. Its foreign policy had some semblance of real capabilities behind it. In a sense, subsequent history provides confirmation of this assessment in that, while most other countries ended up aligning their foreign policies to the requirements of the US as the hegemon after the end of the Cold War, particularly in relation to the NPT and the acquisition of nuclear weapons, India hewed to its own distinctive line. Besides a modicum of material capabilities during the initiation of nonalignment and its heyday up to the mid-1950s, India was also strong in soft power. Under a capable leadership, it had successfully managed its political consolidation; the relatively smooth installation of democracy and its legitimization gave

[29] Rajendra K. Jain (ed.), *US–South Asian Relations, 1947–1982* (New Delhi: Radiant Publishers, 1983), 23.
[30] Nehru, *Independence and After*, 213.

India a unique place among the new states. Because of these advantages, India approached the world with a considerable degree of self-assurance.

It can be reasonably maintained therefore that India's foreign policy of independence was not without a rational basis in capabilities, both hard and soft. However, while capabilities can and do often manifest themselves in foreign-policy goals, they do not do so automatically; rather, they do it through influencing the perceptions of decision-makers. In India's case, the top leadership was not unaware of India's relative capabilities. But the passion which it invested in the goal of foreign policy of independence seems to indicate that the goal originated in a different source, for that leadership came to office because it had led a movement that was extraordinary in the annals of nationalism. Rebelling against British imperialism, the nationalist movement fundamentally sought a revitalization and reworking of India's ancient civilization for the modern era. Sustained over nearly two-thirds of a century, it had been transformed into a genuine mass movement and mass organization in the 1920s under the leadership of Mahatma Gandhi, who brought to it the novel methodology of nonviolence for purposes of mass mobilization. A series of mass agitations made for ever-widening circles of popular support for the nationalist movement. Millions took part in popular agitations, hundreds of thousands went to prison in the cause of the movement, and thousands got killed for it, whether through bullets or the smashing of skulls by the empire's security forces. Independence thus did not come easy to India. The sheer determination and discipline to confront the imperial forces on a sustained basis cannot but arouse awe. India wrested, it was not granted, independence. Indeed, like nonalignment later, India's nationalist movement became a model for countries struggling for national independence in Asia and Africa.

The nationalist movement in India was led by a genuinely nationalist leadership, given to sacrifice for the cause of independence. For many, prison had become a second home, and police persecution a routine experience. By independence, Nehru had spent some ten years in jail, which was about the norm for the top Congress leaders. Interestingly, the nationalist leadership did not identify itself with any single foreign ideology. Instead, it struck a distinctive path. It was sternly opposed to Western imperialism, but it was also committed to political liberalism; it was hostile to communism, but it also favored democratic socialism and planned economic development. Foremost, it was dedicated to India and its interests. When this leadership took over power provisionally in 1946 and more fully in 1947, it would have consequently been unthinkable for it and unacceptable to it to exchange the newly won independence, climaxing a struggle of more than six decades, for a new subordination to either superpower. The foreign policy of independence was thus rooted in the specific historical experience of India; it was simply a manifestation and a continuation of the nationalist movement. The aim of the foreign policy of independence had thus been set by the nationalist movement. However, that aim would not have been sustainable without some semblance of corresponding capabilities.

Potential capabilities and major-power role: At independence, India's was an agricultural economy without a modern industrial base that could provide the military capabilities for a major-power role. However, in the eyes of the Indian leadership, the country's economic backwardness was not an immutable condition. No doubt, the leadership was wrong in believing that ten to fifteen years was all that was necessary for the revolutionary transformation of an agricultural economy into an industrial one, but the determination was there to initiate and push through the industrialization effort as quickly as possible. The leadership therefore saw considerable power *potential* in India.

It is here that an already-discussed important feature of India's situation enters into the picture – size. There is first the size of territory, which is given by the existing boundaries of the state. There is then the size of the population. Interestingly, Samuel Huntington refers to the colorful phrase "demography is destiny";[31] demography's importance was conveyed dramatically when President Richard Nixon justified the opening of relations with China on the grounds of a billion people with nuclear weapons. India, too, at the beginning of the twenty-first century is a country of a billion people, but even half a century earlier, with about one-third that size, it was the second-most populous country in the world. Size, in turn, has a fundamental implication for major-power status. If industrialization of a country is essential to provide an economic base for military capabilities for the sake of national security, then a successful industrialization of India would not merely furnish the economic and military capabilities to assure a foreign policy of independence and the national security associated with it. Rather, it would in combination with India's very size propel it into the group of major powers.

What is interesting is that the Indian leadership, particularly Nehru, was keenly aware of the country's potential and its relationship to the conduct of foreign policy. When Nehru became the head of the interim

---

[31] Samuel P. Huntington, *The Clash of Civilizations and the Remaking of World Order* (New York: Simon & Schuster, 1996), 198.

government, the question came up as to whether India should contest for a seat in the UN Security Council. Nehru was very clear in his mind that India should run, even if it were to lose, and gave a power-based rationale for the choice in an internal government memorandum:

Whatever the present position of India might be, *she is potentially a Great Power.* Undoubtedly, in future she will have to play a very great part in security problems of Asia and the Indian Ocean, more especially of the Middle East and South-East Asia. Indeed, India is the pivot round which these problems will have to be considered. I need not go further into this matter as the importance of India to any scheme of Asian security is vital. *It is absurd for India to be treated like any small power* in this connection. Whether we succeed in getting into the Security Council or not, I think we should take up this attitude at the beginning and throughout that India is the center of security in Asia and that, therefore, India must have a central place in any council considering these matters. ... the fact remains that it is India that counts in the security and defence of both these regions far more than any other country. Thus, it would seem to be the obvious course that India, by virtue of her geographical and strategical position, resources and latent power, should be a member of the Security Council.[32]

In another internal memorandum, dated January 18, 1947, Nehru maintained: "Actually we are not a Power that counts; potentially we are very much so."[33] Similarly, about two weeks later, Nehru more sharply underlined the linkage between potential power and foreign policy:

While India's present position with her rapid advance towards complete freedom and industrial growth has to be emphasized, her potential power must always be kept in view. In the long range it is this that counts in foreign policy, and every far-seeing statesman bases his policy accordingly.[34]

The notion of India as potentially a major power was not something that occurred to Nehru as if in a sudden flash on becoming the head of the interim government in 1946. Rather, it had its backward linkage in time to the days of the nationalist movement. In 1944, while in jail, he reflected on the future in his *Discovery of India;* though deeply conscious of the looming threats to national unity, he believed:

She is one of the very few countries which have the resources and capacity to stand on their own feet. Today probably the only such countries are the United States of America and the Soviet Union. Great Britain can only be reckoned as

[32] *SWJN–SS,* vol. I, 439–40; emphasis added.
[33] *ibid.,* 472.
[34] *ibid.,* 581; emphasis added.

one of these if the resources of her empire are added to her own, and even then a spread-out and disgruntled empire is a source of weakness. China and India are potentially capable of joining that group. Each of them is compact and homogeneous and full of natural wealth, manpower, and human skill and capacity.[35]

The idea of India as a potential major power was held more generally than just by Nehru. As Prasad points out, "the nationalist movement instilled a yearning for a decisive voice in world affairs." Indeed, the Congress felt that it was only the lack of independence that had deprived India of a permanent seat on the UN Security Council.[36] One would have imagined that the partition of the subcontinent would have induced some rethinking and modification of the view, but the notion of India as a major power was carried over unamended into the period after independence. In March 1948, Nehru told the Constituent Assembly somewhat emphatically:

obviously we are not a great military Power, we are not an industrially advanced Power – India even today counts in world affairs, and the trouble that you see in the United Nations or the Security Council is because she does count, not because she does not count. ... If we had been some odd little nation somewhere in Asia or Europe, it would not have mattered much. But because we count, and because we are going to count more and more in the future. ... it is merely the fact that *we are potentially a great nation and a big Power,* and possibly it is not liked by some people that anything should happen to strengthen us.[37]

A year later, he reminded the same assembly to look at India's foreign policy "from the wider point of view that I have placed before it, that is the emergence of India and Asia in the modern trend of human affairs, the inevitability of India playing an important part by virtue of *her tremendous potential,* by virtue of the fact that she is the biggest political unit in terms of population today and is likely to be in terms of her resources also. She is going to play that part."[38] Nehru thus rejected the status for India as an object of the major powers in favor of the role of a subject coordinate with those powers. A few years later, in 1954, he noted significantly:

[35] Nehru, *The Discovery of India* (New York: The John Day Company, 1946), 535.
[36] Bimla Prasad, *The Origins of Indian Foreign Policy: The Indian National Congress and World Affairs, 1885–1947* (Calcutta: Booklands Private Limited, 1960), 253, 221.
[37] Nehru, *Independence and After,* 219; emphasis added.
[38] *ibid.,* 244; emphasis added. China at the time was divided between the Communists and the Nationalists.

Leaving these three big countries, the United States of America, the Soviet Union and China, aside for the moment, look at the world. There are much advanced, highly cultured countries. But if you peep into the future, and if nothing goes wrong – wars and the like – the obvious fourth country in the world is India.[39]

In the light of the preceding analysis, it emerges that the goal to become a major power, the determination to protect that goal from subversion by internal and external forces, and the endeavor to build the capabilities to assure it over the longer run, if not in the short run, were fundamental to Nehru's grand strategy in the world arena. In this reading, the foreign policy of independence emerges not just as a desirable end in itself, nor just as a way-station to a major-power role, but as the specific means of a presently weak but still substantial and potentially strong power to protect the attainment of that goal in the future. For to have aligned with a superpower was to have that goal undercut and foreclosed. The scope and space for a future major-power role created by a foreign policy of independence thus appears not as an unintended consequence of that policy but as its very aim.

An activist global role

If asserting a foreign policy of independence from the opposing power blocs was not daring enough, India under Nehru soon after independence sought to play an activist role in world affairs. It attempted to insert itself into the international system to exercise influence at the global level as if it were already a major power, even though it lacked the necessary "hard" economic and military capabilities for the role. It explained the activism by declaring that staying out of the blocs did not imply neutrality or indifference to world affairs, and it justified the involvement with global issues beyond its region on the ground that the shrinking of space had inextricably linked the fate of all states. In a world politically and militarily divided between two hostile blocs, India therefore sought to bring to world affairs what it thought was a distinctive voice and approach from a newly emergent Asia, and it refused to see either bloc in the black-and-white terms that the other wanted. In large part, this stance was a reflection not only of its own recent historical experience, but also of its internal diversity and ideological pluralism.

[39] Jawaharlal Nehru, *Jawaharlal Nehru's Speeches: Volume III: March 1953–August 1957* (New Delhi: Publications Division, 1958), 264.

The growth of antagonism with the hegemonic power: Although India was not aligned with either bloc, its position on a wide range of issues nonetheless often ran counter to that of the US. This was not a consequence of India deliberately seeking to annoy or hurt the US, but because of the structural position of the US in the international system as the hegemonic power, which additionally headed an alliance system that included the major imperialist powers of the time. India insistently pushed on to the international agenda issues such as world peace and nuclear disarmament; decolonization in Asia and Africa; racial equality and an end to the racial policies of the colonial and white regimes in Africa, particularly South Africa; aid for development in the newly independent states; and restructuring the UN to give greater voice to Asia and Africa. These were normative issues that were close to India's own experience of imperial oppression, national liberation and economic backwardness. They were also expressive of the aspirations and urges of much of the colonized or newly independent world in Asia and Africa. Symbolizing soft power, they earned India, even if not for too long, a leadership role in the developing world. On the other hand, the US felt that these issues impinged on its interests and those of its allies and affected its crusade against communism. What irked the US and its allies was that on many of these issues India's position, though independently arrived at, paralleled that of the Soviet Union, which for reasons of its own opposed Western imperialism and supported decolonization.

US anger at India began early, even before independence arrived. What is ironic is that in the early years of its independence, despite its formal stand of nonalignment and its disillusionment with US and British policies that it thought were unfair and injurious to its national interests, particularly on Kashmir, India was virtually aligned with the Western bloc.[40] Its economic and military ties, amounting to near-dependency, were with the West; they were nonexistent with the Soviet Union. Fearful of the intentions of the communist bloc, with which its diplomatic ties at the time were minimal, India had further chosen to become a member of the Commonwealth of Nations. That only enhanced the Soviet distrust of India, with the Soviet Union convinced that India's independence was fake and that it still remained a British colony. The Soviets called Nehru a "lackey" of British imperialism, and similarly the Chinese communists labeled him a "running dog" of imperialism. Meanwhile, India determinedly crushed the communist insurgency in various parts of the country, and demonstrated its fundamental political preferences by opting for democracy. Early on, in 1948, Nehru

[40] Gopal, *Nehru*, vol. II, 57.

instructed his office that the US and UK be told that there was little possibility of India joining up with the Soviet Union in either war or peace.[41] Nehru at the time even entertained the thought of joining the US bloc; in a moment of suspension of caution, but still with an element of calculation, he asked Krishna Menon: "Why not align with the United States *somewhat* and build up our economic and military strength?" At the same time, however, his official biographer adds, "he was not prepared to pay the price of subservience to the foreign policy of the United States."[42]

It was with the Korean War, when India took what it thought was an equidistant position between the two blocs – after having initially joined the US and its allies in the UN's condemnation of North Korean aggression – that India's bona fides as an independent international actor began to be established. With considerable diplomatic finesse, India now pushed itself into assuming a mediatory role for itself as between the two blocs. That role, while useful to some extent in extricating the US from an extremely difficult military and political situation in Korea, was deeply resented by the US and its allies. Indeed, the US vetoed any role for India in the subsequent talks at Geneva; as one Canadian diplomat expressed it, "the Americans were at their most bloody-minded vis-a-vis the Indians in this period."[43] Still, in the end India forced itself again into an uninvited mediatory role there. India's rationale for inserting itself in this fashion in negotiations on world issues was that the rigidity between the two blocs threatened peace, while it had access to both. In due course, the offering of a mediatory role became the trademark of Indian diplomacy, and India earned considerable international applause for its dedication and efforts to advance peace and peaceful coexistence.

It seems, however, that India went further. It attempted to mobilize support, on the basis not of hard power but of the soft power of the appeal of its ideas, from the increasing number of newly independent states across the developing world for positions that favored their interests on issues that were of concern to them. This activity was unacceptable to the US, as it reduced its area of potential influence, and was a source of consternation and resentment to the superpower. However, the US suspected India to be engaged in a more sinister enterprise than just pushing for peace, conciliation, and the legitimate economic and political interests of the developing countries. The US believed India to be audaciously engineering a gigantic realignment of political forces in

[41] *ibid.*, 45.
[42] *ibid.*, 59.
[43] Escott Reid, cited in Gopal, *Nehru*, vol. II, 172.

the world to the disadvantage of the US as the hegemon, a notion that would seem to fit in with Subrahmanyam's point that Nehru was following a strategy of balance of power. Such an attempt at balancing would not be outside the realm of possibility in view of Nehru's general belief that the contest between communism and containment of communism was a mask for the real issue, which was, in the words of his official biographer, "a struggle for mastery between the two powers."[44] A critical role in convincing the US about this alleged endeavor was played by the US Ambassador to India, Loy W. Henderson, soon after India's independence.

In a long telegram in 1951, Henderson told Washington of a grand design or master plan that he saw at work in Nehru's foreign policies, under which Nehru sought to detach China from the Soviet bloc and Japan from the US alliance.[45] The underlying immediate goal of Nehru in this plan was taken to be the formation of a common front with these two Asian giants under the slogan of "Asian nationalism" in his bid for "attainment [of] united Asia in which he can play important role." On Washington's instructions to remind Nehru of "possible consequences to India if GOI fol[low]s present course in fo[reig]n relations," Henderson expounded his views to Nehru on India attempting to draw Japan away from the US, which would mean "it would be fallacious for either US or India [to] believe our differences were merely superficial." Nehru tried to disabuse Henderson of any such notion, rejecting the whole line of thought as "erroneous."[46] He, however, apparently failed to dissuade Henderson from his perception of India's alleged strategic design, for although the view on the framework of Nehru's foreign policy may initially have been Henderson's personal one, it came to be more generally accepted in the US government. After the transfer of power to the Republican administration, a secret National Security Council study not only referred to Nehru's "dreams of making India a great power" and "dreams of South Asia under his leadership, rising to become a great 'third force' in the world," but also asserted: "India would like to separate Japan from its close association with the United States."[47] What is clear here is that, whether warranted or not, Washington began to see India as a serious rival for influence in the developing world and a threat to the integrity of its alliance system.

[44] Gopal, *Nehru*, vol. II, 274.
[45] *FRUS 1951*, vol. VI, 2179–81.
[46] *ibid.*, 2182–5.
[47] *FRUS 1952–1954*, vol. XI, 1096 117.

The legacy of the nationalist movement: Even though it was lacking in material capabilities, India had taken on a globally activist role. As with the foreign policy of independence, it would seem that behind that role lay patterns of thought and behavior established during the nationalist movement; here, too, there was continuity with the freedom struggle. Since the 1920s, the Congress had taken a very active interest in global affairs. It would have been only too human for Nehru and his close associates to have, apart from the requirement of consistency with past principle, carried the intellectual and political baggage of the nationalist movement into independent India.

During the years of the nationalist struggle, which was a powerful formative influence in the intellectual and political life of its leaders and participants, the Congress adopted certain important political positions on world issues. First, there was active sympathy and support for nationalist struggles against imperialism across Asia and Africa. Second, because of its own experience with racism, the Congress expressed vehement opposition to fascist and Nazi regimes. Indeed, Prasad notes the linkage between these wider sympathies and India's desire for a voice in world affairs:

Deriving sustenance from an idealistic concern with the welfare of humanity at large, this yearning became so strong that, between 1936 and 1939, it sometimes led to a tendency to give more importance to contributing to the solution of major world problems than to furthering India's interests.[48]

Third, while not naive about political suppression in the Soviet Union, the Congress was very impressed with the Soviet achievement of turning a backward country into a major power. At the same time, there was deep disappointment that the US had chosen, in order to placate Winston Churchill on the permanency of the British Empire, to remain largely silent during World War II on India's struggle for freedom; indeed, the Congress saw the US as being in collusion with British imperialism, notwithstanding brave declarations about freedom, such as the Atlantic Charter.[49]

In considerable measure, Nehru's opposition to power politics and alliance formation derived from his hostility to imperialism and Nazism, both of which he saw as inherent in power politics. While discussing the geopolitical "heartland" and "rimland" theories of Mackinder and Spykman, he wrote in 1944:

[48] Prasad, *The Origins of Indian Foreign Policy*, ch. 4.
[49] *ibid.*, 241–2.

All this looks very clever and realistic and yet is supremely foolish, for it is based on the old policy of expansion and empire and the balance of power, which inevitably leads to conflict and war. Since the world happens to be round, every country is encircled by others. To avoid such encirclement by the methods of power politics, there must be alliances and counter-alliances, expansion, and conquest. But, however huge a country's domination or sphere of influence becomes, there is always the danger of encirclement. ... The only way to get rid of this danger is by world conquest or by the elimination of every possible rival.[50]

Nehru's own position was that: "There really seems no alternative between world conquest and world association; there is no choice of a middle course." In common with modern-day institutionalists, he thought rationality itself ought to lead the world to cooperate: "Self-interest itself should drive every nation to this wider cooperation in order to escape disaster in the future and build its own free life on the basis of others' freedom."[51]

It is clear that the foreign-policy preferences of the Congress leadership sprang out of its experience with imperialism, and they had been formed over a considerable period of time. They were sincerely held and could not be easily or quickly given up, even if it were desirable or necessary, on assuming power after independence. India undoubtedly lacked capabilities, but the Congress leadership had been socialized into not being deterred from taking what it believed to be the morally correct positions against stronger political forces. Moreover, the leadership was apparently influenced by what it believed to have been a successful experiment in overthrowing British imperialism, even though the Congress had lacked material capabilities and means of violence. Interstate relations were, of course, different, but in an age of fundamental transformation, with the massive realignment of power in the international system in the wake of World War II and the nationalist upsurge in the colonial world, it was easy to be convinced of the potency of ideas alone in moving masses and elites.

The pursuit of an activist global role, however, had some serious consequences insofar as the excessive fascination for it led to the neglect of other important tasks, including national security. Political leaders have only a finite amount of time and energy for the various tasks confronting a state. To the extent that the leadership focused excessively on pursuing an activist global role, there was less time and energy available for other tasks. Subrahmanyam has pointed out that national security was important to Nehru, and that he had correctly evolved and followed

---

[50] Nehru, *The Discovery of India*, 540.
[51] *ibid.*, 540.

policies of realism and balance of power, but that these policies were not implemented by the bureaucracy properly or in timely fashion in the area of national defense. This does not seem, however, to be an adequate explanation, for it is precisely the function of the top leadership to see that policies are fully executed; it is not sufficient to have them only be formulated if they are not implemented. An inordinate preoccupation with global activism could not have left adequate scope for attention to questions of implementation of policy in respect of national security and other issues. In such manner, global activism inherently carried the potential for policy distortions that were likely to be costly.

Moralism and antipower themes

It is not only that India asserted a foreign policy of independence and pursued an activist global role, but also that it heavily invested its foreign policy with a moral and idealistic dimension that stood in direct opposition to the reigning values of the major Western powers. India denounced the power politics and balance-of-power policies as likely to lead to war; instead, it took its stand in favor of international cooperation. As against the military preparations for war, it emphasized negotiations. Instead of containment and overthrow of communism, it advocated peaceful coexistence; and instead of bargaining from strength, it pleaded for a policy of conciliation. In part, the visceral opposition to power politics and balance-of-power policies stemmed from India's experience with Britain using Indian troops and resources for its wars and expeditions in the interests of the empire. But doctrinally the origin of the various moralistic and idealistic planks in India's foreign policy lay in Gandhi's leadership of the nationalist movement. To a movement that was in danger of becoming moribund, Gandhi brought vitality and strength, activism and action-orientation, through a peculiar weapon of the weak – a willingness to bear self-suffering while mounting active resistance against oppression through disciplined nonviolence and noncooperation in the face of violence used by the oppressors. The abhorrence for the use of means of violence in this strategy of passive resistance was embedded in a wider complex of ethical ideas, which included other injunctions, such as ends do not justify the means, to be fearless in the face of challenges, and to never harbor hatred for one's enemies.

Nehru and some of his colleagues initially looked upon passive resistance as only a useful tool against British imperialism, but gradually they internalized its value system. However, it is no simple matter to put passive resistance into practice by statesmen in office, for such idealism runs counter to the pervasive realpolitik characteristic of interstate relations and provides no defense against external threats to security. Nehru himself gave frank expression to the inherent dilemma in a speech before the Constituent Assembly in March 1949:

we were bred in a high tradition under Mahatma Gandhi. That tradition is an ethical tradition, a moral tradition and at the same time it is an application of those ethical and moral doctrines to practical politics. ... And with that idealism and ethical background we now face practical problems and it becomes an exceedingly difficult thing to apply that particular doctrine to the solution of these problems. ... So we have had these conflicts in our minds and these conflicts continue and perhaps there is no final solution of these conflicts except to try continually to bridge the gulf between the idealism and the practice which is forced upon us by circumstances.[52]

A comprehensive view of Nehru's foreign policy would indicate that he subscribed simultaneously to: the tenets of realism insofar as he sought to protect and foster India's national interests, including defense, foreign-policy autonomy and the acquisition of a major-power role; and a certain idealism imbibed from the doctrine of passive resistance, which found expression in active support for a policy of peace and peaceful coexistence. Nehru was quite clear as to what his role as foreign minister was; he explained:

Whatever policy you may lay down, the art of conducting the foreign affairs of a country lies in finding out what is most advantageous to the country. We may talk about international goodwill and mean what we say. We may talk about peace and freedom and earnestly mean what we say. But in the ultimate analysis, a government functions for the good of the country it governs and no government dare do anything which in the short or long run is manifestly to the disadvantage of that country.

Therefore, whether a country is imperialistic or socialist or communist, its Foreign Minister thinks primarily of that country.[53]

Nehru's instructions to India's diplomats were to look at issues first from the viewpoint of India's interests and only then on their merits.

On the other hand, Nehru was not defensive about his idealism, claiming that today's idealism is tomorrow's realism.[54] More practically, he resolved the tension between the two by pointing to two different ways of looking at foreign policy. One narrow way was where a country pursues its interests without paying heed to its impact on others or the

---

[52] Nehru, *Independence and After*, 233–4.
[53] *ibid.*, 204–5.
[54] Nehru, *India's Foreign Policy*, 51.

consequences for the long term. A second broader view, however, considers that:

the interest of peace is more important, because if war comes everyone suffers, so that in the long-distance view, self-interest may itself demand a policy of cooperation with other nations, goodwill for other nations, as indeed it does demand.

Consequently, Nehru, like the modern-day institutionalists, had decided "to look after India's interests in the context of world cooperation and world peace."[55] Still, it is doubtful whether Nehru ever effectively integrated the two elements of realism and idealism. Their continuous, if uneasy, balancing and bridging was bound to be problematic in the face of the centrality of power politics in interstate relations. At the same time, the element of idealism was no mere mask for realism. The classic case of the impact of idealism on India's foreign policy was that of Goa. Nehru tolerated an oppressive Portuguese colonialism on Indian soil for fourteen years before taking military action to oust it, for fear that he would be accused of hypocrisy in foreign policy.

More generally, it would seem that the advocacy of the themes of peace and peaceful coexistence, and their institutionalization in the nonaligned movement, had the deleterious effect of handcuffing India from a straightforward pursuit of its national interests. The requirements of national security in some sense stood in tension with India's moral posture at the global level. It would not be surprising at all if constant evocation of peace and morality in the affairs of the state would not, in line with the theory of cognitive dissonance, affect state behavior just as much in the realm of national security as in the case of decolonization in Goa. After the security debacle in 1962, Nehru acknowledged, more in regret, that "our whole mentality has been governed by an approach of peace," and that, "We had been conditioned for 30 years by Mahatma Gandhi and his gospel of peace which had left a powerful imprint."[56] This conditioning, plus the priority to economic planning, led to devaluing defense preparedness: "we were anxious to save money in defense. ... we were very stingy about defense spending. ... we possibly agreed to about one-tenth of what they [the army generals] had asked for, and nine-tenths we did not agree to."[57]

[55] Nehru, *Independence and After*, 205.
[56] Jawaharlal Nehru, *Jawaharlal Nehru's Speeches: Volume IV: September 1957–April 1963* (New Delhi: Publications Division, 1964), 235, 403.
[57] Nehru, *Speeches*, vol. V, 188, 190.

Perpetually "carrying the banner of peace everywhere"[58] affected national security in another way also. Even if the US was disenchanted with India's global activism, Nehru's endeavors on behalf of peace and conciliation between the two blocs earned him a lot of praise around the world; even the Saudi king called him the prince of peace. The kind of adulation that Nehru received both at home and abroad for his efforts can be heady stuff for any leader. Note, for example, Nehru's observation in 1953 in a letter to the chief ministers:

I have been watching, with restrained pride and pleasure as well as an ever-growing sense of responsibility and humility, the growth of India's prestige in the world. ... That praise will remain locked in my mind and heart and will give me strength for greater effort in the cause of the country we hold dear.[59]

It is understandable if in some circumstances such an individual were not too eager to pursue policies that would disturb or damage the image based on idealism. It is not surprising that at crucial moments in India's relations with China, Nehru was reluctant to bring up the issue of the exact definition of the boundary between the two countries, for fear that it may undermine the atmosphere of friendship between them. Later, when relations turned sour between the two countries on the border question, Nehru kept the Indian people in the dark for a considerable period of time, apparently on the consideration that it would arouse the masses, besides revealing him as naive.

The shift in foreign policy, 1954–1964

History is a seamless web, and therefore any watertight periodization is likely to be limiting. It would be difficult to maintain that one day in 1954, India's foreign policy underwent a sudden shift in which idealism was completely overpowered by realism. Indeed, some of what are regarded as important accomplishments for the idealistic aspect of Indian foreign policy – such as Bandung in 1955, Suez in 1956, and the formal founding of the nonaligned movement in 1961 by the troika of Nehru, Nasser and Tito – were still in the future. But it is plausible to suggest that the balance between the two elements began to shift in favor of realism starting in 1954, with India forced to accord greater attention to the problems of national security in response to pressures from the international system as well as the regional subsystem.

[58] *ibid.*, 198–9.
[59] Gopal, *Nehru*, vol. II, 166.

In a sense, India could afford to be relaxed earlier about national security because it did not see any immediate threat on the horizon which it could not cope with by itself.[60] Moreover, regardless of its aspirations on the international scene – for the moment, expressed in idealistic terms – India was basically a status quo or satisfied power on the subcontinent, and therefore it did not need to expand its military capabilities. However, beginning with 1954, national security moved to the center of India's concerns, and the centrality of the issue progressively increased as the decade advanced. As a consequence, the reign of idealism was short-lived in India's foreign policy. It is not the case here that India earlier did not pay attention at all to defense and acquisition of military capabilities, but rather that this was overshadowed by the very heavy focus on diffuse pacifist and antipower goals at the global level. Nor is it the case that suddenly in 1954 India went in for massive rearmament, but rather that it was compelled to attend to questions of national security with greater seriousness. It speaks volumes about the attention, or rather the lack of it, to defense that India's military expenditures were only about 2 per cent of GNP during the 1950s, implying virtually unilateral disarmament.

However, the pacifist and antipower themes were never completely exorcised over the following decade, because in some sense the legitimacy of India's foreign policy rested on their continued evocation, while inadequate capabilities left no other recourse. For the true realist observer, Indian foreign policy has always remained a victim of a certain naivete and tender-mindedness, even as the pacifist themes and the associated nonaligned movement became an albatross for India in pursuing its national interests. As time went on, the contrast between the idealism, more fully present in the earlier period, and the more security-oriented policies of subsequent years became increasingly striking. Only with the end of the Cold War, which finished the Soviet Union as a superpower and also as a result the nonaligned movement, could India be liberated, if then, from the constraints of its idealistic past, and to base more fully and openly its foreign policy on its security concerns. However, the trend in this direction was inaugurated in 1954 by the entry of major powers into the security affairs of the subcontinent, and was further accentuated by experience with war in 1962 and, after Nehru, in 1965 and 1971.

---

[60] *ibid.*, 44. In 1956, Nehru stated: "So far as the external danger to India is concerned, the only possible danger is from Pakistan. There is no other danger – not even the remotest danger." His biographer thought that this assessment showed "a grave deficiency of judgement." *ibid.*, 302.

The revenge of realism I: US military aid to Pakistan

The US decision in February 1954 to launch a program of massive military aid to Pakistan for the modernization and expansion of its armed forces was a momentous development for the international politics of the subcontinent. It constituted the first open intervention in the postwar period by a superpower in the affairs of the subcontinent, which had until then been outside the central conflict between the two blocs. A considerable degree of controversy exists about the issue. US spokesmen and much US scholarship take the military aid to have been aimed at the containment of the Soviet Union, and treat any unfortunate consequences for India in terms of the threat to its security from Pakistan as only an unintended result.[61] However, to view it as containment aimed at India as the regional power follows as a logical conclusion from the theoretical argument of the realist scholar George Liska,[62] especially as India was a "rebellious" middle power that refused to be satellized. But the issue cannot be settled by reference to theory alone. Sufficient and compelling evidence has been provided elsewhere in support of the proposition that India itself was the specific target of regional containment by the US.[63] It should suffice here to note that Vice-President Richard Nixon, who played a key role in the decision, argued for military aid to Pakistan "as a counterforce to the confirmed neutralism of Jawaharlal Nehru's India."[64] Nixon regarded India and the US as rivals for influence in Asia and, demanding a firmer course toward India, urged that "an early practical step in that direction would be to strengthen the friendlier nations in this orbit, beginning with Pakistan."[65]

However, this preference for strengthening Pakistan in a balance-of-power move against India was not something new to the Eisenhower

---

[61] See, for example, Dennis Kux, *India and the United States: Estranged Democracies 1941–1991* (Washington, DC: National Defense University Press, 1992) xiii, 109–15, 218 (note 1); Robert J. McMahon, *The Cold War on the Periphery: The United States, India, and Pakistan* (New York: Columbia University Press, 1994), 177; and Richard Sisson and Leo E. Rose, *War and Secession: Pakistan, India, and the Creation of Bangladesh* (Berkeley: University of California Press, 1990), 47–8.

[62] See George Liska, "The Third World: Regional Systems and Global Order," in Robert E. Osgood *et al.*, *Retreat from Empire* (Baltimore, MD: Johns Hopkins University Press, 1973), 326.

[63] See Baldev Raj Nayar, *American Geopolitics and India* (New Delhi: Manohar, 1976); and Baldev Raj Nayar, *Superpower Dominance and Military Aid: A Study of Military Aid to Pakistan* (New Delhi: Manohar, 1991).

[64] Ralph de Toledano, *Nixon* (New York: Henry Holt, 1956), 164.

[65] *New York Times*, December 9 and 10, 1953. See also Escott Reid, *Envoy to Nehru* (Delhi: Oxford University Press, 1981), 102.

administration, or more specifically Dulles and Nixon, but rather was of long standing. Early on, Nehru in 1950 was aware of the US intent to strengthen Pakistan as a rival to India; in a letter to his sister, he stated:

It does appear that there is a concerted attempt to build up Pakistan and build down, if I may say so, India. It surprises me how immature in their political thinking the Americans are! They do not even learn from their own or other people's mistakes; more especially in their dealings with Asia, they show a lack of understanding which is surprising.[66]

Nehru believed that the continuous encouragement of Pakistan by the US and UK had made Pakistan intransigent and occasionally carried the two countries on the subcontinent to the brink of war.

Earlier, it has been seen how the territorial consolidation of India under Nehru had provoked the US in 1950 to think precisely along the lines of using Pakistan to balance off India: "a strong Muslim bloc under the leadership of Pakistan, and friendly to the US, might afford a desirable balance of power in South Asia."[67] Instead of viewing the consolidation of a state in the developing world positively, the US saw in it the threat of a new Japan and, quite early in India's career as an independent state, some in the US began thinking of containing it even though this was not policy yet. This pattern of thinking was indicated by a memorandum in September 1949 from the Deputy Assistant Secretary of State Raymond A. Hare to Ambassador-at-Large Phillip C. Jessup:

India has emerged from World War II as the strongest power in Asia. Its position of dominance will probably increase as its power potential is developed. We have *no great assurance that India in the future will ally itself with us* and we have some reason to believe that it might not. Pakistan, if given reasonable encouragement, might prove the more reliable friend. In certain circumstances, therefore, *a strong Muslim bloc under Pakistan leadership could provide a very desirable balance of power in Asia.* Until we know more about how the future alignment of power is to be shaped, therefore, we should take no action which would indicate that we do not favor Pakistan's endeavor to form a Muslim bloc.[68]

It is noteworthy that, shortly after the decision to provide military aid to

---

[66] Gopal, *Nehru*, vol. II, 63.
[67] *FRUS 1950*, vol. V, 1499.
[68] Jain (ed.), *US–South Asian Relations*, 23. Seemingly, Nehru was in agreement; as he put it in 1951: "Pakistan was easy to keep within their sphere of influence in regard to wider policies, while India was an uncertain and possibly not reliable quality." Cited in Kux, *India and the United States*, 89.

Pakistan, the US Ambassador to India, George Allen, interpreted the decision not as countering communism but as defeating Nehru:

This decision has been *serious defeat for Nehru*. I hope with time *it will undermine his entire concept of neutralism in this region*. If this develops *it will be a major victory for US policy*.[69]

Vice-President Nixon had earlier voiced similar sentiments when he spoke at the National Security Council on December 16, 1953. He argued that it would be a "fatal mistake to back down on the proposed aid package solely because of Nehru's objections; such a retreat would risk losing most of the Asian-Arab countries to the neutralist bloc."[70] Of equal importance is the fact that the weapons-mix provided to Pakistan by the US was, as Ambassador Chester Bowles pointed out, meant for use against India in the plains of the subcontinent rather than against the USSR or China in the mountainous areas.[71] Senator Fulbright's conclusion that the military aid to Pakistan was aimed against Nehru and "designed to force his hand"[72] converged with Nehru's own perception that the US decision-makers "imagine that an alliance between Pakistan and the US would bring such overwhelming pressure on India as to compel her to change her policy of non-alignment," or "that they have completely outflanked India's so-called neutralism and will thus bring India to her knees."[73] Nehru essentially saw the US as diplomatically coercing India by promoting its encirclement through a ring of alliances.[74]

The US decision on military aid to Pakistan, by posing a direct threat to India's security, brought questions of defense preparedness to the fore for India. However, eager not to have defense expenditures affect India's investment plans for economic development, Nehru attempted for the moment to ease the pressure by diplomacy rather than by acquisition of weaponry or by military alignment. He moved toward closer diplomatic relations with the Soviet Union and China and inaugurated a euphoric period of friendship with them. In other words, Nehru attempted to create a *balance of power*, but through political rather than

[69] *FRUS 1952–54*, vol. XI, 1350–2; emphasis added.
[70] Quoted in MacMahon, *The Cold War on the Periphery*, 170.
[71] Chester Bowles, *Promises to Keep: My Years in Public Life 1941–1969* (New York: Harper & Row, 1971), 478.
[72] Selig S. Harrison, "India, Pakistan and the US–II," *New Republic*, 141 (August 24, 1959), 21.
[73] Kuldip Nayar, *India after Nehru* (Delhi: Vikas, 1975), 52; Gopal, *Nehru*, vol. II, 185.
[74] Gopal, *Nehru*, vol. II, 254.

military means. There followed considerable economic aid from the Soviet Union for India's ambitious plans to build heavy industry, including steel plants. At the same time, by its reluctance to align with the Soviet bloc, India signaled to the US that it was still available for competitive bidding.[75] It was this policy of friendship with the Soviet bloc without aligning with it that brought large amounts of economic aid from the US, including substantial quantities of PL-480 foodgrains, in order to prevent India from an even closer embrace with the Soviet bloc. However, as Pakistan re-equipped, modernized and expanded its armed forces with technologically sophisticated weaponry from the US, there was increasing anxiety in India about security. In this manner, the US as the global hegemonic power became the instrument for driving home the lessons of realpolitik to India. Meanwhile, in 1958, the military took over power in Pakistan through a coup d'état. That made no difference, however, to the military aid program of the US, which indeed strengthened the relationship with Pakistan in 1959 through a new agreement. It is ironic, then, that realpolitik held the US as the world's most powerful democracy and Pakistan as a military dictatorship together as military allies, while it drove India as the world's largest democracy and the Soviet Union as the leader of the communist bloc closer together.

The revenge of realism II: The India–China War

The final blow to India's global role and its pacifist thrust was delivered by the India–China War of 1962, in which it suffered a severe defeat. The war revolved around the issue of clashing claims on borders, with India maintaining that the borders were defined by treaty, custom and geography, while China argued that they were a colonial inheritance and therefore unacceptable. Initially, in the euphoria over Asian solidarity, the two sides had been reluctant to bring up the issue. However, the revolt in Tibet and the fleeing of the Dalai Lama to India put the relations on a reverse course. Meanwhile, the Chinese had occupied large parts of what the Indians regarded as their territory, and the Indians vowed to oust them. Hurt nationalist pride in the context of a democratic system prevented India from abjuring rigidity in its position. More fundamentally, India had behaved irresponsibly as a state by spending a mere 2 per cent of GNP on defense. India may have done this on rational grounds so as not to affect long-term economic development, but the price paid was enormous. India acted irresponsibly, too, first by neglecting its borders and then by not accepting the

[75] Pran Chopra, *India's Second Liberation* (New Delhi: Vikas, 1973), 9.

consequences of its neglect. When India woke up to its monumental error, it was too late. The antimilitary attitudes of Nehru and his defense minister, Krishna Menon, further compounded the deficiencies in India's military preparedness and higher direction of war.

The issue of the military reverses at the hands of China went beyond military preparedness to India's conceptual approach to international affairs. Stunned by the reverses, Nehru admitted that "we were getting out of touch with reality in the modern world and were living in an artificial atmosphere of our own creation. We have been shocked out of it, all of us."[76] He now poignantly acknowledged what must have been an enormously painful lesson:

this world is cruel. We had thought in terms of carrying the banner of peace everywhere, and we were betrayed. China has betrayed us; the world has betrayed us. Our efforts to follow the path of peace have been knocked on the head. We are forced to prepare for a defensive war, much against our will.[77]

The war crushed the reputation of Nehru as well as that of India and its army, for it dramatically revealed how a country with such high ambition was not able even to protect its own borders.

The war with China in 1962 unhinged India. Some keen observers averred that India's foreign policy now lay in ruins. There were three issues that India faced: coping with the immediate war situation; the fate of its posture of nonalignment; and the acquisition of military capabilities for the longer term. In the face of the crushing advance of the Chinese forces, India, in what was a humiliating compulsion, appealed to all to provide it military help. It met with enormous sympathy; the US and other Western powers rushed in shipments of immediately needed arms, and the US promised air cover for India's cities. The Soviets showed understanding, but were unable to provide any immediate concrete help because they were preoccupied with the Cuban Missile Crisis, and also because of the fear that supporting India would further fracture the Soviet bloc. Eventually, after inflicting severe blows to the Indian armed forces and having taught India a lesson for antagonizing China,[78] the Chinese forces declared a unilateral cease-fire and withdrew to what they maintained were their original positions. In the face of the contrast in the responses of the two blocs, many Indian leaders urged Nehru to jettison nonalignment. Despite the initial panic, however, Nehru refused to take the plunge, for in his view such a step would be detrimental to India's national interests in the long run.

[76] Gopal, *Nehru*, vol. III, 223.
[77] Nehru, *Speeches*, vol. V, 198–9.
[78] Gopal, *Nehru*, vol. III, 230.

The problem of acquiring military weapons proved at first problematic. In view of the initial US response to the crisis, India expected the US to help with arms. As the immediate crisis passed, however, the US adopted a different stance and, in the words of an inside participant in the State Department of the time, "seized upon India's acute need for US assistance as a lever to force the Indians to make concessions to the Pakistanis in regard to Kashmir, which no democratic Indian Government could make and survive." Moreover, Washington procrastinated and would not come to a decision, since key officials were "strongly opposed to a five-year program to help modernize the Indian armed forces, largely on the grounds that it would disrupt our relations with Pakistan."[79] What was of crucial concern to India was the US insistence that India make a prior commitment to join it in opposing communism globally.[80] This was unacceptable to India, since it would mean opposition to the Soviet Union, not just China, and more generally it would have perhaps made India into a US satellite. The hardline US position was based on the assumption that India was helpless and "had no place to go but to the United States."[81] At that point, India found the Soviet Union eager to help; there thus started a long-term arms-acquisition relationship with the Soviet Union which continued unbroken until the collapse of the USSR in 1991.

In summary, the US arms-supply relationship with Pakistan and the India–China War together constituted a turning point in India's foreign policy. India was shaken out of its idealism to come to terms with the threats to its immediate national security. The two events taught powerful lessons in realism to the Indians, principally the decisive importance of maintaining a balance between goals and capabilities. While India continued to pay homage to nonalignment, it was forced to modify its foreign policy in important ways in the direction of realism. First, by the sheer salience and urgency of the new priority to national security, India was compelled to move away, though not altogether entirely, from its earlier global activism and its focus on pacifism and mediatory roles. Its own neighborhood and the region, rather than global politics, emerged more important. Second, India had perforce to build advanced military capabilities and this drew India closer to the Soviet Union, for that was the only place the means for such capabilities were available on reasonable terms. While formally India remained nonaligned, strategically it had tilted toward the Soviet Union. The international system no longer

---

[79] Bowles, *Promises to Keep*, 439.

[80] William J. Barnds, *India, Pakistan, and the Great Powers* (New York: Praeger, 1972), 195.

allowed India the luxury to abjure power politics or balance-of-power policies. That notwithstanding, India's fundamental intent was to build capabilities domestically on a self-reliant basis. Though chronologically the building of such capabilities followed the initiation of US military aid to Pakistan, its conceptual foundations were of long standing.

The economic strategy for undergirding independence

In the postwar period, the chief objective of economic development in the less-developed countries has been taken to be mass welfare, but statesmen have always known of the central importance of economic capabilities to national security and national power. In this light, Nehru did not simply envision India as a future major power, but his grand strategy encompassed economic planning precisely for that end. Nehru may have been an idealist, especially in the short term, but he was also a realist, particularly for the long term.

Nehru's awareness of the operation of realpolitik in the world led him to place heavy emphasis on economic self-reliance. A fundamental aim with him was not just to raise standards of living, but also to assure India's political independence and foreign-policy autonomy. He recognized that realpolitik matters in economic affairs, which led him to envisage the creation of a rather self-sufficient economy with its own metal-making, capital-goods and strategic industries. It is this vision which forms the centerpiece of the Second Five Year Plan (1956–1961), initiated in the mid-1950s. Formally, the Second Plan was based on the premise that India's rapid industrialization required India to take the route of building local heavy industry in order to remove the constraint against long-term growth represented by the absence of capital goods. Important economists argued that India needed to build its own metal-making and capital-goods industries because of "export pessimism." But, in reality, the goal was "economic independence" and, beyond that, of political independence based on local wherewithal for defense. Abundant evidence has been provided elsewhere for the proposition that considerations of realpolitik bore heavily with India's planners in launching the economic strategy for autarkic industrialization through building local heavy industry.[82]

Even though public attention was mostly focused on the improvement of living standards as the goal of economic planning, the motivation of building national power through heavy industry was no state

---

[81] Bowles, *Promises to Keep*, 440.
[82] See Baldev Raj Nayar, *The Modernization Imperative and Indian Planning* (New Delhi: Vikas, 1972), ch. 3.

secret, even though ignored by media and scholarship. Nehru repeatedly emphasized from countless platforms, varying from parliament to business associations, that heavy industry was key to national power and defense. He underlined that heavy industry was essential for the country's independence, not simply in economic terms but also in defense:

> But the Five Year Plan is the defense plan of the country. What else is it? Because, defense does not consist in people going about marching up and down the road with guns and other weapons. Defense consists today in a country being industrially prepared for producing the goods and equipment of defense.[83]

His statement before a business association in 1960 provides a flavor of his view on the centrality of heavy industry for independence:

> In fact the only ultimate protection of our country is to advance on the economic and industrial front and make our country strong in that respect. War today is not merely a question of some gallant soldiers behaving gallantly. It is essentially a question of the industrial might of a nation, of the productive apparatus of a nation. Therefore, even from that restricted point of view of war – which I hope we shall never have to face anywhere – nevertheless even from that point of view, it is the industrial strength of a nation that counts, as well as of course the prosperity of the people.[84]

What is noteworthy is that, as with his views on the international system and foreign policy, Nehru had arrived at his understanding of the bearing of realpolitik on economic strategy long before he became prime minister.[85] He felt that without industrialization a country could not maintain its independence, and that industrialization required building local heavy industry, otherwise the country would be dependent on the outside world and therefore vulnerable. On this point of equipping India with an independent industrial base, there was largely agreement among Indian nationalists except the Gandhians. Where they differed was over the agency that would own and manage the heavy industries. Nehru and his fellow socialists were able to get their way in making the state assume control of what came to be called the "commanding heights" of the economy.

---

[83] Nehru, *Speeches,* vol. III, 39–40.

[84] Federation of Indian Chambers of Commerce and Industry, *Proceedings of the Thirty-third Annual Session Held in New Delhi on the 27, 28, and 29 March 1960* (New Delhi: 1960), 15.

[85] Dorothy Norman (ed.), *Nehru: The First Sixty Years,* 2 vols. (New York: The John Day Company, 1965), vol. I, 697, vol. II, 179; Nehru, *The Discovery of India,* 407–8.

Many today would consider Nehru's choice of the public sector to have been in serious error, because of the enormous waste and inefficiency that it entailed, while his supporters continue to insist on the historical necessity of the interventionist state in view of what they assume to be the contemporaneous incapacity of the Indian capitalist class. Regardless, the heavy-industry strategy itself was rooted in Nehru's larger view of the working of the international system, which states could not change, yet had to function within. To examine the strategy in economic terms alone is therefore to take a limited view of the world.

Science and technology for strategic autonomy

The choice of technological strategy by a nation is intimately linked to the larger conception that a nation has of itself and its role in the world. The thrust for national independence which is evident in Nehru's foreign policy and economic strategy also informed his science-and-technology (SAT) policy. Nehru's SAT model was extraordinarily ambitious, encompassing several key components. First, there was the broad-front licensing strategy involving a massive import of foreign technology through a wide-ranging net of foreign collaborations in order to save time in industrialization. A second component related to the rapid creation of specific mission-oriented institutions for research and development in selected areas where generation of local technology was considered essential. This component rested on the assumption that there were certain areas of high or sensitive technology, such as nuclear energy and defense equipment, where other countries would not allow exports or would do so under conditions which would compromise India's sovereignty. Accordingly, India must be in a position to conduct its own research and development in these areas. A third component consisted of creating a broad-based general-purpose structure of research and development through a wide network of high-quality science laboratories in the public sector. Finally, in order to staff the various research institutions, the fourth component required a drastic increase in SAT manpower through rapidly expanding and upgrading SAT education.

As in the case of economic strategy, a high degree of earnestness is evident in Nehru's implementation of the SAT model. To begin with, government expenditures on scientific research witnessed exponential growth under Nehru, expanding about tenfold in real terms; as a share of GNP, they went up from 0.05 per cent to 0.31 per cent. The total stock of trained SAT manpower expanded almost four times from 188,000 in 1950 to 732,000 in 1965. Of special significance is the distribution of research-and-development expenditures among the different agencies as indicative of the priorities of Nehru and his advisors. Of the major research-and-development agencies, the Department of Atomic Energy (DAE) was the chief beneficiary; in 1958–59, its research-and-development expenditures amounted to Rs 77.6 million (constituting 33.8 per cent of the total for all agencies), followed by the Council of Scientific and Industrial Research (16.2 per cent) and the Defense Research and Development Organization (6.5 per cent). By 1965–66, DAE's dominant position had slipped, but it still ranked at the top (29.3 per cent); meanwhile, expenditures on defense research had shot up to 14.2 per cent in 1965–66.[86] Taken together, nuclear and defense research expenditures amounted to roughly half of all of India's research-and-development expenditures at the end of the Nehru era.

The dominant goal in Nehru's SAT model was national independence. Although Nehru accepted the notion that there were no national boundaries to science, he insisted:

Nevertheless, there is a special importance for science in a country which is not to be wholly dependent on other countries, and which has to build some capacity for self-growth, self-reliance. We are developing that, I believe, in this country. We have to develop that spirit in other ways, too, in industry and technology, so that we may not be merely dependent on others.[87]

In Nehru's world-view, the policy linkages followed this sequence of prerequisites: national independence → self-reliant industrialization → heavy industry → science and technology → SAT capacity.

Nehru's concern over technological independence is especially manifest in the field of nuclear technology, where he noticed and experienced the operation of "technological protectionism" in an extreme form. Accordingly, he was insistent that India should not lag behind in this area: "we are determined not to go in for making atomic bombs and the like. But we are equally determined not to be left behind in the advance in the use of this new power."[88] Equally, he was anxious to avoid dependence on others:

There is one aspect of this subject which I should like to mention because it has some political bearing. It is very necessary for us not to depend too much on outside sources. If we depend too much on others for fissionable material, then, inevitably, that dependence may affect us in the sense that other people may try to affect our foreign policy or any other policy through that dependence.[89]

[86] For the tables, see Baldev Raj Nayar, *India's Quest for Technological Independence*, 2 vols. (New Delhi: Lancers, 1983), vol. I, 243–50.

[87] Nehru, *Speeches*, vol. V, 146.

[88] Nehru, *Speeches*, vol. IV, 436; Nehru, *Speeches*, vol. III, 513.

[89] Nehru, *Speeches*, vol. III, 517–18.

Nehru therefore resisted the imposition of restrictive international regimes in the nuclear field.

The strong emphasis by Nehru on nuclear research was matched by strong US suspicion and distrust, and that too from the very beginning. Interestingly, in late 1948 Undersecretary of State Lovett advised the newly appointed US Ambassador to India, Loy W. Henderson: "The aspirations of Indian officials in atomic energy development appear illimitable." While the US was eager to obtain monazite and beryl from India for its own use, it refused to reciprocate in exchange to help India in its nuclear-energy program. In order to advance "disenchantment" in India about nuclear energy, the US wanted that "the Indian officials be given frank appraisal of the difficulties ahead in their ambitions toward atomic energy development."[90] Subsequently, however, both as a consequence of the competition with the Soviet Union and the Atoms for Peace Program, the Eisenhower administration agreed to cooperate with India in setting up the Tarapur nuclear power plant.

Nehru's legacy in nuclear research was ultimately ambiguous. The overwhelming part of the legacy was against nuclear weapons. Nehru abhorred the atom bomb, and worked ceaselessly for nuclear disarmament. On the other hand, he developed the country's nuclear capabilities to the point where, if it wished, it could exercise the nuclear option. At the same time, he was not shy of admitting that, if circumstances warranted it, India may have to develop nuclear weapons. Before independence, on August 25, 1945, shortly after the dropping of the atom bombs over Hiroshima and Nagasaki, Nehru gave a considered view of his position at a press conference in answer to the question, "Would the future government of India have atom bombs in its armoury?":

So long as the world is constituted as it is, every country will have to devise and use the latest scientific methods for its protection. I have no doubt India will develop its scientific researches and hope Indian scientists will use the atomic force for constructive purposes. But if India is threatened, it will inevitably try to defend itself by all means at its disposal. I hope India in common with other countries will prevent it being used.[91]

That answer was in character with his general approach to foreign affairs. After independence, though most of his comments speak to his opposition to nuclear weapons, he did admit before the Constituent Assembly in April 1948 of their possible employment by India:

[90] *FRUS 1948*, vol. I, 758–65.
[91] Letter by A.P. Saxena, "Nehru & the Bomb," *Times of India* (New Delhi), July 8, 1998.

Indeed, I think we must develop it [atomic energy] for peaceful purposes. Of course, if we are compelled as a nation to use it for other purposes, possibly no pious sentiments of any of us will stop the nation from using it that way.[92]

There can be a plausible criticism that Nehru's SAT planning was over-ambitious and costly for a developing country. However, this criticism fails to take into account the genuinely innovative aspect of India's strategy, indeed unique among developing countries, in respect of acquiring capabilities with potential for employment in defense but without collapsing under the weight of the cost of building them. It did so in nuclear research, as later in space research, by amortizing the development of such capabilities largely against their use for civilian purposes. No other state had attempted that strategy until then; most of the established nuclear states devoted their early nuclear efforts to the military realm, and only later used the technology and materials developed in that process for civilian purposes.

Summary and conclusions

Two opposing views exist on Nehru's foreign policy, with one stressing that it followed the tenets of realism, and the other maintaining that it was inspired by idealism. Neither view is correct, if taken in its bald form. Both realism and idealism were manifest in Nehru's foreign policy, but their strength varied over time. Nehru's foreign policy has often been described and identified as simply nonalignment. That, however, provides only a limited view of his policy. A first step toward a more nuanced understanding of his foreign policy requires that it be seen temporally in a more differentiated manner. Two distinct periods are discernible, one from 1946 to 1954, and the other from 1954 to 1964. In the first period, idealism essentially predominated over realism, whereas the reverse was the case in the latter period.

Three distinctive features stand out in the foreign policy of the first period. First and foremost, there is the pursuit of an independent foreign policy, which was rooted in the consciousness of India's potential for a major-power role, once its capabilities became more fully developed. Fundamentally, the potential was linked to India's size in terms both of territory and of population, even though the existing low levels of economic and military capabilities inhibited India from assuming that role for the present. To join any of the two superpower blocs was seen as mortgaging India's eventual emergence as a future major power;

---

[92] Cited in General Khalid Mahmud Arif, *Working with Zia: Pakistan's Power Politics, 1977–1988* (Karachi: Oxford University Press, 1995), 358.

it would have run counter also to the legacy of a genuine national-liberation movement sustained over some six decades. State activity was animated by the concern to protect and to foster this power potential. Besides the foreign policy of independence, there were two additional features: an activist global role, and opposition to power politics, which derived from the legacy of the Indian nationalist movement.

The second period reflects the revenge of realism on the idealism of the first period. It was activated by threats to India's national security as a result of the emergence of a militarily strengthened Pakistan following the massive supply of sophisticated weaponry to that country by the US as part of a policy of regional containment aimed at India; it was further reinforced by the actual border war with China in 1962, which was devastating in its impact on India. The consequent shift to greater realism resulted in a reduction of goals by way of India shedding much of the global activism and paying greater attention to the neighborhood in which its security was implicated. The earlier moralism and pacifism were also downgraded. However, the foreign policy of independence, which encompassed the protection of the potential for a major-power role, continued to be a central feature of India's state behavior. Still, in practice India had to tilt toward one or the other superpower, depending on where the resources it required were available.

Enlightening as the temporal differentiation of the two periods may be, the focus on foreign policy alone, especially when understood merely as nonalignment, is not adequate in fully comprehending the significance of Nehru's broader role in finding a place for India in the world. For that, the concept of grand strategy is more productive of understanding. Nehru's vision of India as aiming for a different location as a major power in the international system of the future led him to a multifaceted effort toward the building of capabilities for a strong India with both hard and soft power. This effort is manifest in the political consolidation of India – not just in territorial integration, but also in installing, legitimizing and fostering a liberal-democratic regime and in adopting an accommodative ethnic strategy – as well as in conceptualizing and implementing an economic policy and a science-and-technology policy (especially in the nuclear arena) which were aimed at undergirding the goal of economic and political independence. This wide-ranging effort, rather than simply the foreign policy of independence, provides a true measure of Nehru's vision and practical endeavor in building India. By the same token, Nehru as a result of his legacy set high standards for his successors, to whom were passed the vision and the uncompleted tasks.

5 Strategy in Hard Times: The Long March for Capabilities, 1964–1990

Jawaharlal Nehru, India's first prime minister, left behind for his successors a daunting legacy of foreign-policy challenges in regard to both ends and means, or goals and capabilities. His enduring legacy was a grand strategy, organized around the fundamental aim of a foreign policy of independence rather than one subordinate to either of the two superpowers, the US or the Soviet Union. Associated with it was also the aspiration, largely implicit but at times explicit, for India to become a member of the major-power system.

Nehru's strategy was surely marked by a certain grandeur, and it was an open question whether his successors would be able to rise to the challenge of its demands. There is, indeed, a line of argument that maintains that, until almost the end of the twentieth century, his successors lacked both the vision of India as a major power, and the will and capacity to build and mobilize the requisite capabilities to achieve it. For example, Ashok Kapur holds that up to 1998 the various governments at the center after Nehru, headed by the Congress Party or former leaders from that party, were befuddled by a Gandhian and Nehruvian morality. Accordingly, they were too weak-kneed politically to make a determined push for a major-power role for India in defiance of the major powers, particularly the US. More specifically, they are said to have lacked the political and moral capacity to make a clear and public definition of India's strategic priorities, or the determination to pursue them. In this view, it was only the end of rule by such leaders, at the hands of a different political elite, with a different ideological commitment, that marked a departure from the previous pattern of relative passivity in favor of a more active pursuit of a major-power role.[1] This argument represents a softer version of a more severe indictment by Brahma Chellaney that states that "naivete in foreign policy has afflicted almost all Indian governments," that "Indian foreign policy has not been organized around a distinct strategic doctrine," that "Indian

[1] Presentation by Ashok Kapur at McGill University, Montreal, December 1999.

diplomacy subsist[s] on dreams," and that "India has distinguished itself by reposing trust in adversaries and then crying foul when they deceive it"; it considers India to be a "lamb" as against the "wolf" of China and the "jackal" of Pakistan, believing that "the 'lamb' status is in keeping with its intrinsic disposition and meek objectives."[2]

These strong views parallel the theoretical arguments of George Perkovich. For him, "India's development of nuclear weapon capability only vaguely responded to an ill-defined security threat," and:

domestic factors, including moral and political norms, have been more significant in determining India's nuclear policy. ... India has been torn between a moral antagonism toward the production of weapons of mass destruction, on one hand, and on the other hand, an ambition to be regarded as a major power in a world where the recognized great powers rely on nuclear weapons for security and prestige.[3]

Again, he states: "domestic factors, including individual personalities, have been at least as important as the external security environment in determining nuclear policy." He underlines that realism has been proven wrong, since according to the theory India "would or should have built a survivable, retaliatory nuclear arsenal *long ago* given its threat environment."[4]

Perkovich, however, does more than emphasize the importance of unit properties in questioning the relevance of the realist model. He makes the Indian pattern of nuclear behavior stand on a different footing from that of all the other nuclear weapons states (NWSs), for whom national security was the paramount consideration in going nuclear. Without dismissing national security altogether as a cause for India's nuclear quest, he seriously downgrades it by repeatedly questioning it on grounds of various acts of omission and commission, such as no prior-threat analysis, no prior strategic doctrine, and no involvement of the military in decision-making, or the drive of the nuclear scientists for glory. He also downplays the concern for national security by drowning it under a multitude of other factors (economic and political constraints, national identity and moral values). Further, he argues that the security threat posed by China since the early 1960s, especially since the 1964 Chinese nuclear tests, did not result in a clear strategy or a dedi-

---

[2] Brahma Chellaney, "Hug, Then Repent," *Hindustan Times,* January 26, 2000. The reference to animals draws on the work of Randall L. Schweller.

[3] George Perkovich, *India's Nuclear Bomb: The Impact on Global Proliferation* (Berkeley: University of California Press, 1999), 6.

[4] *ibid.*, 445, 453, 454.

cated nuclear weapons program on the part of India. This contention is used as a critique of realism. In this welter of considerations, however, it should have been important to distinguish national identity and moral values from economic and political constraints in questioning the claims of realism. For policy that is emergent from taking economic and political constraints into account is based on a strategic calculus, whereas national identity and moral values have to do with ultimate ends.

Kapur, Chellaney and Perkovich have adduced a powerful line of argument. There may well be considerable merit in it. However, in contrast, we take the position that, even though influenced by the high idealism of Mahatma Gandhi and Nehru, the Congress or Congress-background leaders were nevertheless, by and large, no less eager to push for a major-power role and to develop the capabilities appropriate for it. This chapter takes for granted as a point of departure that these leaders, either as active participants in an authentic nationalist movement or as inheritors of the mantle of that movement, shared the aspiration to make India a major power. Even though most successive leaders have shared the aspiration, even if only implicitly, they were nonetheless heavily constrained in any active pursuit of it as a result of India's severe contemporaneous vulnerabilities, both external and internal. Indeed, their stance of ambiguity and reluctance to actively seek a major-power role can be said to have reflected an acute appreciation of the weakness of India's capabilities and the political obstacles that stood in the way of enhancing them. It attests to their innate capacity at maintaining a reasonable balance between goals and capabilities.

The ends-means balance was, in part, dictated by India's democratic state structure and its immense social diversity in the context of economic backwardness. No blitzkrieg strategy for the building up of capabilities could perhaps be mounted without endangering the internal political structure and social fabric; the building of capabilities had necessarily to be gradual and incremental. At the same time, India's leadership had to contend with severe external constraints stemming both from hostile neighbors and from the major powers, with the two often linked through alliances. Still, the leaders persisted steadily, if slowly, in the endeavor to advance economic and military capabilities. Indeed, from a long-run perspective, their effort emerges as a long march to building capabilities and attenuating constraints, as if teleologically led by the aim of transforming India into a major power, but watchful at every turn that a wrong move may prove fatal.

In developing the above position, the present chapter, first, summarily looks at the parlous foreign policy and domestic situation inherited by Nehru's successors, partly as a result of his policies and partly as a consequence of the external environment. It then examines the specific external and domestic challenges faced by Nehru's successors. Since the period covered after the passing away of Nehru is quite long, the treatment here of the performance of Nehru's successors is limited to the years from 1964 to 1990. The year 1990 is a convenient cut-off point since the end of the Cold War at the time marks the creation of a new semi-unipolar world with its own unique challenges – which, no doubt, were already in gestation. The next chapter will deal with the period from 1991 to 2001. The present chapter revolves around four different phases, delineated by the dominant feature characteristic of each phase: (1) 1964 to 1971: avoiding marginalization; (2) 1971 to 1974: recovery of middle-power role; (3) 1975 to 1984: middle-power role under pressure; and (4) 1985 to 1990: pushing economic reform and proceeding to nuclear weaponization, even if reluctantly.

Nehru's foreign and domestic legacy

Nehru had from 1947 to 1964 dominated the Indian political scene as a colossus in respect of both its external relations and its internal development. Despite this domination and his obvious dedication to the noble causes of peace and peaceful coexistence, the truth of the matter is that at Nehru's death India faced multiple crises of enormous severity which, in considerable part, flowed from his policies, regardless of how well-intended their origins may have been. Driven by the keen desire to quickly establish the sovereignty of a long-colonized but newly independent state, to firmly solidify the national identity of a diverse society, to rapidly push the modernization of its underdeveloped economy, and to rally the people behind all these causes, Nehru adopted policies which had as their essential characteristic an enormous imbalance between goals and capabilities. This was true as much of his foreign policy as it was of his internal economic policy, and it led to consequences that could not but terribly constrain his successors.

In the sphere of external relations, the foreign policy of independence and global activism was a challenge to the superpowers, principally the US, and could not really be sustained given India's poor capabilities. It called forth from the US the policy of military aid to Pakistan as a means to the regional containment of India. Thus emboldened, Pakistan became intransigent in its disputes with India, while India had to increase its defense expenditures to meet possible threats to its security from Pakistan. More shattering for India's international stature and domestic economy was the violent conflict with China. The long-term impact of that conflict, and the subsequent regional containment of India by China through military assistance and diplomatic support in a de facto alliance with Pakistan, made India highly dependent on the

Soviet Union for arms. These developments radically deflated India's image in the developing and nonaligned world. More seriously, India's doubling of its defense expenditures in response to the conflict resulted in destabilizing the economy and, therefore, the polity.

In the internal sphere, Nehru's highly ambitious industrialization effort, which was really beyond the country's resources, and the simultaneous neglect of agriculture led to major economic disequilibria and dislocations. The Second Five Year Plan (1956–1961) faced a serious foreign-exchange crisis within two years of its being launched, and had then to be rescued through additional economic aid from the US and its allies. The Third Five Year Plan (1961–1966), which essentially repeated the industry-focused strategy of the Second Plan, was even more dependent on foreign economic aid for its implementation. The contradiction between India's pretensions in regard to a foreign policy of independence and its increasing dependence on foreign aid was starkly apparent. The Third Plan was in trouble soon after its inauguration, but the economic situation was aggravated by the India–China War of 1962. The consequent rapid increase in defense expenditures unhinged the economy. High inflation and extreme shortages of essential commodities followed. The successor leadership had the awesome task of coping with the consequences of dependencies that Nehru had left behind, and it was nearly overwhelmed by it. Perhaps too harshly, but as India's adversary, Pakistan's Foreign Minister Bhutto observed the overall scene at Nehru's demise with keen penetration:

By the time he died, India's foreign policy was in utter confusion. He left his country in an orphaned condition, neither aligned nor non-aligned, with a beggar's bowl in its hands. He witnessed the shambles of his foreign policy from his deathbed. … From its lofty height of idealism, the foreign policy of India was brought down to dust. Contradictions began to manifest themselves at every step, causing India to sink into an abyss of gloom.[5]

Avoiding marginalization, 1964–1971

If one were to commence this period two years prior to Nehru's death, it becomes obvious that the decade from 1962 to 1971 has been the most critical in India's post-independence history from the viewpoint of survival as an independent entity with its territorial integrity intact. It was a period of trial by fire. It saw three wars; indeed, the period is

[5] Zulfikar Ali Bhutto, *The Quest for Peace: Selections from Speeches and Writings, 1963–65* (Karachi: Pakistan Institute of International Affairs, 1966), 73.

bracketed by a war at the beginning and a war at the end, with still another war occurring in between. The war with China in 1962 had extremely destabilizing consequences for the economy and polity. Having been dependent on Nehru as a charismatic leader for more than a decade and a half, the polity had its future thrown into question by his death in 1964. China's nuclear test in October 1964 caused further public dismay about India's security. In this situation of an already weakened and demoralized country, Pakistan seized the opportunity and launched a series of military encounters that culminated in war in 1965. The two wars of 1962 and 1965 together were a profound learning experience in realpolitik for the elite and the nation. They instructed them, though not entirely fully or successfully, to come to terms with functioning in the real world, where force matters in interstate relations, rather than remain in the relatively make-believe world of idealism.

The economically destabilizing consequences of the two wars were then joined by the forces of nature, which inflicted unprecedented droughts in two successive years. With famine staring it in the face, the country was thrown at the mercy of the US for food supplies to stave it off. Dependence on the US for economic and food aid, and dependence on the Soviet Union for military equipment, placed India under tremendous pressure, leading to the fear of being turned into a foreign-policy satellite of both superpowers. Further, the two superpowers agreed to institute another international regime in the nuclear arena which, by barring nuclear tests by any state beyond the five powers that had already tested, raised the prospect of a permanent marginalization of India in international affairs. If successful, the projected regime would have had the consequence of closing the door on India's quest for a major-power role and of reducing it permanently to an object.

Subsequently, as the US, with a new Republican administration under Richard Nixon, sought to restructure the world balance of power, India was threatened with greater marginalization, since the only place envisaged for it in that order was as an object. Further, as Pakistan faced internal disintegration as a consequence of the policies of its garrison state, it sought to shift its internal political problems through a massive expulsion of its population from East Pakistan to India. In the ensuing war, the US and China, which had come together as part of the US design for geopolitical restructuring, supported Pakistan, while India had to seek the backing of the Soviet Union. During the period as a whole, India thus faced a situation that was often acute and desperate. However, during this decade of extreme troubles, two astute leaders, Lal Bahadur Shastri (who died in 1966) and Indira Gandhi, guided India in overcoming the various crises, within the limits of the country's democratic structure and its weak capabilities.

The 1965 war

In a sense, the roots of the 1965 war between Pakistan and India lay in the India–China War of 1962. For one thing, the latter war brought Pakistan and China closer together in their hostility toward India. The increasing cooperation that followed between the two countries led to the belief in Pakistan that China would come to its aid in any conflict with India. The 1962 war, however, had led to another consequence that had a serious impact on Pakistani thinking. It persuaded the Indians to mend their defenses, and they launched on a long-term program of re-equipment and expansion of their armed forces. This program threat-ened the military advantage in technologically superior weaponry that Pakistan had gained through the massive military aid provided by the US since 1954. Pakistan now faced the prospect that, as India's re-equipment program would go into top gear, India would be able to fore-close the military option for Pakistan to seize Kashmir in the future. It was therefore rationally opportune for Pakistan to strike before India's armed forces were strengthened.[6] In part, Pakistan was also misled by the cacophony of India's democracy into believing that, following Nehru's death, the Indian leadership was weak and divided, and that the country was well on its way to disintegration. Pakistan was further emboldened in undertaking the risk by an expectation that the security guarantees against international communism under the 1959 agreement with the US on cooperation would apply also to any conflict with India.[7]

In an attempt to test the Indian political leadership and army, Pakistan launched a minor military operation in the Rann of Kutch, in western India. The Indian army's performance was undistinguished, and the Pakistanis were confirmed in their poor opinion of the oppo-nent, derived in part from their own cultural perceptions[8] and in part from India's recent reverses in the war with China. Not known to them, however, was the fact that India had deliberately chosen not to divert its major forces to the Kutch front in the belief that the real war was likely to come in Kashmir and the Punjab. Meanwhile, as the Indians com-plained about the use of US weaponry against them, despite the earlier US assurances that the armaments were meant only to be used in the

---

[6] See T.V. Paul, *Asymmetric Conflicts: War Initiation by Weaker Powers* (Cambridge: Cambridge University Press, 1995), 115–17.

[7] G.W. Choudhury, *India, Pakistan, Bangladesh, and the Major Powers: Politics of a Divided Subcontinent* (New York: The Free Press, 1975), 113; Dennis Kux, *The United States and Pakistan, 1947–2000: Disenchanted Allies* (Washington, DC: Woodrow Wilson Center Press, 2001), 132.

[8] See Altaf Gauhar, "Four Wars, One Assumption," http://www.pakistanlink.com/opinions/99.html.

fight against communism, they were brushed off by the Pakistani president, General Ayub Khan, with the comment that the weapons were meant for use and not to be put in cotton wool.

Pakistan then used the same tactic that it had employed for the initial invasion of Kashmir in 1947. Under Operation Gibraltar, it infiltrated a major force of guerillas into the Kashmir valley to disrupt the state, with the expectation that it would be joined by a local insurrection that would facilitate Pakistan's taking over of the state in the name of a popular uprising. In the event, no insurrection took place. The Indians reacted by attacking the staging bases of the guerillas across the cease-fire line. When the Pakistanis responded with a full-scale attack in Jammu and Kashmir, the Indians faced the nightmare of the state being cut off from the rest of India, with their forces bottled up in the state and available for decimation by Pakistan. Under the leadership of Prime Minister Shastri, diminutive in size but firm of will, the Indians did the unthinkable. To relieve the pressure in Kashmir, they carried the war to the Punjab front and shortly stood at the gates of Lahore. The war involved the massing for battle of the largest phalanx of tanks since World War II. Meanwhile, colluding with Pakistan, the Chinese threatened to intervene and their ultimatum to India was "not a paper threat."[9] But Shastri refused to panic. The war soon wore down to a stalemate, with the Indians relieved that they had been able to hold a technologically superior enemy at bay.

The war had major consequences for the subcontinent. First of all, it restored a measure of pride and self-confidence to the Indians. As General J.N. Chaudhuri, chief of staff of the Indian army at the time, remarked privately a few years later, the blood of Indian officers and men in the 1965 war served to wipe off the black mark on India's forehead from the 1962 war.[10] The war once again underlined to the Indians the importance of defense preparedness and the place of force in international affairs. Second, the war resulted in the decline of US influence in the subcontinent. After the outbreak of the war, the US cut off economic and military aid to both India and Pakistan. Third, there was a corresponding rise in the influence of the Soviet Union in the affairs of the subcontinent. Increasingly pulled into the conflict in Vietnam, the US conceded to the Soviet Union the initiative to settle the aftermath of the India–Pakistan War. With US blessing, the Soviets called the antagonists to Tashkent in early 1966. They pressured India to agree to a settlement whereby it returned the captured territories to Pakistan, while

---

[9] Choudhury, *India, Pakistan*, 190.

[10] Conversations with General J.N. Chaudhuri, after his retirement, at McGill University, Montreal, in 1969 and 1970.

Pakistan largely promised not to use force to resolve its problems with India.[11] The Soviet Union then replaced the US for a few years as the security manager of the region. In part, the consequences of the new arrangement were adverse for the Indians; as against its earlier hostile stance toward Pakistan, the Soviet Union now took a more equidistant position in the continuing conflict between India and Pakistan, even inaugurating an arms-supply relationship with the latter. Though this turn of events caused lot of heartburn and anger in India, the Indians were helpless in view of their own dependence on the Soviet Union for military equipment.

Fourth, the war consolidated the friendship between China and Pakistan into a de facto alliance, with China quickly replacing Pakistani losses of armor and other equipment. Fifth, the most serious consequences of the war were for Pakistan's polity and economy. The war and its conclusion created divisions within the leadership, and triggered large-scale political turmoil. The sharp increases in defense expenditures that followed resulted in the destabilization of the economy and undercut the regime's claim to having achieved "a decade of development." There was widespread unrest and agitation in both wings of the country, which finally brought down the regime of General Ayub Khan. Most importantly, the war led to the chain of events which culminated in the disintegration of Pakistan in 1971. During the war, India had refrained from attacking East Pakistan, even though it had been left completely defenseless in the expectation that an Indian attack there would invite Chinese intervention. The Pakistani neglect reinvigorated the autonomy movement there, which finally resulted in secession.

Despite the war having ended to India's relative satisfaction, that outcome was not certain at its beginning. Indeed, foreign observers expected the war to go in Pakistan's favor, in view of: the largesse of advanced weaponry supplied and training provided by the US; the greater cohesiveness of the Pakistani army because of its narrow ethnic base compared to the multiethnic composition of the Indian army; the self-image of West Pakistan as a modern Prussia; and the Islamic elan of its society and army. The Indians may have had a quantitative edge, but their assets were thinly spread across a vast front against both Pakistan and China. The ultimate fortunes of the war had turned on a single but crucial tank battle, in which a significant proportion of Pakistani armor was destroyed. However, the major-power system was directly implicated in the outcome as well. If the US had decided not to be neutral in the

---

[11] Choudhury, who had official access to the Pakistani minutes of the conference proceedings, discusses the negotiations over the use of no force. Choudhury, *India, Pakistan*, 50–3.

larger cause of containing a radical China, and if it had not cut off arms aid to Pakistan, or if the Chinese had actually intervened, the situation would have become desperate for the Indians. In a sense, the war confirmed to the Indian elites the lesson of self-reliance in economics and defense so that the country's fate did not remain at the disposition of the major powers.

The food crisis of the mid-1960s

That a country's survival can be put under threat not only through physical violence by foreign powers, but also internally by the failure of crops, is abundantly underlined by India's food crisis in the mid-1960s. In turn, such a failure can also reverberate in international politics and have serious repercussions for foreign policy as the country's dependencies are laid bare. Already a food-deficit country at the end of World War II, India became even more dependent on food imports. As population exploded with the decline in mortality rates, India seemed to be inexorably marching toward a Malthusian disaster, the potential for which was partially revealed by the unprecedented and successive two droughts in the mid-1960s. In 1965–66, foodgrains production fell by about one-fifth to 72.3 million tonnes and remained roughly at that level the following year. A US National Security Council study described the resulting desperate situation:

For India the prospect was one more drought, one more year of submission to US demands, one more year of exposure to the world as paupers. This outlook produced a sense of frustration, pessimism and fatalism.[12]

India became heavily dependent on food imports from the US; in the five years from 1964 to 1968, it imported over 38 million tonnes of foodgrains, with over 10 million tonnes in 1966 alone. Face to face with issues of survival for a large part of its population, the leadership could obviously have had little stomach for charting out strategic priorities for a future role in international affairs.

Assisted by an extremely capable minister for agriculture, C. Subramaniam, however, both Lal Bahadur Shastri and Indira Gandhi showed great vision and determination in pushing through, against strong opposition from diverse sources, the Green Revolution strategy. In a few years, this strategy brought India independence from food imports. Still, until such a denouement could occur, Mrs. Gandhi had

---

[12] Dennis Kux, *India and the United States: Estranged Democracies, 1941–1991* (Washington, DC: National Defense University Press, 1992), 255.

to contend with the serious foreign-policy consequences of food dependency and found that the US, which earlier had been anxious to offload its food surpluses, now imposed stringent conditions and sought to modify India's foreign policy. President Lyndon Johnson personally took charge of the decision-making on food shipments and, in what came to be known as the "short tether" policy, deliberately delayed each ship authorization until the very last minute. US officials often justified Johnson's actions on the basis of the need to push India into changing its agricultural policy. However, this is an inaccurate claim, since the Indians had already changed that policy.[13] What was really at issue was changing not agricultural policy but foreign policy, especially in respect of Vietnam, where the Indians had been critical of the intense US bombing.[14]

Interestingly, the depiction of Johnson's "short tether" treatment of India as stemming from his presumed desire to strengthen India agriculturally sits uncomfortably with his equally determined stance on keeping India weak militarily by dismissing its national security concerns as of little consequence. The US rejected India's request for a military-aid package to strengthen itself against China after the India–China War; the core of the package was F-104 aircraft, which the US had supplied to Pakistan. It also refused to provide any security guarantees against a potential nuclear threat, even as it placed enormous pressure on India to sign the NPT. On the other hand, Johnson decided to strengthen Pakistan militarily by reopening the supply line on spare parts for arms, and to secretly pressure third countries to supply major US equipment, such as tanks, to Pakistan.[15] Further, having forced devaluation on India, the US was not forthcoming on economic aid in the amount promised before the devaluation.

These events of recent history seem remote now. However, they serve as an apt reminder of the need for a more adequate appreciation of the crises that the Indian leadership faced during the period and the tremendous international pressures under which it operated. They should also persuade strategic analysts to temper the tendency toward hypercriticism of the leadership for failing to miraculously leapfrog India to major-power status.

---

[13] See Chester Bowles, *Promises to Keep: My Years in Public Life* (New York: Harper and Row, 1971), 530. See also the testimony of Congressman Dole, cited in *ibid.*, 529–30.

[14] Bowles, *Promises to Keep*, 526, 531, 534–5.

[15] See Kux, *United States and Pakistan*, 173.

Economic and political crises

The food crisis was part of a larger economic crisis that India confronted in the 1960s. As the rate of economic growth slowed during the Third Five Year Plan (1961–1966), as the country encountered serious economic bottlenecks under its command economy, as inflation escalated under the impact of additional defense expenditures, and as the food crisis exploded, the leadership came under pressure to change the earlier economic strategy on which until then there had been a national consensus. Under Shastri, India shifted economic policy to a greater emphasis on agriculture when it adopted the Green Revolution strategy. The World Bank then weighed in with a new wide-ranging package of policy measures designed to liberalize the economy. After Shastri's death, Mrs. Gandhi took the first step toward liberalization by drastically devaluing the rupee in June 1966. A key consideration in undertaking devaluation was the dependence of the ambitious Fourth Five Year Plan (1966–1971) on US aid. As the second successive drought occurred soon after, devaluation proved to be a failure. Severe inflation followed and the population groaned under its impact. Also, the foreign-aid donors failed to fulfil their part of the devaluation bargain; the expected World Bank aid did not materialize in the measure that had been promised. India then seemed to confront an economic doomsday. In the absence of increased aid, the government proved unwilling to risk further opening up of the economy. The lesson was a bitter one; as one economic decision-maker averred: "Never again would India allow itself to become so vulnerably dependent on external assistance."[16] Moreover, there was a political backlash against the government for having surrendered to foreign powers on devaluation. All this put an end to liberalization and the Fourth Plan.

Meanwhile, the economic crisis generated more serious political repercussions. The food shortages and high inflation caused great misery to the public. There were food riots and massive protests, and the leftist parties called for strikes to shut down the economy. There were serious threats to law and order, and the problem was compounded by China's calls to local Maoist guerilla groups to rise up against the regime in a series of revolts across India. India's very existence seemed to be at stake; it was as if the prognoses of disintegration proclaimed in the oft-repeated question "After Nehru What?" were turning out to be true. When new elections were being held in 1967, the London *Times* correspondent Neville Maxwell pronounced the verdict that these would be India's last elections.

[16] Cited in *ibid.*, 261.

In this picture of gloom, the Congress Party faced an uphill battle in the elections. Unlike the Nehru era, when democracy was largely formal, it had now become substantive, and an aroused electorate inflicted severe reverses on the Congress Party. Even though the party was returned to power at the center, its majority had been drastically cut. At the same time, the party was defeated in eight of the states, giving way in many cases to multiparty coalitions, which made for increased political instability. What is more, following the electoral debacle, the party became internally polarized between the left and right wings, and finally split in 1969. Mrs. Gandhi was able to continue in power only because of the support from the Communist Party of India and some regional groups. The 1960s thus saw a period of marked political instability and uncertainty, and it is in this environment that the political leadership had to make crucial foreign-policy decisions. Subsequently, in 1971, Mrs. Gandhi fought elections on a radical program and won a strong mandate. That victory proved critical in her ability to handle the Bangladesh crisis, but the masses had meanwhile been aroused and the resulting constraints on the leadership in a democratic system had acquired greater strength.

Escaping the NPT net and retaining the nuclear option

The India–China War of 1962 was a mindset-shattering event, a watershed in national psychology, a transforming divide that moved national security to the center of India's concerns. Coming soon after this war and the death of Nehru, the Chinese nuclear test in 1964 caused great consternation in India, among both the elite and the public, and gave a permanent nuclear cast to the concern for national security. Thereafter, the threat to national security became the stimulus for the focus on matters nuclear. Its impact on strategic thinking was profound and should not be allowed to be confused by references to other extraneous concerns, such as morality and prestige, or the particular state of India–China relations, or the nature of Chinese intentions.

India then began a long search for ways to cope with the perceived challenge to its security – no doubt, without possibly threatening its economy, polity and national autonomy, but still first and foremost addressed to the quest for national security. It is from this search that there issued a series of policies in successive incremental steps in order to ensure long-term national security without seriously damaging the economy and polity, and without arousing its adversaries in the neighborhood and among the major powers to even greater hostility that would undermine its strategic interests. These policies included: the exploration for a nuclear umbrella, the rejection of NPT and preservation of the nuclear option, the undertaking of a "peaceful nuclear explosion," the posture of nuclear ambiguity, the launching of missile development, the adoption of covert or opaque deterrence, and finally the testing of nuclear weapons and the claim to the status of an NWS. To neglect or understate this progressively deepening line of policy development, stemming from the concern with national security, in favor of priority for other factors that made for the delay in arriving at the final destination[17] is to turn reality on its head. There is no warrant in realism that the response to the acquisition of nuclear weapons by rivals must be instantaneous, even if the cost is economic bankruptcy and a broken-back state. Realism is a theory and an approach, not a military tactic; it stresses prudence and taking account of a strategic situation in its entirety.

In the wake of the Chinese nuclear test in 1964, India's nuclear czar, Homi Bhabha, assured Indians that his agency could produce a nuclear device for testing within eighteen months if it were so authorized by the government. Some have disputed India's technical capacity at the time to have produced such a device within the designated time limit.[18] Whether that contention is correct or not, Bhabha's declaration has to be seen in the context of assuring a disconcerted public. In any case, any promise of delivering an atomic device within eighteen months depended not just on government authorization but also on adequate funding. Nonetheless, it was clear from the declaration that at that moment in time India had no nuclear capability for defense or deterrence. The important question that arose therefore for the political leadership was as to what ought to be done to protect national interests in case a nuclear threat from China were to materialize. The question emerged in the context of the troubling political uncertainty in the wake of Nehru's death, and it continued as a cause of concern during the entire period while the country went through the 1965 war, the food crisis of the mid-1960s, the political turmoil of the late 1960s following the decline of popular support for the Congress Party and the break-up of the party, and the war of 1971. Prime Minister Shastri publicly raised the issue of a possible nuclear umbrella over India from the major powers other than China, but the response was negative or evasive. The Indians were then simply left to fend for themselves. Faced with the potential nuclear threat from an adversary with whom it had just recently fought a war, yet deterred from undertaking a full-scale nuclear weapons program by the costs involved, Shastri settled on the middle ground of advancing India's technological capabilities in the nuclear arena, at least as a start.

---

[17] Perkovich, *India's Nuclear Bomb*, 6.
[18] *ibid.*, 86.

He endorsed in 1965 Bhabha's proposal for a "peaceful nuclear explosion." This was the first step in what turned out to be a long road – in view of the economic and political constraints – to acquiring a nuclear deterrent.

The superpowers did not just refuse to provide guarantees against possible nuclear threats, however; rather, they set out determinedly instead to block India from acquiring an independent nuclear deterrent. They decided on a treaty to prevent the addition of any new nuclear powers to the existing number of five. While this move was formally aimed against all non-nuclear states, its specific immediate target was India, for there were hardly any other states at the time that had both the incentive and the technical capacity to go nuclear. To be sure, it may also have been in the interests of the superpowers to have prevented Germany and Japan from acquiring nuclear weapons, but both were already under the US nuclear umbrella and did not have a strong incentive to have a nuclear capability of their own. India alone at the time had both the capacity and the incentive, since it had failed to obtain guarantees of protection against a possible nuclear threat. It is interesting that the US often justified its policies toward India by the latter's closeness to the Soviet Union; yet here were the two superpowers joined together in launching a course that had as its chief purpose to disarm India permanently in the nuclear arena.

The question of possessing nuclear weapons and of preventing others from obtaining them was not unconnected with the issue of graduation of a middle power to major-power status, on the one hand, and, on the other, the preservation of such status by the existing major powers against the claims of what they regarded as new interlopers. For it was clear that the proliferation of nuclear weapons would erode, to some extent, the military power of the US, for example. That was, indeed, the underlying rationale for the new treaty, which is made clear by the deliberations within the Johnson administration. The Gilpatric Committee, which had been set up by President Lyndon Johnson to study the challenge of proliferation, recommended to the US government in 1965 that it bar the further spread of nuclear weapons, for "as additional nations obtained nuclear weapons, our diplomatic and military influence would wane," and that they would "eventually constitute direct military threats to the United States." The committee thus underlined a fundamental conflict of interest between the US as the global power and India as a middle power. Its report was highly influential in guiding the decision process and it led to the NPT. Perkovich adds: "This understanding of U.S. interests in nonproliferation remains operative today."[19]

---

[19] ibid., 102.

India's various objections to the treaty drafts were brushed off for the simple reason that, as one authority recognizes, "India may have had logic, principle, and the 1965 negotiating mandate on its side, but the United States and the other nuclear weapon states had power on their side."[20] In the face of the determination of the superpowers to push the NPT, India had four options. First, it could forgo the acquisition of nuclear weapons in the future and sign a treaty that barred new nuclear powers from emerging. India, however, found the treaty to be unacceptable because of its fundamentally discriminatory nature insofar as it allowed some powers to have nuclear weapons while denying them to others. There was no incentive in the treaty for India to sign. It provided no solution to the problem of how to deter potential nuclear threats to its security or to defend against them. Second, India could press for universal nuclear disarmament, which if it were to occur would put an end to nuclear weapons and thus obviate a nuclear threat to India. That is the position that India took in the negotiations and consistently afterwards, opposing any artificial distinction between those who had tested nuclear weapons by 1967 and all others. However, it encountered a brick wall on this from the major powers who, while eager to impose constraints on others, would not countenance any on themselves. This therefore was no option at all, only a public posture.

Third, India could refuse to sign any treaty of the kind and undertake an immediate program for the acquisition of nuclear weapons for purposes of deterrence and defense. The political costs of such a program would be immense, for it would mean defiance of the superpowers on whom India was dependent economically and militarily. As a State Department study in 1966 assessed the situation, the Indian leadership was reluctant to explode a nuclear device soon because of "US pressures against proliferation, particularly at a time when India is so dependent on the US to help alleviate India's critical food situation," even as it recognized that India would do so "within the next few years" and "proceed to produce weapons."[21] More critical was the question of the stupendous economic costs, especially given the parlous economic situation in which India already was placed. If India were under an authoritarian or totalitarian regime, the masses could be coerced into accepting such costs, but India's democratic framework barred imposing additional deprivations on society and was therefore a crucial constraint. Indeed, a premature thrust for nuclear weapons would have been adverse for India's national security.

[20] *ibid.*, 127.
[21] *ibid.*, 115.

Fourth, India could refuse to sign the NPT and, in view of the political and economic costs, not undertake an immediate program of acquiring nuclear weapons, but retain the nuclear option for the future through a long-term stretched-out program of research and development, leaving open the option to be exercised when the circumstances were more propitious. It is this fourth alternative that India chose against the pressures of the major powers when the treaty was opened for signature in 1968, and it stuck with it for three decades substantively and a half-decade technically. In choosing this option, it is clear that India was mindful of its constraints. These constraints, no doubt, included food and economic dependence on the US and military dependence on the Soviet Union, but most importantly they included domestic constraints in terms of India's political structure and the population's low threshold of tolerance of additional deprivations. At the same time, notwithstanding these constraints, the Indian leadership demonstrated defiance of the superpowers by refusing to accede to a treaty in respect of which both the US and the Soviets had exerted enormous pressure.

Formally, India rejected the treaty on moral and political grounds – the discriminatory nature of the treaty, the lack of balance in obligations between nuclear and non-nuclear powers, the absence of constraints on continued expansion and improvement of the nuclear arsenals of the existing nuclear powers, and the lack of movement toward universal nuclear disarmament – but the underlying logic for its rejection was strategic; that is, to retain India's nuclear option, to be exercised at a circumstance and time of its own choosing. This inner stance does not represent lack of adequate attention to national security, but rather a judicious evaluation that takes full account of all the factors, economic and political as well as technological. After all, one is talking here of a mere developing country, even if large in size and population. To claim that the Indian leadership was really not serious about developing nuclear capabilities because it did not get the military to do a prior-threat analysis at that stage, as Perkovich has argued, is to jump the gun. Quite the contrary, there needs to be a prior demonstrated capacity to conduct a nuclear explosion before bringing the military into decision-making. It would have been the height of presumption to get the military involved when even a tested device did not exist. Meanwhile, the terminology of "peaceful nuclear explosive" was appropriate for declarations about peaceful intent to mitigate pressures from the superpowers.

US global restructuring, and the Bangladesh War

The continuing involvement of the US in the Vietnam War had weakened it in its competition with the Soviet Union. Under the circumstances, the US under President Richard Nixon developed a new strategy to restructure the global balance of power. To place constraints on the Soviet Union's expanding role, to persuade Moscow to make concessions, and to facilitate its own extrication from Vietnam, the US entered into a rapprochement with China as a major player on the side of the US in the world's balance of power. Nixon's policy change was audacious, and it transformed the geopolitics of the postwar world. The new geopolitical shift changed the US stance toward India by eliminating the rationale for the earlier limited US support to India as part of a policy of economic competition with the Soviet Union and of military containment of China. On the contrary, the US recognized that China in its new role as the third major player in international politics had its own legitimate interests in South Asia, primarily in respect of the regional containment of India through support of Pakistan. In his foreign-policy report of 1971, Nixon outlined the new thrust of US foreign policy:

We will try to keep our activities in the area in balance with those of the other major powers concerned. ... We will do nothing to harm legitimate Soviet and Chinese interests in the area. We are equally clear, however, that no outside power has a claim to a predominant influence, and that each can serve its own interests and the interests of South Asia by conducting its activities in the region accordingly.[22]

It became clear that the role India was fit for in the Nixon administration's grand design was that of an object, not just of the US but of all the major powers. The grave implications of the design for India soon unfolded in the administration's actions during the Bangladesh crisis.

As the autonomy movement became ascendant in East Bengal, the Pakistani military regime cracked down ferociously in March 1971 in an effort to wipe out the entire political and intellectual elite of the province, and to ethnically cleanse the province of its religious minority. US consul general Archer Blood in Dacca cabled Washington about the "mass killing of unarmed civilians, the systematic elimination of the

---

[22] Richard M. Nixon, *United States Foreign Policy for the 1970s: Building for Peace* (February 25, 1971), in *Weekly Compilation of Presidential Documents*, vol. VII, no. 9 (March 1, 1971), 341.

intelligentsia, and the annihilation of the Hindu population."[23] The military crackdown forced 10 million refugees to flee to India, largely to the politically explosive state of West Bengal. After East Pakistan emerged as independent Bangladesh, the government declared that a total of 3 million had died in the conflict (although other sources put the figure at half that at the most). It is impressive that, in the face of this immense human tragedy, the Nixon administration offered no critical comment about the activities of the Pakistani military regime, nor did it show much sensitivity to India for the massive burden placed on it with the influx of refugees. Surprisingly, US arms continued to trickle to Pakistan, even though such support had been officially suspended.

The Nixon administration's passivity, despite the US public's condemnation, can be understood only in the light of the monumental US geopolitical move – at the time, still shrouded in secrecy – to restructure the global balance of power, with Pakistan serving as the go-between for the US and China. As the rapprochement between the US and China, with the assistance of Pakistan, became public knowledge, there was consternation in India. The Nixon administration then stunned India by warning it not to expect any US help in case of intervention by China in any war between India and Pakistan. Confronted by the obvious bias of the Nixon administration, and the apparent tacit alliance between the US and China directed against it, India finally decided to defy the US in the Bangladesh crisis. The key consideration that weighed with India in its refusal to reconcile itself to the new situation created by Pakistan was the threat of its own destabilization that the continuing civil war posed and the unacceptability of 10 million refugees remaining permanently in India, which it regarded as "indirect aggression." India resorted to a daring act of balance of power by entering into a semimilitary treaty with the Soviet Union, intended as diplomatic and military insurance in the event that the crisis erupted into violent conflict.

When Pakistan formally initiated the war by attacking several airfields in north India on December 3, 1971, and India reacted, the US administration reflexively condemned India as an aggressor and came out fully in support of Pakistan. Were it not for Soviet vetoes, US actions at the UN Security Council would have rendered India's situation hopeless. Subsequently, Jack Anderson of the *Washington Post* released secret documents, known as the Anderson Papers, which revealed the administration's wholly one-sided approach. The documents showed Kissinger telling the Washington Special Action Group on December 3, in reference to President Nixon, "He wants to tilt in favor of Pakistan," and

---

[23] Stanley Wolpert, *Zulfi Bhutto of Pakistan: His Life and Times* (New York: Oxford University Press, 1993), 156.

again on December 8, "we are not trying to be even handed. There can be no doubt what the President wants. The President does not want to be even handed." Kissinger also asked for the group's advice as to "what the next turn of the screw might be" in relation to India.[24]

Despite the formal US suspension of shipment of all military supplies to both India and Pakistan on the outbreak of the war, the US administration was complicit in the transfer of F-104 aircraft to Pakistan from Libya and Jordan. The US also added a strategic dimension to its political-diplomatic opposition to India. During the course of the war, the US pressed China to intervene in the conflict militarily. State Department documents record Kissinger as telling China's Ambassador to the UN, Huang Hua: "When I asked for this meeting, I did so to suggest Chinese military help to Pakistan, to be quite honest."[25] In any case, the Chinese did not intervene, perhaps for fear of Soviet reaction, but the US did. In a show of force, the US dispatched a naval task force, headed by the nuclear aircraft carrier USS *Enterprise*, into the Bay of Bengal. In Kux's assessment, the episode "etched an image of US hostility into the Indian historical memory."[26] No physical confrontation took place between India and the US because, before the task force reached there, the Indians had already accomplished their war aims with the surrender of the Pakistani forces.

The US rationale for its intervention on Pakistan's side in the conflict was that its credibility was at stake with China in terms of standing by an ally, and that China was essential to the larger US strategic design for the containment of the Soviet Union. Kissinger wrote in justification in his memoirs that "we had to act with determination to save larger interests and relationships."[27] It was poor comfort for India, however, that its survival had been put at risk in the larger US design to restructure the world. That the US chose to side with the military dictatorship in Pakistan and the communist regime in China against the democratic government in India hardened Indian perceptions into cynicism about US attitudes to Indian interests.

---

[24] See Vinod Gupta, *Anderson Papers: A Study of Nixon's Blackmail of India* (New Delhi: Indian School Supply Depot, 1972); and Jack Anderson, *The Anderson Papers* (New York: Random House, 1973), 203–69.

[25] Kux, *United States and Pakistan*, 202.

[26] Kux, *India and the United States*, 342.

[27] Henry Kissinger, *The White House Years* (Boston: Little, Brown & Co., 1979), 898. See also Maya Chadda, *Paradox of Power: The United States in South West Asia, 1973–1984* (Santa Barbara, CA: ABC–Clio, 1986), 36.

An interim assessment

Foreign-policy and strategic decisions are not made in a vacuum where some ideal design can be executed. Nor are they simply a function of the brilliance of a leadership – though that matters a lot – for the leadership has to work within the constraints of the international system and of the domestic society and polity. As one astute observer of the period noted:

> The general international environment, dominated by the US and the Soviet Union, was hostile to the development of India as an independent power center challenging their respective assumptions of security management and order. The regional environment was not conducive to the realization of India's goal of insulation from great power conflicts.[28]

In view of the period's many economic and political crises, internal and external, it is difficult to see how the leadership in India could have drastically improved on its performance in advancing national interests. Given the limitations of the nation's existent capabilities and the nature of its political system, it is unrealistic to expect that there would have been any dazzling breakthroughs in respect of international status, national defense and the nuclear option.

What is striking in the light of the multiple crises during the period is the resilience of the political system and the sobriety of its leadership in maintaining a reasonable balance between goals and capabilities. The leadership pulled India through an awfully difficult period when its bargaining position was extremely weak, given the dependencies in the economic, food and military fields, while some among the major powers eagerly sought to tighten the screws on India to satellize and marginalize it. At the same time, within its constraints, the leadership endeavored to expand the nation's capabilities, both economic and military. In respect of economic capabilities, the major policy innovation was the Green Revolution strategy to eliminate dependence on food imports. In the military arena, defense expenditures were increased in response to new threats. Special mountain divisions were raised for defense against China; the army was expanded and the air force was upgraded, with the MiG-21 as its workhorse. Local manufacture of MiG-21 was begun, and work on materializing the nuclear option continued apace; a space program was started, even if initially only for civilian purposes. However, apart from the Green Revolution, the economic sector was largely marked by stagnation. Economic development was hobbled by massive state ownership and bureaucratic controls. Economic

[28] Surjit Mansingh, *India's Search for Power: Indira Gandhi's Foreign Policy, 1966–1982* (New Delhi: Sage, 1984), 55.

liberalization was initiated, but was soon aborted amid protests from political and ideological forces, partly because of its potential for increased foreign ownership in India.

Recovery of middle-power role, 1971–1974

At independence, India had emerged as the pre-eminent power in South Asia. However, India's pre-eminent or middle-power role was soon countermanded by the US and China through their alliances with Pakistan. During the 1960s, India labored strenuously under the pressures of the regional containment policies of the US and China, compounded by its own economic and political vulnerabilities, which took it almost to a breaking point.

With the separation of Bangladesh from Pakistan as a consequence of the 1971 war, a new strategic environment seemed to emerge in which India's position as the pre-eminent power was apparently resurrected. In a moment of hubris, inspired by an exaggerated notion of the change in the strategic environment, India sought US recognition of "the new realities" in the subcontinent; in other words, of its resurrected position. Such recognition would have entailed the abstinence by external powers from interfering in the affairs of the region, since that allegedly, in India's view, led only to regional conflict. However, India had to be mistaken in any expectation of such recognition, as conflict between major powers and independently oriented middle powers is a relatively persistent feature of international politics.

For the moment, India refused to have any external power, whether the US or the Soviet Union, preside again over the settlement of the war, as had occurred in 1966, because it wanted to see the international affairs of the region develop as an autonomous system in which it was the system-builder. Accordingly, the heads of government of India and Pakistan, Indira Gandhi and Zulfikar Ali Bhutto, met in early 1972 in Simla without any third-party presence. They came to an agreement, known as the Simla Agreement, whereby India agreed to return captured territories and 90,000 prisoners of war in return merely for a Pakistani pledge to resolve issues of conflict between the two countries on a bilateral basis only. Indian critics attacked their government for its naivete in expecting Pakistan either to abide by its commitment or to end its running and ruinous conflict with India.

The US did momentarily respond with recognition of the changes in the strategic situation of the region. Deputy Assistant Secretary of State James Noyes stated in early 1973 that, "A new power alignment in South Asia has emerged from the crisis, India is now unquestionably the major power in the area," and that "India is actually in terms of the sub-

continent itself in being very much the dominant power."[29] President
Nixon, too, graciously acknowledged:

India emerged from the 1971 crisis with new confidence, power and responsibilities. This fact in itself was a new political reality for the subcontinent and for all nations concerned with South Asia's future.

He further characterized India as a "major power" as a result of "its new
power in the region."[30] He also removed the irritant between the two
countries in the form of the accumulating US holdings of Indian
currency as proceeds from the earlier PL-480 food shipments.

As part of India's assertion of its new role, it asked the US to shut
down its economic aid mission, especially in view of the US having cut
off economic aid during the Bangladesh War, and it renounced the buying of US food in the future on a concessional basis. In this manner,
Indira Gandhi decided to remove one symbol of dependency on the US.
Much to the annoyance of the US, India integrated into the Indian federation in 1975 its protectorate of Sikkim – which had become a center
of international intrigue – at the request of the territory's legislature.
More dramatically, India also tested in May 1974 what it referred to as
a "peaceful nuclear explosive." The immediate provocation that triggered developments leading to the test was the US intervention in the
Bangladesh War of 1971 by way of sending a naval task force against
India. The test was, however, equally directed at the Soviet Union as a
show of independence. Though the official US reaction to the test was
restrained, there was deep anger in the Nixon administration at this act
of defiance of US policy on nuclear proliferation. Having defied the US
in this manner, however, India's nuclear program went into an indefinite hibernation, and that only signaled to the superpowers to apply
renewed pressure.

As if in recognition of India's new putative role, Henry Kissinger
made a trip to India in late 1974, the first substantive visit of a US secretary of state since John Foster Dulles in the mid-1950s, and declared:
"The United States recognizes India as one of the major powers of the
world and conducts its policy accordingly."[31] These various gestures of

---

[29] US House of Representatives, Committee on Foreign Affairs, *United States Interests In and Policies Toward South Asia* (93rd Congress, 1st Session; March 12, 15, 20 and 27, 1973), 79, 94.

[30] Richard M. Nixon, *United States Foreign Policy for the 1970s: Shaping a Durable Peace* (May 3, 1973), in *Weekly Compilation of Presidential Documents*, vol. IX, no. 19 (May 14, 1973), 577–85.

[31] Kux, *India and the United States*, 328.

the US toward accommodation with India, however, remained at the symbolic level, lacking in much substance. Even these gestures lasted only until such time as India had leverage with Pakistan by way of the captured territories and prisoners of war, and until a decent interval of time had erased the moral stigma that had attached to the Nixon administration as a result of its having sided with a genocidal regime in Pakistan.

Middle-power role under pressure, 1975–1984

The phenomenon of a resurrected middle-power role lasted only for a few short years. India soon encountered the re-emergence of vulnerabilities, both internal and external. In the first flush of victory in the Bangladesh War, India had exaggerated its accomplishment in having created a new strategic environment. While it had moved forward somewhat, the movement was not sufficient to alter the pattern of behavior on the part of the major powers toward the region. In part, this was a function of the fact that, while India had succeeded in splitting Bangladesh from Pakistan, it was not able to inflict a decisive defeat to the military in West Pakistan. After a short gap in time, therefore, the earlier patterns of behavior reappeared. At the same time, India's internal vulnerabilities became more pronounced in the economic and political arenas, which demanded greater attention than international affairs.

Extended US regional containment

Although the US made gestures of symbolic accommodation toward India after the Bangladesh War, it would have been an unwarranted expectation that it would cease the pursuit of policies appropriate to a major power in relation to a middle power. Indeed, along with such gestures, the US was already prescribing what it considered proper behavior for India. The US also cast a net of protection over the other states in the subcontinent which had friendly relations with China, and it reverted to calling Pakistan an ally after suspending such characterization during much of the 1960s. No meeting of high officials of the US and Pakistan could take place without referring to "strong US support for Pakistan's independence and territorial integrity … as a guiding principle of American foreign policy."[32] Similarly, though not as forcefully, US protection was extended to Nepal as well. In his 1973 foreign-policy statement, President Nixon sought to instruct India about the international behavior expected of it. He stated: "India's policy toward

---

[32] *Department of State Bulletin*, no. 1970 (October 15, 1973), 486.

its neighbors on the subcontinent and other countries in nearby parts of Asia is now an important determinant of regional stability, which is of interest to us." Again, he reminded India: "Every major power – now including India, with its new power in the region – has a basic responsibility toward the international system to exercise its power with restraint." He also called its attention to the disparity in power between India and the US, and sought to disabuse it of the notion of any attempt at exclusion of US intervention in the region: "United States policies globally and regionally will support the independence of South Asian nations. ... This is our responsibility as a great power ..."[33]

In reality, the US took itself to be the dominant power in the subcontinent and, in that role, it reserved for itself the role of determining the appropriate strategic balance within the subcontinent. What was more disturbing from the Indian viewpoint was the accumulating evidence that the net of protection cast over non-Indian states in the region was part of a more comprehensive strategic arrangement that encompassed: collaboration with China, with its accelerated military cooperation with Pakistan based on common hostility to India; and the development of military ally Iran as a surrogate balancer in the subcontinent alongside Pakistan. This arrangement was besides the intensification of the US military presence in the Indian Ocean, including the establishment of the base at Diego Garcia.

What newspaper columnist Joseph Alsop described as "the partial and informal Chinese-American alliance"[34] had serious implications for South Asia in that both the US and China focused on support to Pakistan to countervail India, as part of their larger strategy both against the Soviet Union and against Indian ambitions about being the preeminent power in South Asia. In an exchange with Congressman Lee Hamilton over the US and China viewing "South Asia in a similar perspective from a strategic point of view," Assistant Secretary of State Alfred Atherton agreed, "We have a certain common view in that respect."[35]

China was not the only element in the US strategic calculus about the subcontinent. Following the inauguration of the Nixon administration, the US began building up "loyalist" Iran as a regional power. Toward this end, the US made major arms transfers to Iran in the 1970s. These

---

[33] Nixon, *Shaping a Durable Peace*, 577–85.
[34] Joseph Alsop, "Thoughts Out of China," *New York Times Magazine*, March 11, 1973.
[35] US House of Representatives, Committee on Foreign Affairs, *South Asia, 1974: Political, Economic, and Agricultural Challenges* (93rd Congress, 2nd Session; September 19 and 24, 1974), 34.

arms transfers may have been aimed against other powers in terms of regional balance, but India also was a target of such balancing.[36] It is noteworthy that the US decision on arms transfers to Iran came in May 1972, when hardly six months had passed since India's victory in the Bangladesh War. The "sweeping" decision to supply Iran "virtually any weapons system it wanted," "unprecedented for a non-industrial country," was "based upon broad geostrategic and political considerations rather than exacting calculations about the balance of power in the Persian Gulf."[37] Secretary of State Kissinger himself emphasized that, as a result of "the stabilizing role that Iran has played in both Middle East *and South Asia* policy, we have found it to be in the national interest of the United States and the interest of regional stability to cooperate with Iran" through arms transfers.[38] It is not surprising then that the *Guardian* (July 9, 1973) remarked that "in India's eyes, American objectives are much wider and include – apart from building up an anti-Soviet bulwark … – a considered policy to build up a counterpoise to India, now that Pakistan can no longer play this role."[39]

It is against this background of the developing extended containment of India from outside the region that the US decided in 1975 to resume arms supply to Pakistan through first removing the embargo that had been placed during the Bangladesh conflict. The decision contradicted the repeated declarations in the previous few years that the US intended to stay out of any arms supply to the region. What is more interesting is that the rationale proffered made patent that India was the intended target of the resumption of arms supply.[40] Secretary Kissinger argued:

to maintain an embargo against a friendly country with which we have an allied relationship, while its neighbor was producing and acquiring nearly a billion dollars' worth of arms a year, was morally, politically and symbolically improper.

He emphasized that:

[36] A more elaborate and documented analysis on this point is available in Baldev Raj Nayar, "Regional Power in a Multipolar World," in John W. Mellor (ed.), *India: A Rising Middle Power* (Boulder, CO: Westview Press, 1979), 147–9.
[37] US Senate, Committee on Foreign Relations, *US Military Sales to Iran* (A Staff Report, July 1976), 5, 41, 43.
[38] *Department of State Bulletin*, no. 1941 (September 6, 1976), 314; emphasis added.
[39] Cited in Choudhury, *India, Pakistan*, 223.
[40] The issue is more thoroughly discussed in Baldev Raj Nayar, *American Geopolitics and India* (New Delhi: Manohar, 1976), ch. 6.

it seemed to us an anomaly to embargo one country in the world, to be the only country in the world to be embargoing this country, when its neighbor was not exercising a comparable restraint.[41]

Not international communism, but India was the reference point in this rationale. Interestingly, the US chose to ignore the supply of Chinese arms to Pakistan and the gigantic transfer of US weapons systems to Iran and Saudi Arabia, which had strategic implications for India. As part of the new arms-supply policy, the Ford administration began considering a Pakistani request for A-7 fighter-bombers.

The relationship between the US and Pakistan after the removal of the arms embargo was not altogether smooth, however, as other issues cropped up between the two countries, such as: the dispute over the Pakistani plan to buy a plutonium-processing plant from France; the military coup in Pakistan in 1977; the different even if transient outlook of the Carter administration in respect of military governments; the imposition of US sanctions in line with the Symington Amendment; and the Pakistan government's turning a blind eye in 1979 while anti-American Islamic mobs attacked US citizens and set fire to the US embassy in Islamabad.

India's vulnerabilities to the fore again

While it was eager, on the one hand, to firm up its role as the pre-eminent power in the region in the wake of the Bangladesh War, and while it had to contend, on the other, with the US and China endeavoring in tacit cooperation to undercut that role, India experienced severe internal turmoil. That led to the declaration of a state of emergency in June 1975. It would be easy to personalize the event and blame it on the authoritarian inclinations of Indira Gandhi, but that would tend to neglect the structural causes that lay behind it. First and foremost, there was the decline of the Congress Party as the single dominant party, which had been made evident in the electoral debacle in 1967 and in the subsequent split of the party in 1969. Second, the first half-decade of the 1970s was a time of serious economic deterioration as a consequence of the impact of the Bangladesh conflict, in terms not only of coping with the influx of 10 million refugees, but also of higher defense expenditures and taking care of 90,000 prisoners of war, the termination of US economic aid, the renunciation of concessional food aid, the persistent economic stagnation and decline over four years, the sudden escalation of oil prices in 1973 at the dictation of OPEC, and raging

---

[41] *Department of State Bulletin*, no. 1864 (March 17, 1975), 322.

inflation. The agony of the public in the face of galloping inflation and widespread shortages of essential goods, including food, burst forth into riots and violence, striking at the government in one fashion or another. The general atmosphere of gloom and impending doom affected everyone, and reached its climax in 1974–75, which one government report described as "a year of unprecedented economic strains in the history of independent India."[42]

The acute economic crisis and the resulting social disorder were soon transformed into a political crisis as the opposition not unexpectedly moved in to exploit the public discontent by mounting a major offensive against the government. The noted socialist leader Jayaprakash Narayan (known as JP) rallied the opposition parties across the political spectrum in a massive movement against Mrs. Gandhi. Another socialist leader, George Fernandes, masterminded a strike by 2 million railway employees with a view to shut down the railway system. Mrs. Gandhi suspected a "foreign hand" in the agitation against her. In a secret cable, divulged by Seymour Hersh, US Ambassador Moynihan warned Kissinger that disclosures of CIA involvement in the overthrow of President Allende of Chile confirmed Mrs. Gandhi's "worst suspicions and genuine fears" about US policy in India, adding:

Her concern is whether the United States accepts the Indian regime. She is not sure but that we would be content to see others like her overthrown. She knows full well that we have done our share and more of bloody and dishonorable deeds. ... She thinks we are a profoundly selfish and cynical counter-revolutionary power.[43]

But the real causes of Mrs. Gandhi's predicament were internal. Perceiving a political upheaval generated by the opposition forces led by JP, Mrs. Gandhi imposed a state of emergency in the country. The resulting authoritarian regime continued for over a year and a half. When Mrs. Gandhi ordered new elections in early 1977, the results were cataclysmic; she and her party were defeated by a ragtag coalition of several parties that had been hurriedly put together under the umbrella of the Janata Party.

While many hopes were attached to the Janata Party, it failed to deliver because of its internal squabbles. The Janata government proclaimed that its aim was to correct alleged distortions in foreign policy by working for "genuine non-alignment." The stance of its prime minister,

---

[42] S.D. Punekar (ed.), *Economic Revolution in India* (Bombay: Himalaya Publishing House, 1977), 107.
[43] *New York Times*, September 13, 1974.

Morarji Desai, was highly and rigidly moralistic. In his personal opposition to nuclear weapons, he may have also retarded the development of India's nuclear capabilities. The government was a confused lot; in some ways it reinforced the idealistic strain in the Nehruvian legacy by raising hopes about friendlier relations with India's neighbors by one-sided concessions, ignoring the fact that antagonism toward India originated in their own perceptions of national interest. The government was, however, not long enough in office to have had much sustained impact. The noteworthy event of its period in office was the visit to India by President Jimmy Carter in 1978, as part of a strategy to cultivate "regional influentials."

The quarrels within the coalition resulted in the collapse of the government. New elections then brought Indira Gandhi back to power at the beginning of 1980 after a lapse of three years. While she had to cope with the issue of Soviet intervention in Afghanistan and the resulting massive inflow of US arms to Pakistan, her major focus had to be on the internal front, where she had to face increasing threats to national unity and political stability. The sources of these threats lay in India's structural profile of ethnic diversity and economic underdevelopment. These elements are not novel to India; in many ways, India is a political marvel in that it has operated a moderately successful federal and democratic political system while most of the developing countries have endured long stretches of authoritarian or military rule. No political system can, however, adequately satisfy all political groups in a country undergoing modernization, even as democracy intensifies their social mobilization. Some groups are bound to become alienated, and sometimes political leaders use one group or the other for their electoral purposes. In India, the alienation at this time was partly aided by a worldwide rise in religious fundamentalism, which had spillover effects in the subcontinent.

Three areas of India were particularly affected, Punjab, Kashmir and the north-east region, but at this time the Punjab posed the gravest problem. Terrorism and violence became rampant in that state. India suspected Pakistan's intelligence agencies of having had a big hand in coordinating the activities of the militants, assisting in their being smuggled in and out over a porous border, and supplying them with weapons, explosives and drug-trafficking money. Pakistan's capacity to handle this kind of activity had, ironically, been advanced by the training provided by the CIA to its intelligence agencies in connection with the ongoing war in Afghanistan. Sikh militants turned the Golden Temple of Amritsar – the holiest of Sikh shrines – into a fortress of opposition and armed struggle against the government. Eventually, Mrs. Gandhi tired of the long drawn-out campaign of violence and terror, and she made

the awfully difficult and painful decision to order the military to intervene and blast its way into the temple to oust the militants. The action
infuriated the entire Sikh community, and the anger finally consumed
Mrs. Gandhi when her bodyguards, who were Sikhs, assassinated her in
1984. This and other ethnic conflicts weakened India, threatened its
national integration, and showed up its internal vulnerabilities, which
hobbled the country's economic progress and international endeavors.
They also made vivid the possibilities of exploitation by external powers
as a leverage against India.

The Soviet intervention in Afghanistan

By the late 1970s, Afghanistan had for several years been in political turmoil, partly because a Marxist regime without much of a popular political base was overly eager to aggressively and quickly modernize a
strongly conservative population, and partly owing to the covert activities of outside powers, not excluding Pakistan and the US, to overthrow
the regime. When the regime's existence was under threat in late 1979,
it called for military intervention by the Soviet Union to save it. The war
between the Soviet and Soviet-backed forces and the anti-Marxist guer-
rilla forces, with sanctuaries in Pakistan, created new security threats for
the military regime in Pakistan, besides resulting in a massive influx of
refugees.

India refused to join in the US-led condemnation of the Soviet
Union, maintaining that all external interventions needed to be taken
into account, not only the most recent one, that public condemnation
was not likely to lead to a Soviet withdrawal, and that all foreign intervention should cease. However, while its refusal to join in public condemnation earned it the hostility of the US, its own private protests to
the Soviet Union did not work either. In reality, India was inhibited
from a more active role by its own dependence on Soviet supplies of
arms even as the US was reluctant to supply arms to India. India's concern over Soviet intervention in Afghanistan was expressed indirectly
through seeking a better relationship with the US. Fundamentally, what
India feared more than the Soviet intervention was possible US military
aid to Pakistan to counter the intervention, which would change the balance of power in the region. That fear came to pass sooner than it antic-
ipated.

One consequence of the war between India and Pakistan in 1971 had
been the discrediting of the military in Pakistan and the replacement of
its rule by an elected political leader, Zulfikar Ali Bhutto. In early 1975,
the US removed the embargo on arms supplies – imposed during the
war – to Pakistan as an ally, but it was soon disconcerted by the

Pakistani drive to acquire nuclear capabilities. In April 1977, the US was constrained to suspend project aid to Pakistan because of the latter's contract to procure a nuclear reprocessing plant from France. Meanwhile, in July 1977, the military under General Zia ul-Haq overthrew Bhutto, and then hanged him in 1979 in what was regarded as a judicial murder. The new military regime refused to yield to US pressure to cancel the contract with France, and the Carter administration then stopped further military and economic aid to Pakistan.[44] The aid was restored a year later, after France bowed to pressure and cancelled the contract, but relations between the US and Pakistan remained strained. In 1979, the US stopped aid once again over concerns relating to Pakistan's uranium-enrichment program.

The Soviet military intervention in Afghanistan in December 1979, however, resulted in a fundamental change in US policy. On the one hand, the US elevated the strategic relationship with China to a de facto alliance, and on the other it began to court Pakistan assiduously as a frontline state. At first, Pakistan dismissed as "peanuts" a $400 million aid package for eighteen months that was offered by the Carter administration, but then eagerly accepted the Reagan administration's offer of a five-year aid package worth $3.2 billion. On Pakistani insistence, the US agreed to supply F-16 aircraft; the insistence apparently derived from the aircraft's ability to carry nuclear weapons. US government spokesmen routinely announced that the aid package would not affect the regional balance of power, but also let it be known that there was no accompanying condition as to what countries the arms could or could not be used against. After five years, the US reached another agreement with Pakistan on a six-year aid package in the amount of $4.02 billion.

In exchange for the aid package, Pakistan agreed to be the conduit for the supply of US arms, training and funding to the Afghan guerillas organized by Pakistan's Inter Services Intelligence (ISI) in an Islamic holy war against the Afghan government and its Soviet backers. During the entire anti-Soviet conflict in Afghanistan, Pakistan maintained the myth that it had nothing to do with the arms supplies to the guerillas. General Zia told President Reagan, "We've been denying our activities there for eight years. Muslims have the right to lie in a good cause." Similarly, he informed the US Defense Secretary: "I'll lie to them like I have been lying to them for the past ten years."[45] The US thus became, in what proved to be a short-sighted policy, an ally of Islamic fundamentalism in Afghanistan. Later it may rue having given birth and

---

[44] General Khalid Mahmud Arif, *Working with Zia: Pakistan's Power Politics 1977–1988* (Karachi: Oxford University Press, 1995), 352.

[45] Kux, *United States and Pakistan*, 289.

training to fanatic terrorists and equipping them with modern weaponry like Stinger missiles, but at this time it found them eminently useful. By the same token, the ISI was turned into a powerful force in the military, politics and external affairs of Pakistan; in turn, it tried to husband US supplies for its own purposes and to establish a regime in Afghanistan that would be in Pakistan's orbit and thus give Pakistan "strategic depth" in its conflict with India. The ISI also found additional resources for itself in drug trafficking from the poppy fields of Afghanistan.

The US was extremely successful in eventually forcing the Soviets to withdraw in humiliation from Afghanistan in 1989, a revenge for its own defeat in Vietnam. However, the longer-term results of the US and Pakistani involvement in Afghanistan for South Asia were enormously damaging. First, it undermined the economic, social and political fabric of Pakistan. It intensified the rise of Islamic fundamentalism in Pakistan, brought about an alliance between the ISI and fundamentalist forces, made violence pervasive in the social life of Pakistan through the generation of what has been known as "the drug and Kalashnikov culture," and further strengthened the military as a political force in Pakistan. It is difficult to say what other alternatives Pakistan had in the face of the Soviet intervention, but the existing suppression of civil society by the military meant that Pakistan's foreign-policy choices tended to represent less the pursuit of the overall national interest of the country than the interests of a single interest group; that is, the military.

Second, because of its contingent needs in Afghanistan, the US also became an accessory to the nuclearization of South Asia, notwithstanding its positions on nonproliferation and rogue states. Nearly a year after the nuclear tests in South Asia in 1998, US Deputy Secretary of State Strobe Talbott stated in an article:

Largely in reaction to developments in India, Pakistan had already concluded that it, too, must have nuclear weapons. It sought and received help from China, which further stoked India's mistrust of both nations. ... During this period, the United States and others were trying to halt proliferation by penalizing countries trafficking in dangerous material.[46]

However, this all too abbreviated history of the Pakistani nuclear and missile program, and of the assistance to it from the outside, overlooks the US's own complicity in that program. It is noteworthy that, prior to the agreement on the US aid package, Pakistan had informed the US,

---

[46] Strobe Talbott, "Dealing with the Bomb in South Asia," *Foreign Affairs*, 78 (March–April 1999), 110–22.

in the words of General Zia's chief aide General Arif, that "Pakistan would neither compromise on her nuclear programs nor accept any external advice on internal matters"; in turn, Secretary of State General Alexander Haig assured that "Pakistan's nuclear program would not become the linchpin of the new relationship." Arif further noted in relation to Afghanistan:

> So strong was the US concern that, as a measure of tactical necessity, she temporarily relegated her concern about Pakistan's nuclear program to the backburner. ... The Soviet military intervention in Afghanistan suddenly eased external pressure. Pakistan's nuclear program remained irksome for the US administration but it no longer was an obstacle in developing a closer relationship with her. The other Western countries and agencies followed the US lead. It became expedient for the West to coexist with the ground reality in Pakistan.[47]

In its confrontation with the Soviet Union, the US thus set aside its concerns over nuclear proliferation and exempted Pakistan for six long years from the requirements of the Symington Amendment. Indeed, after five years it renewed the aid program with a larger amount. The US also turned a blind eye to the growing China–Pakistan nuclear cooperation.

Third, the military aid provided by the US and the nuclear capabilities achieved by Pakistan as a frontline ally of the US emboldened Pakistan to take risks with India by launching on a campaign of "low intensity warfare" against it. Fourth, the forces of fundamentalism and holy war unleashed in the Afghan war with the aid of the US and Pakistan, and the specialized training provided to the ISI in the conduct of terrorism and guerilla warfare, did not remain confined to the Afghan theatre after the Soviet withdrawal. These forces soon made the world their playground, with India a special target. The year 1989 is noteworthy not only for the Soviet withdrawal, but also for the escalation of cross-border state-sponsored terrorism and violence by Pakistan in the Indian state of Kashmir. The US, no doubt, accomplished its Cold War objectives, but it left behind a strategic muddle in South Asia, which barely a dozen years later would rebound on the US itself.

Building economic and military capabilities

Faced with the security concerns arising out of the military regime being in power in Pakistan, the major arms sales to Iran and Saudi

---

[47] Arif, *Working with Zia*, 341, 347, 368. See also Kux, *United States and Pakistan*, 257.

Arabia as allies or benefactors of Pakistan, the lifting of the US arms embargo on Pakistan, and the subsequent massive military aid to Pakistan, India reacted by increasing its defense expenditures and purchasing new weapons systems. Historically, because of the reluctance of the Western countries, particularly the US, to sell arms to India at economic prices, India had been dependent on the Soviet Union. However, India chafed at the excessive dependence on the Soviets and was eager to diversify by buying arms from the West. India's preference for Western equipment lay in its more advanced technology. India bought Mirage 2000 aircraft from the French, Jaguar bombers from the British, and submarines from the Germans. It was less successful with the US, despite discussions about some possible purchases. As a former US foreign-service official pointed out: "In Washington, despite the improvement in atmospherics, many officials, especially in the Defense Department where anti-Indian and pro-Pakistani sentiments persisted, did not like the idea of selling weapons to India."[48] Indeed, the US vetoed the sale of the Swedish aircraft Viggen to India, since it was powered by an American engine.

The usual US reservation on sale of arms to India was the possible leakage of its technology to the Soviets. The Indians took the reluctance to be indicative of the US interest in not strengthening India per se, and particularly not against its military ally, Pakistan. Dual-use technology was in any case barred to the Indians in view of their refusal to sign the NPT. After the meeting of President Reagan and Prime Minister Indira Gandhi at Cancun in 1981, India and the US reached an agreement to facilitate transfer of non-dual-use technology, but the agreement was in effect subverted in implementation. India continued to be denied one sophisticated item after another. As Sridharan noted:

US policy toward Indian high-tech purchases was not one of flat rejection, but one of prolonged delay – sometimes as long as two years – in clearance. ... the policy of delays in export licensing since the mid-1970s was meant to derail Indian projects. Delays were undeclared sanctions. ... because they effectively halted investments in a program until the product became obsolete or would be so by the time it materialized after the clearance was obtained.[49]

Particularly interesting was the fate of India's request for the Cray XMP-24 supercomputer for weather research. For fear that it may be

---

[48] Kux, *India and the United States*, 394.
[49] Eswaran Sridharan, *The Political Economy of Industrial Promotion: Indian, Brazilian, and Korean Electronics in Comparative Perspective, 1969–1994* (Westport, CT: Praeger, 1996), 188–90.

used in nuclear and missile development, the US was willing to offer only a much less powerful computer, Cray XMP-14. The irony is that the US was at the time engaged in a massive transfer of technology to China, a communist country, but was highly restrictive in relation to India, a democracy; realpolitik proved more powerful than shared values.

Given the experience in obtaining defense equipment or technology from the West, India felt justified in its policy of self-reliance. It had already demonstrated its capacity to explode a nuclear device, but had refrained from exercising the nuclear option in terms of a nuclear weapons program. Its reluctance perhaps stemmed from the high economic costs that the program would entail, particularly in view of the economic sanctions that it would surely provoke. India may also have felt that, given the particular world configuration of power at the time, it had tacit nuclear protection from the Soviet Union. Again, it may have believed that exercising the nuclear option would be premature in the absence of the means for delivery, especially in relation to China. That the concern over the nuclear threat was nonetheless strongly felt – given that three nuclear powers existed or operated in its neighborhood (China, the Soviet Union and the US), and that Pakistan was working furiously on a clandestine nuclear program under the direct auspices of its military – is evident from the decision in 1983 to undertake the Integrated Guided Missile Development Program (IGMDP), with the intent to develop a whole array of missiles, including IRBMs. Though abstaining from exercising the nuclear option, the leadership cannot be said to have been particularly nonvigilant in nuclear matters. Through the IGMDP, it was working to add one more building block to a potential balanced structure of nuclear deterrence. Given the deteriorating strategic situation in its neighborhood, India also planned another nuclear test in 1983, but reluctantly gave it up in response to US pressures when the preparations for it were discovered through satellite surveillance.[50] Contrary to Perkovich's position, this level of activity does not betoken any moral reservations on the part of Mrs. Gandhi about "the morality and worth of nuclear weapons" or having been "misled into the nuclear test" of 1974 by the nuclear establishment;[51] rather, it represents a measured response in the overall calculation of costs and benefits.

It is noteworthy also that the Indian leadership did not have a narrow view of building capabilities, confined to the defense arena alone.

[50] K. Subrahmanyam, "Indian Nuclear Policy – 1964–98 (A Personal Recollection)," in Jasjit Singh (ed.), *Nuclear India* (New Delhi: Knowledge World, 1998), 26–53.

[51] Perkovich, *India's Nuclear Bomb*, 188.

Rather, its view encompassed advancing overall economic capabilities. India's economy had been largely stagnant broadly for a decade and a half from 1960 to 1975; indeed, it had seen much turbulence over the period, marked by frequent crises. Marxist analysts referred to the economic situation as "structural retrogression" and assumed it to be self-perpetuating in the absence of structural (that is, revolutionary) change. It is to the credit of Mrs. Gandhi that she initiated a reversal in economic policy in 1974 from her past radicalism in order to put the country on a higher growth path. Her move was decisive but the country's accumulated ideological mindset was too heavily weighted against dramatic change. Nonetheless, the middle of the decade of the 1970s marks India pulling away from the earlier slow-paced pattern of "the Hindu rate of growth." On her return to power in 1980, Mrs. Gandhi pursued liberalization in small doses and that, too, largely by stealth in order to fend off attacks from the entrenched and powerful left on grounds of having betrayed the path of socialism. These were small beginnings but they were essential to the initiation of liberalization. It is important to remember that these beginnings in India grew out of its own experience rather than being a consequence of pressures from the West or in imitation of Margaret Thatcher and Ronald Reagan.

Walking on two legs: Economic reform and nuclear weaponization, 1985–1990

The beginning of this period was both turbulent and full of hope. The assassination of Mrs. Gandhi in October 1984 was followed by large-scale murderous rioting and violence in north India in reaction. India's survival seemed under grave threat. On the other hand, the succession of her son Rajiv Gandhi as prime minister promised youthful and dynamic, even if unproven, leadership to take India, as he himself articulated it, into the twenty-first century as an advanced country. The massive electoral mandate won by him and his party a few months later in early 1985 provided assurance that fulfillment of the promise was within grasp. The open launching of economic liberalization soon after, the public attack by him on political bosses and corruption as part of a promise to revitalize the Congress Party, the reordering of relations with the US on a friendlier course, and the willingness to use power to accomplish foreign-policy goals in the region – all this betokened a more confident and assertive India. These developments in India coincided with a wave of worldwide change; in the USSR, Mikhail Gorbachev succeeded a tired and old leadership and launched the Soviet Union on a promising course of openness and economic and political restructuring, while in much of the developing world economic liberalization and political democracy became the new watchwords.

However, India soon stumbled in the promise. The liberalization process stalled, the future of Rajiv Gandhi came under a cloud because of charges of corruption in defense purchases, his party failed to win the 1989 elections, and political instability and frequent changes in government followed through much of the next decade, which was also marked by violence, generated both from within and from without. Meanwhile, it was surreptitiously, but certainly momentously though reluctantly, decided in the late 1980s to finally go in for a nuclear deterrent in response to Pakistan's acquisition of nuclear weapons with Chinese help and US indulgence.

Pushing economic liberalization

After Mrs. Gandhi died in October 1984, Rajiv Gandhi, her son and political successor, adopted liberalization as the centerpiece of his political program, declaring it as essential for building India as an advanced industrial power. At the beginning, he was helped by the fact that he had won the most powerful electoral mandate in India's history, basically on account of sympathy for the martyrdom of his mother and the threat seen to India's national integration. His open espousal of economic liberalization was truly path-breaking, for no Indian prime minister, indeed no-one in high office, had done so thus far. In a series of highly visible and salient actions, Rajiv Gandhi seemed to initiate a new economic course for India. These actions marked an acceleration of the liberalization policies adopted by Mrs. Gandhi earlier, with the course apparently intended eventually to take the country out of the inherited socialist framework altogether. While his vision was ambitious, Rajiv Gandhi did not envisage an immediate paradigm shift and an overthrow of the old system; rather, his aim appeared to be to carry out incremental revisionist change within the overall framework of the old system.

Interestingly, Rajiv Gandhi took to the new course when India faced no immediate economic crisis. His liberalization stemmed, to a considerable degree, from his personal orientation, especially his fascination with modern technology and computers. However, he was also influenced by the apparent success of the earlier liberalization policies, even as he realized that, despite it, India's growth rate had been insufficient to make an impact on domestic poverty, while at the same time the country was becoming increasingly marginalized internationally. The situation of marginalization was becoming more and more unacceptable to the new leadership. Rajiv Gandhi now sought to reinterpret the concept of self-reliance, which as India's overall national aim in the past had, in the main, been interpreted as requiring the country to produce domestically whatever it could, regardless of considerations of cost. In his reinterpretation, rather than implying autarky, self-reliance meant "the development of a strong, independent national economy dealing extensively with the world, but dealing with it on equal terms."[52]

To a certain extent, the new policies represented a continuity with the process of gradual reform that had been under way for a decade. But they also signified a marked shift. In the first place, there was an acceleration in the pace of change. Furthermore, the change was proclaimed boldly and forthrightly. Second, the policy changes were carried out along a broad front. Third, they were presented without being justified in the name of fostering socialism. The key feature of the changes was reliance on the private sector – instead of the public sector – as the engine of economic growth in the future, and to that end to provide the required resources and appropriate environment for the private sector. The public sector was expected to play a complementary but subsidiary role to the private sector, concentrating primarily on the infrastructure. Designed to influence both the supply side and the demand side, the changes were particularly manifest in taxation, industrial licensing and trade policy.

Although economic liberalization was welcome to the upper and middle classes, it made the government politically vulnerable because it came to be identified with the rich. The trade unions and the communist parties were particularly opposed to liberalization, declaring it to be a reversal of established national policies and a surrender to imperialism. Surprisingly, the first serious challenge to the government on the issue came from key segments within the Congress Party, which were concerned about electoral prospects in the face of being labeled a party of the rich rather than of the poor, as it had traditionally considered itself. As a consequence, Rajiv Gandhi's assertive liberalization soon became moderated and attenuated, indeed arrested. His government was particularly unsuccessful in reforming the public sector.

Despite the setback to his economic program, Rajiv Gandhi nonetheless changed the nature of the debate on the economy; as against the earlier ideological hegemony of socialism and mercantilism, it now became legitimate to regard liberalization as an appropriate alternative economic strategy. Even though he lost the 1989 elections, perhaps for causes unrelated to the economy, he left behind the legacy of his 1991 election manifesto, which the Congress Party posthumously claimed as a mandate for a paradigm shift to economic liberalization. Also, the

---

[52] India, Planning Commission, *Seventh Five Year Plan, 1985–90* (New Delhi: Government of India, Planning Commission, 1985), v.

economy saw a slight acceleration in the annual growth rate, from 5.4 per cent during the Sixth Plan (1980–1985) under Mrs. Gandhi to 5.8 per cent during the Seventh Plan (1985–1990) under Rajiv Gandhi. Some improvement in productivity, resulting from the several doses of liberalization since 1974, may have played a part in the better economic performance. However, a major factor in the higher growth rate was that the state followed an imprudent expansionary policy, relying for expanded investment and populist subsidies – in a shift from its traditional fiscal and monetary conservatism – on successive large fiscal deficits and external commercial borrowings. The regime's fiscal profligacy was, indeed, laying the basis for a future economic crisis. The higher growth rate on the back of fiscal deficits was in the long run just unsustainable.

Still, the average growth rate of about 5.5 per cent during the 1980s did mark a break from what had been regarded as the perennial "Hindu rate of growth" of about 3.5 per cent. The higher economic growth rate possibly inclined India's decision-makers to spend more on defense for the modernization of its armed forces, and it also apparently imparted greater self-confidence in foreign policy and national security, as evident in relation to Sri Lanka, the Maldives and Nepal. This is not to suggest, however, that the consequence was necessarily the cause – that is, that economic liberalization had been inspired by strategic motives. It is difficult to find evidence for a direct link between the liberalization measures undertaken and strategic considerations. Nonetheless, India's decision-makers could not be said to have been oblivious of the link between economy and security; after all, Nehru's economic strategy of self-reliance was based on precisely the acknowledgement of such a link.

More particularly, strategic considerations cannot be altogether excluded from the initial opening to liberalization that started with Mrs. Gandhi in 1974, even though the immediate stimulus was an economic crisis. For Mrs. Gandhi was a past master at realpolitik; comparing herself with her father, she maintained that, "He was a saint who strayed into politics. ... I am a tough politician."[53] The ultimate tribute to her sense of political realism was paid by Henry Kissinger, himself a connoisseur of realpolitik. In his book about his years at the White House, Kissinger stated that one reason Nixon and Mrs. Gandhi totally despised each other was that they were both keen practitioners of realpolitik, and that "Mrs. Gandhi had few peers in the cold-blooded

---

[53] Kux, *India and the United States,* 287. Apart from Mrs. Gandhi's self-perception, Mansingh makes repeated references to her practical and pragmatic political orientation. See Mansingh, *India's Search for Power,* 2, 16, 24, 26–7, 32, 34–5, 196.

calculation of the elements of power. ... Mrs. Gandhi was a strong personality relentlessly pursuing India's national interest with single-mindedness and finesse."[54]

In the light of this assessment, it is not far-fetched to assume, though it is still speculative, that Mrs. Gandhi could well see that India's slow economic growth created foreign-policy costs. After all, she had felt personally humiliated in asking for food shipments from the US, and had vowed not to be put in that position again. She also knew of the foreign-policy consequences of weakness on the food front; she had perforce to remain guarded about too much criticism of the US bombing of Vietnam in view of India's food dependence. Consequently, she had worked determinedly to make India self-sufficient in food. Similarly, as a mark of independence, she had renounced going in for concessional food imports. During the Bangladesh crisis in 1971, she had inquired of her key economic advisor, I.G. Patel, "whether we have the power of sustaining ourselves if the Americans go against us?" She must have been impressed by the economic significance of his reply: "For the first time we have a thousand crores in foreign exchange reserves and foodgrains are in our granary."[55] Again, though not successfully, the Fifth Five Year Plan (1974–1979), framed under her direction, aimed to work for zero net foreign aid. Given this background, she could not have been unaware that a weak economy was inconsistent with foreign-policy independence, and that she had therefore to alter economic course, no doubt for economic reasons, but also for strategic reasons. However, if – despite her assessment and that of her successors about the centrality of rapid economic growth and their eagerness for economic reform to that end – India has largely been an economic laggard and considerably resistant to reforming an entrenched system in the absence of a crisis, a key reason has been its political framework of democracy in the context of a continental polity of awesome diversity. Though it does not always guarantee success in reform, authoritarianism has its advantages.

Crossing the nuclear Rubicon, reactively and reluctantly

Except for 1990, Rajiv Gandhi was prime minister during the period under consideration, 1985 to 1990. This was a critical time, not only for momentous strategic changes in the region but also in the world, particularly the Soviet Union, where Mikhail Gorbachev succeeded an effete and old leadership. Rajiv Gandhi had come to office suddenly, largely as an inexperienced, idealistic young man. In line with his grand-

---

[54] Kissinger, *The White House Years*, 848, 879–80.
[55] Pupul Jayakar, *Indira Gandhi: A Biography* (New Delhi: Viking, 1992), 223.

father's idealism, he spoke with passion against nuclear weapons and against India acquiring them. He developed an image "as a crusader for disarmament."[56] Not surprisingly, he was one of the moving spirits behind the Six-Nation Five-Continent Initiative that resulted in the Delhi Declaration in May 1985 by India, Argentina, Tanzania, Greece, Sweden and Mexico, calling on the nuclear powers to immediately cease testing, development and production of nuclear weapons. In his visits abroad, he repeatedly stressed: "We are for complete nuclear disarmament, dismantling of weapons, and the destruction of stockpiles. We would like this to take place as soon as possible." On the question of India acquiring nuclear weapons, he time and again took the stand:

We have no intention to produce a nuclear weapon. We don't want a nuclear weapon. We think it is wrong, it is bad, it would not help the total world system. ... To go nuclear will be our *last choice*.[57]

He believed that acquisition of nuclear weapons by India would be counterproductive for its economic and political development.

Yet being against nuclear weapons did not mean that he was against the rise of India as a major power. He told the US Congress in June 1985: "I dream of an India strong, independent, self-reliant, in the front rank of the nations of the world in the service of mankind."[58] Indeed, his period in office saw India become more assertive in power terms in the region. His readiness to help foil a military coup when asked to do so by the legitimate government of the Maldives, his intervention in Sri Lanka with an Indian peacekeeping force to help the government curb a secessionist insurgency, his use of trade restrictions against Nepal when it threatened India's strategic interests vis-à-vis China, and his encouragement to the army chief of staff in the modernization of India's defense forces – all these are testimony to his not being insensitive to the uses of power. And, finally, when after 1987 the evidence became overwhelming of US inaction in the face of the Pakistani acquisition of nuclear weapons with the assistance of China, he took the plunge and secretly authorized going nuclear, notwithstanding his personal sentiments to the contrary. India was now confronted with a situation where two ardently hostile nuclear powers that were deeply in collusion sat on its borders. "Faced with these harsh realities," says Subrahmanyam, Rajiv Gandhi gave the "go-ahead" to the nuclear establishment in 1988 "to

---

[56] Subrahmanyam, "Indian Nuclear Policy," 43.
[57] Kathleen Healy, *Rajiv Gandhi: The Years of Power* (New Delhi: Vikas, 1989), 32–7; emphasis in the original.
[58] *ibid.*, 6.

proceed with the Indian weapons program. The Agni was successfully test-fired in May 1989. It could not have been an easy decision for Rajiv Gandhi."[59] By 1990 India had, as a consequence, developed a nuclear deterrent in response to Pakistan's prior acquisition of nuclear weapons capability. India, like Pakistan, had thus become a de facto nuclear-weapons power. The nuclear Rubicon was in reality therefore crossed in the late 1980s, even though the nuclear tests that caused such global uproar were to come a decade later. In the face of these facts, it cannot therefore be maintained that the Indian leaders, especially those belonging to the Congress Party, had shied away from responding to the nuclear threat on moral grounds.[60] When the moment required it, they took the appropriate decision, and the crucial determinant in the decision was the perceived threat to national security.

George Perkovich has argued that India's nuclear program, unlike the corresponding programs of the other nuclear powers, originated not in threats to its security, but arose for reasons of international prestige, national identity and the significance of nuclear capabilities as a symbol of modernity. He maintains that, prior to the Chinese nuclear tests, "international security considerations played little role in shaping Indian nuclear policy." Although Nehru "recognized that nuclear weapon capability could enhance India's status and power in the Western-dominated world whose logic he understood well," he states: "Bhabha and Nehru took India to a unique position of restrained nuclear weapon capability with little regard for particular security concerns." Instead:

the main motivations for India's initial plans to acquire the means to produce nuclear explosives had more to do with Bhabha's and Nehru's beliefs that nuclear technology offered India a shortcut to modernity and major power status.

Such mastery of science would also allow India to "transcend its recent colonial past" and "refute racially tinged stereotypes about the capacities of Third World scientists."[61] In this manner, Perkovich tends to downgrade, largely by assertion, the security motive, and overlooks the abundant evidence in his own work, which contradicts his position. For example, security was at the core of Bhabha's concerns at his address to the Pugwash conference in 1964 before the Chinese tests, and it moved to the center of national debate after the tests.[62] The choice of an appro-

---

[59] Subrahmanyam, "Indian Nuclear Policy," 44.
[60] See Perkovich, *India's Nuclear Bomb*, 6.
[61] *ibid.*, 14–15, 47, 59.
[62] *ibid.*, 60–1, chs 2, 4.

priate nuclear strategy to meet the challenge to security is an altogether different matter, however.

More broadly, in relation to the nature of security threat just prior to the Chinese tests – that is, allegedly the absence of such a threat – Perkovich and others who share his views betray a misconception of what a threat to security means. Does a security threat mean only a declaration of belligerent intent by adversaries, or does it not also mean disparity in capabilities in relation to declared or potential adversaries? Does it only mean a clear and present danger of physical attack, or does it not also mean the prospect of political domination, coercive diplomacy, political blackmail, or even an adverse balance of power? If there exists a disparity in capabilities and, as a consequence of that disparity, also the potential for political domination, then a security threat exists for the country with the lesser capabilities, even if it only be latent for the moment. The disparity in terms of nuclear capabilities is not something that can be bridged overnight in the face of an eruption of actual threat, but requires preparation over a long period of time.

Summary and conclusions

An analysis of India's relationship to the world over about the quarter of a century after Nehru finds little basis for the view that the successor leadership over this period lacked either the Nehruvian vision about India's role as a major player in the world, or his commitment to the building of the economic and military capabilities appropriate for such a role. Such a view has been based on an inadequate appreciation of the severe constraints, both internal and external, under which the leadership had to function. The internal constraints derived, first and foremost, from the long-term condition of India's underdevelopment and the limited resources that went with that condition. What is especially worthy of note is that in the early part of this period the leadership faced a series of awesome crises, which arose, in considerable measure, from Nehru's own economic policies. The economic crises, which directly affected the lives of hundreds of millions of people in areas as critical as food, did not afford the successor leadership the luxury to launch a rapid march to the acquisition of strategic capabilities. Besides the pressures of these crises, the very nature of India's political system placed severe limits on any forced build-up of such capabilities. Necessarily, the path had to be gradual and incremental.

Moreover, the leadership confronted constraints from the external environment by way of war, containment and restrictive international regimes on the part of one or another set of adversaries. Yet, through all this, the leadership continued to build, block by block, India's strategic capabilities to a point where, when the moment was opportune, India could test nuclear weapons and stand up as a declared NWS. Under the circumstances in which it was placed after the Nehru era, for the leadership to have attempted to act beyond what it actually did would have been adventuristic, to say the least. To be sure, the Indian leadership carried – perhaps not to the degree that Nehru did – ideals handed down by the nationalist movement and its leading lights such as Gandhi and Nehru, but it was not handcuffed by morality when it came to safeguarding India's national interests. Partisan attacks aside, the record abundantly speaks to the constancy and consistency of commitment to national interests on the part of the Indian leadership. What determined its actions was not morality but the circumscribing condition of constraints. It avoided, however, the extremes of panic and adventurism. To be prudent in the face of constraints, as the successor leadership was, is not the same thing as to be lacking in vision and will.

Of more critical significance has been the failure of the political leadership on the economic and social fronts in respect of achieving rapid economic growth, removing poverty and investing in the social sectors. The need for reform has been evident to the leadership, but in terms of determined action it has been a prisoner of the system in which it is located. Many entrenched groups who benefited from over four decades of the command economy are loath to lose their economic and social privileges, and therefore oppose reform. Political democracy enables such groups to block or scuttle reform, for democracy is nothing but a mirror of society, and it often tends to politically privilege those who are socially powerful. Reform in these circumstances tends to be slow. The comparison with China, no doubt, is relevant. However, as Marx maintained, men make history, but they do so within the constraints of their social situation. Taking the comparison with China too seriously ought necessarily to entail the recommendation for either revolution or dictatorship.

6   After the Cold War: Adaptation, Persistence and Assertion, 1991–2001

The end of the Cold War, marked by the unraveling of the Soviet bloc in 1990 and more dramatically by the unexpected disintegration of the Soviet Union in 1991, transformed the nature of the international system from a bipolar order to a semi-unipolar one that was now presided over by the US as the sole superpower. The event also sparked a profound resurgence of US, and in a broader sense Western, triumphalism. With its awesome capabilities, including those emergent from the revolution in military affairs (RMA), the US was, in the aftermath of the end of the Cold War, now determined to remain the sole superpower. This determination was set forth in an emphatic fashion in the draft Defense Planning Guidance Paper of 1992:

> Our first objective is to prevent the reemergence of a new rival, either on the territory of the former Soviet Union or elsewhere. ... This is a dominant consideration ... and requires that we endeavor to prevent any hostile power from dominating a region whose resources would, under consolidated control, be sufficient to generate global power. ... Our strategy must now refocus on precluding the emergence of any potential future global competitor.[1]

Following the lead of the guidance paper, one US scholar demanded, more colorfully, that the US "be the global hegemon of the regional hegemons, the boss of all the bosses."[2] The US political leadership itself was not far behind in expressing this self-perception of the US as the one indispensable nation. As a consequence, the key feature of the US strategy to retain and perpetuate its position as the sole superpower has been containment of the second tier of the major powers, existing or aspirant, unless they are willing to bandwagon with the US as

---

[1] Cited in Barry R. Posen and Andrew L. Ross, "Competing Visions for U.S. Grand Strategy," *International Security,* 21 (Winter 1996–97), 5–53. The draft paper was subsequently revised after severe criticisms around the world following its unauthorized publication.

[2] James Kurth, cited in Posen and Ross, "Competing Visions," 36.

subordinate allies. The chief mechanism in this policy of containment of other contending powers has been the conventional technique of counter-balancing them through alliances, explicit or tacit. Another mechanism has been the creation and fostering of international regimes which would freeze or limit the nuclear and missile capabilities of its rivals, and also to prevent the rise of any new powers with such capabilities.

Despite the evident rise of the US to the status of the sole hegemonic superpower in the new semi-unipolar system, and the seeming permanence of that arrangement, it is apparent that the world has also seen a substantial diffusion of power. Indeed, some realist scholars have maintained that it is inevitable that new challengers opposed to the US will rise in the wake of the demise of the Soviet Union.[3] Already, the diffusion of power can be seen in the rise of Japan as an economic superpower (even though it has seen some decline over a decade during the 1990s), as well as in the emergence of China as a potential challenger to the US. Equally, the European Union (EU), with Germany as its economic core and France and Britain as its nuclear core, may also eventually turn out to be a challenger as it advances further its economic cohesion and develops its independent military identity. Russia, too, as the successor to the Soviet Union, may see a market-driven economic revival and acquire the economic muscle to undergird its still massive military arsenal.

Other regional powers that are dominant in certain territories may also seize their opportunities as they emerge to claim their due as major powers through the acquisition of the appropriate nuclear and missile capabilities. In addition, the major powers in the second tier may form alliances among themselves to counter the hegemony of the sole superpower. The present ascendance of the US to hegemonic status in a semi-unipolar system does not therefore guarantee a continuance of that position, and it has to constantly remain on guard and endeavor to hold on to it through various mechanisms. Moreover, beyond the state-level challenges, there are now the substantial subnational threats posed by terrorist groups as evident in the September 11, 2001, attacks in New York and Washington, DC. On the other hand, notwithstanding the diffusion of world power, the existential disparity in power between the US and the second tier of the major powers is so massive – and the incentives, both economic and political, to cooperate with it are so over-

---

[3] Christopher Layne, "The Unipolar Illusion: Why New Great Powers Will Rise," *International Security*, 17 (1993), 5–51; Kenneth N. Waltz, "The Emerging Structure of International Politics," *International Security*, 18 (1993), 44–79.

whelming – that every major power, existent or aspirant, is compelled to continue or to adopt a policy of *engagement* with the US.

Regardless, the end of the Cold War confronted India with a new strategic situation of the semi-unipolar system, in which the Soviet Union was no longer available as a political, economic and security anchor, and in which nonalignment had been rendered meaningless since a leverage-providing rival bloc had disappeared. As a consequence, India stood out, as Huntington was to describe it, as a "lonely" and "friendless" power.[4] In the face of this situation, for which it was hardly prepared, India had perforce to adapt its international posture and to work out new political equations with the major powers. Unfortunately for it, the circumstances for such adaptation were hardly propitious. For, as the end of the Cold War was under way, India was going through the throes of the end of the political hegemony of the Congress Party. The resulting coalition governments between 1989 and 1991 made not only for political instability, but also for political turmoil and violence as a result of their penchant for populist measures. Additionally, as a consequence of the withdrawal of the Soviet forces from Afghanistan in 1989, Pakistan was on an ascending curve of assertiveness, and it vigorously diverted its energies to foster and sustain a major long-term insurgency against India through inducting *jihadi* (crusader) guerillas into Kashmir.[5] Even when new elections in 1991 restored the Congress Party to power, the Congress initially suffered from the handicap of lacking a majority in parliament. It was nonetheless to the new Congress government led by Prime Minister P.V. Narasimha Rao that the task of adaptation was entrusted for execution over the succeeding half-decade. However, when the Congress took over power, adaptation to the new international situation was a lesser priority in the face of an overwhelming economic crisis.

The end of the Cold War coincided with the shooting into prominence in worldwide perception of another international phenomenon, that of economic globalization, in which, too, the US was the most powerful actor. A key consequence of globalization has been the expansion of the market at the expense of the state, which has had to be redesigned or re-engineered so as to render it less controlling and interventionist in relation to the economy. Among the less-developed countries (LDCs), the process of globalization has often been advanced through the forced opening up of their economies by structural adjustment programs

[4] Cited in J. Mohan Malik, "India Goes Nuclear: Rationale, Benefits, Costs and Implications," *Contemporary Southeast Asia*, 20 (August 1998), 103.

[5] Dennis Kux, *The United States and Pakistan, 1947–2000: Disenchanted Allies* (Washington, DC: Woodrow Wilson Center Press, 2001), 305, 316, 321–2.

imposed by the international financial institutions like the IMF and the World Bank. Some enthusiasts of globalization predict that the increased pace of international economic integration would, as markets come to dominate the state, make the state irrelevant. It is true that economic issues have acquired greater salience in world affairs, and that they today exercise increased influence over the conduct of bilateral relations. However, the state with national security as its primary function continues to remain central for its population and in international politics. The stories about its impending demise are highly exaggerated.

While there has, no doubt, been pressure on the LDCs to go in for economic liberalization, many of them have also come to realize the need for the same on account of the costs of economic insulation. For economic insulation has had distortionary effects by way of: slower rates of economic growth; high-cost, and therefore uncompetitive, economies; shortages of goods and necessities; and large-scale smuggling. India, too, had been suffering such consequences over the years, and accordingly it had for some time been contemplating economic-policy reform. However, starting in 1990, it was confronted with an economic crisis of major proportions, in which it teetered on the verge of defaulting on its debt repayments. The new Congress government under Narasimha Rao thus had to confront not only the task of adaptation to the new international political configuration emergent from the end of the Cold War, but also the task of coming to terms with the awesome economic crisis. This chapter therefore initially looks at the response to the economic crisis and then to the task of foreign-policy adaptation, not only under the Congress government, but also under subsequent coalition governments. The discussion is divided into six parts: (1) economic liberalization; (2) engagement with the US and other major powers; (3) tightening of the nuclear noose by the major powers; (4) defiance of the major powers by India on nuclear testing; (5) the aftermath of the defiance; and (6) the new challenge of global terrorism.

Economic liberalization

The stalling of the economic reforms after 1987, combined with the fiscal profligacy of the state during the 1980s, had made the balance of payments critical by the end of the decade, a situation that was compounded by political instability under coalition governments. With Iraq's invasion of Kuwait in 1990 and the resulting Gulf War in early 1991, the economic situation in India erupted into a full-blown economic crisis. In response, soon after coming into power in mid-1991, the new Congress government resorted, in cooperation with the IMF and World Bank, to a major program of economic restructuring, consisting not only of short-term economic stabilization, but also of a longer-term structural adjustment.[6] Although there was continuity in this endeavor with the reforms implemented during the previous decade, there was at the same time a clear acceleration of the reform process and thus a break with the earlier reforms. The new government openly embraced globalization and liberalization with obvious enthusiasm, and made a paradigm shift in the nation's economic posture. Opting in favor of the market over the state, it started the process of dismantling along a broad front the system of physical controls associated with the inherited command economy.

The currency was sharply devalued and gradually made fully convertible on the current account. The licensing system was almost completely abolished for imports, while tariffs were reduced drastically. The doors were substantially flung open for foreign investment. Also, the entire structure of industrial licensing was demolished, restrictions on the expansion and diversification of industrial capacity were reduced or removed, and many areas hitherto reserved for the public sector were thrown open to the private sector. True, not all that was desired or intended was achieved. However, there was substantial movement in the direction of globalization and liberalization. Indeed, the World Bank emphasized that "India has fundamentally altered its development paradigm" and that the reforms "have ended four decades of planning and have initiated a quiet economic revolution."[7]

Although 1991 marked a policy breakthrough, a fuller change from a command economy to a market economy was a task only for the long haul. India's democratic political structure imposed constraints on the pace of change; change could only be gradual and incremental, not of the "big bang" or "shock therapy" variety, even if the latter had been desirable. Frequent changes in government that were a feature of the 1990s also slowed reform, especially when the government lacked a majority in the upper house. Even though all governments persevered to carry forward the liberalization process, regardless of their original ideological predilections, the process of reform remained excruciatingly slow. Successive governments found it especially difficult to resolve the problem of persisting fiscal deficits; to privatize state-owned enterprises; to institute reforms in the labor sector; and to restructure the debt-ridden and loss-making state electricity boards.

[6] The issue of economic policy reform is more thoroughly examined in Baldev Raj Nayar, *Globalization and Nationalism: The Changing Balance in India's Economic Policy, 1950–2000* (New Delhi: Sage, 2001).
[7] World Bank, *India: Five Years of Stabilization and Reform and the Challenges Ahead* (Washington, DC: 1996), xvii, 31.

Despite the constraints and the limits to reform, the Congress government managed the economic stabilization program extremely skillfully and smoothly under the able leadership of Finance Minister Manmohan Singh. Even though distributional problems persisted, there was no decline in national income, economic recovery was quick and the economy was placed on a higher growth path. Economists are likely to differ as to the causes of growth, or even question whether there has been real growth, but with a growth rate of over 5 per cent the period of liberalization since the early 1980s does mark a higher growth path for the economy (see Table 2). It is unlikely that any strategic motives underlay the economic restructuring at the beginning of the 1990s. The economic crisis was an overwhelming concern of the leadership, whose attention was directed toward overcoming it. There was nonetheless an underlying concern that the earlier economic model had failed in relation to the two key goals of the republic's founding fathers: making India a major economic player in the world, and raising the standards of living of the population. This concern was sharply deepened when seen in the context of the rapid growth in the economies of East Asia, including China.

Table 2 *GNP growth: Five-year average rates (at 1993–94 prices)*

Years	Rate (%)
1951–52 to 1955–56	3.7
1956–57 to 1960–61	4.2
1961–62 to 1965–66	2.8
1966–67 to 1970–71	4.8
1971–72 to 1975–76	3.3
1976–77 to 1980–81	3.4
1981–82 to 1985–86	4.8
1986–87 to 1990–91	6.1
1991–92 to 1995–96	5.5
1996–97 to 2000–01	6.2

Source: Calculated from data in Government of India, *Economic Survey 2000–2001* (New Delhi: Ministry of Finance, 2001), S–4. The annual rate for 2000–01 has been taken to be 5.2 per cent on the basis of the story "NCAER Cuts 2001/02 GDP Growth to 4.8%," http://www.timesofindia.com, December 28, 2001. Projections for the year 2001–02, a year featuring a worldwide economic downturn, place growth at between 4.5 and 5.5 per cent.

Regardless, the economic liberalization undertaken had a double-edged impact on national security. The immediate response to the economic crisis in 1991 by way of economic stabilization was adverse for defense preparedness, since the brunt of the slashing of budgetary expenditures was borne by the military. However, economic liberalization also had a different kind of impact on India's strategic situation. By putting India on a higher economic growth path, by adding substantially to India's foreign-exchange reserves, and by making possible access to foreign investment instead of the earlier sole reliance on official foreign aid, liberalization provided the political elite a sense of greater confidence about managing the economy. No doubt, India continued to face high fiscal deficits from one year to the next, but the better performance of the economy instilled faith that the economy was no longer predestined for slow growth. What that performance did was to provide assurance that India could withstand the imposition of economic sanctions by the US and its allies in case it needed to defy them over the nuclear option. In that sense, economic power in the shape of better economic performance through liberalization and military power in the shape of the later exercise of the nuclear option were intimately connected. This is a connection that seems to have been lost on the economic nationalists, who wish to insulate India from the world economy even as they want an India with greater economic and military muscle.

An unintended consequence of economic liberalization was, as a result of the removal of state controls over the economy and the exploitation of India's particular endowment, the sparking of an explosion of computer-software exports and of the high demand in the Western world, especially the US, for India's computer professionals. This new phenomenon not only helped India in the sphere of invisible foreign-exchange earnings, but it also to some extent dented the worldwide perception of India as solely a backward economy, and it instead enhanced its image as a country of some exceptional technological strengths.

Seeking engagement but resisting containment

With the Soviet Union gone as a pillar of security, India was compelled by considerations of national security to rework its relations with the major powers, the key ones being the sole superpower, the US, India's chief arms supplier, Russia, and India's principal long-time adversary in Asia, China. India under Narasimha Rao attempted to accomplish this in a considered overall strategy of seeking constructive engagement with all these powers. The important elements of the strategy were: to work for positive relations with the major powers, to abjure provocation and confrontation in dealings with them, to resolve bilateral problems in a practical manner through identifying areas of agreement as a basis for building mutually beneficial relationships, and to avoid moralizing and ideological posturing on issues that were important to them. At the same time, under this strategy, India was equally determined to remain firm on issues of fundamental importance to its strategic interests.[8] Because, for their own reasons, some of the major powers had adopted a policy of regional containment toward India, both through alliances and through instituting restrictive and discriminatory international regimes, India was fully resolved to resist and counter their efforts in this direction.

Despite the apparent novelty of the strategy, there was continuity at the same time with earlier policies, even though these had then been practised under the rubric of nonalignment. India had diversified relationships with the two power blocs, and there was consequently no need for an altogether radical departure requiring rapprochement with any of the major powers in repudiation of earlier policy. What essentially became necessary now were adjustments in the relations with the major powers in the changed geopolitical context. No doubt, the earlier ideological posturing had involved staking positions often on grounds of moral and universal principles, but this stance encompassed such principles as mere code words for considered national interests.

Nor for that matter, at the same time, had the geopolitical situation changed so radically with the end of the Cold War as to eliminate the central features that have long been part and parcel of the working of the international system. Interstate conflict, even in a muted form, remains the defining characteristic of international politics, and states continue to resort to the classic mechanism of balancing, in both its hard and soft varieties, to secure their national interests. There is, undoubtedly, often a tendency to exaggerate the impact of contemporaneous momentous events such as the end of the Cold War. However, old enmities do not as a result always easily vanish, nor do old patterns of alliances always easily come to a sudden end; nor are old hurts and defeats in violent contests always easily forgotten. The central features of international politics have a strange habit of reasserting themselves. *Plus ça change, plus c'est la même chose.* Under the circumstances, what would be ideally desirable from India's viewpoint would be harmony, but not condominium, among the major powers, so that India would not be pulled into their conflicts. A second-best situation would be, on the assumption that China would remain a long-term adversary and a security threat, good relations with both the US and Russia as support-

[8] See J.N. Dixit, *My South Block Years: Memoirs of a Foreign Secretary* (New Delhi: UBSPD, 1996), 177–8; and J.N. Dixit, *Across Borders: Fifty Years of India's Foreign Policy* (New Delhi: Picus Books, 1998), 293.

ive powers that were at the same time on friendly terms with each other. While India may devoutly wish for either of these situations, it is not within its control or capacity to bring them about. The worst possible scenario for India would be a hostile US allied with its adversaries.

Managing the US's regional-containment policy

In its new position as the sole superpower in a semi-unipolar system, the US sought, particularly after the Gulf War in 1991, a wide-ranging engagement with the various powers in an effort to build a "new world order" under its hegemonic leadership. Although India was not of central importance in this strategy of engagement, the US nonetheless considered it to be an important regional power in Asia. Moreover, India was seen as a potentially attractive economic partner now that it had opted for liberalization and was enacting economic-policy reforms to open its economy to foreign trade and investment.

For its part, India under Narasimha Rao was eager for a closer relationship with the US in the changed structure of world power. India's policy of engagement with the US was not entirely novel, however. After all, Indira Gandhi and Ronald Reagan had seemed to launch the two countries on a friendlier course after their meeting in Cancun in 1981. Similarly, Rajiv Gandhi had advanced relations between the two countries by signing in 1985 a "memorandum of understanding" to promote technological cooperation. If, despite these efforts, there was little actual advance in relations, it was because the US was single-mindedly focused at the time, insofar as South Asia was concerned, on getting the Soviet Union out of Afghanistan. The memorandum of understanding on technology transfer therefore remained, in practice, substantially a dead letter. There was too much US suspicion about India's relationship with the Soviet Union and too much US commitment to Pakistan as a frontline ally to give the latter cause for annoyance; as a consequence, the US was unwilling to contribute to building India's technological capabilities.

The new circumstance of a changed geopolitical context following the end of the Cold War was perhaps more propitious for an improved relationship. Indeed, there was some increase in military cooperation by way of conducting a minor joint naval exercise in 1992. However, the approaches of the two states to their mutual relations were working fundamentally at cross-purposes. India sought through its strategy of constructive engagement to improve relations so as to build its capabilities and, especially, to protect its nuclear option, whereas the US under President George Bush (senior) sought precisely to contain India's capabilities and, more critically, to divest it of its nuclear option. This was no recipe for success in building fruitful relations. India found itself under insistent pressure from the US to cap, roll back and eventually eliminate its nuclear capabilities, a formula that was passed on to the Clinton administration. The most visible and concrete expression of the Bush administration's opposition to India's nuclear and missile capabilities was its determined effort to persuade the new Russian government to cancel in 1993 the contract to supply cryogenic engine technology for India's civilian space program.

India's relations with the Clinton administration, which came to power in 1993, got off to a bad start. Part of the reason was that the new administration made nuclear nonproliferation and Kashmir the centerpiece of its policy toward South Asia. Nuclear nonproliferation was, of course, a matter of deep concern to the wider US strategic community. However, the antiproliferation lobby was particularly strong in the new Democratic administration, and India was a special target for pressure because of the belief that Pakistan would follow suit once India agreed to US prescriptions. The first Clinton administration, no doubt, sought increased interaction with India, but without any larger shared strategic purpose, for India did not figure as of much importance on the US radar screen. One purpose in such enhanced interaction was to advance the economic relationship, with the US encouraging India to continue on the path of liberalization. The larger purpose, however, was the regional containment of India in respect of nuclear capabilities.

Many proposals were put forward by the US in order to disarm India in the nuclear arena. India, however, remained opposed to piecemeal solutions, such as a nuclear-free zone for South Asia, and to other proposals. The Clinton administration also successfully persuaded France to stop supplying nuclear fuel for the commercial reactor at Tarapur. Apart from its vehement insistence on nuclear nonproliferation, the administration wanted India to desist from developing and testing missile capabilities. India, however, defiantly refused to oblige, and tested the intermediate-range ballistic missile Agni in January 1994. What caused great consternation to India was that, while the Clinton administration was thus energetically pursuing the goal of eliminating India's nuclear capabilities, it was promoting a policy of strategic engagement with China. To India, it seemed that, rather than building a balance of power in Asia that would involve the major powers in Asia, including Russia, Japan and India, apart from the US and China, the US appeared determined to work for a condominium over Asia in strategic partnership with China, in the belief that it had sufficient capabilities to manage China by itself. Adding to India's concerns was the fact that, while the US was focused on eliminating India's nuclear capabilities, it decidedly overlooked or underplayed the transfer of nuclear and missile technology by China to Pakistan, and the persistence of such transfer even after China joined the NPT in 1992 and agreed to abide by several Missile Technology Control Regime (MTCR) norms.[9] In sum, the US was rewarding China for its proliferation activities, while continuing to punish India through sanctions and pressures for its restraint.

The nonproliferation issue was, in turn, heavily implicated in Kashmir, because the two parties in conflict over that territory were already de facto nuclear powers, and President Clinton considered Kashmir to be the most dangerous place in the world. What set the proverbial cat among the pigeons, however, was what India regarded as inflammatory statements in 1993 by Assistant Secretary of State Robin Raphel, who seemed to question the very validity of the legal instrument of accession of Kashmir to India.[10] Nothing could have raised hackles in India more, nor pleased Pakistan more, than that particular stance of the State Department. Despite India's earlier determination not to let acrimony creep into the relationship, senior Indian ministers reacted with harsh statements of their own. To the Indians, the new US stance on Kashmir signified a reorientation of policy on the part of the Clinton administration toward Pakistan, for the administration also sought to revive the arms-supply relationship with that nation.[11]

India's eagerness to seek engagement with the US thus ran smack into the American policy of containment during the first Clinton administration. Engagement therefore proved to be fruitless: "Indo-US political relations were in the doldrums" even as economic relations "continued to expand."[12] Despite the end of the Cold War, the fundamental reality was that the interests of the US as the sole superpower and of India as an aspirant major power stood in contradiction to each other. India's strategy of engagement was based on the exaggerated expectation that "the US would be willing to accept India's political, technological and economic aspirations without any reservations in the transformed international scenario."[13] This was an unwarranted assumption, for, given its new role in a semi-unipolar system, the US was even more assertive in respect of having the world conform to its preferences on how the globe should be ordered. The common attribute of democracy was a poor reed on which to build a strong relationship. Furthermore, the US saw Pakistan as performing a useful role in coun-

---

[9] Kux, *United States and Pakistan*, 282–6, 332–3.

[10] *ibid.*, 327–8.

[11] The efforts at renewing the arms relationship with Pakistan during the Clinton administration are recounted in *ibid.*, 326–32.

[12] Dixit, *My South Block Years*, 203.

[13] *ibid.*, 204.

terbalancing India, and thus in persuading the latter to act in accord with US policy. Bent as the US was on selective nuclear nonproliferation, and determined as India was to preserve its nuclear option until there was a commitment on the part of the P-5 for universal nuclear disarmament, the two powers seemed set on a collision course.

Salvaging the arms relationship with Russia

India's strategic relationship with the Soviet Union had begun to crumble even before the latter disintegrated. Once Mikhail Gorbachev came to power in 1985, the Soviet Union reoriented its overall global strategy, making collaboration with the US and an end to hostility with China the centerpieces of its diplomacy. In the process, little remained of the rationale for the earlier strategic convergence with India. The Soviet Union then placed India and Pakistan on an equal footing in its foreign policy. With that ended the Soviet policy of invariably supporting India in the disputes between the two countries of South Asia.

Ironically, after the disintegration of the Soviet Union, Russia continued that newly developed Soviet policy in view of its larger strategic architecture of integrating itself with the West. Indeed, so overwhelming was the contemporaneous thrust to integrate with the West that Russia rejected all policy that it thought was associated with the former Soviet Union. The strategic neglect of India flowed naturally from that particular stance. This was a grievous setback for India, and its relations with Russia deteriorated and entered a period of considerable uncertainty. When Russia did become more receptive to Indian overtures subsequently, it was for its own reasons. It was only the later nationalist backlash following Russia's disappointment with the West in treating it as an object and as a potential adversary (given the West's commitment to enlarging NATO) that led Russia to make a strategic shift, though not a wholesale one. Russia then became more assertive vis-à-vis the West and began to cultivate areas that it had hitherto neglected or ignored.[14] Therefore, it was only after Russia had thus reconfigured its strategic calculus that China and India once again, as a result, became the recipients of Russian affection. Although not in the same measure as in the past before Gorbachev, there were two other reasons why India was again attractive as a partner: as a major arms market for a cash-strapped Russia, and as the most powerful state in a region located close to Russia.

At the same time, Russia was extraordinarily important to India. With some 70 per cent of its arms imports dependent on the former Soviet

---

[14] Hannes Adomeit, "Russia as a 'Great Power' in World Affairs: Images and Reality," *International Affairs*, 17 (1995), 35–68.

Union, salvaging as much of the earlier relationship as possible was most crucial to India. Therefore, it sought to settle as quickly as possible emergent problems between the two countries, most importantly the Indian debt to Russia for past supplies and, relatedly, the rouble–rupee exchange rate. Yeltsin visited India in early 1993, and negotiations led to the resolution of the two issues, though more to the satisfaction of the Russians, as India made most of the concessions in the interest of a longer-term relationship. Yeltsin assured the Indians of the continued high importance of India to Russia for both strategic and economic reasons, and he underlined the convergence of interests between the two countries.[15] A new treaty of "friendship and cooperation" was signed between the two countries, but it lacked the semimilitary clauses of its predecessor. Other agreements were also signed, relating to technology and defense cooperation. Yeltsin also promised to abide by the earlier Soviet contract with India to supply cryogenic technology for its civilian space program.

Even though the Yeltsin visit generated considerable enthusiasm in India, the relations between the two countries saw little improvement in substance. For one thing, Yeltsin soon caved in to US pressure on the contract for cryogenic technology. For another, later in the year, Russian Foreign Minister Andrei Kozyrev, contrary to Yeltsin's assurances, downgraded relations with India by taking policy positions on nuclear nonproliferation and Kashmir strictly in line with that of the US and its allies.[16] It was only after the victory of the nationalists in new elections in 1995 that the process of improvement began in bilateral relations.[17] But there could be no restoration of the situation that existed prior to Gorbachev, for China was now an important partner for Russia, economically and strategically.[18] Such a situation could only add to the Indian determination to be self-reliant in deterrence capabilities, even while cultivating Russia for the arms-supply relationship and as a balancing factor in relations with the other major powers.

[15] Dixit, *My South Block Years*, 220.
[16] *ibid.*, 223.
[17] Adomeit, "Russia as a 'Great Power'," 59.
[18] On Russia's arms sales to China, see Zalmay Khalilzad *et al.*, *The United States and a Rising China: Strategic and Military Implications* (Santa Monica, CA: Rand, 1999), 50–2.

Warily engaging China as adversary

The engagement with China had begun long before the end of the Cold War. The turning point in the relationship came with the visit to China of Prime Minister Rajiv Gandhi in 1988, when the two countries agreed to set up a joint working group to resolve the border dispute. A key element in the forward movement was the Indian concession not to insist on a prior resolution of the border dispute, though without shelving it, but to move on to improve relations in other areas. The process of engagement was carried further in 1991 when China's Premier Li Peng visited India. In 1993, Narasimha Rao went to Beijing on a return visit, and signed the important "agreement on the maintenance of peace and tranquility" along the line of actual control as a confidence-building measure. The same year China agreed to replace France in the supply of nuclear fuel for the commercial reactor at Tarapur. Other exchanges of high-level officials followed, including the visit by Chinese President Jiang Zemin in 1996. During this period, China also appeared to distance itself somewhat from its earlier stance of one-sided support of Pakistan in its disputes with India.

Despite the apparent improvement in relations as a result of India's policy of engagement, there was one highly disturbing element in the relationship which had a deep impact on India. Throughout this period of improving relations and the bonhomie associated with the official exchanges, China continued unremittingly on a course of supplying nuclear and missile equipment and technology to Pakistan, in addition to vast quantities of other weaponry. China's military relationship with Pakistan, building the country as a military counterweight against India, was of long standing, going back to the early 1960s, but the more recent nuclear and missile element was putting India at a serious disadvantage. This new element served as an "equalizer" between Pakistan and India, eroding the latter's superiority in conventional arms. Moreover, it made India's strategic situation unenviable insofar as Pakistan's nuclear and missile capabilities were, being derived from China, proven ones, as against India's untested devices.

China's nexus with Pakistan on India's western flank was not the only variable in the equation. On India's eastern flank, China also found a military regime in Myanmar suffering from diplomatic isolation and developed a military relationship with it, rendering it a virtual client state. In return, China obtained observation facilities in Myanmar's Coco Islands in the Bay of Bengal to monitor India's missile testing. In addition to Pakistan and Myanmar, China cultivated India's other smaller neighbors, both politically and militarily, as if to surround India with a ring of containment. It also vastly increased its military capabilities in Tibet.

Behind the smokescreen of cordiality between India and China, which had been apparent in the early and mid-1990s, there thus lay a different reality altogether. Engagement between the two countries was based not on trust, but simply on convenience to avoid a flare-up on the border, which could spin out of control. Behind the mask of engagement was the reality of deep mistrust and enduring rivalry between the two adversaries. In their continuing rivalry, India as the less powerful of the two states has, no doubt, long been fearful of China. However, China, too, considers India a potential challenger to its regional ambitions. For in Asia, India is one country that has the size, power potential, and even some determination to counterbalance China. Indeed, as much is recognized by China, for it assesses "India to be an ambitious over-confident, yet militarily powerful neighbor with whom it may eventually have to have a day of reckoning."[19] Malik sharply underlines the strategic conflict at work:

The major objective of China's Asia policy has been to prevent the rise of a peer competitor, a real Asian rival to challenge China's status as the Asia-Pacific's "Middle Kingdom". ... Beijing has always known that India, if it ever gets its economic and strategic act together, alone has the size, might, numbers and, above all, the intention to match China. In the meantime, perceiving India as weak, indecisive and on the verge of collapse, all that was needed, from Beijing's perspective, was to keep New Delhi under pressure by arming its neighbors and supporting insurgency movements in India's minority regions. That is why over the years, Beijing has pursued a policy of containment of India and encirclement by proxy. All of India's neighbors have obtained much of their military arsenal from China – 90 per cent of China's arms sales go to countries that border India.[20]

Compounding India's strategic situation, beyond China's evident encirclement strategy in South Asia through the instrumentality of India's neighbors, was the growing disparity in the economic and military capabilities between the two powers, as well as the developing equations between China and the major powers. Spurred by its leaping economic growth since the late 1970s, China was augmenting its military capabilities at a rapid pace. Ironically, in the 1990s its build-up of capabilities was aided by the supply of more sophisticated equipment and technology provided by Russia. No longer could India have the advantage of relatively more modern Russian equipment compared to China's earlier indigenous copies of obsolete Soviet-supplied technology.

[19] Gary Klintworth, "Chinese Perspectives on India as a Great Power," in Ross Babbage and Sandy Gordon (eds), *India's Strategic Future: Regional State or Global Power?* (Houndmills, UK: Macmillan, 1992), 96.

[20] Malik, "India Goes Nuclear," 194–5; emphasis added.

More critically, the US seemed to endorse China's hegemonic ambitions in Asia and to endow legitimacy on its aim to manage the security affairs of South Asia. For one thing, the US acquiesced in China's transfer of nuclear and missile equipment and technology to Pakistan. Second, it directly boosted China's own nuclear and missile capabilities by allowing export of US satellite and nuclear technology. This action could not but arouse anxiety in New Delhi. Third, by making this transfer of technology conditional on Chinese restraint in arms exports, but only to Iran, the US sent India a message about its positive view of Chinese arms exports to Pakistan. Fourth, rather than balancing China, the US's public embrace of that country through proclaiming a "strategic partnership" with it further alarmed India. Krauthammer accurately portrayed the consequence for India of such a China-first US policy in Asia: "There is nothing quite like a US–China strategic partnership to put the fear of God in India."[21] India was thus truly a "lonely" and "friendless" power. Finally, after 1995, "Clinton administration officials had been asking China to take a greater interest in South Asia, virtually conceding South Asia as China's 'sphere of interest'."[22] India was therefore left to its own devices to find a way out of this strategic predicament.

In brief, then:

India saw China aiding Pakistan, militarizing Tibet while steadily improving its own nuclear arsenal and cementing ties to the military regime in Myanmar – in effect encircling India – while at the same time being courted by the United States.[23]

Given the strategic situation that it confronted, India faced a choice between two courses. Already "encircled" by China's containment policy, India could acknowledge China as the hegemonic power in Asia and submit to it as a client state. Or, more consistent with its inherited commitment to national autonomy and an independent foreign policy, India could stand up and resist the Chinese and US plans on the disposition of Asia and South Asia, and indeed become a factor itself in counterbalancing China in Asia. The second course could not, however, just be a function of Indian wishes; rather, India would need to acquire the requisite economic and military capabilities, not least the missing element of their nuclear component, and the determination to build them.

---

[21] Charles Krauthammer, "Clinton's China Grovel," *Washington Post*, June 5, 1998, cited in Malik, "India Goes Nuclear," 199.
[22] Malik, "India Goes Nuclear," 198–9.
[23] *ibid.*, 199.

The nuclear noose tightens around India

The year 1995 saw a defining moment in India's view of the developing situation in respect of the international regime for nuclear nonproliferation. The periodic review of the NPT had been scheduled for that year, and India had mistakenly assumed that the NPT review conference would be critical of the P-5 in not meeting their part of the bargain by way of taking the world toward universal nuclear disarmament. India, however, underestimated the immense power of the US to persuade the conference to abide by its wishes. US diplomacy was extraordinarily skilful, and it was highly successful in steering the conference to its goal of obtaining the indefinite extension of the treaty, even as the P-5 refused to make any commitment to fulfil the obligations about the elimination of nuclear weapons.

From India's perspective, the indefinite extension of the NPT was a turning point. It drove home the message with clarity that the US and the other P-5 members were not serious about nuclear disarmament, only determined to see that the others remain disarmed in the nuclear arena. India concluded that the earlier pretense by the P-5 about fulfilling mutual obligations undertaken in the treaty was a mere charade. The Indians feared that the indefinite extension of the treaty would make permanent what India considered to be a global *nuclear apartheid*. US diplomacy had proven to be very clever in accomplishing its ends. But it led to a fierce determination in India to demonstrate that it was not bound by the unequal bargain of the review conference. As an earnest of its determination, the government planned to conduct a nuclear test in 1995. However, it was forced to recoil from it, even if momentarily, after the preparations for the test were detected in American satellite pictures and the US warned India of the serious consequences that would ensue.

Flushed with the success of its diplomacy in regard to the NPT regime, the US in 1996 pushed for a Comprehensive Test Ban Treaty (CTBT) at the Conference on Disarmament (CD) in Geneva. The timing for the treaty seemed ripe; France had already conducted a series of nuclear tests in 1995 and China was in the process of doing so. On the surface, the draft treaty was nondiscriminatory in that it barred future nuclear tests by all powers. India could hardly make inequality and discrimination a ground for objection. However, the treaty did nothing about the existential division of the world into nuclear haves and nuclear have-nots. India insisted that a time-bound commitment be included in the treaty for the elimination of nuclear weapons, while the US and the other P-5 members adamantly refused to countenance any such proposal. Moreover, the draft treaty allowed simulation and laboratory tests at the subcritical level, which meant that the P-5 would continue to refine and improve their nuclear arsenals while the other powers would be excluded from acquisition of tested, and therefore reliable, nuclear weapons. The treaty as drafted was therefore unacceptable to India, but it made known that it would not be a block to its being concluded.[24]

At that point, believing that India under the circumstances would continue to retain the nuclear option, an entry into force (EIF) clause was included in the treaty at the insistence of China, among others, which required that forty-four nuclear-capable countries sign the treaty before September 1999 for it to become effective. While superficially the number of countries required to sign the treaty was large, the real target was, as the British delegate revealed, India.[25] With overwhelming support favoring the draft treaty, the P-5 thought that India was cornered and would not dare to veto the treaty. However, India did the unthinkable and refused to subscribe to the consensus. And it advanced concerns relating to its national security for its opposition to the treaty, not some moral principles.

The US was not deterred by India's veto, however. It used the stratagem of having its allies bring the issue directly before the UN General Assembly and getting it endorsed there. The treaty was accordingly opened for signature. A review conference on the treaty was scheduled for 1999. Having refused to subscribe to the treaty, India strongly suspected that the review conference was intended to impose sanctions, like the ones already in effect against Iraq,[26] on those who would be recalcitrant in regard to the treaty. India then came to the conclusion that the door was closing on its nuclear option; indeed, that the option would vanish into thin air. The considered assessment of one of the more intellectual of India's recent foreign secretaries was that "the relevance of measured ambiguity with respect to our nuclear weapons program and missile capacity is coming to an end."[27] Ironically, the CTBT conference's rush to making the treaty enforceable on pain of sanctions precipitated the very consequence that it was designed to avert; that is, India declaring, after its nuclear tests in 1998, that it stood as a nuclear weapons state (NWS).

---

[24] See Arundhati Ghose, "Negotiating the CTBT: India's Security Concerns and Nuclear Disarmament," *Journal of International Affairs*, 51 (Summer 1997), 247–8.

[25] Dinshaw Mistry, *India and the Comprehensive Test Ban Treaty*, ACDIS Research Report (Champaign: University of Illinois at Urbana-Champaign, September 1998), 21, 93 (note 74).

[26] Malik, "India Goes Nuclear," 192.

[27] Dixit, *Across Borders*, 298.

Defiance: A reprise on going nuclear

In May 1998, India stunned the world by a series of nuclear tests and by proclaiming itself to have become a nuclear weapons state. Since then there has been an abundance of analysis and speculation as to the factors that led India to take this unprecedented step, largely out of character with its conventional reactive and risk-averse state behavior.[28] Some attribute the causes to systemic factors relating to competition among the major powers, existing and aspirant; others invoke regional and bilateral factors relating to threat perceptions to explain the tests; still others regard domestic factors pertaining to party ideology and party competition as the most critical. For a momentous event such as daring to conduct nuclear tests and to declare the country to be a nuclear weapons power, no single explanation is likely to prove adequate. All three factors therefore need to be taken into account. Since the issue has been hanging fire over several decades, it would seem even difficult to isolate any particular factor as having priority. However, as the story unfolds below, it will be seen that systemic and subsystemic factors have compelling force as explanation. For a clearer understanding of India's motives in its long drive toward the acquisition of nuclear capabilities, three different elements are distinguished here: (1) the deeper structure of conflict in nuclear proliferation; (2) the immediate precipitant in the secret decision in 1988 to acquire a covert nuclear-weapons capability; and (3) the specific events leading up to the nuclear tests in 1998. If the US looms large in the discussion that follows, that is only testimony to its hegemonic power in the global order, and does not imply any exceptional virtue or vice as a state.

The deeper structure of conflict in nuclear proliferation

At least since the mid-1960s, India and the US have been locked in a

---

[28] See, among others, Mohammed Ayoob, "Nuclear India and Indian–American Relations," *Orbis,* 43 (Winter 1999), 59–74; Sumit Ganguly, "India's Pathway to Pokhran II: The Prospects and Sources of New Delhi's Nuclear Weapons Program," *International Security,* 23 (Spring 1999), 148–77; Malik, "India Goes Nuclear," 191–215; T.V. Paul, "The Systemic Bases of India's Challenge to the Global Nuclear Order," *Nonproliferation Review* (Fall 1998), 1–11; George Perkovich, *India's Nuclear Bomb: The Impact on Global Proliferation* (Berkeley: University of California Press, 1999); Damodar Sardesai and Raju G.C. Thomas (eds), *Nuclear India in the 21st Century* (New York: Palgrave, 2002); Itty Abraham, *The Making of the Indian Atomic Bomb* (London: Zed Books, 1998); and Ashley J. Tellis, *India's Emerging Nuclear Posture: Between Recessed Deterrent and Ready Arsenal* (New Delhi: Oxford University Press, 2001).

fundamental conflict over nuclear proliferation. India has been insistent on retaining the nuclear option unless there is universal nuclear disarmament, while the US has been determined to prevent India in particular, but also others in general, from either acquiring nuclear weapons or having the option to do so. At the same time, the US has refused to countenance any consideration of, let alone any commitment to, giving up its own nuclear weapons. Under the US leadership, the major-power system worked out a new international regime, the key pillar of which has been the NPT. The regime was intended to bar others from acquiring nuclear weapons while allowing the major powers to retain and expand their nuclear arsenals, even as they vaguely agreed to negotiate in good faith for arms control and nuclear disarmament. India refused to sign the NPT, and it exploded a nuclear device in 1974 as a reminder of its capabilities. It refrained, however, from acquiring nuclear weapons and waited to see the seriousness with which the major powers took their pledge on nuclear disarmament. Its wait was in vain, for the nuclear arsenals of the major powers continued to expand and improve (*vertical proliferation*), even as these powers continued to insist on barring new additions to the nuclear club (*horizontal proliferation*).

The questions arise as to why India wanted to adopt the course of retaining the nuclear option in the first place and why the US wanted it to desist from that course. Fundamentally, the issue has been one of national autonomy against foreign domination, or more specifically, Indian autonomy against Western, in particular US, domination. There is strong historical continuity in this respect on both sides. For the past half-millennium, the world, with Asia as a prominent part of it, has been dominated by a succession of Western powers. The latest of these dominant powers is the US, which has been hegemonic since World War II, but particularly so since the end of the Cold War. On the other hand, India, which had suffered conquest by the British, and then colonial rule under them for nearly two centuries, places high value on national and strategic autonomy on account of its established nationalism resulting from a long and sustained nationalist struggle. While national autonomy may be an unrealistic goal for a minor power, India has seen itself not only as a middle power that is pre-eminent in its region, but also as a potential major power. Despite the fact that both the US and India have been political democracies, the US thrust for hegemony, in one shape or another, and the Indian thrust for autonomy set the two countries on a long-term course of political conflict.

As discussed in chapters 3 to 5, one strand in the US exercise of its hegemony against India's claims or pretensions to national autonomy has been the regional containment of India through a long-term, though occasionally interrupted, military alliance with Pakistan. To the Indians,

the US–Pakistan alliance has looked suspiciously close to the collaboration between the British colonial regime and Pakistan's predecessor
organization, the Muslim League, which was designed to thwart Indian
nationalism. Another strand in the hegemonic behavior of the US has
been the long and determined opposition to India retaining its nuclear
option, let alone exercising it. The basis for this opposition lay in what
the Gilpatric Committee had expressed as the fear that "our diplomatic and military influence would wane" if more states acquired nuclear
weapons.[29] But "diplomatic and military influence" does not fully con-
vey the serious consequences of nuclear weapons when viewed from the
other side, for the possession of nuclear weapons by some and the exclusion of others from such possession make the latter militarily and politically vulnerable to the former. This has not been merely a question of
Indian fears; it has also been of US calculation. Intervening in the
debate on the question of whether nuclear weapons make for stability or
instability in international politics, one adviser to US policy-makers
states:

There are reasons for opposing proliferation as a matter of policy, regardless of
whether one is an optimist or pessimist in the command-and-control debate –
and not for any antinuclear bias, as [David J.] Karl darkly suggests. Under every
condition, nuclear proliferation complicates *the ability of the United States to project power abroad* and in many cases *may embolden other states to resist US efforts to
impose its will.*[30]

The US's will to dominate became even more expansive after the collapse of the Soviet Union and the end of the Cold War. This more
expansive version was most forcefully articulated by the Bush administration in 1992 in the draft Defense Planning Guidance Paper. In a no-
nonsense fashion, the paper expressed the US's determination, as
indicated earlier, to make its first strategic priority "to prevent the
reemergence of a new rival, either on the territory of the former Soviet
Union or elsewhere."[31] Such a prescription seems quite appropriate,
given the overwhelming power and global reach of the US. On the other
hand, the proliferation of nuclear weapons is bound to erode, to some
extent, the military power of the US, as the influential Gilpatric
Committee on Nuclear Proliferation had concluded more than a quarter of a century earlier.

---

[29] Perkovich, *India's Nuclear Bomb,* 102.
[30] Peter D. Feaver, "Proliferation Pessimism and Emerging Nuclear Powers,"
International Security, 22 (Fall 1997), 185–92; emphasis added.
[31] Cited in Posen and Ross, "Competing Visions," 5–53.

What is noteworthy here is that the draft defense guidance paper was not simply addressed to all-and-sundry regional powers. Rather, the same paper made it clear that India was a specific target by declaring: "We should discourage Indian hegemonistic aspirations over the other states in South Asia and the Indian Ocean." In contrast, it recommended the rebuilding of "a constructive US–Pakistan military relationship."[32] The paper revealed a strong presumption that US primacy across the globe, and therefore in all the regions, was benign, while the influence of other powers, even if restricted narrowly to their own regions, was inherently malign and, in the name of world order, therefore rightly deserving of containment. What the draft guidance paper made clear was that containment as a strategy was a continuing policy directed at regional powers and not necessarily related only to the Soviet Union, which had since ceased to exist.

The practical manifestation of this approach was evident in the US attempt to foil any accretion to India's deterrent capabilities and, to the extent possible, to cripple them. The US began applying pressure on India on the nuclear question "from 1991 onwards,"[33] after the US had emerged triumphant in the Cold War against the Soviet Union and in the Gulf War against Iraq. These pressures came via specific sanctions and the creation and strengthening of ad hoc international regimes on the part of the existing nuclear powers and their allies. In 1992, the US imposed sanctions against the Indian Space Research Organization (ISRO), as well as the corresponding Russian contracting agency Glavkosmos, on account of ISRO's contract to obtain cryogenic technology from Russia for India's space program. The sanctions placed a two-year ban on export of US equipment to both agencies, on any US-government contracts with them, and on imports from them into the US. The Indians protested that the technology was meant for its civilian satellite program and not for military purposes. Continued US pressure finally coerced Russia into canceling the contract. It was the belief of security experts that "this setback significantly damaged India's long-range missile capabilities."[34] What is impressive in this episode is the intense personal involvement of the US president, vice-president and secretary of state in order to thwart the development of India's missile capabilities, and the great lengths to which the US went to provide

---

[32] *New York Times*, March 8, 1992, A14.
[33] K. Subrahmanyam, "Indian Nuclear Policy – 1964–98 (A Personal Recollection)," in Jasjit Singh (ed.), *Nuclear India* (New Delhi: Knowledge World, 1998), 46.
[34] Alexander A. Pikayev, Leonard S. Spector, Elina V. Kirichenko and Ryan Gibson, *Russia, the US and the Missile Technology Control Regime* (IISS Adelphi Paper 317; Oxford: Oxford University Press, 1998), 70.

incentives to Russia for the purpose. Meanwhile, the US began to put pressure on India to bend on the issue of nuclear and missile capabilities by actively involving itself in the Kashmir issue in the early years of the first Clinton administration. Interestingly, Assistant Secretary of State Robin Raphel justified her critical stance on Indian policies by revealing her belief, at a Carnegie Endowment Study Group seminar organized by Selig Harrison, that India had pretensions to importance which the US should not encourage in any way, and nor should it feed India's inflated ego.[35]

In brief, behind the different positions of the US and India on nuclear proliferation lay a deeper structure of conflict between the US as the hegemonic major power and India as both a middle power and a potential major power. That deeper structure of conflict bore vitally on India's autonomy and national security, but the issue could not be altogether disentangled from the question of international status. If the existing major powers were determined to retain the sole right to possess nuclear weapons and to exclude all other powers from such possession, they had unwittingly made the possession of nuclear weapons the very definition of a major power. It should then occasion little surprise that, given India's self-perception as a potential major power, this stance of the major powers made it mandatory that it, too, must have deterrence capability.

The precipitant in the 1988 nuclear decision

In its eagerness to mobilize Pakistan behind the US effort to organize the fundamentalist Islamic guerilla forces to overthrow the Marxist regime and defeat the Soviet forces in Afghanistan, the US under the Reagan administration provided large-scale military aid to Pakistan throughout the 1980s. In view of the importance of its objective, the US reconciled itself to forgoing its nonproliferation concerns in relation to Pakistan.

However, as evidence surfaced of Pakistan relentlessly pursuing its goal of acquiring nuclear weapons with the help of China and with clandestine purchases of equipment across Europe and North America, public concern mounted in the US. Chinese aid to Pakistan's nuclear program had been extensive. As CIA Director James Woolsey was to observe subsequently before the Senate Governmental Affairs Committee in February 1993:

[35] Interview with Selig Harrison at the Century Fund, Washington, DC, December 16, 1999.

Beijing has consistently regarded a nuclear armed Pakistan as a crucial regional ally and as a vital counterweight to India's growing military capabilities. And
building on a close and extensive cooperation effort, Beijing prior to joining the
Non-Proliferation Treaty in 1992 probably provided some nuclear-weapon-
related assistance to Islamabad that may have included equipment.[36]

The Chinese aid is said to have ranged from providing critical equipment, such as ring magnets, to a model design for the bomb, and to
actually testing a Pakistani bomb at Lop Nor. Chinese aid was no less
extensive for the Pakistani missile arsenal and missile development program.

The Reagan administration sought to deflect the mounting public
pressure for imposing sanctions by encouraging adoption of the Pressler
Amendment of 1985, which made aid conditional on an annual certification by the president that Pakistan was not in possession of a nuclear
device. Throughout the remainder of its term, the Reagan administration regularly and readily provided such certification, even though by
1987 it was clear to all that Pakistan had acquired nuclear capability.
That year, President Zia ul-Haq told *Time* magazine (March 30), "you
can write today that Pakistan can build a bomb whenever it wishes."
Washington simply responded with what amounted to "an aye and a
wink."[37] In the face of overwhelming evidence of the Pakistani acquisition of nuclear capability with Chinese assistance and US indulgence,
India felt that it had to respond, especially when changes on the international scene were turning adverse to its interests.

The ascendancy of Mikhail Gorbachev in the Soviet Union, with his
policy of openness and restructuring, meant the removal of the earlier
tacit Soviet nuclear guarantee for India, and also an end to the avail-
ability of the Soviet veto in the UN Security Council. India was now on
its own in terms of its security. At the same time, the decline of the nonaligned movement liberated India from its moralistic constraints to pursue its own national interests. In this situation, Rajiv Gandhi, who until
then had opposed acquisition of nuclear weapons, decided that there
was no choice for India but to go nuclear. It is in this manner that India
and Pakistan became de facto nuclear powers. Only in 1990, after the
Soviet forces had withdrawn from Afghanistan the previous year, did
President George Bush take the position that it was no longer possible
to provide the necessary certification that Pakistan did not possess a
nuclear device. To most observers, it seemed that the US had for an
entire decade turned a blind eye to the Pakistani acquisition of nuclear

[36] *Arms Control Reporter*, April 1993, cited in Sumita Kumar, "Pakistan's
Nuclear Weapon Program," in Jasjit Singh (ed.), *Nuclear India*, 179.
[37] Kux, *United States and Pakistan*, 285.

capabilities in the cause of pursuing its own interests. Only when Pakistani help was no longer needed in Afghanistan did the US pick up once again the refrain of nonproliferation in South Asia.

The events leading up to the 1998 tests

With the end of the Cold War, the US had already made nuclear non-proliferation a central concern of its foreign policy. The new Democratic administration under President Clinton then picked up the issue with single-minded fervor. In relation to South Asia, the administration's goal was set "to cap, roll back, and eliminate" nuclear capabilities in the region. Its principal target was India, for it was assumed that once India agreed, then the US would be able to persuade Pakistan to fall into line. However, the US suffered from a grievous handicap in this endeavor. That handicap related to having been a military ally of Pakistan over the years, having been indulgent toward Pakistan's nuclear ambitions during the 1980s, and having been permissive toward China in respect of its assistance in building up the nuclear and missile capabilities of Pakistan. The US nonetheless played its cards with great finesse and seemed to be irreversibly tightening the noose around India's nuclear option so as to make it ineffective.

First of all, in 1995 the US was spectacularly successful in getting the NPT extended permanently in a one-sided bargain, where non-NWSs were to abjure forever the acquisition of nuclear weapons. The US, however, failed to realize that in Indian eyes this was a turning point, for the permanent extension of the NPT endowed legitimacy on nuclear weapons of the existing powers without any reciprocal obligation to bring about their elimination. India saw the US attempt to eliminate its nuclear option not only as a direct threat to its national security, but also as foreclosing its rise to the status of a major power.

Contributing to the Indian determination was the growing evidence on the US permissiveness toward the China–Pakistan collaboration in nuclear and missile matters. In 1991, the US had placed sanctions on China and Pakistan for the transfer of missile-related technology, including mobile launchers for M-11 missiles, but these were waived after China agreed to abide by the MTCR. The US once again, in 1993, applied sanctions against Pakistan's space agency and the Chinese ministry of aerospace industries on account of the supply of M-11 components, but revoked them against the latter a year later on China agreeing to a ban on exporting missiles exceeding specified load and range. In 1995, strong evidence surfaced in the US that China had supplied M-11 missiles, not just components. However, the Clinton administration, in order to avoid sanctions against China in the cause of its higher strategy of engagement with that country, announced that it had not yet made a determination. Surprisingly, it could not reach a determination to either confirm or deny over the succeeding years. Yet Congressman Curt Weldon stated in 1996: "In fact, the missiles are there – our intelligence community has affirmed this beyond a reasonable doubt – and for the purposes of US law it is irrelevant whether the missiles have become operational."[38]

Earlier, CIA Director John M. Deutsch had testified before the Senate Intelligence Committee that there was little ambiguity about the CIA's assessment on the supply of M-11 missiles to Pakistan, and among China's proliferation activities were "nuclear technology to Pakistan, M-11 missiles to Pakistan and cruise missiles to Iran."[39] The failure of the Clinton administration to arrive at a determination on Chinese activities and its increasingly deferential approach toward China were the source of great anger in India, reminding it of the collusion between China, Pakistan and the US in 1971. Indian strategic analyst K. Subrahmanyam put the issue with great clarity:

By 1994, India not only knew of the arrival of the missiles in Pakistan, it also became once again evident that the US was tilting toward Pakistan and China in shielding the arrival of the missiles – a tilt which continues till today with the US forfeiting all its credibility in pretending that it is not able to reach a finding on the M-11 missiles.[40]

In 1995 the Brown Amendment, pushed forward at the instance of the Clinton administration, also allowed the supply of more F-16 aircraft to Pakistan, as if to legitimize and reward Pakistani nuclear proliferation activity.

In this situation, India was in no mood to be bound by the strengthened international regime by way of the permanent renewal of the NPT. Prime Minister Narasimha Rao ordered preparations for a nuclear test in late 1995. It is a different matter that the test had to be aborted under US pressure after the discovery of the preparations in US satellite pictures. Then national elections intervened to preclude further action by India on this score, while the election results brought into power a new coalition government. Meanwhile, the US pushed further its advantage by hustling in a Comprehensive Test Ban Treaty (CTBT) in 1996 at the

[38] *Arms Control Reporter*, June 1996, cited in Kumar, "Pakistan's Nuclear Weapon Program," 183.

[39] V.P. Dutt, *India's Foreign Policy in a Changing World* (New Delhi: Vikas, 1999), 55.

[40] Subrahmanyam, "Indian Nuclear Policy," 50.

UN Conference on Disarmament. That the treaty negotiations came after tests by France and China seemed highly opportunistic. With the apparent overwhelming support mobilized by the US in favor of the treaty, India seemed to have been successfully cornered and marginalized. It defied the US, however, by daring to veto a consensus on the treaty. The US and its allies then resorted to the unusual step of having the CTBT brought directly to the floor of the UN General Assembly and having it endorsed there, in the process resolutely overriding the national-security concerns of a substantial power through procedural maneuvers.

For the Indians, the US position could carry weight only with those who were already under its protection, or did not have the capability of developing a nuclear option, or did not have the national goal of being an independent center of power. India fitted none of these categories. If sanctions were to come anyway for not submitting to the CTBT, thought the Indians, then why not let them be invoked in reaction to a definite act of defiance through nuclear tests while making a transition to the status of an NWS. In any case, the tested and proven nature of the equipment and technology received by Pakistan from China made it compelling for the Indians to test their already-assembled nuclear devices. That Pakistan would follow suit was not unexpected. The fact that the US remained largely passive in the face of the Pakistani test of the Ghauri missile in April 1998 only reinforced India's determination. Meanwhile, the coming into power of a multiparty coalition led by the more nationalist-minded BJP added greater spine to that determination, and the nuclear tests followed in May. Indeed, some have held the domestic change of the replacement of risk-averse governments of the past by a risk-acceptant BJP-led government in 1998 to be an important factor in the nuclear tests.[41] But the question arises: Why did risk-averse governments come to be replaced by a risk-acceptant one? To be sure, electoral outcomes are complex affairs, especially in a society as diverse as India's. However, it would certainly be to ignore an important part of social reality if one were to neglect the contribution that the conduct of the P-5 themselves at the NPT-renewal and CTBT negotiations made to "nuclear nationalism" in India, not only among the elites, but also, through an aroused media, among the electorate.

In announcing the nuclear tests to a stunned world in May 1998, India ascribed the break in previous policy to the progressive deterioration in its security environment, particularly in respect of China's mounting nuclear capabilities and its clandestine transfers of nuclear

---

[41] Tellis, *India's Emerging Nuclear Posture*, 79–80, 206, 208.

technology and equipment to Pakistan. Those who were critical of the tests countered that there was no immediate threat to India's security that would have justified this extreme step. This divergence in positions arises from two different conceptions of "threat." Following the analysis by Steven Walt on "balance of power" and "balance of threat," we take the stand that a major power or an aspiring major power is not only concerned about balancing against immediate security threats, but also about balancing against the increasing power of its actual and potential adversaries.[42] The negative responses of Russia and China to the US acquiring missile defense systems arise not necessarily from an imminent threat, but precisely from the fear of future threats and of the decline of their relative power positions as a result of the change in the strategic balance.

To established powers and rising powers, what matters is not the present intentions of rival powers, but their relative capabilities, both present and prospective. This is evident in the way the major powers continuously innovate and acquire new weapons systems. If other major powers are advancing rapidly, the affected state is likely to view the increase in their power as constituting a longer-term threat to its security, for the powers that have as a result acquired superior capabilities may use them as and when opportunity arises in future military-crisis situations. In India's case, the issue of an immediate threat from China is less significant, while the widening gap between China and India, as well as its longer-term implications, are most crucial here. Even if Beijing does not hold any malign intent toward India at the moment – a highly questionable assumption – this situation may well change as a rapidly strengthening China exerts its power on its neighbors. Furthermore, China is likely to view India's power position with contempt and continue to treat it as a power equivalent to Pakistan, while placing itself in the category of major powers with special rights to involve itself in the management of South Asian security affairs. Arguably, India saw a widening gap between itself and the relevant powers in nuclear capabilities, and acted to correct the situation, even if not in full measure. Besides this, nuclear capabilities are not something that can be quickly acquired off the shelf when an actual and present danger to national security arises. Nor could India as a rising power consider the intentions of the established major powers toward it to be particularly benign, because the previous two decades, and especially the preceding two years, had witnessed a furious determination on the part of

---

[42] Steven Walt, "Alliance Formation and the Balance of World Power," *International Security*, 9 (Spring 1985), 3–43.

the major powers to shut off India forever from acquiring nuclear capabilities while they continued to retain and upgrade their own.

More crucially, India's action was a matter of its self-redefinition as a major power; it was also an important signal to the major-power system to treat its claim to such status seriously. As Tellis notes, "great-power status in the international system has been defined primarily by a state's possession of comprehensive military capabilities, which today include, among other things, the possession of nuclear weapons."[43] India's aspiration to be recognized as a major power had, no doubt, been of long standing, but it had gone into eclipse as India struggled to cope with a series of economic and strategic crises in the 1960s and 1970s. As India regained some of its self-confidence in the 1990s, following the quickening of economic growth, it was eager to transit from its middle-power status into the major-power system. India now also laid claim to a permanent seat in a future reformed UN Security Council. A permanent membership of the UN Security Council has since the end of World War II been a proxy for major-power status by virtue of the unique privilege of the veto. Moreover, it is significant that the present P-5 are the only ones recognized as NWSs under the NPT. The accession to power of a more nationalist-minded government in India in 1998 resulted in a decisive attempt to bring a convergence between its claim for major-power status and its capabilities. Regardless of the claim, it is nuclear capabilities that are perceived to be critical, for what matters in international politics is the substance of power, and not necessarily the formal status that such capabilities may bring. The P-5 themselves had underlined that fact by refusing to renounce their own nuclear capabilities, even as they strenuously endeavored to bar all others from acquiring them.

The aftermath of the tests: Punishment and engagement

India's nuclear tests were a momentous event. They removed once and for all the ambiguity surrounding India's nuclear policy. The tests and India's simultaneous declaration of having become an NWS constituted a bold challenge to the existing major-power system in that it embodied a declaration that the present status hierarchy in the international system was no longer acceptable and needed to be modified by accommodating India. The immediate reaction of the major powers was one of automatic rejection. This was quite natural, since the admission of an additional member into the major-power system, or even to acknowledge

[43] Tellis, *India's Emerging Nuclear Posture*, 153.

the power credentials of that state, would necessarily reduce the influence of the existing members of a select club. However, it would also have been extraordinary for the five major powers to maintain unity on the issue on a sustained basis, for over time they would diverge in their positions on the issue, consistent with the overall compatibility of the national interests of each power with those of the new claimant.

The US: Supplementing containment with engagement

In reacting to India's nuclear tests, the US was the most crucial among the major powers, given that many states, particularly its allies (chief among them the UK, Germany and Japan) took their cue from it over international issues. Anger was the instant reaction to India's nuclear tests, and it immediately led to a strategy of punishment by way of quickly isolating India politically and hurting it economically through the imposition of sanctions. To make India submit to its wishes, the US threatened to internationalize the Kashmir issue. The Clinton administration's anger stemmed not only from the very surprise of the tests, but also from their spelling a major diplomatic failure for the US in that India had, through its act of defiance, undercut the longstanding US aim and endeavor to contain it through the careful construction of international regimes (such as NPT, CTBT and MTCR).

In its campaign to isolate India politically, the US attempted to mobilize the other major powers in a number of international forums to join with it in the condemnation of India and in the imposition of economic sanctions. Secretary of State Madeleine Albright was particularly energetic in this effort, and she and her spokesman James Rubin frequently spoke in tough language to India. With the intent to make an example out of India for any other state contemplating proliferation, the Clinton administration warned India of the devastation that the sanctions would inflict on its economy. At the meetings of the P-5, G-8, CD and UN Security Council, the US urged others to condemn and punish India by following its model of imposing severe economic sanctions. A special meeting of the P-5 in Geneva, organized at the prompting of the US, rejected the claims of India and Pakistan to be recognized as NWSs. The UN Security Council, in early June 1998, enacted Resolution 1172, which consolidated the various demands made on India and Pakistan by the major powers at the different forums. Later referred to as "benchmarks," these demands included the signing of NPT and CTBT, and the halting of development of nuclear weapons.

Of particular note in this regard is the role that the US accorded to China in isolating India. With his contemporaneous thrust of engagement and partnership with China, Clinton announced a new and important policy initiative in mid-June 1998 to involve China in resolving the differences between India and Pakistan, presumably on the premise that the US and China had a common interest in stability in South Asia. At month's-end, the presidents of the US and China jointly demanded that India and Pakistan renounce the use of nuclear weapons. While in China, Clinton declared: "We [the US and China] are now pursuing a common strategy to move India and Pakistan away from further testing and toward a dialogue to resolve their differences on outstanding issues."[44] Characterizing such joint intrusion as betraying a "hegemonistic mentality" of an era long past, India rejected it. India reminded Beijing and Washington that it was "most ironical" that they should now be prescribing norms on nuclear nonproliferation when they had actually been complicit, directly and indirectly, in the proliferation of nuclear weapons and delivery systems in the region.[45]

The initial reaction of punishment by way of political isolation and economic sanctions was, however, soon supplemented by strategic engagement. Hardly had a full month passed after the tests when the US began negotiations with India in an effort to seek a new basis for the relationship with it. These negotiations were carried out between US Deputy Secretary of State Strobe Talbott and India's special envoy Jaswant Singh, later designated foreign minister, at some one dozen meetings at different locations over the next two years. This strategic engagement was unparalleled in the relationship between the two countries in terms of its prolonged, sustained and serious nature. Strategic engagement, termed so by the parties themselves, had become necessary because India had confronted the US with the already accomplished fact of the tests, shown its determination to be an NWS and, with unusual self-confidence, refused to be intimidated by economic sanctions. Moreover, the US isolation and punishment of a democracy did not comport well with the simultaneous campaign of the Clinton administration to befriend China. For its part, India could not but be eager for a rapprochement with the hegemonic power. Desirous of being seen as a responsible power, it had already shown its sensitivity for US nonproliferation concerns by declaring a moratorium on further tests and by committing itself to no-first-use of nuclear weapons.

The central issue in the negotiations was that of reconciling the diametrically opposed positions of the two sides on the nuclear problem,

[44] N.C. Menon, "China Shares America's Interest in Stable Asia," http://www.hindustantimes.com, June 13, 1998; "Further Tests by India, Pak to be Prevented: Clinton," http://www.hindustantimes.com, June 30, 1998; Harvey Stockwin, "India, Pakistan on the Wrong Side of History, Says Clinton," *Times of India,* July 4, 1998.

[45] "Clinton's Suggestion has Complicated Sino-Indian Ties," *Times of India,* June 15, 1998.

with India determinedly insisting that nuclear weapons were essential to its security, while the US with its global interests was focused on non-proliferation.[46] During the long period of negotiations between the two states, references were often made to their "strategic dialogue" and "strategic partnership," and to their being "natural allies." However, in substance, India was treated very much as an object on which the US made demands for compliance in respect of signing the CTBT, participating seriously in multilateral negotiations on the Fissile Material Cut-off Treaty (FMCT), showing strategic restraint in the development and deployment of delivery systems, exercising stricter export controls on sensitive materials, and engaging in a serious dialogue with Pakistan.[47] On most of these issues, India was amenable, but at its own pace, consistent with its aim of developing a "credible minimum nuclear deterrent."

Although the two states reached no final resolution of the nuclear issues dividing them, there was a partial readjustment on the part of the US to the new realities on the ground. Through much of the 1990s, the US had sought the progressive elimination of India's nuclear capabilities. However, it now seemed to partially accept, but not without equivocation, that, in Talbott's words, "only the Indian Government has the sovereign right to make decisions on what sorts of weapons and force posture are necessary for the defense of India and Indian interests." The fact of the US being reconciled to India's nuclear possession was further evident in his statement that signing the CTBT and FMCT would not preclude India from having a credible nuclear deterrent.[48] Moreover, in asking India to be more explicit about what it referred to as its credible minimum nuclear deterrent, he implied that no longer at issue was the deterrent itself, but its precise scope and content. Also, in having President Clinton visit India in March 2000, without India having signed the CTBT, the US signaled its acceptance of the new situation.

India also strengthened its case for nuclear possession by the restraint it displayed at the time of the invasion from Pakistan in the Kargil sector during the summer of 1999. India's behavior, evidencing maturity and a sense of responsibility as a power, stood in sharp contrast to the nuclear bluster of key Pakistani decision-makers. The military coup in Pakistan in the wake of the Kargil crisis further damaged Pakistan's rep-

---

[46] "India Yet to Bridge Gap with US on CTBT, Says Jaswant," *Economic Times*, September 18, 1998; Strobe Talbott, "We Are for a Qualitatively Better Relationship with India," http://www.hinduonnet.com, January 14, 2000.

[47] For an analysis of the US–India interaction, see Dinshaw Mistry, "Diplomacy, Sanctions, and the US Non-proliferation Dialogue with India and Pakistan," *Asian Survey*, 39 (1999), 753–71.

[48] Talbott, "We Are for a Qualitatively Better Relationship."

utation. The changing image of the two South Asian powers was apparent in the different manner in which Clinton treated the two countries on his visit, emphasizing cordiality on an extensive tour of India, and handing out blunt talk during the brief stopover in Pakistan. The US also showed greater sensitivity to India's position that disputes in the subcontinent needed to be settled bilaterally, and that Pakistan must first cease exporting violence to India before a dialogue could take place. Better relations between India and the US were also aided by expanding economic ties, even as the influential US community with an Indian background urged the US Congress and the Clinton administration for closer relations with India. In sum, the Clinton administration had by its end evidently moved the relations from "estrangement"[49] between the two democracies to "engagement." Reflective of the change was the usage by Clinton and Vajpayee and their spokesmen of the terms "strategic partners" and "natural allies" for the two nations. The US also made references to India being an emerging global or major power, which were pleasing to Indian ears.

The partial accommodation accorded to India by the US, and the evident cordiality between the two that was on display on mutual visits by the executive heads, however, masked continued serious divergence in strategic aims. To the end of his administration, the US under Clinton proved unwilling to officially, explicitly or unambiguously acknowledge India as a nuclear power and it was unbending on its longstanding objective of disarming India in the nuclear arena. Nor, for that matter, was there any US offer of support for India's aim to be a permanent member of the UN Security Council, despite the occasional references to India being an emerging global power or major power. There were thus severe limits to the accommodation proffered by the US.

Of particular interest in this connection was the forceful statement made by Talbott in late 1998 that:

we remain committed to the common position articulated by the UN Security Council, the G-8 and others, notably on our shared long-range goal of universal adherence to the Nuclear Nonproliferation Treaty. This is a crucial and immutable guideline for our policy.[50]

[49] The credit for the description belongs to Dennis Kux, *India and the United States: Estranged Democracies, 1941–1991* (Washington, DC: National Defense University Press, 1992).

[50] Strobe Talbott, "US Looks to India's Emergence as a Global Power," *Times of India*, November 13, 1998.

In thus referring to the NPT, Talbott underlined the aim of eliminating India's nuclear capabilities. Similarly, Undersecretary of State Thomas Pickering made it bluntly clear to the Indians that any possible support for India to have a permanent seat in the UN Security Council was conditional on India signing both the NPT and the CTBT.[51] Indeed, he made such a prospect conditional also on securing a regional consensus, in effect giving Pakistan a veto on India's candidacy. Nor was the Clinton administration averse to using the leverage of the sanctions to extract nuclear renunciation from India. The lesson for India in all this was that in order to be treated as a subject, rather than as an object, there was no alternative to building its own power capabilities, even while employing diplomacy to avoid disruption of the overall relationship.

China: Persistent in its opposition to a nuclear India

Despite the surface normalcy and mutual exchange of visits of high officials in the early and mid-1990s, there was an enormous amount of distrust in India of China because of the continuing transfer of nuclear and missile technology to Pakistan, and the Chinese insistence on the entry into force clause during the CTBT negotiations. The tests certainly aggravated the situation further. Moreover, India had already queered the pitch even prior to its nuclear tests. As a new nationalist-minded government took over power in New Delhi in 1998, its Defense Minister George Fernandes referred to China as "potential threat number one" in view of China's encirclement of India through its military ties with India's neighbors. The description understandably caused a diplomatic furore in China, but it was in reality no different from the belief of China's military that India constituted the "largest potential threat."[52]

China's immediate response to the tests had been marked by restraint. However, the divulgence by the White House of the contents of Prime Minister Vajpayee's letter to President Clinton, naming China as the principal reason for undertaking the tests, turned China's reaction into severe anger. Condemning the tests, China charged that, through undertaking them, "the Indian government attempts to dominate the South Asian region and also wants to provoke a nuclear arms race in the region." It then went on to state that "the international com-

---

[51] Aziz Haniffa, "No Seat for India Without NPT, CTBT Pact: US," http://www.economictimes.com, April 29, 2000.

[52] China, Central Military Commission, *Can the Chinese Army Win the Next War?* (Beijing: 1993), 6, cited in Ashok Kapur, "China and Proliferation: Implications for India," *China Report*, 34 (1998), 401–17.

munity should adopt a common policy position in strongly demanding India to immediately stop its nuclear development program." Reporting on the statement, one foreign analyst commented that "the only surprise in all the Chinese comments was the implicit assertion that China was the only Asian state permitted to possess nuclear weapons."[53] In return, India justified its position by referring to China's own behavior:

> If China, with a large nuclear arsenal built with the experience of over 44 tests, felt compelled to test again in July 1996 (when the CTBT was in the final stages) for its own security, then it should be possible to understand the rationale of India conducting a limited number of tests after a 24-year long period of voluntary restraint.[54]

Of particular interest, beyond China's rhetoric, was its energetic role as chairman at the P-5 and UN Security Council meetings in June 1998, which laid down the "benchmarks" for compliance by India and Pakistan. Interestingly, President Clinton and President Jiang Zemin agreed in Beijing in June "to continue to work closely together, within the P-5, the Security Council and with others" to tackle the situation that had arisen as a result of the nuclear tests in South Asia. India vigorously objected to such joint interference, but was rebuffed by the Chinese with the comment that both China and the US were major powers and, as such, had a responsibility for preventing a nuclear arms race in behalf of the common interest of the international community.[55]

The anger and the chill in relations as a result of India's nuclear tests lasted the longest with China among the major powers. The process of normalization nonetheless began two months after the tests, when it was apparent that the US was already engaged with India in a serious dialogue. In the subsequent interaction, there were exchanges of visits by high-level officials. However, much as in the case of the US, this seeming return to normalcy in bilateral relations stood in sharp contrast to China's other activities as a major power on the global scene concerning nuclear issues. As one Indian analyst pointed out:

> China's two-pronged policy is to continue to oppose India's nuclear aspirations and deny it any new political status at par with China through its emergence as

[53] Harvey Stockwin, "Halt Hegemonistic Tendencies: China," *Times of India,* May 17, 1998.
[54] K.K. Katyal, "Indian Envoy to China Called for Consultations," *Indian Express,* May 20, 1998.
[55] B. Raman, "Sino-Indian Relations: A Chronology," South Asia Analysis Group, http://www.saag.org/papers/paper49.html.

a de facto nuclear weapon power, while at the same time not allowing this to affect bilateral relations.[56]

Accordingly, China repeatedly insisted on India signing not only the CTBT, but also the NPT, and thus renouncing its nuclear weapons capability. Indeed, China displayed annoyance with the US for engaging in a strategic dialogue with India. China's Director General of Arms Control and Disarmament made particularly manifest China's persistence in its tough-minded opposition to India's nuclear capabilities. He sternly told a Washington conference of nonproliferation experts: "It is a direct violation of UN Security Council Resolution 1172 to negotiate, or to even discuss, with India on India's so-called minimum nuclear deterrence capability." He further asserted: "It is also unhelpful to publicly support India's permanent membership in the UN Security Council soon after its nuclear tests."[57] Nothing could have been clearer than that statement that China continued to regard as unacceptable both India's elevation to the status of a nuclear weapons power and India's claim to a permanent seat in the UN Security Council. By the same token, the statement also drew attention to the limits to normalization of relations between the two countries.

Russia and France: Pillars of support for India

Russia's initial reaction to India's nuclear tests in 1998 was somewhat confused; different officials spoke in different voices. There was, no doubt, expression of disappointment at the tests, but it was largely muffled, and there was none of the anger that was displayed by the US and its allies as well as by China. As a major power, Russia was part of the consensus at the various multilateral forums of the major powers, such as G-8, P-5 and the UN Security Council. At summit meetings with the US and China, Russia also agreed that India and Pakistan could not be recognized as NWSs. However, Russia did not take the lead in attacking India or making demands on it. Crucially, for India, Russia's opposition to sanctions at the various international forums prevented the imposition of collective sanctions. Russia also refused to halt arms exports to India. In these respects, Russian behavior was sharply different from the US and its special allies (the UK, Germany and Japan).

Before the end of the year, Russia had moved to an even more positive approach toward India; in the process, it elevated India to a global role. Russia spoke in favor of a multipolar world, with India as one of

[56] *ibid.*
[57] *ibid.*

the poles. Later, it proposed a strategic partnership among Russia, China and India as a counterbalance to the hegemonic power of the US. Going further, Russian Prime Minister Yevgenii Primakov signed a joint declaration with India in New Delhi to the effect that "Russia considers India, an influential member of the international community, to be a strong and appropriate candidate for permanent membership of an expanded UN Security Council."[58] In this manner, Russia became the first major power to extend explicit support for a permanent seat for India in the Security Council, and it did so unconditionally.

Russia's muted reaction to India's nuclear tests was very welcome to India, but it was not entirely unexpected, since Russia had already made a strategic shift that was of political benefit to India. However, what was a source of immense relief and absolute delight to India was the obvious but unusual restraint and moderation with which France greeted the tests. Privately, France let the Indians know that it could live with a nuclear India,[59] and officially it announced that it did not see sanctions as an appropriate response to the tests. France showed unusual understanding for India's reasons for going nuclear, chiefly the Chinese nuclear and missile help to Pakistan while the West turned a blind eye with a view to advancing its commercial interests in China.[60] Like Russia, France was also part of the consensus at the international forums of the major powers; however, like Russia, it opposed sanctions.

Going beyond reacting to the tests, France opened a strategic dialogue with India and there were exchanges of visits by high-level officials. French cultivation of India at the time was simply critical in that it undermined the effort mounted by the US and its special allies to isolate India politically. French officials were extremely forthcoming in referring to India as a major power and endorsing its claim – indeed, its right – to a permanent seat on the UN Security Council. Thus, National Assembly Speaker Laurent Fabius affirmed that "India will be and already is a major player,"[61] while Foreign Minister Hubert Védrine declared that "in the changing international order India has a right to be in the enlarged Security Council."[62] To top it all was the enthusiastic endorsement by President Jacques Chirac that: "India is naturally

[58] Jyotsna Bakshi, "Russian Policy towards South Asia," *Strategic Analysis,* 23 (8, 1999), 1367–97.
[59] K.K. Katyal, "The French Connection," http://www.hinduonnet.com, April 17, 2000.
[60] Ramesh Mulye, "France Not Wary of Nuclear India,
[61] "France Does Not Want to Internationalize Kashmir Issue: French Speaker," *Times of India,* September 17, 1998.
[62] "France Backs India's Claim for UN Council Seat," http://www.timesofindia.com, April 16, 2000.

destined to become a permanent member of the UN Security Council. France supports and will support your candidature."[63]

Triggered by the nuclear tests, France's response was an unexpected one. True, President Chirac's visit to India a few months before the tests – when a different government in New Delhi was on its last legs – had given the Indians the opportunity to get a sympathetic ear for their concerns. However, by and large there had not been much substance in the relationship between the two countries. The explanation for France's recent posture toward India in the wake of the tests rests on its construction of a new strategic framework to cope with the hegemonic power of the US in a unipolar world. France regards the concentration of power in the US, which it labels as a "hyperpower," as ominous for the other international actors. As a counter to the unipolar system, France therefore wishes to push for a cooperative multipolar system. It is that endeavor at geopolitical restructuring which explains France's strategic posture toward India.

France conceptualizes the present structure of world power as being constituted, besides the US as the hyperpower, by the next tier of seven "powers of global influence," which include France, the UK, Germany, Russia, China and Japan, "as well as India (àll the more if it enlarges its vision, still regional)."[64] In the French view, it is this tier that will shape the future multipolar system. No doubt, France envisions a role for itself as a leader, but in partnership with Germany and the UK, of a united Europe in the multipolar system. However, it is remarkable that it regards India as fit for a distinct pole in that system. One official at the French foreign office stated that "India is one of the countries that will be master of all the elements of power and it could become a factor of stability."[65] Similarly, an admiral of the French navy averred when in Bombay (Mumbai) that India has "all the parameters of power."[66] Indeed, the nuclear tests were instrumental in France according a place to India as a major power in its framework of a multipolar world. The tests were a proof to the French of India's determination to be a major power. As one French defense official put it, "the tests put them on the

---

[63] "France Backs India for UN Council," http://www.timesofindia.com, April 19, 2000; and K.K. Katyal, "France Backs India for Council Seat," http://www.hinduonnet.com, April 19, 2000.

[64] Hubert Védrine, *Les Cartes de la France à l'heure de la Mondialisation* (Paris: Fayard, 2000), 9, 13, 17.

[65] Interview, Paris, July 12, 2000.

[66] Rear Admiral Herve Giraud, commanding officer of the French naval forces in the Indian Ocean, in "France N-Sub Here Ahead of Joint Exercise," http://www.timesofindia.com, November 13, 2000.

map."[67] The tests were also important in adding a dimension that in the postwar world has been associated with the major powers – nuclear weapons – which earlier had been missing in India's profile of capabilities; they made India's hard capabilities more complete. Of course, it remains to be seen whether a multipolar world can be developed in the near future. What is pertinent here is the support extended by France to India at a critical time, and the conceptual framework that led to it. Understandably, France has the expectation that India would reciprocate by providing commercial opportunities for it.

Overview

The relatively short period of about two and a half years after India's nuclear tests in May 1998 witnessed enormous changes in India's relations with the major powers. Most of the major powers reacted with instant condemnation of the tests. Several of them sought to isolate India politically and to punish it economically through sanctions, suspension of economic aid, and denial of loans from the international financial institutions. They held before India the specter of its economic collapse in the face of the sanctions. The major powers correctly perceived in the nuclear tests, along with India's declaration that it now stood as a nuclear weapons power, the rise of a challenger, albeit a limited one by virtue of its essential moderateness. However, even before two years had passed, the political scene had undergone a vast change.

Initially, the major powers presented a common front, but the surface unity did not last long. Russia and France left no doubt, by word and deed, of their different approach through opposition to sanctions and political ostracism. France's posture, which issued out of its grand strategy to restructure the world in a cooperative multipolar direction, proved invaluable as a means for India to break out of its political isolation. In failing to form a joint front in imposing either sanctions or isolation on India, the behavior of the major powers made it obvious that India had created a new world in which nuclear weapons were no longer a monopoly of the P-5. With enormous self-confidence, India proved unrelenting in the face of the sanctions and diplomatic isolation. It also demonstrated the resilience of its economy to stand up to the punishment of the sanctions.

Under the circumstances, the US took the initiative in opening up a strategic dialogue with India. The result of the unusually long dialogue with India was a tacit and partial accommodation on the part of the US to India as a de facto NWS, even as the US remained formally

---

[67] Interview, Paris, July 12, 2000.

committed to its ultimate aim of nuclear nonproliferation. Once the US was seen as engaged with India, its special relationship with the UK, Germany and Japan moved these allies to proceed in the same direction. China emerged as the single major power that placed India outside the ring of engagement for the longest time. It sternly emphasized the importance of literally sticking to the decisions of the P-5 and the UN Security Council, and it was visibly irritated with the US for entering into a strategic dialogue with India. China's critical and more cautious approach to India's nuclear tests and its global ambitions is understandable in the light of the longstanding adversarial relationship between the two countries. It is also explicable in view of China's strategic interest in precluding the rise of any other Asian power to the status of an NWS or to permanent membership of the UN Security Council. Nonetheless, China, too, finally came around to resuming the course of normalcy in its relations with India and to entering into a security dialogue with it.

The ending of India's isolation was evident in the visits to India of high-level officials from all the major powers. The high point among these exchanges was, of course, the visit to India by President Clinton. But there were also visits by the Russian prime minister, the Russian president and the Japanese prime minister. In addition, the foreign ministers of France, Germany, the UK and China made trips to India. Moreover, by the end of the period, India had entered into arrangements for strategic or security dialogue with all the major powers, with most of them referring to India as a strategic partner. Beyond the major powers, India became a strategic partner of the EU and held its first dialogue with it in June 2000. This event was particularly significant, not only because earlier the EU had been the site of bitter criticism of India for its nuclear tests, but also because all the other dialogue partners of EU are members of the G-7 or P-5. India is the only dialogue partner of EU that is not a member of either of these two groups. That event put India in the same category as China and Japan, these being the only three powers from Asia. Furthermore, Russia and France as two major powers have extended enthusiastic support for a permanent seat for India on the UN Security Council. The US and the UK have also seen merit in India's credentials but have been less forthcoming by way of emphatic support.

Within two years of the tests, there had been a sea change in the treatment of India by the major powers. Condemned and ostracized at the beginning, India was now seen as involved in a strategic engagement with all of them. India was also now taken seriously, even if not universally, as a candidate for major-power status. This is quite a contrast from its earlier marginal position in the world prior to the tests. Paradoxically, this turn of events was stimulated precisely by the nuclear tests. The relationship between the tests and the new status was astutely noted by an admiral of the French navy, who remarked: "The nuclear tests have given [India] a different place in the world and India's relationship with different countries is also on a different plane now."[68] The tests were clearly the trigger for refashioning relations between India and the major powers. Some Indian analysts had maintained before the tests that the world would make a lot of noise at the beginning, but would finally adjust once India showed the will and determination to be a major power and went in for nuclear weapons. It is perhaps crude to suggest that there may be merit in the position that they took. Comforting as such a conclusion would be, however, it would seem premature, for the road to the full-fledged status of major power is a long and tortuous one.

The new Bush administration and the war on terrorism

The shrinking of geographic space with the advance of economic globalization has linked the destinies of nations that are removed from each other by thousands of kilometers, while the diffusion of advanced technology has made even powerful nations vulnerable to damaging attacks by small but fanatically dedicated groups. Together, they seem to have accelerated the pace of history. The terrorist attacks on the US on September 11, 2001, employing hijacked civilian aircraft as missiles to destroy the twin towers of the World Trade Center in New York and a wing of the Pentagon in Washington, DC, provided dramatic testimony to the impact of globalization and the power of technology. Causing nearly 3,000 deaths, the attacks left the US deeply wounded, and its mainland, for the first time in some two centuries, was shown to be vulnerable to attack. The event led to the repeated use of the cliché that, in the wake of the terrorist attacks, the world had changed irreversibly and that it would never be the same again. As the US rose to the challenge, it was able, through the use of massive air power and the help of local disaffected elements, to defeat the Al-Qaeda terrorists in their home base and to overthrow the Taliban regime in Afghanistan, which had harbored them. In the process, the US foreign-policy posture also underwent a significant change in focus. At the same time, the recently elected Republican president, George W. Bush, emerged from the shadows of an uncertain legitimacy and controversial mandate – because of the wrangles over the election results – as a popular and decisive war

[68] Giraud in "France N-Sub Here."

leader. Equally, the war and its aftermath was not without impact on the configuration of US relations with the nations of South Asia.

Deeply conscious of the overwhelming power of the US, and of the foundations of that power in the nation's immense technological prowess, the Bush administration had come to office in January 2001 with a deep unilateralist impulse. Even before the elections, a Republican-dominated Senate had refused to ratify the CTBT. Now the new administration was determined to push the US's technological advantage in space to the hilt by erecting a National Missile Defense (NMD) system, regardless of the restrictions of the ABM treaty and the opposition of Russia and China, and the indifference of much of Europe. Nor was the new administration sympathetic to the Clinton legacy of seeking a strategic partnership with China. Quite the contrary, it regarded China as a competitor (that is, a challenger), not a partner. The administration's unilateralist impulse was also evident in areas other than the strategic, such as the rejection of the Kyoto Protocol, which sought to protect the earth's atmosphere from excessive gas emissions.

Strangely, however, the Bush administration sought not only to continue the latter-day Clinton legacy of seeking engagement with India, but to deepen the relations between the two countries, and on short order, too. The signs were propitious even before the administration took office. In the election campaign, Bush made some very favorable references to India, while his national security advisor, Condoleezza Rice, underlined the strategic importance of India in an article in an influential journal:

It [the US] should pay closer attention to India's role in the regional balance. There is a strong tendency conceptually to connect India with Pakistan and to think only of Kashmir or the nuclear competition between the two states. But India is an element in China's calculation and it should be in America's, too. India is not a great power yet, but it has the potential to emerge as one.[69]

After the elections, Bush emphasized the theme of the common commitment to democracy as the force behind the drive of the two countries for closer relations. There may also have been included in the calculus, if only tacitly, the factor of treating China as a competitor. The Indians were only too eager to reciprocate. When the Bush administration announced its plan for the NMD, perhaps the only positive response, and in the most enthusiastic of terms (even if subsequently qualified

[69] Condoleezza Rice, "Promoting the National Interest," *Foreign Affairs*, 79 (January–February 2000), 45–62.

somewhat), came from India. This support was partially motivated by India's own desire for acquiring a theater missile-defense system against China and Pakistan. The same kind of enthusiasm was evident later after the terrorist attacks, when India offered all possible help and facilities in the US fight against terrorism (no doubt because of its own situation as a longstanding victim of terrorism).

For its part, as a symbol of the high regard it now held India in, the Bush administration dispatched a high-level official, Deputy Secretary of State Richard Armitage, to India, among a select few countries, to explain the plan. In addition, Armitage made statements about the high importance the US now attached to India as a strategic partner, and about elevating the relationship to new and unprecedented levels of cooperation in many fields, including defense. Similarly, the new Assistant Secretary of State for South Asia, Christina Rocca, welcomed "India's new global status" during her confirmation hearings in May 2001.[70] Certainly, cooperation in defense became increasingly manifest. While the administration was keen on good relations with Pakistan, too, it informed the Indians that India would be treated in its own right and not in reference to US ties with Pakistan. It also sent an eminent strategic expert, Robert Blackwill, as ambassador to India and made other favorable gestures, such as an impromptu meeting by President Bush with India's Foreign Minister Jaswant Singh. The administration also assured India repeatedly that the sanctions imposed in the wake of the nuclear tests would soon go, but always qualified the assurance as dependent on an overall review of the issue, and not on a decision specific to India.

Ironically, when the sanctions were finally removed, they did not wait on any review but were simply the by-product of the removal of sanctions against Pakistan. Of course, the withdrawal of sanctions was a tacit acknowledgement of the two countries as nuclear weapons powers. The terrorist attacks on the US made a dramatic shift in the relative importance of South Asian powers in the eyes of the administration. Before September 11, Pakistan under General Pervez Musharraf was largely in diplomatic isolation, not merely because of the nuclear tests, but also because of the overthrow of the legitimate democratic government by the military in 1999 and the lack of a definitive promise on the holding of fresh elections. Pakistan had even been suspended from membership in the Commonwealth, while important officials from the major powers, excepting China, avoided making a side trip to Pakistan when visiting India. Pakistan's economy was also in deep trouble, in part because of the sanctions, and the international financial institutions were being tough with the regime on conditionalities. All that changed with the terrorist attacks, however.

As the US sought to build a coalition against the Taliban regime and the Al-Qaeda terrorists, Pakistan emerged as of key strategic importance because of its geographic location. Apparently, the US gave Pakistan an ultimatum to either join the war against the terrorists or be counted as being their accomplice. Considering that Pakistan had been instrumental in installing the Taliban regime in the first place and was its chief ally, with the ISI intimately involved in supporting the regime, it was a tough choice. In a dramatic political somersault, Musharraf became a frontline ally of the US, in an ironic twist, in the war against terrorism. Pakistan now made available to the US the use of its air space and some air bases, and even allowed the stationing of US armed personnel on its territory, at the risk of provoking fundamentalist elements.

In one sense, the switch spelt a grievous failure of policy for Pakistan, since it lost the strategic asset created in Afghanistan by way of a penetrated client regime. The new forces that came to power in replacement in December 2001 held deep resentment, even hostility, toward Pakistan for having forcefully intervened earlier in Afghan affairs and for having foisted a tyrannical regime in the name of a common Islamic ideology. One of the first diplomatic acts of the new regime was to reestablish Afghanistan's former relationship with India. On the other hand, Pakistan was the chief beneficiary among the allies in the US war against terrorism, since not only were the sanctions removed, but economic largesse poured in from the US and other allies, and the international financial institutions. More importantly, Pakistan's president, General Musharraf, rose to high esteem in the estimation of the Bush administration, and he was lauded greatly for his decisive leadership and dynamism. The Bush administration could not escape the predicament, however, that all earlier US administrations had faced, for its closeness to the military regime in Pakistan was received with some annoyance in India, putting some distance in the relationship with the latter. The dilemma was deeper, though, for Pakistan itself was hostage to fundamentalist and terrorist groups within, which it had nurtured in the past; even the regime's own institutions were not immune to sympathy with these groups or to penetration by them. As these elements became more active, or were allowed to become more active, in India (in compensation for their defeat in Afghanistan), including a deadly attack on its parliament in December 2001, and India expressed readiness to respond forcefully, the Bush administration had to walk a tightrope between the two nuclear powers.

Notwithstanding the resurrection of the US alliance relationship with

Pakistan and supply of US economic aid, in a deeper sense the consequences of the spotlight on Pakistan, as a result of the US's encounter with terrorism, have been adverse for Pakistan. For, more and more, Pakistan has come to be seen as the sponsor, breeder and sanctuary of terrorism. The feelings may be shared by the administration, even though not expressed for tactical reasons, but the US media has been increasingly blunt about it.[71] However, such a state of affairs in Pakistan poses challenges for both India and the US, and may have the potential for a convergence of interests between them. A full-blown war between India and Pakistan could, on the other hand, place tremendous strain on this relationship.

Summary and conclusions

The most significant consequence of the end of the Cold War was the rise of the US to the status of sole superpower in a semi-unipolar international system. Even though it necessitated adaptation to the hegemonic status of the US on the part of other powers, that event did not eliminate the central features of the international system. The cumulative diffusion of power in the world since World War II assured that interstate conflict and balancing would continue to characterize international politics. Even the US recognized that its "unipolar moment" could not be a permanent one, and consequently it was determined to prevent the rise of new challengers to its hegemony. The principal mechanisms in its strategy of containment toward powers that are or are likely to be possible rivals, globally or regionally, have been of counterbalancing them through alliances and of creating international regimes to constrain the growth of their capabilities. India has been the target of the application of such mechanisms, no less after the end of the Cold War than it was before.

The attempt at the regional containment of India by the US through instituting a nuclear nonproliferation regime intensified after the end of the Cold War; and the effort found unusual cooperation among the P-5 to retain their monopoly of nuclear weapons as a currency of power and status. India found itself in a difficult situation, in that it no longer had the leverage that its earlier friendship with the Soviet Union had provided it. Moreover, the US negligence of the Chinese transfer of nuclear and missile equipment and technology to Pakistan and its embracing of China during the mid-1990s as a strategic partner confronted India

---

[71] See S. Rajagopalan, "US Media Backs India's Stand," http://www.hindustantimes.com, December 27, 2001.

with the prospect not only of US hegemony, but also of US-endorsed Chinese hegemony over it.

However, India proved defiant and, through its nuclear tests, defeated the US attempt to permanently defang it in the nuclear arena. The further US attempt to punish India through economic sanctions did not succeed either, because the major powers could not agree on making them collective. Indeed, some of them, such as Russia and France, saw, once India had shown the determination to be a nuclear power, possibilities of collaborating with it in international politics. Failing to isolate India, even the US then sought to engage it in a strategic dialogue rather than marginalizing it as it had done before. To India, improved relations with the US were important because of the latter's position as the sole superpower and its unsurpassed economic and technological power. The major power that has been the most adversely affected by India's rise to a nuclear weapons power has been China, insofar as that ascent opens up possibilities of undercutting China's claim to sole and unhindered hegemony over Asia. If it could develop its economic and military capabilities further, India could be a factor, in collaboration with others, in providing a military counterweight to China in Asia. That may, of course, lead China to redouble its efforts, long under way in any case, to encircle India. That is a risk, but it is also a challenge for Indian diplomacy, as it is for the polity to build the appropriate capabilities and strategies to counter it.

7   Conclusions: India and the Emerging International Order

This book has had as its subject matter India's long but unfinished journey toward becoming a major power. It has been concerned with questions such as: Has India had the aim to become a major power? Since when? How consistently has it pursued that end? Has it worked to acquire the wherewithal for that end? How consistently? What are the constraints that it has faced in the endeavor? The present chapter summarizes the various issues raised in the book, and then briefly discusses the appropriate strategies that are feasible for India to become a major power, as well as the question of adjustment of the major-power system to the phenomenon of rising powers in an era when the traditional recourse to violence is too risky to contemplate. These issues are of theoretical and empirical significance in the treatment of India's ambition for a major-power role.

The theory: Realism and state behavior

Major power, or more particularly *great power* as conventionally used, is a concept that is central to the paradigm of realism in the study of international relations, as is the related concept of the major-power system. The very centrality of power in realism makes these concepts critical to that paradigm. By virtue of the broad array of capabilities they command, major powers determine, whether in conflict or cooperation, the nature of the international system and its future development in the endeavor to advance their particular interests as regards security and welfare. The international system, as it is presently constituted, is thus essentially a near-oligarchy of the major powers, with the other powers often consigned to the role of objects of the decisions of the major powers. Accordingly, for reasons of their own security and welfare, eligible *middle powers* have it as their ambition to enter the exclusive club of major powers through the expansion of their capabilities. For it is the middle powers, rather than the *minor powers*, who are more likely to have the potential to graduate to the role of major powers, since they are already pre-eminent in their regions, and command sufficient capabilities to resist those decisions of the major powers that are unwelcome to them. However, such ambition can set off a collision with the major powers, for the latter aim instead to reduce the middle powers to the status of minor powers or objects in order to protect their own present status. The typical policy of a major power in response to such situations is *regional containment* of the eligible middle power. It is precisely this line of reasoning that makes realism, especially the classical variety, the ideal framework for examining the issue of the quest of India for a major-power role. However, despite the robustness of its theory and the acuity of its insights on the dynamics of the relationship between major powers and other powers, realism by itself is not fully adequate for understanding the mainsprings of the foreign policy of a nation. There is an important area of foreign policy that realism, it seems, sidesteps.

Realism, both classical and structural, rests on the basic premise that nations in an anarchical international system are confronted by a *security dilemma* as a consequence of the lack of a central authority, which results in a struggle for power among nations in order to assure their security and survival. Nations therefore work, and must work, for their security by augmenting their own capabilities, or by borrowing power through *balance of power* alliances, or both. The central message of realism is that, in coping with the security dilemma, nations must strive for a balance between goals and capabilities, ends and means, for an imbalance between them either invites peril or makes for inadequate realization of the potential for security and welfare. However, security is never permanently assured in the international system, because changes in relative economic strength and technological position, as well as in the goals of the nation and those of its friends and adversaries, lead to the need for constant readjustments in balancing power. Although realism posits this scenario, it provides no assurance that nations will always follow its prescription, only that they will invite punishment by violating it. Indeed, punishment is the primary means through which wayward nations are often socialized into an international system driven by power politics. In all these respects, realism provides useful insights for both theory and policy. However, realism is essentially a theory about the workings of the international system; it is not a theory of foreign policy of individual states.[1] Indeed, the absence of an adequate theory of foreign policy is the Achilles heel of realism. Realism does not tell us why nations at times fail to follow the requirements of the international system in their policies, only that they will incur punishment for doing so.

---

[1] Kenneth Waltz has driven home this point in his *Theory of International Politics* (New York: Random House, 1979), 121–2.

It is curious that realism takes for granted what otherwise ought to be a central issue for theoretical treatment: why some nations are revisionist while others are status quo. As a consequence, while the pertinence of realism to any analysis of foreign policy is almost absolute, national attributes of individual states cannot altogether be ignored.[2]

The practice: India's quest for a major-power role

Even though discussing India's foreign policy in terms of the tension between realism and idealism may seem old-fashioned, it becomes unavoidable, since the leaders themselves have consciously used those terms in reference to their policies. At the same time, India's foreign policy cannot be understood without recognizing the dominant role of Jawaharlal Nehru in founding, consolidating and sustaining it over the long period of seventeen years from 1947 to 1964. However, there exist opposing positions on the nature of his foreign policy, with some believing it to be based on ideals derived from liberalism, Gandhian values and Marxism, while others consider it to have followed the tenets of realism. In fact, both elements were present and Nehru prided himself in combining the two, though it is questionable whether he was successful in effectively integrating them.

What is clear is that Nehru pursued a foreign policy that was beyond India's extant capabilities at the time. He endeavored to follow a foreign policy of independence, refusing to align himself with either of the two Cold War power blocs. Moreover, he attempted to play an activist role in international politics at the global level, mobilizing the developing countries on the basis of the common ideological platform of nonalignment. The effort at a foreign policy of independence is understandable, to a considerable extent, in the light of India's substantial capabilities in comparison with other developing countries – notwithstanding their limited nature from the perspective of the requirements of playing a global role – and also of its regional pre-eminence in South Asia. But the attempt at an activist global role was not justified by the capabilities of a nation in its circumstance of a backward economy and of a polity that had not yet been consolidated. Of course, the lack of adequate capabilities to some extent explains the resort to normative appeals to justice, peace and peaceful coexistence, for these are often the weapons of the

---

[2] In recent years, newer approaches such as *defensive realism* have attempted to rectify this problem. See, for instance, Fareed Zakaria, "Realism and Domestic Politics," *International Security,* 17 (1992), 177–98; and Gideon Rose, "Neoclassical Realism and Theories of Foreign Policy," *World Politics,* 51 (1998), 144–72.

weak. However, the passion with which a foreign policy of independence was pursued on the global scene and with which the appeals were made cannot be said to have issued out of capabilities or the lack of them.

The historical dimension

The explanation for the imbalance between India's goals and capabilities lies, more correctly, in the historical experience of the nationalist movement, which has extended over about two-thirds of a century, and which during the later half of the period was led by Mahatma Gandhi with his doctrine of nonviolence and ethical practice. The Indian nationalists had fought a bitter struggle against imperialism through a nonviolent and ethical strategy of passive resistance, and had identified themselves with most other anticolonial movements through the course of that struggle. India under Nehru therefore could not have suddenly switched on the morrow of independence to subordinating the nation to one power bloc or another, and to forgetting the high ethical ideals that he and others had been socialized into under Gandhi.

There is nonetheless an aspect of India's capabilities that suggests a more rational and realistic basis for a foreign policy of independence and global activism. That has to do with the perception, not only of Nehru but of his other associates as well, that India was a *potential* major power by virtue of its large size in territory and population, as well as its location on the communication routes between Europe and the rest of Asia. Once the country became developed into an industrial power – and the leadership intended to work for that – the role of major power was thought to follow in its train as a matter of course. Added to that assessment was the element of India as the seat of a historic civilization. Nehru deeply believed that in a matter of time India would be among the four or so major powers of the world. Most Indians had come to share that belief with him. The consciousness of India as a nation destined to be a major power was thus a legacy of the nationalist movement.

If India was seriously considered to be a potential major power, then it followed that nothing should be done to foreclose that possibility. It is not certain whether or not Nehru made such a calculation. However, it would seem that joining a power bloc in a subordinate position would in all probability have affected adversely a future assertion of a major-power role, and consequently a foreign policy of independence was essential from that point of view as well. The aspiration for a major-power role became part and parcel of the political and ideological make-up of the successors of Nehru. It was not something that they had always to shout from the rooftops, but all endeavored to see that the potential was realized and, at least, not be allowed to be undermined.

The socialization dimension

The fact that the foreign policy of independence and global activism had its roots in India's historical development could not, however, have compensated for the lack of capabilities. Howsoever justified the policy might have been, it violated the requirement of balance between goals and capabilities. Soft-power capabilities could not substitute for hard-power capabilities. What is more, Nehru did not just assume an independent and activist role; he also neglected defense capabilities relative to possible threats. The cause of that neglect may have been an unconscious devaluation of the instrument of violence with which Nehru may have been inculcated at the feet of Gandhi. However, there can be no doubt that inadequate provision for defense was also a matter of conscious policy so as not to retard the prospects of state-sponsored economic development. Nehru stated on one occasion:

industrialization takes time. What will happen before you are strong enough? You may get knocked down in the course of next ten years. And all your saying "we are not ready for an attack" will not prevent the enemy from attacking you. This is a difficult problem that every country has to face, to balance immediate danger with considerations of better security later on.[3]

Nor can there be any doubt that Nehru was motivated by concerns over excessively boosting the armed forces in an untried polity, which prior to independence had been run by colonial authorities whose sole basis of support was the army and bureaucracy. Basically, with defense expenditures at less than 2 per cent of GNP, Nehru had implicitly adopted a policy of unilateral disarmament.

Through leading the nonalignment movement around the world and opposing the hegemonic superpower of the time, the United States, India impinged on the global influence of that power. It is not surprising, therefore, that the US then undertook – as Liska would have predicted from his realist perspective on the relations between major powers and middle powers – the policy of regional containment of India by counterbalancing it through the building up of Pakistan militarily, beginning in 1954. Sufficient evidence has been presented on the issue in chapters 3 to 5, and there is no reason to belabor the point any

---

[3] Jawaharlal Nehru, *Jawaharlal Nehru's Speeches: Volume III: March 1953–August 1957* (New Delhi: Publications Division, 1958), 42–3.

further. One can interpret the US policy within the realist framework as one of attempting to teach India an instructive lesson on the workings of the international system. By its behavior in reaction, India demonstrated that the lesson was working, for it responded with a counterbalancing act of its own by cultivating China and the Soviet Union, largely at the political level. India also took steps to firm up its defenses, but only modestly, in order to protect its economic development program. However, India still continued with the foreign policy of independence and global activism, as well as inadequate attention to national defense.

The real lesson on the workings of the international system, however, was administered by China, which in 1962 inflicted a stinging defeat on India in the high mountains of the Himalayas. That marked the beginning, for India, of the integration of the means of violence into its foreign policy. From that point started the emphasis on building military capabilities in the here and now, and not simply on laying the industrial foundations for defense preparedness sometime in the future. It was in this fashion that India was *socialized* into the international system, and made to discard by and large the inheritance from the nationalist movement in terms of the stressing of nonviolence and ethical ideals. To a great extent, it dethroned Gandhi in favor of Kautilya. India was thus made to come to terms with the requirements of the international system. It learnt the lesson on the need for balance between goals and capabilities, but at the grievous cost of defeat in war and the resulting international humiliation. The consequence was the muting of the aspiration for major-power status, for territorial security became the immediate priority. However, at the same time there developed in its leadership the tenacity to develop the capabilities – including those that would make feasible a nuclear option – for defense, even in the face of opposition from the major powers. Indirectly, the building of such capabilities would aid as well the cause of obtaining a major-power role, since those capabilities would be built on the base of the substantial size of India's territory and population.

It was not only in the arena of building capabilities that socialization was apparent. It became manifest as well in India's counterbalancing of the triple alliance of the US, China and Pakistan in the early 1970s by entering into a semimilitary treaty with the Soviet Union. It was also evident in India decisively intervening in the Bangladesh War in 1971, in exploding the nuclear device in 1974, in launching the integrated missile-development program in the early 1980s, and finally in exercising the nuclear option through the nuclear tests and the simultaneous declaration of being a nuclear weapons state (NWS) in 1998.

The capabilities dimension

While Nehru neglected defense in the sense of military preparedness for possible near-term security threats, his attention to defense over the longer term constitutes a different story. Of course, it can be argued that Nehru really saw no immediate threat to India's security, and thus the rational choice was to devote attention to the longer term. It was unfortunate for him that international events proved his choice to have been wrong. In any case, when it came to the issue of the longer term, Nehru had a deep intellectual grasp of the requirements for security and for major-power status. As a man of great vision, Nehru worked out a grand strategy for the nation, of which the foreign policy of independence was but one component. The foreign policy of independence represented the nationalist element in Nehru's world-view. A second component was the consolidation of the polity on the basis of a secular state, a democratic political system and an accommodative strategy of national integration – all this because of his liberal values and his regard for the ethnic and linguistic diversity of the nation.

A third component was a highly ambitious, inward-oriented economic strategy that was geared to providing India a massive industrial base, organized around heavy, metal-making, engineering and capital-goods industries. Such an industrial base was designed to equip India to grow economically on a self-sustaining basis, without having to depend on the outside world, and at the same time to provide the sinews of technological and military power. In this respect, Nehru was a realist par excellence. Nehru's personal values were, no doubt, that of a liberal and an internationalist. However, after much reflection, Nehru came to the intellectual understanding that the international system as it was presently constituted, with the struggle for power at its core, required India to proceed in that manner in the economic arena. Nehru had come to this understanding before independence actually arrived.

The fourth component of Nehru's grand strategy was a strong thrust for science and technology through the establishment of higher-level educational institutions, of a series of research laboratories and, most importantly, of a nuclear research organization of vast scope. In founding this last organization, Nehru became the true father of the nuclear tests in 1998. Although Nehru had an abhorrence for nuclear weapons, he was at the same time reconciled to the fact that nations – and India could be no exception – were likely to use the most advanced weapons for defense when threats to their security arose and that they would not be persuaded by sentiment to do otherwise. His strategy for economic development and for the advancement of science and technology are consistent with realist theory's emphasis on capabilities.

Some have argued that Nehru's successors did not have the will or the determination to carry forward Nehru's ambitions to make India a major power and to build the necessary national capabilities for that role. That seems to be largely an unfair conclusion, and it betrays an inadequate appreciation of the challenges posed by crises that are inherent in the development process. In reality, the successors were not much different from Nehru in their commitment to developing India into a major power. However, they were confronted with a concatenation of crises that tied them down to crisis management. In part, these crises were of Nehru's making. First, there was the defeat in the India–China War of 1962, which necessitated heavy defense expenditures, and also heavy dependence on the Soviet Union for arms supplies. Second, the heavy defense expenditures resulted in inflation and, thus, mass disaffection in the population. Third, Nehru's economic strategy had neglected agriculture, which resulted in massive food shortages and pathetic dependence on the US for food supplies. Fourth, Nehru had located most of the new industry in the public sector, which proved to be inefficient. Fifth, the Congress Party under Nehru had become an effete organization, relying primarily on the personal popularity of Nehru as a nationalist hero to win elections. The conflicts within the party finally led to its split, making the government dependent on the support of communist and regional groups to sustain itself in office. Eventually, of course, as mass antigovernment movements developed, India came under a state of emergency in the mid-1970s. Sixth, the aftermath of the India–China War resulted in a collusive strategy on the part of Pakistan and China to keep India pinned down in fire-fighting operations at home, through enormous pressure on its borders and encouragement of internal upheavals. India also had to face two more wars with Pakistan, one in 1965 and another in 1971. In both, Pakistan was largely the instigating party, and in the second one the US and China collaborated in support of Pakistan.

There were also other crises that had nothing to do with the economic and political inheritance from Nehru. There were the economic shocks of the OPEC oil-price hikes in the early and late 1970s. In addition, there was enormous ethnic turmoil in the early 1980s. In short, Nehru's successors were faced with new challenges that did not allow much room for maneuver. Given these crises, what is more impressive is that India defied the superpowers over the NPT, refused to cave in to the US over the conflict in what later came to be Bangladesh, and showed its spirit of independence from both superpowers by exploding the nuclear device in 1974. In the early 1980s, in the midst of all its political troubles, India went ahead with the integrated missile-development program, designed to make the nuclear option meaningful in fact.

Successive prime ministers remained committed to the nuclear option and prepared to go forward with nuclear tests if the circumstances were propitious. It is true that they were cautious, but it can also be said that they were prudent. As the long-delayed economic liberalization began in 1991, it opened new options for India through the higher economic growth it made possible. India could now afford to take some risks. It is this circumstance that made possible the nuclear tests. If India had continued to be dependent on the US for food and for economic aid as it was in the 1960s, or if it had been overwhelmed with economic and political turmoil as it was in the 1970s and 1980s, it would have been difficult for it to contemplate risking this step. Realism does not call for attention only to military capabilities; rather, it requires taking into account the entire range of capabilities, especially economic strength.

The "low posture" dimension

Although India has long had the aspiration for a major-power role, and actually did play a global role in diplomacy in the 1950s, it has been by and large very low-key about it. Its aspiration has not been accompanied by an emphatic thrust for its achievement. There is none of the threatening and confrontational posture that China, for example, has displayed as a rising power. Rather, India's state behavior has been distinguished by moderation and restraint. There has been a marked reluctance as well in the employment of violence; India has lacked the killer instinct in interstate conflict. Rather, India itself has been the victim of wars which others initiated, even if they were weaker in aggregate capabilities. By and large, India has acted as a satisfied power. It has been semirevisionist only at the systemic level, and that, too, only to the extent of demanding a share in international governance consistent with its large size, in terms of both territory and population, and it has done so through methods more appropriate to trade unions. Equally, India has been tepid in building economic and military capabilities. Some of this behavior may have been a consequence of the legacy of Gandhian values and of Hinduism, which has lacked the proselytizing tradition of Christianity or Islam. But it is also a result of the many external and internal constraints that India has faced.

Among the external constraints has been, importantly, the policy of regional containment pursued by both the US and China, as well as the conflict with Pakistan, which taken together have tied India down to its region rather than letting it exert itself on the global scene. The attempt at regional containment by the US and China – not only in their support of Pakistan, but also in their trying to impose international normative regimes on India, especially in the nuclear and missile technology areas – have left India gasping in its rearguard actions to fight them off. Furthermore, if it is true that a country is known by the enemies it keeps, then the conflict with Pakistan has tended to equate India with that country in the eyes of the rest of the world. Pakistan has also taken upon itself the role of blocking by all possible means India's elevation to major-power status. What is unfortunate for India in that context is that there is little it can do to placate Pakistan other than at the cost of its own disintegration and the consequent domination by Pakistan over the subcontinent. Any territorial concessions on its part to Pakistan, especially in Kashmir, are likely to only whet that country's appetite for more.

In its permanent conflict with India, Pakistan is moved not by what India does or does not do, but rather by its own internal dynamics, which have to do with the ideological foundations of its constitutive legitimacy. As long as Pakistan aims at strategic parity with India and remains organized on a sectarian basis, the only possible option open to India seems to be, unfortunately, to proceed on the assumption of a permanent hostility on the part of Pakistan and to take the resulting consequences as they come. Minor adjustments are unlikely to end this conflict any time soon, although confidence-building and nuclear-risk reduction measures may be essential to avert an inadvertent nuclear war. Effective crisis management is equally important, as this dyad tends to generate periodic crises. India will also have to assume that China will most likely support Pakistan in its hostility to India. The key element that is susceptible to a shift in its posture is that of the US, especially in the context of the changing balance of power in the Asia-Pacific region. The US is also perhaps crucial to changing the Pakistani posture toward India. In fact, after the terrorist attack on India's parliament in December 2001, the US emerged as a key player in the political-military crisis between India and Pakistan. At the same time, reducing the level of conflict with neighbors, especially with China, through political and economic interactions could provide opportunities for building up India's strength, especially in the economic arena.

It is not only in its state behavior in the international system that India has been low-key, but equally it has been so in the building of economic and military capabilities. Its approach to building capabilities has been gradual and incremental. India has not shown any of the frenetic pace that is characteristic of the Chinese effort, with the US as its reference point. The fundamental reason for that feature of its behavior is its democratic political system, which in turn is related to the nature of its society. Within that system, only incremental changes are possible or are tolerable to the society or its key groups; blitzkrieg strategies are thus difficult to implement in such a system, except in a situation of war or crisis. One can not expect revolutionary change from such a society. At the same time, India's poor record on removing poverty and improving the economic infrastructure does not add to its attractiveness as a possible major power in the interim.

In summary, realism explains a lot about India's foreign-policy posture, but it does not explain everything. It cannot tell us why India went in for an activist foreign policy at the global level when lacking the capabilities for it. India's record demonstrates no automatic transmission belt between the nature of its capabilities and its foreign policy. Rather, the goals of foreign policy seemed to have derived from historical experience. On the other hand, India's counterbalancing actions in the wake of the conflicts with the US and China underline the robustness of realism. Similarly, India's more quiescent foreign policy on the global scene after the lack of its capabilities was exposed in war is also in line with realism. So also is the tenacity displayed by the elites of an eligible middle power to build capabilities consistent with its geopolitical ambition for a larger role, even if only gradually in a long march.

The future

Through its nuclear tests in 1998, India repositioned itself from being a largely marginal player in the international system to being a serious candidate or contender for major-power status. The tests proved to be the catalyst for the change. They removed the "fence-sitter" quality from Indian nuclear policy, thereby eliminating the ambiguity surrounding it. The existing major powers were divided in their response to the tests on the basis of their strategic interests. Russia and France basically accepted India as a nuclear power, regardless of their own commitment to the NPT, and offered enthusiastic support for its candidacy for a permanent seat on the UN Security Council. Consistent with its position as a long-time adversary, China opposed India on both counts. The US condemned the tests and imposed economic sanctions, but gradually became tacitly reconciled to what seemed like an irrevocable situation of nuclear possession; however, its position on the question of the UN Security Council seat was marked by ambiguity and reservations. The UK did not impose sanctions, but other than that it followed the US in its response. Despite the differences among the major powers, all of them at the end entered into a strategic or security dialogue with India. While India had thus elevated itself from a middle power to become a candidate major power, its success in the endeavor to become a full-fledged major power is not certain. Such success depends on a number of imponderables, some under India's control and others not at all. There are both internal and external factors involved, the former relating to capabilities and patterns of state behavior, the latter pertaining to the evolving nature of the global balance of power and of international governance.

Capabilities

First and foremost in the question of elevation to major-power status come capabilities. Since such elevation is dependent on the other major powers, there must be some incentive for them to concede on this point, and capabilities have a significant role to play here. George Modelski makes the important point that the capabilities of a new power should be such as to cause other major powers "to fear" it, but they should also be such as to serve "to attract" them.[4] Certainly, India has a long way to go in both respects, especially when its capabilities are compared with China's. It is noteworthy that it was India's determination finally to exercise the nuclear option that made it a fit partner for others to have a strategic dialogue with, when hitherto they had ignored it or treated it as merely an object. It was the element of fear that persuaded them to move in this direction as they saw a challenger to the major-power system arise. What this suggests is that, for India to be taken seriously, it should proceed energetically toward its declared intention to build a "credible minimum deterrent" based on a triad of delivery platforms on land, sea and air, but without any threatening military postures that could attract intense counteractions.

However, nuclear weapons are designed to serve as a deterrent and are not likely to be actually used except in the case of a supreme national emergency. Accordingly, India would have to keep up with new developments in the field of conventional weapons, especially as they relate to the revolution in military affairs. It would need to integrate its information technology (IT) capabilities into its defense preparedness. Defense, however, does not come cheap. But then the cost of not spending enough on defense can be even more grievous, as India learnt in 1962. Indeed, the numerous crises and the economic retardation that dogged India during the 1960s can all be traced back precisely to the military losses inflicted on India in the 1962 war and the hurried effort to build up defenses. All nations confront the inherent dilemma of balancing guns and butter, and India can be no exception. National defense also presumes internal security and the ability to eliminate domestic threats to India's integrity as a nation-state.

To focus on military preparedness alone, however, is to take only a

---

[4] Observations made during a round-table at the Brookings Institution, Washington, DC, December 15, 1999.

limited view of national capabilities. Economic capabilities need to move in tandem with those of defense, otherwise a state can end up bankrupt and broken-backed, and thus made more vulnerable; the two types of capabilities are intimately linked. As Paul Kennedy points out, wealth and power are requisites for each other.[5] If too little is spent on defense, the result is military vulnerability, as India witnessed in 1962. If too much is spent on defense, it can undermine long-term economic growth by taking resources away from investment, as happened in the case of the Soviet Union. The conclusion, then, is compelling: wealth and power must move forward in a mutually supportive way. Success in the economic arena is also likely to advance the political and economic integration of the nation.

The question of assuring adequate economic growth necessarily leads to the issue of economic reform. India built up a largely insulated economy over the period of three decades following the adoption of the Second Five Year Plan in 1956. Even after seven years of economic liberalization following 1991, India remained in 1998 about the least open economy among countries with populations of over 50 million.[6] Yet there are strong voices, especially among the ideological right and left, against liberalization and, linked to that, globalization; there is a fervent clamor in favor of an insulated economy. There is a strange contradiction in the position of the ideological right in that it wants India to be a strong nuclear power with a global role, and at the same time demands a closed economy that is cut off from the world. In the circumstance of a closed economy, the crucial question arises: what is there to attract other major powers to accord India such a role?

In many things, such as acquisition of nuclear and missile capabilities or aspiration to become a major power, China as an adversary has been both a stimulus and a model for India to advance on those fronts. The same lesson must hold in the economic arena, where China is vastly more open to trade and foreign investment. By virtue of its large open market, China has become a source of economic attraction even for its competitors or adversaries. In the process, it has assured for itself a rapid rate of economic growth and a flourishing economy, which has allowed it to invest heavily in military modernization. India can do no better than follow the Chinese example and become an attractive economic partner for other global players, which outcome can then also have political and strategic spillover effects. A nation has to affect the

[5] Paul Kennedy, *The Rise and Fall of Great Powers: Economic Change and Military Conflict from 1500 to 2000* (New York: Random House,1989), xvi.

[6] See Baldev Raj Nayar, "Opening Up and Openness of Indian Economy," *Economic and Political Weekly*, 36 (September 15, 2001), 3529–37.

interests of other nations in order to give them a stake in its own well-being and advance. Developing countries have to fear, not so much globalization as being passed over by it, and thus becoming economically marginalized in the global economy. That, however, is not a recommendation for a mindless headlong rush into globalization, but rather for a well-thought-out program for it that provides for appropriate capacity for adjustment of the domestic economy. Toward that end, state capacity needs to be strengthened even as some existing economic functions, such as excessive state ownership and state controls, are shed. Areas of modern economic endeavor where India has special strengths, such as IT software and pharmaceuticals, need to be promoted in order to "brand-name" India as an attractive economic partner.

Moreover, for the sake of higher economic growth, it is necessary for India to participate fully in rule-based international economic organizations, such as the World Trade Organization (WTO); the critics who advocate quitting WTO are mistaken in their position, since rule-based organizations work more to the benefit of weaker economic players than power-based ones. At the same time, it is incumbent on India to develop the national capacity to cope with adjustment problems that arise from being a member of the WTO and other such organizations. It is most interesting that China endeavored eagerly to enter the WTO. Indeed, India should press to enter other such organizations, like APEC and even the G-8. Equally, for higher growth, action closer to home is necessary by way of a common market for South Asia, though because the group of nations within South Asia is a fractious lot, not much hope can be placed on it. However, given the continental size of its own economy, a more fruitful path for India is to fully integrate it into a domestic common market by removing the internal barriers to trade.

The military and the economy do not exhaust the arena of capabilities. Fundamental to them both is the integration of the polity. It is difficult for others to take a nation's quest for a major-power role seriously if millions of its citizens live in abject poverty and squalor. India has been particularly remiss in adequately attacking the problem of poverty. Of course, this should not be allowed to detract from India's aspiration to become a major power, because all major powers have their seamier side that they seek to hide from the public eye. Associated with poverty-removal is advancement in literacy and education. An illiterate population is poor support for global ambition. A global role demands a population that understands the world in which the nation operates and takes its responsibilities about the nation's role in the world seriously. In fact, universal literacy could help mitigate other social evils that bedevil India, even as it improves the quality of life.

Equally critical are political and integrative capabilities. Here, again, there is a contradiction between the principal stated goal of most of the major political parties to make India a global economic and military power, and the actual behavior of many of them, especially the BJP, in setting groups against other groups on the basis of community, religion and caste in the pursuit of their narrow political, especially electoral, interests. What such parties seem to forget is that the secular, democratic fabric of India is a source of immense strength, a strength that can make India a durable and well-integrated major player in the future international order. Indeed, it is India's unique achievement to have been able to engage in nation-building through democracy and secularism for over half a century, a feat largely unparalleled in the developing world. Focusing excessively on debilitating internal issues – such as building temples on contested sites and suppressing minority rights – is likely to take India away from its central goals of speedily achieving internal cohesion, prosperity and international status.

State behavior

A nation that aspires to a major-power role needs to be involved actively in global issues, no doubt consistent with its capabilities. It has to do so not on an "episodic"[7] basis, but on a sustained one. Involvement with global issues means to be strategically engaged with the world's balance of power and to interact with the major powers on issues that concern them. Traditionally, India's participation at the global level has been through the nonaligned movement, which functioned, to put it uncharitably, in a mendicant's role in relation to the major powers, asking either to be left alone, or begging for special treatment or concessions because of the condition of indigence of its members. Whatever the satisfaction it provided to the elites of developing countries, the nonaligned movement was actually an albatross for India in truly pursuing its own national interests. Emotionally though not formally, India has perhaps already left, if only by neglect, the nonaligned movement in the wake of the end of the Cold War. The movement has, in any case, disintegrated because the catchment area for recruitment to it – that is, the developing world – has become highly differentiated internally. Some of what were earlier developing countries have graduated to the ranks of developed countries (such as South Korea), while others are more exploitative of their poorer cousins than the developed countries (such as the oil-exporting nations), and still others have worked out their own arrangements as members or associates of Western trading blocs (for

---

[7] The notion is from Dennis Kux. Interview, Washington, DC, December 15, 1999.

example, Mexico). India's declaration of itself as an NWS has also made it a less relevant member to what still remains of the nonaligned movement.

In any case, because of its diminished relevance, the nonaligned movement has occupied a less important role in India's overall foreign policy after the end of the Cold War, and particularly after India's acquisition of nuclear weapons. However, India has yet to liberate itself from being excessively preoccupied with South Asia. As an aspiring major power, India needs to transcend its vision beyond the region. Through an astute but flawed, because costly, diplomacy, Pakistan has been able to amass large resources from multiple sources to maintain its mortal enmity with India. At one time in the 1960s, Pakistan was getting arms aid from the three political giants of the time: the US, the Soviet Union and China. In the 1970s and 1980s, the US and China collaborated in providing it with economic and military aid. In the 1990s, Pakistan largely counted on China and the Islamic bloc. However, in the pursuit of its single-issue foreign policy of enmity with India, Pakistan has wrecked its own economy and polity. Piecemeal concessions are not likely to placate Pakistan, and the territorial concessions that Pakistan wants may result in India's disintegration. In any case, no such concessions are likely, for democracies rarely yield to nondemocracies for fear of electoral setbacks.[8] The alternative for India is to build its own economic and military capabilities in line with its potential and aspirations, without being confrontational about it, and to become militarily and economically so preponderant that Pakistan would have to face the choice of reconciling itself to the situation, even if only over the long haul. Indeed, a scenario similar to the lowering of strategic goals by Mexico and Canada vis-à-vis the US, as a result of the latter's assumption of overwhelming preponderance, is not implausible and may well be a precondition for peace in South Asia. Meanwhile, India could also make use of the post-September 11 and post-Afghan War strategic environment in the region to put pressure on Pakistan to modify its territorial ambitions, and perhaps convert the current line of control dividing the two countries into a permanent border, while providing limited autonomy to the Kashmiri people.

India's public relations on Kashmir have often been weak. In fact, there are strong arguments, not only legally in terms of the instrument of accession, but also politically and morally, in support of its position: perhaps more Muslims live in India than in Pakistan; the Indian liberal-democratic and secular polity offers more political freedom to Muslims

---

[8] See Paul Huth, *The Democratic Peace and Territorial Conflict in the 20th Century* (Cambridge: Cambridge University Press, 2003).

than most other Muslim countries do; living conditions on the Indian side of Kashmir are better than on the Pakistani side; another partition on religious grounds may result in more strife and marginalization of the Muslims in India; and an independent Kashmir, organized on theocratic lines, has the potential to become another Taliban-style Afghanistan, and thus a geopolitical nightmare for all. Further, territorial revisions in Kashmir could violate a key norm of postwar stability – that is, the territorial integrity norm – which proscribes the alteration of interstate boundaries through the use of force.[9]

Engaging strategically with the global balance of power would require a different mindset than that which India has been accustomed to in the past. India's association with the nonaligned movement was largely based on ideology, rather than the pursuit of its national interests; even when India acted out of its interests, it was interpreted as emerging out of ideology, as in the case of its friendship with the Soviet Union. This is quite in contrast with the behavior of China, which in a historical rupture in 1971 switched to an alignment with the US on the basis of its perceived strategic interests and, in the process, graduated to a major-power role. It was not deterred by its communist ideology from aligning with the capitalist West, because that is what realpolitik demanded. Indeed, that is the pattern of state behavior that is associated with major powers. In rejecting the position of the ideologues in the ruling party, China acted in the manner that Hans Morgenthau had advised the practitioners of foreign policy to do: to "pursue real interests" and forgo the "shadow of worthless rights."[10] Shades of such behavior, but only just that, have appeared more recently in the case of India as well, such as on the occasion of allowing US planes to refuel in India during the war in Iraq in 1991 and the Afghan War in 2001. But it is most telling that the first instance took place only furtively, and when it was exposed a halt was called to it. Again, after the Bush administration announced its determination in 2001 to go ahead with national missile defense, the government was daring enough to endorse it, partially driven by India's own need for such defensive systems. Noteworthy, however, is the opposition's attack on the government for sacrificing India's traditional foreign-policy posture. Of course, breaking from the old mindset does not only mean leaning toward the US, but going where national interests lead the nation, and that includes maintaining national and foreign-policy autonomy.

[9] On this, see Mark W. Zacher, "The Territorial Integrity Norm: International Boundaries and the Use of Force," *International Organization*, 55 (Spring 2001), 215–50.

[10] Hans J. Morgenthau, *Politics among Nations*, 6th edn. (New York: Alfred A. Knopf, 1985), 588.

The evolving balance of power

The passing of the bipolar system has created new opportunities for India by liberating it from being too closely tied to the apron strings of the Soviet Union. India was never a satellite of the Soviet Union, even as its status as the founder and advocate of the nonaligned movement gave it some room for diplomatic maneuver and allowed it to keep lines of communication open with the US. Yet some constraints did follow from having been too close to the Soviet Union, arousing in the process suspicion in the US about India's real inclinations and affiliation. However, the end of the Cold War also led to a semi-unipolar international system with the US as the hegemonic power, and India had to adjust to it. There was enormous pressure by the US throughout the 1990s on India over nuclear nonproliferation and its relations with Pakistan. At the same time, while the US continues to be the hegemonic power, the "unipolar moment" has perhaps passed and there is increasing diffusion of power in the world. Indeed, India's assertion of its nuclear capabilities in 1998 was part of this diffusion process. There is increasing evidence of tendencies toward multipolarity in the international system. There are pressures on the part of Russia, France and China toward the same end, and India, too, is determined to be an independent pole. The world, then, seems to be returning to the traditional pattern of several major powers, even though one of them is hegemonic. That development will inevitably lead to balance-of-power policies among them.

The return to the pattern of shifting balances of power will open new opportunities for India, as well as confront it with tough choices. Indeed, the post-September 11, 2001, global power configuration illustrates this. While the common enemy, terrorism, has brought about a rapprochement between the US and Russia, India has benefited from becoming a part of the coalition. The US opposition to India buying arms from Russia and Russian concerns over India–US military cooperation have dwindled. Even China seems to want to get closer to India economically in order to prevent a full-blown US–India alliance relationship. However, as the terrorist threat recedes, there is likely to be the re-emergence of state-centric balancing of power. With the US insistent on deploying NMD and China on increasing its offensive nuclear capability to counter it, US–China competition is likely to occur. India's natural tendency in the past has been to stay out of power politics, even though eventually national-security concerns compelled it to react through counterbalancing. If in the context of the present world India wants its claim to major-power status to be taken seriously, then it will not be able to avoid participation in the balancing process more actively, even if surreptitiously. India will have to devise a grand strategy that would allow it to play the game more effectively. It would need to make all possible efforts to participate in the global balance of power without provoking intense rivalries and counterbalancing by other major powers and smaller states.

Why India needs to acquire major-power status is a question often raised by opponents and skeptics alike. Should a country with such immense poverty focus on military balancing and the associated security behavior of a major power, instead of putting all its efforts in removing its socioeconomic maladies? Is it power for the sake of power, or power for some larger goal that India is seeking? States may have many and varied goals, but power is a requisite for their achievement. Within the constraints of an anarchical international system, all states seek national security, political autonomy and economic welfare to the extent possible. But the achievement of these goals by nations is often a function of their power. Without power, either self-owned or borrowed, there can be no national security. Effective power implies that a state possesses decision-making and problem-solving capabilities. A powerful actor is more autonomous to make independent choices and it is less vulnerable to the choices that others make. A major power by definition is a state that has an effective voice in the chief councils of the world, where crucial decisions are made that affect itself and the international community at large. A power that is not a major power is often at the "receiving end" of international politics. Other powerful actors, when making decisions, treat the power concerned as an object, not as a subject whose interests need to be taken cognizance of. Being a successful major power curtails the chances of becoming a victim of the politics of other major powers in various spheres. It reduces uncertainties for itself and its allies.

However, there is considerable danger in becoming obsessed with skewed power capabilities provided by the military component alone, as evident in the Soviet case. In the contemporary international order, a state requires comprehensive and balanced power capabilities in order to claim and retain major-power status. Prudence is the watchword here. It requires the state to command both hard-power and soft-power resources and to use its power to improve the quality of life for its citizens, to become more efficient in running its economy and society, and to work for security and peace for itself and the wider international community. India needs power capabilities if it is to achieve such goals.

As Schweller points out, how a rising power is dealt with by the established powers will be based on whether it is risk-acceptant or risk-averse.[11] A risk-acceptant revolutionary power will be dealt with by balancing and deterrence strategies, while a risk-acceptant nonrevolutionary power may be tackled through engagement. The problem, though, is that the established powers have little incentive to engage a timid, risk-averse rising power, since it is unlikely to challenge the status quo in any meaningful way. India has been basically risk-averse, while China has pursued a combination of risk-acceptant and risk-averse strategies. India would need to prudently do the same. The task for India, then, is not to appear too revolutionary or risk-acceptant and thereby provoke encirclement, but not too risk-averse either, and to use all avenues for engagement to further its major-power ambitions. The possibilities for engagement will largely be a function of hard-power and soft-power resources, and of how these resources of a rising power affect the interests of the established major powers and the international order itself. Economic and military power are crucial here because power and plenty go hand in hand, as discussed earlier. An economically powerful state will attract the engagement of other major powers, as it will be of consequence to the world economy and the global trading system.

The likely pattern of balancing will, however, not be altogether the same as in the traditional balance-of-power system. That is so because it will operate in the context of a different world, where the presence of nuclear capabilities places constraints on violent conflict between a hegemon and challengers, while increasing economic cross-dependencies place limits on conflict because of the economic damage they can cause. The likely pattern will be a combination of both cooperation and competition within any single dyad of major powers. This applies as much to the case of the relationship between the US and China, which is believed to be the likely next challenger to the hegemonic position of the US, as to any other relationship.

The US relationship with China has seen many changes in the postwar period. From a mortal enemy during the 1950s and 1960s, China in the 1970s and 1980s became a de facto ally of the US in the larger conflict between the US and the Soviet Union. During the 1980s and 1990s, the economic interdependence between the US and China grew tremendously, and the two have learnt to behave with restraint, notwithstanding episodic flare-ups of conflict. Despite the diplomatic turbulence resulting from the Tiananmen debacle, the 1990s were marked by a strategic partnership between the two, at times at the cost of India. With the growing power of China, the US is likely to perceive China as

---

[11] Randall L. Schweller, "Managing the Rise of Great Powers: History and Theory," in Alastair Iain Johnston and Robert S. Ross (eds), *Engaging China: The Management of an Emerging Power* (New York: Routledge, 1999), 1–31.

a competitor, even as economic ties will tend to dampen, but not remove, the competition. To assure that the world order does not unravel in an uncontrolled manner, the US may well organize an open or tacit alliance against China's growing power. If so, the US would want a closer strategic relationship with India.

Such a development may provide an opportunity for India to maneuver for a major-power role. Parenthetically, it can be noted that, in the case of China after its Cultural Revolution ended in the late 1960s, it was not its earlier diplomatic ties with other nations, but rather the opening of its relations with the US that led to its formal recognition as a major power through its assumption of the permanent seat on the Security Council, until then occupied by Taiwan. Meanwhile, interestingly, there is evidence of a growing coincidence of interests between India and the US because of several factors. Among these factors are: the traditional adversary relationship between India and China as large rival powers on the land mass of Asia, plus their unsettled border dispute, China's unwillingness to recognize Sikkim as an integral part of India, its opposition to recognition of India as an NWS, its reticence over India's candidacy for a permanent seat in the UN Security Council, and, importantly, its de facto alliance with Pakistan and its role in making Pakistan a nuclear and missile power; the growing economic ties between India and the US, with the US as India's number-one trading partner and the predominant destination of India's software exports and trained personnel; the considerable influence of the growing US community of Indian origin, which has a vested interest in fostering good relations between the two countries; and the perceived need for increasing military, especially naval, cooperation between the two countries in the Indian Ocean in order to assure safe movement of oil and other vital commodities. Given the traditional tendency of India to distrust the US, it remains to be seen how this relationship will play out. It may depend partly on the US relationship with Russia, which is an arms supplier of critical proportions for India. Given the past US reluctance to supply arms to India, India would be loath to harm its relationship with Russia. Equally, India would be wary of how far it can go in antagonizing China by a closer relationship with the US in view of China's veto power over India's prospects in the UN Security Council. On the other hand, could it be that India may be wooed by both sides? China may well want to avoid antagonism on two fronts, in East Asia as well as in the Himalayas. An intense Cold War style rivalry between the US and China may create problems for India, whereas limited strategic rivalries could offer more room for maneuver.

International governance

The present system of international governance is fundamentally a legacy of the postwar settlement following the end of World War II. More than half a century has passed since, but the formal institutional structure remains largely the same, as evident in the shape of the UN Security Council, where ultimate power inheres only in the P-5. There has been some accommodation, as in G-7, of the powers that were defeated in World War II but have risen again under US occupation and protection. However, from the perspective of Latin America, Africa and Asia (other than China), there has been little change. The structure therefore lacks legitimacy for them. The entire structure is of Western design and construction, preserves Western power, and serves Western interests. Take, for instance, the UN Security Council. Why, for example, should the UK and France continue to be permanent members after the decline of their power, while India and Brazil are denied such status? As Bracken points out:

That France and Britain retain permanent seats on the UN Security Council while India and Indonesia, or for that matter Japan, do not, is, of course, ridiculous. This is but one example among many of an institution that has not changed to reflect the new conditions of Asia's significance. ... The challenge to the West is not only one of managing a complicated integration of new countries into a world order that it has run for centuries. It is a challenge of self-conception. The challenge comes from the realization that the West's conception of itself is that of a leader that shapes international security and economic affairs. The long era in which Asia was penetrated by outside powers is coming to a close. An age of Western control is ending, and the challenge is not how to shape what is happening but how to adapt to it.[12]

Moreover, there is the question of ideological consistency in the stance of the Western powers. These powers are in the forefront of advocating democracy around the world as the ideal mechanism for governance at the domestic level, but refuse to acknowledge its relevance on the international scene. There is thus a fundamental contradiction in the position of the West, for which no rationale has been offered. It would seem that the UN Security Council needs to be widened to accommodate vast populations that are now excluded from the same privileges that the P-5 have. The same consideration applies to the G-7; some feel that it is necessary to "encourage the G-7 to broaden its membership to include Russia (which is already included in most discussions), Brazil, China,

---

[12] Paul Bracken, *Fire in the East: The Rise of Asian Military Power and the Second Nuclear Age* (New York: Harper Collins, 1999), 169–70.

and India."[13] India holds more than one-sixth of humanity; going by any standards of proportional representation (the key electoral system of multiethnic democracies to maintain internal peace and justice), India's case seems the strongest of all. Going by Westphalian juridical equality does not solve the problem of adequate representation for large segments of humanity in international institutional governance, since it simply equates India with Bhutan in membership rights. As India is one of the few countries in Asia, beyond China and Japan, capable of contributing to systemic stability, it seems geopolitically essential that India should be integrated as an effective participant and agent for stability in the region.

The exclusion of vast portions of the globe from institutions of international governance would tend to discredit such institutions. It would also tend to arouse extremist elements among nationalists in countries that feel they are excluded for perverse reasons; such a development could have unforeseen consequences for world order, given the possession of nuclear weapons by some of them. The rise of global terrorism is a manifestation of this exclusion of vast regions from global governance, although the religious element has given it a civilizational facade. The world needs to work out arrangements for peaceful accommodation of new rising powers in the nuclear era. Perhaps the Community of Democracies could, if it is firmly and finally established, provide an avenue of participation to a wider number of countries, but it is presently conceived of more like a club, without any role in international governance.

Summing up

India has strong credentials for a major-power role. Even major powers that are reticent about coming forward to support India in its aspirations recognize as much. The case for accommodation toward India's aspirations has been cogently put by an Australian scholar:

there would be advantage in not obstructing the gradual achievement of these aspirations. This is not only because they are largely inevitable but also because many of India's fundamental values and interests are broadly compatible with those of the West. India's deeply entrenched democratic heritage, its successful market economy, its open culture and English language and its role as a rising, strong but essentially status quo power provide a basis for enhanced relationships.[14]

[13] W. Bowman Cutter, Joan Spero and Laura D'Andrea Tyson, "New World, New Deal: A Democratic Approach to Globalization," *Foreign Affairs*, 79 (March–April 2000), 80–98.

[14] Ross Babbage, "India's Strategic Development: Issues for the Western Powers," in Ross Babbage and Sandy Gordon (eds), *India's Strategic Future: Regional State or Global Power?* (Houndmills, UK: Macmillan, 1992), 153–69.

Bibliography

Abraham, Itty. *The Making of the Indian Atomic Bomb: Science, Secrecy and the Postcolonial State.* London: Zed Books, 1998.

Adams, John. "India: Much Achieved, Much to Achieve." In *India and Pakistan: The First Fifty Years,* eds Selig S. Harrison, Paul H. Kriesberg and Dennis Kux. Washington, DC: Woodrow Wilson Center Press, 1999.

Adomeit, Hannes. "Russia as a 'Great Power' in World Affairs: Images and Reality." *International Affairs,* 17 (1995), 35–68.

Agarwal, Pradeep, *et al. Policy Regimes and Industrial Competitiveness: A Comparative Study of East Asia and India.* Houndmills, UK: Macmillan, 2000.

Ahmad, Akhtaruddin. *Nationalism or Islam: Indo-Pakistan Episode.* New Delhi: D.K. Agencies, 1982.

Akbar, M.J. *Nehru: The Making of India.* London: Penguin Books, 1988.

Akram, Lt. General A.I. "Security and Stability in South Asia." In *The Security of South Asia,* ed. Stephen P. Cohen. Urbana: University of Illinois Press, 1987.

Alagappa, Muthiah. "International Politics in Asia: The Historical Context." In *Asia's Security Practice,* ed. M. Alagappa. Stanford, CA: Stanford University Press, 1998.

Alamgir, Jalal. "India's Trade and Investment Policy: The Influence of Strategic Rivalry with China." *Issues and Studies* 35 (May–June 1999), 105–33.

Anderson, Jack. *The Anderson Papers.* New York: Random House, 1973.

Arif, General Khalid Mahmud. *Working with Zia: Pakistan's Power Politics, 1977–1988.* Karachi: Oxford University Press, 1995.

Asia and American Textbooks. New York: Asia Society, 1976.

Ayoob, Mohammed. "Nuclear India and Indian-American Relations." *Orbis,* 43 (Winter 1999), 59–74.

"India's Nuclear Decision: Implications for India–U.S. Relations." In *India's Nuclear Security,* eds Raju G.C. Thomas and Amit Gupta. Boulder, CO: Lynne Rienner, 2000.

Azam, Ikram. *Pakistan's Geopolitical and Strategic Compulsions.* Lahore: Progressive Publishers, 1980.

Babbage, Ross. "India's Strategic Development: Issues for the Western Powers." In *India's Strategic Future: Regional State or Global Power?* eds Ross Babbage and Sandy Gordon. Houndmills, UK: Macmillan, 1992.

Bajpai, Kanti P., and Amitabh Mattoo eds *Securing India: Strategic Thought and Practice*. New Delhi: Manohar Publishers, 1996.

Bakshi, Jyotsna. "Russian Policy towards South Asia." *Strategic Analysis* 23 (8, 1999), 1367–97.

Barnds, William J. *India, Pakistan and the Great Powers*. New York: Praeger, 1972.

Besant, Walter. *The Rise of the Empire*. London: Horace Marshall & Son, 1897.

Bhutto, Zulfikar Ali. *Foreign Policy of Pakistan*. Karachi: Pakistan Institute of International Affairs, 1964.

The Quest for Peace: Selections from Speeches and Writings, 1963–65. Karachi: Pakistan Institute of International Affairs, 1966.

Bowle, John. *The Imperial Achievement: The Rise and Transformation of the British Empire*. London: Secker & Warburg, 1974.

Bowles, Chester. *Promises to Keep: My Years in Public Life 1941–1969*. New York: Harper & Row, 1971.

Bracken, Paul. *Fire in the East: The Rise of Asian Military Power and the Second Nuclear Age*. New York: Harper Collins, 1999.

Bradnock, Robert W. *India's Foreign Policy since 1971*. London: Pinter Publishers, 1990.

Brass, Paul R. "India: Democratic Progress and Problems." In *India and Pakistan: The First Fifty Years*, eds Selig S. Harrison, Paul H. Kriesberg and Dennis Kux. Washington, DC: Woodrow Wilson Center Press, 1999.

Brecher, Michael. *India and World Politics: Krishna Menon's View of the World*. New York: Praeger, 1968.

Bull, Hedley. *The Anarchical Society*. New York: Columbia University Press, 1977.

Burr, William ed. *The Kissinger Transcripts*. New York: The New Press, 1998.

Byman, Daniel L., and Kenneth M. Pollack. "Let us Now Praise Great Men: Bringing the Statesman Back In," *International Security* 25 (Spring 2001), 107–46.

Calleo, David. *The German Problem Reconsidered: Germany and the World Order, 1870 to the Present*. Cambridge: Cambridge University Press, 1978.

Chadda, Maya. *Paradox of Power: The United States in South West Asia, 1973–1984*. Santa Barbara: ABC-Clio, 1986.

Chandler, Robert W. *The New Face of War*. McLean, VA: Amcoda Press, 1998.

Chase, Robert, Emily Hill and Paul Kennedy eds. *The Pivotal States: A New Framework for U.S. Policy in the Developing World*. New York: W.W. Norton, 1999.

Chaudhuri, Nirad C. *The Autobiography of An Unknown Indian*. London: Macmillan, 1951.

Cheema, Pervaiz Iqbal. "American Policy in South Asia: Interests and Objectives." In *The Security of South Asia: American and Asian Perspectives*, ed. Stephen Philip Cohen. Urbana: University of Illinois Press, 1987.

Chellaney, Brahma. "After the Test: India's Options." *Survival* 40 (Winter 1998–99), 93–111.

Chengappa, Raj. *Weapons of Peace: The Secret Story of India's Quest to be a Nuclear Power*. New Delhi: Harper Collins, 2000.

Chopra, Pran. *India's Second Liberation*. New Delhi: Vikas, 1973.

Choudhury, G.W. *India, Pakistan, Bangladesh, and the Major Powers: Politics of a Divided Subcontinent*. New York: The Free Press, 1975.

Christensen, Thomas J. *Useful Adversaries: Grand Strategy, Domestic Mobilization, and Sino-American Conflict, 1947–1958.* Princeton, NJ: Princeton University Press, 1996.

"Posing Problems without Catching up: China's Rise and Challenges for U.S. Security Policy." *International Security* 25 (Spring 2001), 5–40.

Claude, Inis. *Power and International Relations.* New York: Random House, 1964.

Cohen, Stephen P. *Arms and Politics in Bangladesh, India, and Pakistan.* Buffalo: State University of New York, Council on International Studies, 1973.

"The United States, India and Pakistan: Retrospect and Prospect." In *India and Pakistan: The First Fifty Years,* eds Selig S. Harrison, Paul H. Kriesberg and Dennis Kux. Washington, DC: Woodrow Wilson Center Press, 1999.

"India Rising." *Wilson Quarterly* 24 (3, Summer 2000), 32–53.

Cutter, W. Bowman, Joan Spero and Laura D'Andrea Tyson. "New World, New Deal: A Democratic Approach to Globalization." *Foreign Affairs* 79 (March–April 2000), 80–98.

Desai, Meghnad. "Capitalism, Socialism, and the Indian Economy." In *India: Joining the World Economy,* eds Kalyan Banerji and Tarjani Vakil. New Delhi: Tata McGraw-Hill, 1995.

de Toledano, Ralph. *Nixon.* New York: Henry Holt, 1956.

Dittmer, Lowell, and Samuel S. Kim eds. *China's Quest for National Identity.* Ithaca, NY: Cornell University Press, 1993.

Dixit, J.N. *My South Block Years: Memoirs of a Foreign Secretary.* New Delhi: UBSPD, 1996.

Across Borders: Fifty Years of India's Foreign Policy. New Delhi: Picus Books, 1998.

Dockrill, M.L., and Brian McKercher eds. *Diplomacy and World Power: Studies in British Foreign Policy, 1890–1950.* Cambridge: Cambridge University Press, 1996.

Doyle, Michael W. "A Liberal View: Preserving and Expanding the Liberal Pacific Union." In *International Order and the Future of World Politics,* eds T.V. Paul and John A. Hall. Cambridge: Cambridge University Press, 1999.

Dulles, Foster Rhea. *America's Rise to World Power 1898–1954.* New York: Harper & Row, 1955.

Dutt, V.P. *India's Foreign Policy in a Changing World.* New Delhi: Vikas, 1999.

Epstein, William. *The Last Chance: Nuclear Proliferation and Arms Control.* New York: The Free Press, 1976.

Feaver, Peter D. "Proliferation Pessimism and Emerging Nuclear Powers." *International Security* 22 (Fall 1997), 190–1.

Federation of Indian Chambers of Commerce and Industry. *Proceedings of the Thirty-third Annual Session Held in New Delhi on the 27, 28, and 29 March 1960.* New Delhi: 1960.

Foran, Virginia I. "Indo-US Relations after the 1998 Tests: Sanctions versus Incentives." In *Engaging India: US Strategic Relations with the World's Largest Democracy,* eds Gary K. Bertsch, Seema Gahlaut and Anupam Srivastava. New York: Routledge, 1999.

Gaddis, John Lewis. *The Long Peace: Inquiries into the History of the Cold War.* New York: Oxford University Press, 1987.

Galtung, Johan. "A Structural Theory of Aggression." *Journal of Peace Research* 1 (1964), 95–119.

"On the Way to Superpower Status: India and the EC Compared." *Futures* 24 (November 1992), 917–29.

Ganguly, Sumit. *The Crisis in Kashmir.* Washington, DC: Woodrow Wilson Center Press, 1997.

"India's Pathway to Pokhran II: The Prospects and Sources of New Delhi's Nuclear Weapons Program." *International Security* 23 (Spring 1999), 148–77.

Ghose, Arundhati. "Negotiating the CTBT: India's Security Concerns and Nuclear Disarmament." *Journal of International Affairs* 51 (Summer 1997), 239–61.

Gilpin, Robert. *War and Change in World Politics.* Cambridge: Cambridge University Press, 1981.

Gopal, Sarvepalli. *Jawaharlal Nehru: A Biography* (3 vols). Cambridge, MA: Harvard University Press, 1976.

Gordon, Philip. *A Certain Idea of France.* Princeton, NJ: Princeton University Press, 1993.

Gordon, Sandy. *India's Rise to Power.* New York: St. Martin's Press, 1995.

Gould, Harold A. "U.S.–Indian Relations: The Early Phase." In *The Hope and Reality: U.S.–India Relations from Roosevelt to Reagan,* eds Harold A. Gould and Sumit Ganguly. Boulder, CO: Westview Press, 1992.

Green, Michael J. "The Forgotten Player." *The National Interest* 60 (Summer 2000), 42–9.

Gupta, Akhil. *Postcolonial Developments: Agriculture in the Making of Modern India.* Durham, NC: Duke University Press, 1998.

Gupta, Dipankar ed. *Social Stratification.* Delhi: Oxford University Press, 1991.

Gupta, Vinod. *Anderson Papers: A Study of Nixon's Blackmail of India.* New Delhi: Indian School Supply Depot, 1972.

Gusterson, Hugh. "Nuclear Weapons and the Other in the Western Imagination." *Cultural Anthropology* 14 (1999), 111–43.

Hall, David K. "The Laotian War of 1962 and the Indo-Pakistani War of 1971." In *Force without War,* eds Barry M. Blechman and Stephen S. Kaplan. Washington, DC: The Brookings Institution, 1978.

Hall, John A. *International Orders.* Cambridge: Polity, 1996.

Hall, John A., and G. John Ikenberry. *The State.* Minneapolis: University of Minnesota Press, 1989.

Harries, Meirion, and Susie Harries *Soldiers of the Sun: The Rise and Fall of the Imperial Japanese Army.* New York: Random House, 1991.

Harrison, Selig S. "India, Pakistan and the US-II." *New Republic* 141 (8–9, August 24, 1959), 20–5.

"A Nuclear Bargain with India." Paper presented at the conference "India at the Crossroads," at the Southern Methodist University, Dallas, Texas, March 27, 1998.

Harrison, Selig S., and Geoffrey Kemp eds. *India & America after the Cold War.* Washington, DC: Carnegie Endowment for International Peace, 1993.

Healy, Kathleen. *Rajiv Gandhi: The Years of Power.* New Delhi: Vikas, 1989.

Heeks, Richard. *India's Software Industry: State Policy, Liberalisation, and Industrial Development.* New Delhi: Sage Publications, 1996.

Heimsath, Charles H. "American Images of India As Factors in U.S. Foreign Policy Making." In *Race and U.S. Foreign Policy during the Cold War,* ed. Michael L. Krenn. New York: Garland Publishing, 1998.

Herz, John. "Idealist Internationalism and the Security Dilemma." *World Politics* 2 (January 1950), 157–80.

Hitchcock, William I. *France Restored: Cold War Diplomacy and the Quest for Leadership in Europe, 1944–1954.* Chapel Hill: University of North Carolina Press, 1998.

Hoffmann, Stanley. "France: Two Obsessions for One Century." In *A Century's Journey,* ed. Robert A. Pastor. New York: Basic Books, 1999.

Holsti, Kalevi J. *Peace and War: Armed Conflict and International Order.* Cambridge: Cambridge University Press, 1991.

The State, War and the State of War. Cambridge: Cambridge University Press, 1996.

Hoyt, Timothy D. "Indian Military Modernization, 1990–2000." Unpublished paper, Georgetown University, July 2000.

Huntington, Samuel P. *The Clash of Civilizations and the Remaking of World Order.* New York: Simon & Schuster, 1996.

"The Lonely Superpower." *Foreign Affairs* 78 (March–April 1999), 35–49.

Huth, Paul. *The Democratic Peace and Territorial Conflict in the 20th Century.* Cambridge: Cambridge University Press, 2003.

Inden, Ronald. *Imagining India.* Cambridge, MA: Blackwell, 1992.

India, Ministry of Finance. *Economic Survey 2000–2001.* New Delhi: Government of India Press, 2001.

India, Planning Commission. *Seventh Five Year Plan,* 1985–90. New Delhi: Government of India, Planning Commission, 1985

International Institute for Strategic Studies. *The Military Balance 2000–2001.* London: IISS, 2001.

Isaacs, Harold R. *Images of Asia: American Views of China and India.* New York: Harper Torchbooks, 1972.

Jain, Rajendra K. ed. *US–South Asian Relations, 1947–1982.* New Delhi: Radiant Publishers, 1983.

James, David H. *The Rise and Fall of the Japanese Empire.* London: George Allen and Unwin, 1951.

James, Lawrence. *The Rise and Fall of the British Empire.* New York: St. Martin's Press, 1994.

Jayakar, Pupul. *Indira Gandhi: A Biography.* New Delhi: Viking, 1992.

Jervis, Robert. "Cooperation under the Security Dilemma," *World Politics* 30 (January 1978), 167–214.

"Systems Theories and Diplomatic History." In *Diplomacy: New Approaches in History, Theory, and Policy,* ed. Paul Gordon Lauren. New York: Free Press, 1979.

The Meaning of the Nuclear Revolution. Ithaca, NY: Cornell University Press, 1989.

System Effects: Complexity in Political and Social Life. Princeton, NJ: Princeton University Press, 1997.

Jha, Prem Shankar. *India: A Political Economy of Stagnation.* Bombay: Oxford University Press, 1980.

Joffe, Joseph. "Germany: The Continuities from Frederick the Great to the Federal Republic." In *A Century's Journey*, ed. Robert A. Pastor. New York: Basic Books, 1999.

Johnston, Alastair Iain. "International Structures and Chinese Foreign Policy." In *China and the World: Chinese Foreign Policy Faces the New Millennium*, ed. Samuel S. Kim. Boulder, CO: Westview Press, 1994.

Kalb, Marvin, and Bernard Kalb. *Kissinger.* Boston: Little, Brown & Co., 1974.

Kapur, Ashok. *India's Nuclear Option: Atomic Diplomacy and Decision Making.* New York: Praeger, 1976.

"China and Proliferation: Implications for India." *China Report* 34 (3–4, 1998), 401–17.

"Indian Strategy: The Dilemmas about Enmities, the Nature of Power and the Pattern of Relations." In *India: Fifty Years of Democracy and Development*, eds Yogendra K. Malik and Ashok Kapur. New Delhi: APH Publishing Corp., 1999.

Karnad, Bharat. "India: Global Leadership and Self-Perception." Paper presented at the workshop "India as an Emerging Power," at the United Service Institute of India, New Delhi, January 22, 1999.

Kennedy, Paul. *The Rise and Fall of Great Powers: Economic Change and Military Conflict from 1500 to 2000.* New York: Random House, 1987.

Keohane, Robert. "Lilliputians' Dilemmas: Small States in International Politics." *International Organization* 23 (Spring 1969), 291–310.

Khalilzad, Zalmay, *et al. The United States and a Rising China: Strategic and Military Implications.* Santa Monica, CA: Rand, 1999.

Kim, Samuel S. "China as a Great Power." *Current History* (September 1997), 246–51.

Kissinger, Henry. *The White House Years.* Boston: Little, Brown & Co., 1979. *Diplomacy.* New York: Simon & Schuster, 1994.

Klintworth, Gary. "Chinese Perspectives on India as a Great Power." In *India's Strategic Future: Regional State or Global Power?* eds Ross Babbage and Sandy Gordon. Houndmills, UK: Macmillan, 1992.

Kohli, Atul. *Democracy and Discontent: India's Growing Crisis of Governability.* New York: Cambridge University Press, 1991.

Kolodziej, Edward. *French International Policy under De Gaulle and Pompidou.* Ithaca, NY: Cornell University Press, 1974.

Krasner, Stephen D. *Structural Conflict: The Third World against Global Liberalism.* Berkeley: University of California Press, 1985.

Kristof, Nicholas D. "The Rise of China." *Foreign Affairs* 72 (December 1993), 59–74.

Kumar, Sumita. "Pakistan's Nuclear Weapon Program." In *Nuclear India*, ed. Jasjit Singh. New Delhi: Knowledge World, 1998.

Kurian, Nimmi. *Emerging China and India's Policy Options.* New Delhi: Lancer Publishers, 2001.

Kux, Dennis. *India and the United States: Estranged Democracies, 1941–1991.* Washington, DC: National Defense University Press, 1992. *The United States and Pakistan, 1947–2000: Disenchanted Allies.* Washington, DC: Woodrow Wilson Center Press, 2001.

Laitin, David. *Language Repertoires and State Construction in Africa.* Cambridge: Cambridge University Press, 1992.

Layne, Christopher. "The Unipolar Illusion: Why Great Powers Will Rise." *International Security* 17 (1993), 5–51.

Levy, Jack. *War in the Great Power System 1495–1975.* Lexington: The University Press of Kentucky, 1983.

Liska, George. "The Third World: Regional Systems and Global Order." In *Retreat from Empire*, eds Robert E. Osgood *et al.* Baltimore, MD: The Johns Hopkins University Press, 1973.

Lustick, Ian S. "The Absence of Middle Eastern Great Powers: Political 'Backwardness' in Historical Perspective." *International Organisation* 51 (Autumn 1997), 653–83.

McMahon, Robert J. *The Cold War on the Periphery: The United States, India and Pakistan.* New York: Columbia University Press, 1994.

Malik, J. Mohan. "India Goes Nuclear: Rationale, Benefits, Costs and Implications." *Contemporary Southeast Asia* 20 (August 1998), 191–215.

Mansingh, Surjit. *India's Search for Power: Indira Gandhi's Foreign Policy, 1966–1982.* New Delhi: Sage, 1984.

ed. *Nehru's Foreign Policy, Fifty Years On.* New Delhi: Mosaic Books, 1998.

Menon, V.P. *The Story of the Integration of the Indian States.* New York: Macmillan, 1956.

Middleton, Drew. *Retreat from Victory: A Critical Appraisal of American Foreign and Military Policy from 1920 to the 1970s.* New York: Hawthorn Books, 1973.

Midlarsky, Manus I. *On War: Political Violence in the International System.* New York: The Free Press, 1975.

Mistry, Dinshaw. *India and the Comprehensive Test Ban Treaty* (ACDIS Research Report). Champaign: University of Illinois at Urbana-Champaign, September 1998.

"India's Emerging Space Program." *Pacific Affairs* 71 (Summer 1998), 151–74.

"Diplomacy, Sanctions, and the US Non-proliferation Dialogue with India and Pakistan." *Asian Survey* 39 (1999), 753–71.

Modelski, George. "The Long Cycle of Global Politics and the Nation State." *Comparative Studies in Society and History* 20 (April 1978), 214–35.

Morgenthau, Hans J. *Politics among Nations*, 4th edn. New York: Alfred A. Knopf, 1967.

Politics among Nations, 6th edn. New York: Alfred A. Knopf, 1985.

Mueller, John. *Retreat from Doomsday: The Obsolescence of a Major War.* New York: Basic Books, 1989.

Myrdal, Gunnar. *Asian Drama: An Inquiry into the Poverty of Nations*, vol. I. New York: Pantheon, 1968.

Naipaul, V.S. *India: A Wounded Civilization.* New York: Vintage Books, 1976.

Nayar, Baldev Raj. *The Modernization Imperative and Indian Planning.* New Delhi: Vikas, 1972.

American Geopolitics and India. New Delhi: Manohar, 1976.

"A World Role: The Dialectics of Purpose and Power." In *India: A Rising Middle Power*, ed. John W. Mellor. Boulder, CO: Westview Press, 1979.

"Regional Power in a Multipolar World." In *India: A Rising Middle Power*, ed. John W. Mellor. Boulder, CO: Westview Press, 1979.

India's Quest for Technological Independence (2 vols). New Delhi: Lancers, 1983.

Superpower Dominance and Military Aid: A Study of Military Aid to Pakistan. New Delhi: Manohar, 1991.

"India as a Limited Challenger." In *International Order and the Future of World Politics*, eds T.V. Paul and John A. Hall. Cambridge: Cambridge University Press, 1999.

Globalization and Nationalism: The Changing Balance in India's Economic Policy, 1950–2000. New Delhi: Sage, 2001.

"Opening Up and Openness of Indian Economy." *Economic and Political Weekly* 36 (37, September 15, 2001), 3529–37.

Nayar, Kuldip. *India after Nehru.* New Delhi: Vikas, 1975.

Nehru, Jawaharlal. *The Discovery of India.* New York: The John Day Company, 1946.

Independence and After. New York: The John Day Company, 1950.

Jawaharlal Nehru's Speeches: Volume III: March 1953–August 1957. New Delhi: Publications Division, 1958.

India's Foreign Policy: Selected Speeches, September 1946–April 1961. New Delhi: Publications Division, 1961.

Jawaharlal Nehru's Speeches: Volume IV: September 1957–April 1963. New Delhi: Publications Division, 1964.

Jawaharlal Nehru's Speeches: Volume V: March 1963–May 1964. New Delhi: Publications Division, 1968.

"Free India's Role in World Affairs." In *Selected Works of Jawaharlal Nehru: Second Series.* New Delhi: Oxford University Press, 1984.

Nixon, Richard M. *United States Foreign Policy for the 1970s: Building for Peace* (February 25, 1971), in *Weekly Compilation of Presidential Documents*, vol. VII, no. 9 (March 1, 1971).

United States Foreign Policy for the 1970s: Shaping a Durable Peace (May 3, 1973), in *Weekly Compilation of Presidential Documents*, vol. IX, no. 19 (May 14, 1973).

Norman, Dorothy ed. *Nehru: The First Sixty Years* (2 vols.). New York: The John Day Company, 1965.

Nye, Joseph. *Bound to Lead: The Changing Nature of American Power.* New York: Basic Books, 1990.

Ollapally, Deepa, and Raja Ramanna. "U.S.–India Tension: Misperceptions on Nuclear Proliferation." *Foreign Affairs* 74 (January–February 1995), 13–18.

Organski, A.F.K. *World Politics*, 2nd edn. New York: Alfred A. Knopf, 1968.

Organski, A.F.K., and Jacek Kugler. *The War Ledger.* Chicago: University of Chicago Press, 1980.

Oxford Companion to the Second World War. Oxford: Oxford University Press, 1995.

Panikkar, K.M. *Asia and Western Dominance.* London: George Allen & Unwin, 1953.

Pastor, Robert A. ed. *A Century's Journey: How the Great Powers Shape the World.* New York: Basic Books, 1999.

Patel, I.G. *Economic Reform and Global Change.* New Delhi: Macmillan, 1998.

Paul, T.V. "Influence through Arms Transfers: Lessons from the U.S.–Pakistani Relationship." *Asian Survey* 32 (12, December 1992), 1078–92.

Asymmetric Conflicts: War Initiation by Weaker Powers. Cambridge: Cambridge University Press, 1994.

"Nuclear Taboo and War Initiation in Regional Conflicts." *Journal of Conflict Resolution* 39 (December 1995), 696–717.

"The Systemic Bases of India's Challenge to the Global Nuclear Order." *Nonproliferation Review* 6 (Fall 1998), 1–11.

"Power, Influence and Nuclear Weapons: A Reassessment." In *The Absolute Weapon Revisited: Nuclear Arms and the Emerging International Order,* eds T.V. Paul, Richard Harknett and James Wirtz. Ann Arbor: The University of Michigan Press, 1998.

Power versus Prudence: Why Nations Forgo Nuclear Weapons. Montreal: McGill–Queen's University Press, 2000.

"Great Powers and Nuclear Non-Proliferation Norms: China in South Asia." Paper presented at the ISA conference in Los Angeles, March 14–19, 2000.

Perkovich, George. *India's Nuclear Bomb: The Impact on Global Proliferation.* Berkeley: University of California Press, 1999.

Perret, Geoffrey. *A Country Made by War: From the Revolution to Vietnam: The Story of America's Rise to Power.* New York: Random House, 1989.

Pikayev, Alexander A., Leonard S. Spector, Elina V. Kirichenko and Ryan Gibson. *Russia, the US and the Missile Technology Control Regime,* Adelphi Paper 317. International Institute for Strategic Studies, Oxford: Oxford University Press, 1998.

Posen, Barry R. *The Sources of Military Doctrine: France, Britain, and Germany between the World Wars.* Ithaca, NY: Cornell University Press, 1984.

Posen, Barry R., and Andrew L. Ross. "Competing Visions for U.S. Grand Strategy." *International Security* 21 (Winter 1996–97), 5–53.

Poulose, T.T. *The CTBT and the Rise of Nuclear Nationalism in India.* New Delhi: Lancers Books, 1996.

"Viewpoint: India's Deterrence Doctrine: A Nehruvian Critique." *Nonproliferation Review* 6 (Fall 1998), 77–84.

Pradhan, S.D. "Indian Army and the First World War." In *India and World War I,* eds DeWitt C. Ellinwood and S.D. Pradhan. New Delhi: Manohar, 1978.

Prasad, Bimla. *The Origins of Indian Foreign Policy: The Indian National Congress and World Affairs, 1885–1947.* Calcutta: Booklands Private Limited, 1960.

Punekar, S.D. ed. *Economic Revolution in India.* Bombay: Himalaya Publishing House, 1977.

Pyle, Kenneth B. *The Japanese Question: Power and Purpose in a New Era.* Washington, DC: The AEI Press, 1992.

Rajan, M.S. *India and International Affairs: A Collection of Essays.* New Delhi: Lancers Books, 1999.

Raman, B. "Sino-Indian Relations: A Chronology." South Asia Analysis Group, http://www.saag.org/papers/paper49.html.

Reid, Escott. *Envoy to Nehru.* Delhi: Oxford University Press, 1981.

Rice, Condoleezza. "Promoting the National Interest." *Foreign Affairs* 79 (January–February 2000), 45–62.

Robbins, Keith. *The Eclipse of a Great Power, Modern Britain 1870–1992.* New York: Addison-Wesley, 1994.

Robinson, Thomas W., and David Shambaugh eds. *Chinese Foreign Policy: Theory and Practice.* Oxford: Clarendon Press, 1994.

Rose, Gideon. "Neoclassical Realism and Theories of Foreign Policy," *World Politics* 51 (1998), 144–72.

Rosen, Stephen P. *Societies and Military Power: India and its Armies.* Ithaca, NY: Cornell University Press, 1996.

Ross, Robert S. "Engagement in U.S. China Policy." In *Engaging China: The Management of an Emerging Power,* eds Alastair Iain Johnston and Robert S. Ross. London: Routledge, 1999.

Rostow, W.W. *Politics and the Stages of Growth.* Cambridge: Cambridge University Press, 1971.

Rubinoff, Arthur G. "Congressional Attitudes toward India." In *The Hope and Reality: U.S.–India Relations from Roosevelt to Reagan,* eds Harold A. Gould and Sumit Ganguly. Boulder, CO: Westview Press, 1992.

Sahni, Varun. "India as a Global Power: Capacity, Opportunity and Strategy." In *India's Foreign Policy: Agenda for the 21st Century,* vol. I. New Delhi: Foreign Service Institute and Konark, 1997.

Said, Edward W. *Orientalism.* New York: Vintage Books, 1979.

Saini, Krishan G. "The Economic Aspects of India's Participation." In *India and World War I,* eds DeWitt C. Ellinwood and S.D. Pradhan. New Delhi: Manohar, 1978.

Samuels, Richard J. *Rich Nation, Strong Army: National Security and the Technological Transformation of Japan.* Ithaca, NY: Cornell University Press, 1994.

Sardesai, Damodar, and Raju G.C. Thomas eds. *Nuclear India in the 21st Century.* New York: Palgrave, 2002.

Schweller, Randall L. "Managing the Rise of Great Powers: History and Theory." In *Engaging China: The Management of an Emerging Power,* eds Alastair Iain Johnston and Robert S. Ross. New York: Routledge, 1999.

Segal, Gerald. "Does China Matter?" *Foreign Affairs* 78 (September–October 1999), 24–36.

Sen, Amartya. *Development as Freedom.* New York: Anchor Books, 2000.

Sen Gupta, Bhabani. *The Fulcrum of Asia: Relations among China, India, Pakistan and the USSR.* New York: Pegasus, 1970.

"India: The Next Great Power." In *India's Foreign Policy: Agenda for the 21st Century,* vol. I. New Delhi: Foreign Policy Institute and Konark, 1997.

Singh, Jasjit. ed. *Nuclear India.* New Delhi: Knowledge World, 1998.

Singh, Jaswant. "Against Nuclear Apartheid." *Foreign Affairs* 77 (September–October 1998), 41–52.

Defending India. New York: St. Martin's Press, 1999.

Sisson, Richard, and Leo E. Rose. *War and Secession: Pakistan, India, and the Creation of Bangladesh.* Berkeley: University of California Press, 1990.

Snyder, Jack L. "Russia: Responses to Relative Decline." In *International Order and the Future of World Politics,* eds T.V. Paul and John A. Hall. Cambridge: Cambridge University Press, 1999.

Sridharan, Eswaran. *The Political Economy of Industrial Promotion: Indian, Brazilian, and Korean Electronics in Comparative Perspective, 1969–1994.* Westport, CT: Praeger, 1996.

Strange, Susan. "The Persistent Myth of Lost Hegemony." *International Organization* 41 (Autumn 1987), 749–52.

Subrahmanyam, K. "Nehru and the India–China Conflict of 1962." In *Indian Foreign Policy: The Nehru Years,* ed. B.R. Nanda. New Delhi: Vikas, 1976.

"India and the Changes in the International Security Environment." In *India's Foreign Policy: Agenda for the 21st Century,* vol. I. New Delhi: Foreign Policy Institute and Konark, 1997.

"Indian Nuclear Policy – 1964–98 (A Personal Recollection)." In *Nuclear India,* ed. Jasjit Singh. New Delhi: Knowledge World, 1998.

"Eight Months after the Nuclear Tests." Paper presented at McGill University, February 16, 1999.

Talbott, Strobe. "Dealing with the Bomb in South Asia." *Foreign Affairs* 78 (March–April 1999), 110–22.

Tammen, Ronald L., *et al. Power Transitions: Strategies for the 21st Century.* New York: Chatham House, 2000.

Tanham, George K. *Indian Strategic Thought: An Interpretative Essay.* Santa Monica, CA: Rand Corporation, 1992.

Taylor, Jeffrey. "Russia is Finished." *Atlantic Monthly* 287 (May 2001), 35–52.

Tellis, Ashley J. *India's Emerging Nuclear Posture: Between Recessed Deterrent and Ready Arsenal.* New Delhi: Oxford University Press, 2001.

Thomas, Raju G.C. "The Growth of Indian Military Power: From Sufficient Defence to Nuclear Deterrence." In *India's Strategic Future: Regional State or Global Power?* eds Ross Babbage and Sandy Gordon. Houndmills, UK: Macmillan, 1992.

(ed.). *Perspectives on Kashmir: The Roots of Conflict in South Asia.* Boulder, CO: Westview Press, 1992.

Tremblay, Reeta Chowdhari. "Kashmir: The Valley's Political Dynamics." *Contemporary South Asia* 4 (1, 1995), 79–101.

US Department of State. "Text of Joint Pakistan–US Statement." *Department of State Bulletin* no. 1970, October 15, 1973.

Foreign Relations of the United States, 1950: Volume V: The Near East, South Asia, and Africa. Washington, DC: Department of State, Bureau of Public Affairs, 1978.

United States–Indian Educational and Cultural Relations. Washington, DC: Department of State, Bureau of Educational and Cultural Affairs, 1982.

US House of Representatives, Committee on Foreign Affairs. *United States Interests in and Policies toward South Asia* (93rd Congress, 1st Session; March 12, 15, 20 and 27, 1973).

New Perspectives on the Persian Gulf (93rd Congress, 1st Session; June 6, July 17, 23, 24 and November 28, 1973).

South Asia, 1974: Political, Economic, and Agricultural Challenges (93rd Congress, 2nd Session; September 19 and 24, 1974).

US Senate, Committee on Foreign Relations. *US Military Sales to Iran* (A Staff Report, July 1976).

Varnynen, Raimo. ed. *The Waning of Major Wars.* Forthcoming.

Vasquez, John A. "When are Power Transitions Dangerous? An Appraisal and Reformulation of Power Transition Theory." In *Parity and War,* eds Jacek Kugler and Douglas Lemke. Ann Arbor: University of Michigan Press, 1996.

Védrine, Hubert. *Les Cartes de la France à l'heure de la Mondialisation.* Paris: Fayard, 2000.

Vertzberger, Yacov. *The Enduring Entente: Sino-Pakistani Relations 1960–1980.* New York: Praeger, 1983.

Wainwright, A. Martin. *The Inheritance of Empire: Britain, India, and the Balance of Power in Asia, 1938–55.* Westport, CT: Praeger, 1994.

Wallace, Michael D. *War and Rank among Nations.* Lexington, KY: Lexington Books, 1973.

Walt, Stephen. "Alliance Formation and the Balance of World Power." *International Security* 9 (4, Spring 1985), 3–43.

Waltz, Kenneth. *Theory of International Politics.* New York: Random House, 1979.

"The Emerging Structure of International Politics." *International Security* 18 (1993), 44–79.

Weede, Erich. "Overwhelming Preponderance as a Pacifying Condition among Contiguous Asian Dyads, 1950–69." *Journal of Conflict Resolution* 20 (September 1976), 395–411.

Weiner, Myron. *The Child and the State in India.* Princeton, NJ: Princeton University Press, 1991.

Wight, Martin. *Power Politics.* Edited by Hedley Bull and Carsten Holbraad. Leicester, UK: Leicester University Press, 1978.

Wilcox, Wayne A. "India and Pakistan." In *Conflict in World Politics,* eds Steven L. Spiegel and Kenneth N. Waltz. Cambridge, MA: Winthrop Publishers, 1971.

Williams, Marc. *Third World Co-operation: The Group of 77 in UNCTAD.* London: Pinter, 1991.

Wolpert, Stanley. *Zulfi Bhutto of Pakistan: His Life and Times.* New York: Oxford University Press, 1993.

World Bank. *India: Five Years of Stabilization and Reform and the Challenges Ahead.* Washington, DC: World Bank, 1996.

India: Sustaining Rapid Economic Growth. Washington, DC: World Bank, 1997.

The World Development Report, 2000/2001. Washington, DC: World Bank, 2001.

World Economic Forum. *Global Competitiveness Report.* Geneva: The World Economic Forum, September 2000.

Zacher, Mark W. "The Territorial Integrity Norm: International Boundaries and the Use of Force." *International Organization* 55 (Spring 2001), 215–50.

Zakaria, Fareed. *From Wealth to Power: The Unusual Origins of America's World Role.* Princeton, NJ: Princeton University Press, 1998.

Index